Making Government Work

Ernest F. "Fritz" Hollings
with Kirk Victor

The University of South Carolina Press

© 2008 University of South Carolina

Published by the University of South Carolina Press
Columbia, South Carolina 29208

www.sc.edu/uscpress

Manufactured in the United States of America

17 16 15 14 13 12 11 10 09 08   10 9 8 7 6 5 4 3 2 1

Library of Congress Cataloging-in-Publication Data

Hollings, Ernest F., 1922–
    Making government work / Ernest F. "Fritz" Hollings, with Kirk Victor.
      p. cm.
    Includes bibliographical references and index.
    ISBN 978-1-57003-760-3 (cloth : alk. paper)
    1. Hollings, Ernest F., 1922– 2. United States. Congress. Senate—Biography.
    3. Legislators—United States—Biography. 4. United States—Politics and government—
    1945–1989. 5. United States—Politics and government—1989– I. Victor, Kirk.
    II. Title.
    E840.8.H655A3 2008
    328.73092—dc22
    [B]
                                                                          2008008041

This book was printed on Glatfelter Natures, a recycled paper with 30 percent
postconsumer waste content.

For Peatsy

Fritz and Peatsy Hollings, 2004. Collection of the author

CONTENTS

List of Illustrations   *ix*
Acknowledgments   *xi*

Prologue   *1*
1 The Accidental Politician   *7*
2 Taking Charge as Governor   *42*
3 Getting to Know the Kennedys   *84*
4 Getting Started in the Senate   *111*
5 Clement Haynsworth's Nomination to the Supreme Court   *141*
6 The Early Fight to Protect the Environment   *151*
7 The Supreme Court Corrupts Congress   *159*
8 Imperial Nixon, Cautious Ford   *170*
9 The Carter Years: A Time of Big Battles   *181*
10 The Assault on Government   *201*
11 Attacking the Excesses of Reaganomics   *214*
12 Missed Opportunities   *231*
13 The Early 1990s: From Budget Battles to Trade Wars   *246*
14 Protecting the Public Interest   *266*
15 The George W. Bush Years: Reckless Policies Divide the Country   *277*
16 Making Government Work   *304*

Notes   *333*
Index   *345*
About the Author   *359*

ILLUSTRATIONS

Fritz and Peatsy Hollings, 2004   *v*
Lieutenant Governor Hollings with Jimmy and Maude Byrnes
  and Senator Strom Thurmond, 1955   22
The Barnwell Ring's "Bottle Baby," 1958   *40*
Governor Hollings in his inaugural parade, 1959   *43*
Governor Hollings recruiting new business, c. 1959–62   *59*
Senator John F. Kennedy, Senator Olin Johnston, and Governor
  Hollings, 1960   *91*
Senator Hollings, President Lyndon B. Johnson, and General William
  Westmoreland, 1968   *121*
Senator Hollings during his 1969 hunger tour   *134*
Rosalynn Carter, Joan Mondale, and Peatsy Hollings, 1977   *182*
Senators Hollings, Phil Gramm, and Warren Rudman, 1986   *221*
Senators Frank Lautenberg, Hollings, and James Exon, c. 1987   *225*
President and Mrs. George H. W. Bush with Senator and
  Mrs. Hollings, 1989   *239*
The Hollingses and Sally Howie McDevitt, 1994, at fiftieth
  anniversary observances of the Normandy invasion   *256*
The Hollingses with the Clintons, 1998   *272*
Senators Hollings and John McCain, 2003   *281*
The Hollings staff, 2004   *301*

ACKNOWLEDGMENTS

This book could not have been written without the research and expertise of Kirk Victor, and I appreciate his great skills, talent, and good nature. I couldn't begin to tell the story of fifty-two years of public service without thinking how fortunate I have been in having an excellent staff both as Governor and United States Senator. I won't list them all, but recent help who should be acknowledged are Betty Pittleman, John Windhausen, Jami Koontz, Greg Elias, and Ivan Schlager of my staff and Sheila Dwyer and Brian McLaughlin of the staff of the U.S. Senate. My friends at the Charleston School of Law—Allison Jones and Abby Edwards were tremendous in their research. The eminent economist Charles McMillion and my friend Jack Nash of Washington were of terrific assistance. My secretary Patty Kasell worked tirelessly in transcribing, entering the many edits, and making most valuable suggestions. My papers are held by the University of South Carolina in its South Carolina Political Collections. Its staff—Director Herb Hartsook, Lori Schwartz, Dorothy Hazelrigg, and Kate Moore—provided wonderful help in research and improvements in the manuscript. Thanks also to Karen Rood, my project editor at the University of South Carolina Press.

I can hear the pundits predicting that the special interests will never allow government to work. During my years in the Senate, Roger Milliken, the best of corporate America, and the late Evelyn Doobrow, the best of organized labor, worked tirelessly together to maintain our nation's production. The special interests always yield for the good of the country to make government work.

Finally I can't thank the people of South Carolina enough for allowing me to serve them for fifty-two years.

Making Government Work

Prologue

If you are looking for the standard autobiography written by many Senators over the years, this is not the book for you. Those books are often filled with tales of being born in a log cabin, making straight A's in school, and saving the country in World War II. Instead of writing an autobiography, I tell a story of how government once worked and can be made to work again. I skip over growing up in Charleston, education at the Citadel, three years in combat in World War II, law school, and twenty years as a trial lawyer. Instead my aim is to draw on fifty-two years in public service to show how government once worked at the state and federal levels, but today is at a standoff. After World War II many veterans returned home and entered public service in order to solve problems. They jumped into politics before pollsters, TV ads, big money, and the national parties dominated every facet of campaigning and serving in public office.

To the critics who reflexively disparage government, I say look at the record. We in South Carolina would not have emerged from the depths of our economic woes without public policies that helped us catch up with the rest of the nation. When I was first elected to the legislature in 1948, the South was behind the nation but on the brink of vast changes. Racially our country was still segregated. The civil rights movement was just beginning. Unlike many other states in the Old Confederacy whose streets were streaked with blood, South Carolina went through a transformation without a life being lost while I served as Governor.

South Carolina also pursued a different course economically. Many of our citizens were not sharing in the American dream. But change was coming. We raised taxes to pay for the government we provided. We balanced the books. Moody's and Standard and Poor's awarded South Carolina a triple-A credit rating—making it the first state to earn this ranking in the South and allowing South Carolina to finance its economic expansion at a discount. In due course our progress on the racial and economic fronts attracted firms looking to put down roots in a hospitable climate.

During my fourteen years in state government, as I moved up the political ladder from Speaker Pro Tem in the legislature to Lieutenant Governor and Governor, South Carolina's government transformed the state's economy from primarily agricultural to largely industrial based. To make sure our workers had the skills these new companies demanded, we started a highly successful system of technical training that continues to be widely emulated in other states and even across the Atlantic in Ireland. We were the first southern state to tap into the markets in South America. Similarly our trips to Germany nearly fifty years ago were so successful in touting the advantages of having a presence in the Palmetto State that today more than ninety German affiliates and two hundred German manufacturing facilities have roots in our state. We had comparable success in France, where we called on Michelin, the tire manufacturer, which now has four plants as well as its North American headquarters in South Carolina. And we attracted Pirelli from Italy.

Yes, government worked. Like all southern states at the time, we had our troubles, but we brought about change without the carnage that made headlines elsewhere. The culture of the 1950s had split "for segregation" and "against segregation." Political leaders had to choose. None held office without a pledge to continue to fight for the "southern way of life." In 1954, in the famous *Brown v. Board of Education of Topeka, Kansas,* decision, the United States Supreme Court ruled that "separate but equal" public facilities were unconstitutional. But in Kansas secondary schools were already integrated, and Kansas submitted its brief in *Brown* to the Supreme Court without argument. The school-desegregation part of the civil rights movement started in Clarendon County, South Carolina, years before the *Brown* case, and I record the struggle and suffering of the petitioners in the *Briggs v.*

Elliott case, which Thurgood Marshall argued before the Supreme Court as an element of *Brown*.

The ruling in *Brown* did not change the culture of the South. James F. Byrnes, then Governor of South Carolina and a former Supreme Court Justice, fiercely attacked the decision. He proclaimed that *Brown* was unconstitutional, a stance that gave credibility to the widespread resistance movement. Newspapers editorialized against the Supreme Court's ruling. The Ku Klux Klan was regenerated, and White Citizens Councils were formed to continue segregation. "Impeach Earl Warren" billboards sprang up over the South, referring to the Chief Justice who had engineered the unanimous *Brown* decision.

Arkansas Governor Orval Faubus set the standard for southern Governors in 1957 by trying to prevent the integration of Central High School in Little Rock. "Schools are for education, not integration," he said. A mob gathered around the school, intent on physically blocking the entry of nine African American children. President Dwight Eisenhower had no choice but to order paratroopers to join forces with the federalized National Guard to enforce the students' constitutional rights. The school was desegregated. Order was restored.

But in October 1962 at Oxford, Mississippi, peace was not to be. Governor Ross Barnett of Mississippi was a leader in the opposition to the *Brown* decision. He claimed that he fought to preserve the "state's sovereignty" against the United States. The political tempest reached a boiling point. Barnett solicited me to lead a march against the admission of James Meredith, an African American, to the segregated University of Mississippi. I declined. The National Guard was called out to maintain the peace. The Justice Department stationed U.S. Marshals galore around the Mississippi campus. A riot broke out. Two people were killed, and scores were injured.

Amid this violence, Harvey Gantt, a black student, applied for admission to Clemson College, which was segregated. Nearing the end of my term as Governor in January 1963, I summed up my duty as Governor in the phrase *salus populi suprema lex* (the safety of the people is the supreme law). Quietly I laid the groundwork to integrate Clemson and maintain the peace. I called Attorney General Robert Kennedy, informed him of our plans, and said we "do not need U.S. Marshals." On January 9, 1963, I told the state legislators in my valedictory address that the law of the land was clear. All manner of resistance and defiance to stop integration had been tried. "As we meet, South Carolina is running out of courts. . . . This General Assembly must make clear South Carolina's choice, a government of laws rather than a government of men. . . . We of today must realize the lesson of a hundred years ago and move on for the good of South Carolina and the United States." As I spoke, tensions in the Statehouse were palpable. Not long after that address, Clemson was peacefully integrated. In a most trying time, government had worked.

Elected to the U.S. Senate in 1966, I joined a government working at the federal level. Of course we had enormous problems, especially Vietnam. But what impressed me in my first two decades on Capitol Hill was that government made a positive difference in people's lives. Early on I focused on the scourge of hunger that all of us in politics had ignored or swept under the rug. I toured South Carolina to learn the reality of this plague and wrote a book, *The Case Against Hunger.* I was blistered by some prominent politicians in the state for hurting tourism by highlighting such a desperate problem. But when I went back to Washington, lawmakers paid attention when I said that I had seen hunger in my own backyard. We beefed up feeding programs, held the line on George McGovern's Food for Peace, and started the Women, Infants and Children (WIC) Program to attack hunger and malnutrition.

Government also woke up to environmental concerns. We created the National Oceanic and Atmospheric Administration. We attacked pollution by prohibiting dumping in the oceans. All fifty states joined in coastal-zone planning. We instituted the Energy Department and passed legislation that resulted in auto manufacturers producing more efficient vehicles that got more miles for each gallon of gas. And it was our Senate Commerce Committee that had the first hearing on climate change.

Yes, government worked. It even worked when we as a country recognized the important lesson of Vietnam. We cannot occupy the middle of another country. That same issue surfaced in the vitriolic debate over the Panama Canal Treaties. Despite intense political pressure and a cry of "give-away" that some continue to make to this very day, we lawmakers came together and did the right thing. In 1977 we ratified the treaties and gave sovereignty over that area to the people who live there.

Hoping to prevent the cancer of money from wreaking havoc in our political system, we also tried to limit spending in campaigns. President

Richard Nixon signed legislation that we passed in 1971 and 1974 to address our concern that public office was for sale. But such efforts were nullified in 1976, when the Supreme Court in *Buckley v. Valeo* amended the First Amendment by limiting free speech with money. That decision ignited the money chase that infects every aspect of governing today as elected officials are constantly on the fund-raising treadmill.

At about the same time, Washington began to change, as leaders with a far different ideology took charge. This blame-the-government crowd was out to dismantle federal programs. Their irresponsible blueprint included reckless tax cuts coupled with a huge increase in spending for the military. It spelled disaster. Rising deficits. Higher unemployment. Cutting taxes to raise revenue—called "voodoo" by presidential candidate George Herbert Walker Bush—drove us into the ditch as our national debt soared.

As our government failed to open markets and refused to enforce our trade laws, companies outsourced workers and moved offshore. They were determined to find the cheapest labor possible. Our domestic industries, especially textiles, were getting clobbered as they tried to compete against foreign firms unburdened by working standards and benefits to which U.S. workers are entitled. Congressmen's and Senators' attempts to protect our production and economy were thwarted. When Congress moved to protect our industries and our workers, corporate America's well-heeled executives and lobbyists cried "Free Trade, Free Trade," and many Congressmen and Senators, needing their contributions, joined the chorus. Big business, which controls much of the money flowing to campaigns, has anesthetized the public servant.

The business lobby's mantra of "don't provoke a trade war" prevailed as one President after another vetoed lawmakers' efforts to provide protection for U.S. industries. As a result of these ruinous policies, the number of our workers engaged in manufacturing today is the lowest it has been in more than fifty years.

We must rebuild our manufacturing base. The country can't pay for health care and vital improvements in infrastructure unless we create jobs. We can't defend America unless we rejuvenate our industrial base. But presidental candidates avoid the problem of outsourcing. Instead of "it's the economy, stupid," today's campaign slogan in the presidential race is "don't ask; don't tell."

Today, as confidence in our economy continues to slip, Washington is preoccupied with war. There is no greater blunder for our government than to attempt to force-feed democracy as we have done in Iraq.

We squandered the goodwill toward the United States that arose around the world in the wake of the horrific attacks of September 11, 2001. Today our military is stretched thin, and our country is isolated on the world stage.

Government has gone off course. We refuse to pay our bills. Instead we accumulate more debt. We waste billions in interest costs that buy nothing. Our manufacturing base is decimated. All the while casualties continue in a battle for a cause the country thinks a mistake. The Congress flounders in dangerous waters. The greed of capitalism has reached compatibility with the greed of politics. The capitalist is divorced from country to seek profit, and the politician is divorced from country to seek contributions. Desperate needs are ignored.

Despite these problems, this is no time to despair. The government might be in a standoff, but the country is strong. As I show in this book, government has worked before, and we can make it work again.

1

The Accidental Politician

Germany had just agreed to unconditional surrender on May 8, 1945, when my army unit in Fussen, Austria, immediately began training for war in Japan. We were running gas-mask drills and other exercises to prepare for battle when suddenly everything changed. On August 6, as we prepared to board ship for Japan out of Le Havre, France, President Harry Truman ordered an atomic bomb dropped on Hiroshima. Three days later the President ordered a second A-bomb targeting Nagasaki. Next thing I knew World War II was over. Thank God.

I boarded ship headed for the States, reveled at the sight of the Statue of Liberty, and made it home to Charleston, South Carolina, on Thanksgiving evening 1945. I hadn't seen Mother in three years. We had a great reunion and almost immediately began talking about my plans to go to law school.

Like others returning to the States after military service, I was in a hurry. Veterans were playing catch-up. We were eager to put down roots and get to work. I returned to a state that had many problems. Illiteracy was far too common. Pockets of poverty were obvious to anyone willing to see them; our civil rights inequities were beginning to be recognized; and there was no industry to speak of. Those looking for a job were headed out of state. Those issues would be a big part of South Carolina's history in the coming years. I had no idea that I would soon become a player in that story. I wasn't thinking about such weighty concerns.

I had long known I wanted to be a trial lawyer. I got my first taste of what lawyers do as a teenager, when I helped out at my Uncle Ernest's law firm. I dashed from one Broad Street law office to another in Charleston, delivering legal documents. It was exciting to listen in as lawyers swapped stories about their cases and clients and more exciting as I sat transfixed during jury trials. At that young age, I already knew my calling.

But I feared I was out of luck. It appeared to be too late to start law school. First-year students were well into their studies by the end of November. Still I was determined not to postpone school for a year. So the morning after I arrived home, I traveled with Uncle Ernest (J. D. E. Meyer) to see Nelson Frierson, the dean at the University of South Carolina School of Law in Columbia, the state capital.

"You're too late," the dean said.

"Come on," I implored. "I can't wait until next year. You've got to let me try."

I told him that I had always wanted to be a lawyer. I described my work as an office boy in my uncle's law firm when I was a teenager. I explained that I had arrived so late in the year only because I had just returned from three years of combat. I made the invasion of Africa, the invasion of Corsica, the invasion of Southern France—I laid it on thick. If there were any way he could let me in, I assured him, I would make it. I was still in uniform. My uncle, a respected member of the bar, also did some cajoling. "You have to give the veteran a chance," he said.

Finally the dean agreed. "Audit the classes, brief the cases, take the exams in January; and, if you pass, I'll give you credit and you can continue," he said.

I couldn't have been happier. Classmates gave me the list of cases to be briefed, and I worked late every night. I'll never forget Sarah Leverette, the librarian who came early every morning during the Christmas holidays and opened the law library so I could work. I took the exams, and by January 17, 1946—less than two months after I started law school—I had passed the first semester.

In those days veterans were gung ho and not about to get sidetracked with distractions. In fact we were so determined to finish our courses as quickly as possible that when the school administration considered a change in the schedule that would have ended the option of taking three semesters in a year—a plan begun during the war—the veterans raised hell.

We protested and marched on the Statehouse, demanding rights for returning veterans. The demonstrations worked. The university trustees put the kibosh to the change, and the law school continued to offer three semesters a year into the 1950s. By August 1947 I had completed a three-year law program in twenty-one months.

I joined my uncle's firm, Meyer, Goldberg and Hollings, eager to get into the courtroom. Uncle Ernest made it clear to me going all the way back to my days as an office boy that the practice of law is all consuming. "The law is a jealous mistress," he had said. "If you want to be a good lawyer, don't fool with politics."

That advice was easy enough for me to follow. Just as I had been totally focused on my studies in law school, as a member of the bar, I took the same approach. I was not about to get involved in outside diversions. I had no idea about what was going on politically and was not interested in running for office. I dived into trial work. By November I was in court trying my first personal-injury case.

My client had lost an eye in a railroad-crossing collision. Judge Woodrow Lewis, who was presiding, also had lost an eye. So too had the foreman of the jury! As the weather was quite cold, when we broke for lunch, Judge Lewis had three saucers of warm water ready in his chambers. My client, the Judge, and the jury foreman each squirted his glass eye out into the saucer to keep it warm, while they went out in the winter wind. After lunch, they reinserted their eyes. It turned out to be a very rewarding case, as the jury returned a $35,000 verdict. I was a lawyer on the fast track and never happier.

But then the partners—even my uncle—did an about-face. They urged me to take a temporary detour from law that, they promised, would help further my legal career. Although they didn't say it in so many words, the partners were hoping that I could help them out of a problem.

David S. "Rocky" Goldberg, a hard worker and fine lawyer, had been the firm's candidate for the Statehouse in the past two elections. But he had been whipped both times. Now the partners had to decide what to do in 1948. In his previous races, Goldberg had received a substantial vote in Charleston, where he was well known. But the folks in North Charleston, where he didn't have many friends, swapped him off the ticket for a North Charleston boy.

The partners gathered on the second floor in the library during the summer of 1948, lamenting their predicament. They didn't want a three-time loser. But Rocky was ready to run again. He thought he could win, but the partners could not be convinced. Another loss would be embarrassing. Then somebody decided out of the blue that I should jump into the race.

"Let Fritz run," he said. "He's been off to college, war, and law school. He doesn't know the county. He sure doesn't know anybody in North Charleston. But, he'll have an excuse to meet the magistrates, learn the county. If he loses, it won't make any difference."

I immediately reminded my uncle of his "jealous mistress" admonition. But even he took up the chant: "Let Fritz run." Rocky agreed it was a good idea. It was true that I needed to get to know folks in the area and introduce myself to potential clients. It might result in more business for the firm. But initially I resisted. I told them I didn't mind having a reason to go around introducing myself, but they ought to know that there was no way I would get into politics. I explained that no one in my family had ever run for political office. I was really feeling good about my prospects as a lawyer, and I still had a bad taste about politics that stemmed from an incident years before.

In the summer of 1940, Uncle Ernest had taken me to the Republican National Convention in Philadelphia. As the lawyer for the South Carolina Republican Party, he appeared before the Credentials Committee to represent the "Tieless Joe" Tolbert faction of the state party the Friday before the convention opened. Joseph W. Tolbert, who got his nickname because he never wore a tie even when presiding over official functions, was one of the state's most influential Republicans. A bear of a man at 6 feet 5 inches tall and 300 pounds, Tolbert regaled delegates at the convention with stories and humor. Our delegation was committed to Ohio Senator Robert Taft for the presidential nomination. A rival faction of South Carolina delegates, who supported New York prosecutor Thomas E. Dewey, had challenged our credentials. My uncle took up Tieless Joe's case and made a brilliant argument. I had no doubt the challenge would be rejected. But the African American Philadelphia lawyer for the contesting South Carolina delegation made just as good an argument. I had never seen or heard of a black lawyer. The Tolbert group lost its credentials and was kicked out.

I learned later that the whole thing had been fixed. The Credentials Committee was controlled by the Dewey faction and had booted Tolbert to help Dewey. "Crooked politics," I muttered to myself.

Then I found we were just as crooked. After the Tolbert group had lost its credentials, Tieless Joe had somehow obtained the delegate badges. I was told to stand at the side of the hall and give them to the Tolbert delegates so they could get into the convention. Of course we were for Taft for President, but when it was obvious that he was losing, we joined the forces for Wendell Willkie, shouting from the gallery, "We want Willkie! We want Willkie!" It was a fun experience for an eighteen-year-old kid. Willkie was nominated, but President Franklin D. Roosevelt defeated him to win a third term.

Despite my good time at the convention, I also had learned a lesson. I had seen politics behind the ouster of Tieless Joe Tolbert. "You can't win before a fixed jury," I muttered to myself as I returned home. "Politics is crooked."

But the partners in the law firm, including my uncle, were not about to give me a pass because I was so put off by the shenanigans in Philadelphia eight years before. They insisted that I jump into the race for a seat in the South Carolina House of Representatives. They gave me one hundred dollars for promotional cards and said, "Go to it." I didn't like the change in plans, but this turn in my career wound up having a big impact on my thinking about politics and public service.

Back then politics was not organized and certainly not nationalized as it is today. There were no pollsters, no consultants, no TV ads, no yard signs, no fund-raisers—just some bumper stickers and perhaps a newspaper ad the weekend before the election. As I ran for the Statehouse, I had no campaign headquarters or paid staff. The culture of politics was different. Many of those running were veterans. Since we were all Democrats, we didn't have to worry about party pressures. We felt lucky to have survived the war. Now all we wanted was to get our state to share in the postwar boom that much of the rest of the country was experiencing.

As I began my campaign, civil rights issues were beginning to surface. The battle by African Americans to gain voting rights had been addressed by the Supreme Court in a 1944 case, *Smith v. Allwright,* that said all-white primaries in Texas were unconstitutional. South Carolina held similar all-white Democratic primaries, and its legislature responded in a special session by repealing all its laws relating to primary elections. The lawmakers were trying to circumvent the *Allwright* ruling by claiming that Democratic primaries were purely private matters and not subject to state regulation. As such, they argued, the federal government—including the Supreme Court—did not have any control over the voting requirements in the state's "private" primaries.

The National Association for the Advancement of Colored People (NAACP) sent one of its top lawyers, Thurgood Marshall, to make its argument in a challenge to South Carolina's all-white Democratic primaries. Federal Judge J. Waties Waring bought Marshall's argument. In his July 1947 ruling in *Elmore v. Rice,* Waring wrote, "I cannot see where the skies will fall if South Carolina is put in the same class with . . . other states." He added, "It is time for South Carolina to rejoin the Union." We were still fighting the Civil War.

White folks reacted bitterly to the ruling. You would have thought that someone had invaded a private party. They decried this "unheard of" decision that was surely "unconstitutional." The inevitable question arose: Would white candidates solicit the African American vote? During this period, African Americans were disenfranchised. Fewer than 1 percent of blacks in the state were registered to vote in the 1940 elections.[1]

Before long candidates were proclaiming that they wouldn't run in a primary that allowed African Americans to vote. Charlestonian Allen Legare, the most popular member of the Charleston County delegation running for reelection, called a meeting of all the candidates at the courthouse. The question was whether we should withdraw en masse from the primary and run only in the general election. I felt that such a move would be not only awkward but also insulting.

I had just returned from a war in which African Americans bravely fought for our country, right alongside white soldiers. At the end of the campaign in Africa, the 90th AAA (Anti-Aircraft and Artillery Regiment), an all-black outfit from Philadelphia, landed in Oran. I was sent back on special detail to help them get settled. So I had served with black troops in Africa—troops ready to give their lives for the cause. And here we were a few years later, a bunch of white politicians arguing about whether we should remain in the Democratic primary or boycott it in order to avoid African American voters. I couldn't believe it. I was not about to vote to withdraw from the primary. I took the floor and stated my position openly. We broke up without having made a group decision. Several candidates wound up skipping the primary and running only in the general election—and losing. As all this was going on, the *News and Courier,* the daily paper in Charleston, publicly questioned the candidates, asking: "Do you or do you not solicit the Negro vote?"

I was put off by that inquiry. It was perhaps the first time in my political career—but there would be plenty of others—in which my quick tongue got me in a tangle with the media. I thought the *News and Courier* was trying to stir up controversy. I responded to the newspaper's inquiry with a question of my own: "Do you or do you not solicit Negro subscribers and advertisers to your newspaper?" That's all I put down. They stayed angry with me for some twenty years.

Incidentally, to give a sense of the bitter racial undercurrent in the state at that time, I should mention that Judge Waring was absolutely reviled. He and his wife were verbally abused and blistered in newspaper editorials. Their house was vandalized. Waring's ruling, coupled with President Truman's decision in February 1948 to call for passage of sweeping civil rights laws, set loose anger, fear, and hostility throughout the South. Strom Thurmond, South Carolina's Democratic Governor, bolted the party to run on the Dixiecrat presidential ticket against Truman and Republican Thomas Dewey in 1948. He ran on a platform that promised to hold the tide, to fight the courts and to preserve states' rights.

But in campaigning Thurmond was blunter. I personally heard him waxing hot and heavy for segregation because of his fears that "mixing" would produce what he called a "mongrel race." Of course, after Thurmond's death, we all learned that in 1925 he had himself fathered a mixed-race child, Essie Mae Washington-Williams. Thurmond's Dixiecrat race for President marks the first move by southerners to split from the Democratic Party. The so-called Solid South linked to the Democratic Party was not so solid after all. It was beginning to crumble. Eventually the South would shift 180 degrees and align itself with the GOP. That development would make it increasingly difficult for a Southern Democrat like me to survive over the years.

Amid this tumult, I was busy waging my campaign for a House seat. Up and down Charleston's King Street, a main thoroughfare, I handed out cards and urged folks to vote for me. I was inexperienced, but I discovered during the earliest days of the campaign that I had something of a secret weapon. I had gone to Johns Island, where my first stop was the Limehouse Store. It was named for the owner, John Limehouse, a huge man at 300 pounds and well over 6 feet 6 inches. I always had done my homework and knew the names of the merchants ahead of time.

"Mr. Limehouse, I'm Fritz Hollings, running for the Statehouse, and I'd appreciate your consideration," I said.

"Did you say Hollings?" Mr. Limehouse thundered in response.

"Yes, sir."

Pacing back and forth in thought behind the counter, he finally asked, "Have you ever heard of Bubba Hollings?"

"Yes, sir," I answered. "He was my daddy."

"Well," said Mr. Limehouse, pumping his shoulders up and down and looking straight at me, "If you're half as good as your daddy, you'll do all right in Columbia. Put your cards on that cash register."

That scene was repeated numerous times. My promotional cards went into all the grocery stores. That kind of exposure helped candidates win elections. Back then there were no supermarkets. TVs were not yet much of a presence in Charleston. When you went looking for voters, you'd head to the neighborhood grocery stores. Those stores were a gathering place for folks to talk about politics or community affairs or just to swap gossip.

I also learned the lasting impression my dad had made on folks. He was the classic self-made man who ran smack into the Great Depression. He had left high school as a sophomore, worked eight years at various paper companies, and then opened his own shop—A. G. Hollings Wholesale Paper Company. He sold school supplies, paper bags, refrigerators, scales, and other products to the various stores in Charleston and Georgetown counties. The store eventually became the biggest paper company on East Bay Street, with all my uncles and aunts working there. As an enterprising businessman, Daddy put the names of his regular customers and their particular insignia on paper bags that his firm sold. But as times got rough in the Great Depression, he got the calls: "Bubba, they're not paying their grocery bills. I don't have any money to pay for the bags. So don't send them." "Well," Daddy replied, "they've got your name on them and I can't use them. I'll just send them anyway; and, if you get some money, we'll settle up." In those days, everyone looked to "settle up"—never to declare bankruptcy. No way! People were ashamed to "write off" what they owed.

Many merchants were impressed by the way Daddy handled adversity. After his store went out of business, Daddy kept a ledger of his debts. When he found work, he saved money over time and paid back as many of those debts as he could. As I campaigned on King Street, I came to a store where Daddy had settled up years before. Mr. Arnold Prystowsky, the owner, said, "Son, come in the back of the store here, I want to show you something. See these file cabinets [old-time wooden Globe-Wernicke cabinets]? Your daddy gave them to me to settle our accounts." Then, like the other merchants, he said, "Put your cards on the counter there." Daddy was a salesman when he died in 1940, while I was a sophomore at the Citadel. But he was very much alive in my first campaign.

Those stories made me proud. I continued to campaign in the general stores and fire stations, from Edisto to Ladson to McClellanville. Knowing how "Rocky" got treated in the last two elections, I was determined to make a special effort in North Charleston. Up early in the mornings, I went to where local political leaders such as Colie Moss gathered to drink coffee, and I got to know them.

On Election Day folks who voted in the biggest box in the county, North Charleston, cast their ballots in the high-school gym. At seven o'clock, when the polls closed, long lines of voters were still waiting to cast their ballots. The doors were shut with all the voters crowding into the gym. My friend Colie let me in too. I quietly went down the line and asked folks for their votes. The last voter emerged at nine o'clock. About an hour later, I returned to the law-firm library, which was filled with supporters shouting that I was leading the ticket.

I had really worked hard and wound up getting more votes than any of the other sixteen candidates. Everybody thought that Uncle Ernest made the difference for me in that first race, but they were wrong. I knew the key to my victory was Daddy. When he died, he didn't leave anything but a good name, but that good name elected me.

We were sworn into office the Thursday after Election Day. Customarily the leader of the ticket served as chairman of the Charleston House delegation. Having served as a Senate page, I knew enough about the state legislature to know that I really didn't know anything. After all I hadn't even expected to be elected. So I nominated the senior (in age) member, Lionel K. Legge, who already had served for six years in the legislature.

After the ceremonies at the courthouse, Creighton Frampton, the superintendent of education for Charleston County, approached me and said, "Can you meet me tomorrow morning? I want to show you something."

"Yes sir. I'll pick you up at your house at 8:30," I replied.

Early the next day Creighton and I drove over the Cooper River Bridge and turned left on the Mathis Ferry Road. A couple of miles down he told me to pull over next to a large, one-story, rectangular building set on concrete blocks. Called the Promised Land, it served as an elementary school for African American children. We opened the double doors. As we walked into the one-room school on this cold November day, a pot-bellied stove provided heat. This single room housed two classes of forty-three and forty-seven children—all taught by a single teacher.

Mrs. Simmons, the black teacher, called the classes to order, introducing Mr. Frampton. Creighton then presented me as a newly elected member of the legislature. The children dutifully clapped. Embarrassed at their plight, I apologized for interrupting. There was law and order at the Promised Land. Mrs. Simmons didn't have any trouble keeping the students quiet and getting their attention. And they were all dressed neatly. Mr. Frampton exclaimed how proud he was of Mrs. Simmons and the school, thanked her, and we departed.

Outside, Creighton said, "We've got to do something about this, Fritz."

"We sure do," I responded, and then I asked, "What do you suggest?"

"Teachers, buildings, transportation," he said. "They don't have any buses for the little Negro children. It's going to take a lot of money. The white schools are not much better. They have a teacher for each class, but there is a shortage. We don't pay the teachers enough."

That experience was an eye-opener. The law of the land was *Plessy v. Ferguson,* an 1896 Supreme Court decision that had upheld "separate but equal" public schools. But given what I had just seen, I realized that minority education was separate but certainly not equal. As Creighton and I drove back, I learned that Charleston County supplemented teachers' pay, but the average pay for nine months—for a white teacher—was $1,296 while Mrs. Simmons, who was teaching two classes, received only $900 for nine months. Instantly I had a cause. Public education had to be improved—for all students, black and white.

A couple of years later, I recounted this experience to constituents at a Charleston civic club. "There were three little colored children in every desk, and on the walls were the U.S. and South Carolina

Constitutions guaranteeing every child, white or black, an equal chance," I told them. "I don't think you are proud of things like that. I know I am not."[2]

It is noteworthy that I had become aware of this situation not because some teachers' union was lobbying me or some education lobbyist was imploring me to do something. Instead I learned of it because the county superintendent of education was concerned. I never met a lobbyist during my first two years in the General Assembly. During my first ten years in politics, I knew of only five interests that had full-time lobbyists: John Cauthen represented textiles; Walter G. "Buck" Edwards lobbied for the telephone company; Warren Irvin represented the movies; Bob Heilman was the point man for beer; and Nat Turner advocated for banks. All five were skilled representatives for their clients and developed close relationships with influential lawmakers.

It is a far cry from today when everything that moves has to have a hired gun to work the halls of Congress. Back then there was nothing akin to K Street in South Carolina. No political honchos were demanding that lawmakers go along with the party line. Instead, a few superintendents of education had told leaders in the House and Senate about the dual problems of poor pay and a shortage of teachers. Political leaders initially responded with an enhanced program at Winthrop College for Women. As a consequence, Winthrop was producing fine teachers in the late 1940s. But by the 1950s South Carolina's investment in Winthrop was for naught. Many of our best and brightest who had graduated from Winthrop with teaching degrees bolted across the state line for better salaries in North Carolina. The Tar Heel State had enacted a sales tax for public schools in 1934. When I learned this, I didn't think twice. We had to have a sales tax too.

I jumped into my new role as a legislator and was pleased to have landed on the Ways and Means Committee, the most powerful panel in the House. Under the S.C. Constitution (just as under the U.S. Constitution), all measures affecting revenue must originate in the House of Representatives. The Ways and Means Committee holds the key. When I was first elected, House rules required that, before it was allowed, any appropriation for the state's ordinary expenses had to have a certificate from the Comptroller General that the total sought did not exceed the state's estimated total revenues. If South Carolina did not have the revenue to cover it, then the bill would be bucked back to the Ways and Means Committee. It's popular these days in

Washington to talk about "pay as you go" government, but South Carolina adhered to that fiscal discipline sixty years ago.

The lesson I learned in my first days in government was that there was not much money for anything. House members were paid only one thousand dollars per session—and not a penny for travel or expenses. University deans were paid only nine thousand dollars a year. The Governor was paid the sumptuous sum of fifteen thousand! We needed money for everything. Despite the low pay, many of the newly elected legislators who had come from battlefields to serve in the government had a public spiritedness about them. In fact by 1948 some 59 veterans had been elected to serve in the 124-member House—and only 4 of them had been in office before the war.[3]

One of the first bills we took up was the Veterans Bonus Bill. Many states had already approved bonuses for their veterans, but we were not thinking along those lines. I'll never forget Julian Dusenbury, a Navy Cross winner, sitting on the back row just inside the door in a wheelchair. He had lost the use of his legs in combat. At the closing argument, Julian raised himself up on the brass bars provided for him to stand and vote. "Mr. Speaker," piped Julian, "we're all veterans; but we're all South Carolinians, and South Carolina doesn't have the money. I move to table the bill." And the bonus bill was killed.

Early on I began to seek support for a sales tax for public education. I told the story of the Promised Land School countless times. I told how the teacher program at Winthrop was a waste because our newly minted teachers were fleeing the state. I made the case that, unless we paid teachers more and boosted our educational system for all our children, we would never get out of the economic ditch. We needed to put government to work for the people.

My idea was to pass a sales tax whose revenues would be earmarked for public education. I made sure the tax hike proposal was minimal—just 3 percent—and that the revenues it generated could be used only to increase teachers' pay, to repair the schools, and otherwise to improve public education. Of course taxes were no more popular back then than they are today. For politicians, calling for a tax hike was akin to taking hemlock. South Carolina never had passed a sales tax. But how else were we to create the revenue to address our enormous needs? Even Mississippi had passed a sales tax in 1933. We couldn't even say "Thank God for Mississippi."

Ultimately enough of my friends in the House backed this tax hike, but before introducing a bill, I wanted to make sure both chambers supported it. Much to my consternation, when I turned to the Senate, I hit a roadblock. The old-timers there had no intention of paying for anything. In fact they were famous for passing spending measures and sending them over to the House, knowing full well that we would have to amend their bills in order to comply with our rules for fiscal discipline.

The Senate wanted no part of a sales tax for education. Its leaders even refused to consider establishing a joint committee to study the issue. I was not going to take "no" for an answer, so I asked Jim Hunter, the House clerk, if the House could establish just a House committee to study the feasibility of a sales tax for education.

"No, you can't do that," Hunter responded. But the day before we adjourned, he motioned for me to approach the desk. When I did, he said, "I've been studying that for the last few nights and I don't see anything that would prevent just a House Committee from considering it. Why don't you try it?"

That go-ahead was all I needed. But before I could act, we had to settle a disagreement between the House and Senate over the appropriations bill. The Senate wanted to fund the bill with an increase in income taxes. The House was opposed. The two sides could not get together. Eventually I came up with a compromise. I proposed that, rather than passing an income-tax surcharge, we raise taxes one cent on beer, one cent on cigarettes, and one cent on gasoline. The two chambers agreed.

Then, on the last day of the General Assembly in June 1950, I introduced a resolution—passed by a large majority—to appoint a six-member House committee to "study and prepare a sales tax providing for the educational needs of the State of South Carolina."[4] The members knew that we had to meet the "separate but equal" mandate of the Supreme Court in *Plessy*. After the legislature adjourned, the six of us met without pay all summer and fall to hammer out a proposal. We went full bore. We enlisted the help of tax experts, including Otis Livingston, chairman of our Tax Commission, who was very helpful, as was Charles Conlon of the National Federation of Tax Administrators in Chicago. After learning that California and Ohio had the best sales-tax provisions, we merged these into a South Carolina bill. We sent our final proposal to Eugene Shaw, the auditor of North Carolina, to get his comments and suggestions.

Now we had a final bill, but we were "all dressed up with no place to go." We had no idea how we were going to get it passed in the Senate. Then we got a lucky break courtesy of the voters. James F. "Jimmy" Byrnes, one of our state's most prominent citizens, had returned to South Carolina after an illustrious career in Washington. The jaunty Irishman had surprised everybody by running for Governor. I knew that we needed some additional political muscle to pass our proposal, and I figured that Byrnes might be willing to sign on to our proposal.

Byrnes had a distinguished career and might well be willing to go out on a limb in supporting a tax hike. He was well liked by South Carolinians and could make all the difference. He was a legend in the state, a public servant who had worked his way up from humble beginnings to achieve great prominence in all three branches of government.

Raised by his widowed mother, an Irish American dressmaker in Charleston, Byrnes became a political powerhouse, winning elections as Solicitor for the Second Circuit of South Carolina and then going on to the U.S. House of Representatives and the U.S. Senate. He was a leader in helping to enact President Franklin Roosevelt's New Deal. In 1941 Roosevelt appointed him to be an Associate Justice of the Supreme Court. In October 1942—after Roosevelt had declared war following the attack on Pearl Harbor the previous December—the President persuaded Byrnes to step down from his lifetime position on the Court to take a new post. The South Carolinian moved into the East Wing of the White House as director of the Office of Economic Stabilization. Later he headed the War Mobilization Board. It was an impressive portfolio that put Byrnes in a position to shape the civilian aspects of the war effort. During this period, the press even took to calling him "Assistant President" as he ran the country's domestic programs while Roosevelt ran the war.

By 1944 Roosevelt was making noise that Byrnes would be his choice for Vice President. But objections were raised by various interests. Civil rights groups opposed his selection because, they said, he was a segregationist. Organized labor likewise railed against him, charging that he was anti-union. And prominent Roman Catholics objected as well, noting that Byrnes, though once an altar boy, had left the church to become an Episcopalian when he married Maude Perkins Busch of Aiken, South Carolina. In light of those objections, FDR changed course and picked Harry Truman to be his running mate. Truman and Byrnes were close. In fact the morning that Truman was nominated at the convention, he had in his jacket a speech nominating Byrnes as Vice President. Roosevelt had called at the last minute from a cruiser offshore from San Diego saying his choice was Truman.

When Roosevelt died on April 12, 1945, Truman became President and chose Byrnes to be his Secretary of State. As one of the few who knew about the atomic bomb, Byrnes encouraged the President to use it against Japan. Byrnes also quickly made a splash in his new cabinet post. His travels and speeches about the U.S. role in the aftermath of the war gained lots of attention and even made him *Time* magazine's Person of the Year for 1946. All that attention caused friction with Truman, who was displeased that Byrnes seemed to be setting foreign policy by himself. Forced to resign from his post in 1947, Byrnes returned to South Carolina a bitter man.

Truman told me how he relieved Byrnes when we were both in Savannah, Georgia, in March 1962. At that time I was Governor of South Carolina and had been invited to give a toast to the Hibernian Society there on St. Patrick's Day. Having been president of the Charleston Hibernian Society, I welcomed the invitation. I later learned that Truman also would be giving a toast. I had sense enough to shorten my remarks to five minutes. Truman spoke for nearly an hour, during which you could hear a pin drop. Afterwards I praised him for his fine speech and was preparing to return to South Carolina when he said, "Don't you want a drink?"

"Yes, sir," I replied.

"Well, come on up to the room," he said.

As Truman regaled me with all kinds of stories, I couldn't resist asking how he had come to fire Jimmy Byrnes. "Byrnes thought of himself not just as Secretary of State, but in charge of foreign policy," Truman said. He added that Byrnes had been getting lots of attention after a major speech in Stuttgart, Germany, in which he outlined U.S. foreign policy in the postwar era. When he returned to the States, Byrnes landed in New York and went to the broadcast studios of Lowell Thomas, a very prominent journalist. Truman said he happened to be upstairs in the White House when he heard Byrnes describe his trip on Thomas's show. The next morning, when the Secretary of State came to report to the President in the Oval Office, Truman listened respectfully and then told his friend Jimmy, "You reported this last night to Lowell Thomas.

Jimmy and Maude Byrnes, Lieutenant Governor Hollings, and Senator Strom Thurmond, 1955. Collection of the author

Lowell Thomas didn't appoint you. I did. Now that you're looking for another job, I suggest you see Lowell Thomas."

Truman was a good storyteller. It was around 1:30 in the morning when I left. I now had a greater understanding of Byrnes's ill will when he returned to South Carolina. His feelings of resentment help explain how this longtime "Mr. Democrat" shifted gears over the years. He wound up backing Republican Presidential candidates, and in 1968 he even advised Richard Nixon about how to entice rural Southern Democrats into the GOP fold as part of the so-called Southern Strategy.

Still Byrnes surprised everybody when, at age seventy-one, he decided to jump back into politics and run for Governor in 1950. He was easily elected. Even though I had actively supported Speaker of the House Tom Pope over him, Byrnes and I were friendly as neighbors on the Isle of Palms. I had become familiar with his routine. The former Secretary of State spent the day writing a book, and then at five, in good Charleston style, he would come out on his porch and shout, "Fritz, come on over."

I never passed up such opportunities. Those times were a real treat, although my memory of them is a bit hazy because of the wickedly potent old-fashioneds that Byrnes concocted. He fascinated me with stories about larger-than-life figures from World War II, including of course Roosevelt, Winston Churchill, and Joseph Stalin. I just sat there, mesmerized. Byrnes would call these get-togethers "bullbat sessions" because at that time of evening, the bullbats would be diving and flitting low around the houses on the beach.[5]

Governor Byrnes was the most interesting individual I have ever met in politics. And, after he mixed up one of his famous old-fashioneds, he also was one of the most persuasive. So I decided to make the most of our friendship. We hoped to enlist the newly elected Governor to support our proposal for the sales tax, and so I said, "Governor, come join us. I want you to hear us out on this sales tax." I figured that if we could press the case for the tax hike directly to Byrnes, even before his inauguration, we might be able to persuade him to endorse it. Sure, it would mean that one of his first acts as Governor would stir opposition from those arguing that South Carolinians were too broke to pay an increase in taxes. But I knew he would see that we'd be worse off without taking this step.

When the Governor-elect came to the old Ways and Means room just inside the State Capitol, I set out in detail the dilapidated conditions of the African American schools in the state. Other committee members also pressed for the tax hikes as the only way to address our problems in education, including providing decent transportation and boosting teachers' pay. He listened intently to our pitch for about an hour. I told him that we had formed a committee in the House but the Senate had refused to participate. We noted that North Carolina and even Mississippi had already enacted a sales tax and were providing for their schools.

Byrnes clearly was impressed. Underlying the discussion was the fact that, unless we got a sales tax, the state would be in jeopardy—and subject to legal challenges—for failing to provide separate but equal facilities. Obviously he didn't want that to happen on his watch. After a while Governor Byrnes called out to his chauffeur, Willie Byrd, "Call Miss Maude and tell her I will be late for dinner." He listened for another thirty minutes and then turned to us and said: "I never heard of anything like this. I don't know whether I can go along. I'll need some time to study it and I'll let you know."

Here it was, shortly before his inauguration as Governor, and Byrnes really had no idea about the magnitude of this problem. I encouraged him to check it out with Tax Commissioner Otis Livingston, who had worked closely with us in developing the proposal, as well as other experts who helped us. I added that we really wanted his support. Without it we couldn't prevail.

Finally, during Christmas week, the Governor-elect called me and said, "Fritz, I've studied that thing, and damn it, I'm going with it. I want you to get everything you know about it and sit down with my staff. We'll get it."

I was ecstatic. I said, "Thank God. Governor, with your leadership, we can get it done. We can pass it in the House, but the Senate is absolutely opposed."

"I'll get those Senators—don't worry," he replied.

But I did worry. In certain parts of the state, particularly upstate in places such as Anderson, in the foothills of the Blue Ridge Mountains in the northwestern corner, the hostility toward a sales tax was intense. Newspaper editorials argued that we couldn't afford it and that such a tax was regressive. But the state had to afford it. Today, looking back on fifty-two years of public service, I can say that moving the sales tax, rather than regressive, was the most progressive thing I have done.

When the new legislature convened in January 1951, my colleagues made me Speaker Pro Tempore by acclamation. That post put me in a prime position to push the sales tax. Right out of the gate, Byrnes lived up to his pledge of support by saying in his inaugural address that winning approval of the sales tax was the best way to improve the education of all children, white and black. "It is our duty to provide for the races substantial equality in school facilities," Byrnes said. "We should do it because it is right. For me that is sufficient reason. If any person wants an additional reason, I say it is wise."

The new Governor also emphasized that the Supreme Court had upheld "separate but equal" facilities as constitutional but that cases seeking to strike down segregation were pending. "I am hopeful that the Supreme Court will deny this appeal," the Governor said. "I am hopeful, too, that if in a given case there is shown an honest effort to provide substantially equal facilities, it will favorably influence the opinion of the Court."

If the Supreme Court abolished segregation, Byrnes added, such a ruling would "endanger the public school system in many States. The overwhelming majority of colored people in this State do not want to force their children into white schools. . . . Except for the professional agitators, what the colored people want, and what they are entitled to, is equal facilities in their schools. We must see that they get them."

On January 23, the committee issued its formal report, filled with extensive data, including revenue estimates from the sales tax, the state's budget requirements, and a proposal on how resources should be divvied up among school construction, transportation, and teacher salaries. The next day Byrnes weighed in again. He went before the lawmakers and made an emphatic pitch for the tax. He cited our committee as having "rendered a splendid service," and he endorsed our recommendations as "the best plan for an educational program." He added, "I agree with the committee that a retail sales tax is the only source from which we can hope to secure the revenue necessary to give the children of South Carolina the educational opportunities to which they are entitled."

Once Byrnes had weighed in, a lively debate followed in the legislature. I continued my nonstop talking for passage of the sales tax. I insisted that every cent of revenue would go to public education. Opponents said that the state was broke and its citizens poor. My response was straightforward: How are we going to get our children out of the mud? We're stuck. The ox is in the ditch. And we must pull together to get it out.

During the battle the school superintendents put their shoulders to the wheel to make the case.[6] Meanwhile I stayed on the floor day after day, responding to what seemed like endless questioning. Finally, after hearing me go on and on, John Amasa May, the Representative from Aiken County, queried, "Will the member yield?"

"I'll be glad to yield," I responded.

"The trouble with you, Hollings, is that you've got an impediment in your speech."

Thinking of my Charleston accent, I smiled and said, "What's that?"

"Your trouble," exclaimed May, "is you can't listen."

I'll never forget May's lesson. I learned to listen and to rely on plenty of my colleagues to help get that sales tax passed in April.[7]

We wound up with a 3 percent tax on retail sales that produced enough revenue to boost teachers' pay, build new schools, repair old ones, and provide buses for all the children in the state. We were determined to meet our obligation under the law to provide separate but equal facilities for white and black students. The one-teacher and two-teacher schools were on their way to extinction. Of course, while we made good progress in narrowing the gap between white and black schools by making all these improvements, we still had a ways to go before they would be "equal."

In addition to the sales tax, we also passed another measure of great significance. It may seem hard to believe by today's standards, but in 1950 no law was on the books to prohibit lynching. I proposed such legislation in the wake of the infamous Willie Earle lynching case in Greenville, which had ended in 1947 with the culprits going free. We veterans of World War II now serving in the legislature had not fought so that South Carolinians could be free to lynch. Those of us who supported the legislation cited the Earle lynching as a horrific scar on our state's history. It showed the still-potent force of mob rule.

Earle was accused of killing a taxi driver. The twenty-four-year-old suspect fit the description given by the dying man, and he had bloodstains on his jacket. After Earle's arrest, more than thirty men stormed the jail where he was being held and, sometime after 4:30 in the morning, pointed a shotgun at the jailer and took off with the young man. Earle was slashed, tortured, and eventually killed by a shotgun blast. An all-white male jury acquitted the twenty-eight white defendants. The verdict was condemned as a "ghastly farce" by the *Atlanta Journal*.[8]

When I proposed the antilynching measure, several House members walked out, saying that they did not want to be near me during that debate. There were a few redneck objections. I'll never forget Blease Ellison of Lexington standing up during a full session of the House and announcing loudly as he walked out, "I'm not sitting in this chamber with someone who makes such a proposal." He and I later ended up good friends, but his words underscore where racial sentiments were back then.

The first year I proposed the antilynching bill, it failed to pass. But the next year, 1951, it passed overwhelmingly. The grand dragon of the Ku Klux Klan sat in the gallery glaring down during the vote.

Those experiences taught me a great deal about how to pass legislation. I was especially pleased by the passage of the sales tax. Today conventional wisdom says that a politician who supports a tax increase must have a death wish. But in 1950 I had sponsored a tax increase on gasoline, cigarettes, and beer and, just six months later, led the way for the state's first sales tax. Despite such actions I was unanimously elected Speaker Pro Tempore of the House of Representatives in January 1951. People expect their government to respond to their needs. I had responded. The people haven't changed. They still have the same expectations. But politics has become so polluted with pollsters, lobbyists, special interests, national TV, national political parties, and money that the people's needs are often ignored.

Getting that sales tax passed showed that government can work. We were on the path to equalizing our educational facilities. Given the backdrop of the ruling by Judge Waring, elected officials knew that we must act voluntarily or, as Byrnes had suggested, potentially face court orders that might go further than any of us at that time would tolerate. Indeed Byrnes even said in a speech to the South Carolina Education Association on March 20, 1951, "If the Court changes what is now the law of the land, we will, if it is possible, live within the law, preserve the public school system, and at the same time maintain segregation. If that is not possible, reluctantly, we will abandon the public school system."

The stakes couldn't be higher. Governor Byrnes had even gone so far as to put the very preservation of the public-school system at issue. Throughout the 1950s tensions over civil rights issues were never far from the surface. Now that the courts had permitted African Americans to vote in the Democratic primary, pressure was beginning to build in other areas as well.

Of course at that time schools were segregated. No politician who called for anything other than segregated education could remain in office. But I saw no reason for school boards to be segregated. The Charleston County School Board reflected ethnic and religious considerations in its makeup: there was a Greek member, Leventis; a Jewish member, Pearlstine; a Catholic, Runey; and a Protestant, Seignious. But there was no African American member who could provide insight into the needs of black children. As chairman of the Charleston County legislative delegation, I proposed an addition to the board, Joseph W. Brawley, an African American, a college graduate, and a retired mail carrier. I quietly lined up the support of the entire delegation for Brawley.

Then word leaked out, and before long, the name of the Reverend Paul M. Kinports of St. Matthew's Lutheran Church was proposed. The selection of a Lutheran was quite deliberate since my critics knew that I was a Lutheran. They had decided to "put Hollings in his place." No one thought at the time I would vote for an African American instead of a prominent Lutheran minister. But I stuck to my guns. My roommate, Paul Macmillan, and State Senator O. T. Wallace also supported Brawley. But Kinports was elected 6–3. The prevailing sentiment was that our way of life had to be protected. Sure enough, in my campaigns for Lieutenant Governor and Governor, voters were reminded that I was for integration.

"All men are created equal" in the Declaration of Independence was not a reality in the Old Confederacy and surely not in Summerton, South Carolina, a sleepy little southern town fifty miles southeast of Columbia, the state capital. But African American citizens who had served in World War II had gotten the word. Fighting on the front line in Europe and being told to sit in the back of the bus on returning home was bad enough. But providing a bus for white children and none for the black was stark.

Levi Pearson, an African American, had a home in Sumter County, but his children were required to attend Scott's Branch School in Clarendon County and had to walk nine miles each way to school. Pearson fixed up a discarded school bus and went with Reverend Joseph A. DeLaine, a schoolteacher in Clarendon County, to the school board for gasoline money. The superintendent told DeLaine that there wasn't any gas money. When DeLaine asked "Why not?," the superintendent told him that white folks owned property and paid taxes, which provided money for the transportation of the white children. But since the blacks didn't own any property and paid no taxes, there would be no money for buses or gas. At the time Clarendon County provided thirty buses for the whites to attend twelve schools, but the county provided no buses for the black children, who had to travel to sixty-one schools.

Pearson went to Columbia and got Harold Boulware, an NAACP lawyer, to bring suit for "separate but equal" transportation. When the case came on for trial, it was thrown out on a technicality. Although Pearson's children were required to attend the Scott's Branch School in Clarendon County, Pearson's home was just over the line in Sumter County. This enabled the Judge in Clarendon County to throw the case out for lack of jurisdiction. Pearson not only lost the case, but he lost white customers for the timber that he cut; and the bank immediately cut his credit. Not to be deterred, Reverend DeLaine consulted with James M. Hinton, chairman of the state NAACP, and Modjeska

Simkins, a civil rights activist in Columbia. Hinton told DeLaine that, if he could get twenty-five plaintiffs, they would get "that Washington lawyer Thurgood Marshall" to bring a class action, and they would show the white folks that they really meant business. Instead of twenty-five, some seventy-six plaintiffs signed up—children through their parents. The named defendant was Roderick W. Elliott, chairman of the Clarendon County School Board, which was represented by a prominent attorney, Emory Rogers. Noting that the high-powered Marshall was on the case, the board then retained Robert McCormick Figg, a Columbia University law graduate in Charleston who was considered just about the best attorney practicing in federal court in South Carolina.

Upon the filing of the *Briggs v. Elliott* case all hell broke loose. Harry Briggs, a World War II veteran operated a filling station while his wife worked as a maid at a small inn in Manning. Immediately white customers stopped coming to Briggs's station, and blacks were intimidated from patronizing it. Mrs. Briggs lost her job, and maids who had signed the complaint were fired from their jobs. African American farmers were refused seed at the supply store and had to travel all the way to Columbia for seed to plant their crops. All kinds of threats and insults were hurled at the plaintiffs. Tensions were high. In fear for his life and to make a living, Briggs and his wife wound up fleeing to Florida. DeLaine lost his job as principal of Scott's Branch High School, and twice at night vigilantes drove by and shot up his home. On the second occasion, when the Reverend DeLaine—who was threatened several times with being lynched—was forewarned that they were coming again to shoot up his house, he used a shotgun to fire at the car's tire so he could identify the assailants. For this he was charged with "assault and battery with intent to kill." Then on October 10, 1951, DeLaine's home was burned down. The church moved Reverend DeLaine to Lake City, twenty miles away. DeLaine was given a new church, but before long his Lake City church was burned. Shortly afterward, when Reverend DeLaine heard that a mob was heading for him one night, he escaped out of the back door of his home and went across two neighboring fields to a highway, where he caught a ride to Charlotte and then to New York, never to return to South Carolina. The warrant against him remained outstanding for the rest of his life—a decision by authorities to make certain that he would never return home. DeLaine died in 1974, but it was not until

2000 that the South Carolina parole board granted him a posthumous pardon. Despite the pressure on the plaintiffs to drop the case, sixty-six plaintiffs stuck it out—the so-called Summerton 60.

As this violence was occurring, Thurgood Marshall changed his legal strategy. His lawsuit contested not just the equality of transportation but also the right of the State of South Carolina to practice segregation in public schools. The State responded by relying on the South Carolina constitutional requirement of "separate schools . . . for children of the white and colored races." The defense also relied on the well-settled "separate but equal" doctrine of *Plessy v. Ferguson*. The State also contended that as a result of the recently passed 3 percent sales tax, black school facilities were on par with white schools; black teachers' pay had been raised; and transportation to the black schools also had been made equal.

Marshall sought an injunction against state and county officials, a filing that required a three-judge panel hear the case. One of them, Judge Waring, already had caused a ruckus in the state with his earlier ruling that allowed African Americans to participate in Democratic primaries. The Court, by a 2–1 margin, held that it was bound by the precedent of the 1896 *Plessy* case that "separate but equal" facilities were constitutional. But the majority also found that African Americans had not been furnished "educational facilities and opportunities equal to those furnished white persons" and ordered the state to correct the inequities and to report back in six months.

Once again, Waring was the outlier, filing a dissenting opinion that antagonized plenty of the state's white citizens. Waring was gaining notoriety among whites for his liberal views on racial issues. A respected jurist, he had married into a well-connected old Charleston family but then was divorced and married Elizabeth Hoffman, a "redhead liberal" from New York. During the trial Mrs. Waring made a show of greeting and embracing the minority witnesses and inviting them to be seated within the rail. In his dissent Waring was blunt. He wrote that "segregation in education can never produce equality and that it is an evil that must be eradicated."[9] After that decision, Waring was harassed and even received death threats. The Warings got round-the-clock FBI protection, but after so many "invitations" to leave town, the Judge finally did just that. He left his native state and moved to New York—never to return, except for his funeral.

Meanwhile the next stop for the litigation was the United States Supreme Court, where the plaintiffs used Waring's dissent as the basis for their appeal. Initially, the Court returned the case to the district court for a hearing on the state's progress in making the facilities equal. But Marshall argued that equality could not exist as long as the schools were segregated. That argument prompted another review by the Supreme Court. *Briggs* was consolidated with challenges to the law in Kansas, Virginia, Delaware, and the District of Columbia. In fact *Briggs* was the first desegregation case to reach the Supreme Court, and Thurgood Marshall considered it the most important.

To represent South Carolina, Byrnes enlisted John W. Davis, a fine appellate lawyer who had served as Solicitor General in the Wilson administration and had been the Democratic presidential nominee in 1924. He had argued more than one hundred cases before the Supreme Court and was so confident of victory that he agreed to represent South Carolina pro bono. Governor Byrnes, a former Supreme Court Justice himself, knew we had the law on our side but wanted to make certain that we also marshaled all the facts.

The Governor appointed me to help with the defense since I had been the principal author of the 3 percent sales tax that would help to make the African American schools "equal" to those attended by white children. I could be a ready reference for all questions raised about teachers' pay, transportation, and school buildings. Byrnes told me at the time of my appointment that he was confident that South Carolina would win in a walk. He was counting on Chief Justice Fred Vinson to uphold *Plessy,* the long-standing precedent, and to side with arguments favoring state sovereignty.

Robert Figg and I boarded the Carolina Special for Washington, arriving at Union Station at six o'clock on Sunday morning, December 6, 1952, prior to the Tuesday opening arguments. As we had breakfast at the station, Thurgood Marshall walked in, and joined us. Figg and Marshall were both professionals. Not only did they have the utmost respect for each other, but over the months of motions and trial, they had become fast friends. In fact, some years later, when Figg was being considered for an appointment to a Federal District Judgeship, Marshall wrote a letter endorsing the appointment. And at the unveiling of Byrnes's portrait at the Supreme Court, Justice Marshall surprised everyone by greeting Figg in a loud voice and embracing him— almost lifting him off the floor.

On that Sunday morning, they first exchanged pleasantries. As they chatted, Marshall told of his trouble in Cicero, Illinois. An African American family had moved into an all-white neighborhood, and all kinds of commotion had exploded. Threatening telephone calls were followed by drive-by gun shots.

"I had to go to Springfield and get Governor [Adlai] Stevenson to move that family back down to Mississippi for safekeeping," Marshall said. "But don't ever tell anybody. That would ruin me."

I quickly responded: "Don't tell anybody I'm eating breakfast with you or I'll never get elected to another office." We all laughed.

They then started talking about the case. "Let's assume I win, Bob," Marshall said. "The Court has ruled with me. How long do you think it will take for the schools to be integrated?"

Figg paused for a couple of minutes, stroking his chin. Finally he replied, "Thurgood, it's going to take longer than you think. All of twenty-five years."

"Longer than that, Bob," Marshall countered. "It'll be closer to fifty."

I listened attentively. After the breakfast at Union Station, Figg and I learned to our surprise that the Kansas case had been moved up on the docket ahead of the lead case, *Briggs v. Elliott*. I was told that NAACP leader Roy Wilkins was close to the Solicitor General and had the Kansas case moved ahead of *Briggs* so that the NAACP would get a strong start before the Court. Kansas schools already were moving toward integration. It was in a different posture because there were no allegations of gross inequality in school facilities, curriculum, or staff. Indeed the State of Kansas had submitted its case based on briefs and was not even preparing to participate in the oral argument. Realizing that Kansas was not even sending a lawyer, Figg got on the phone to Governor Byrnes to inform him of the changed posture of the case.

Byrnes then called Governor Edward Arn of Kansas and raised sand. This was an historic case, and Kansas was not even bothering to send counsel for oral argument! Kansas was practically admitting we were wrong. He implored Arn to at least send a lawyer to argue. Later that afternoon we learned that an Assistant Attorney General named Paul Wilson, who would be making his first appellate argument, would represent Kansas. We didn't think much of this. After Wilson arrived in Washington, he joined us in our large parlor room at the Wardman Park Hotel, where we argued the various points and critiqued those arguments in order to be thoroughly prepared. We continued until the wee hours of the morning to make sure that Wilson was adequately briefed.

On Tuesday morning we bucked the long lines and crowds in order to get into the Court and secure our seats within the rail. The first order of business was to move my admission to practice before the Supreme Court. Then I spotted the actor Henry Fonda, who was performing in Washington in that period. He didn't have a seat, so I invited him to sit by me.

When Wilson rose for his argument, much to our surprise, he knocked the ball over the fence. Cogent and categorical, he answered all the questions directly and never deviated from his central theme that the Court must rule in our favor because of the long-standing precedent of *Plessy v. Ferguson*. Next came Thurgood Marshall and John W. Davis.

A hush fell upon the Court. Marshall had barely begun setting out his argument when Justice Felix Frankfurter started quizzing him. Other Justices also joined in the questioning. Marshall was clear, incisive, and persuasive. He made his presentation with a down-home, folksy style. He easily responded to the torrent of questions, having prepared many long nights in advance of that moment. Then came John W. Davis, who lived up to his well-earned reputation for eloquence.[10]

No one had argued more cases before the Court than had Davis.[11] He provided a surprising analysis of a twelve-year period at the end of the Civil War when the Reconstruction government of South Carolina integrated the schools. "We have already tried what the Appellants seek," he declared. "There was total chaos."

Later as I reflected on the case, I thought both Davis and Marshall had performed superbly. Many predictions were made as to how the Justices would rule. But instead of a decision, the Court decided that counsel should present further arguments in another hearing in order to address various constitutional issues that they had not sufficiently answered.[12]

Then the dynamics on the Court changed dramatically. Before the Court convened for the rehearing, Chief Justice Vinson died suddenly in September 1953. President Eisenhower picked as the next Chief Justice former California Governor Earl Warren, who had run for Vice President in 1948 and had backed Ike at the 1952 Republican National Convention for the presidential nomination. Years later, after Warren's name became synonymous with a slew of liberal Supreme Court decisions, the President called his choice of the Californian to be Chief Justice one of the worst mistakes of his presidency.

President Eisenhower's comments reflected in part a reaction to the stunning decision rendered by the Warren-led Court, on May 17, 1954, when it unanimously declared that "in the field of public education the doctrine of 'separate but equal' has no place. Separate educational facilities are inherently unequal." A year later the Court decided that such schools must be dismantled "with all deliberate speed."

Lawyers not only represent their clients but also serve as officers of the Court. Accordingly the attorneys for both sides—including Figg, Marshall, and civil rights activist Roy Wilkins—got together to collaborate on the most effective way for the South to come into compliance with the decision. In order to comply with the Court's mandate that desegregation occur "with all deliberate speed," they concluded that the only realistic way to make it work was to integrate the first grade the first year, the first and second grades the second year, and so on. In that way the schools would be integrated peacefully over a twelve-year period. Everybody agreed, but then one of the plaintiff's lawyers rejected that approach. "We shall not be given our constitutional rights on the installment plan," he said.

That position marked the end of any chance for a feasible plan to implement the decision. Instead of complying with the Supreme Court decision and having fully integrated schools by 1966, we made little progress. Marshall was right that integration would be a long time coming. Southerners greeted *Brown v. Board of Education* with anger, fear—and defiance. Twelve years after *Brown*, more lawsuits, demonstrations, and resistance followed. Instead of complying with the decision over a twelve-year period, Scott's Branch School in Clarendon County was almost totally segregated fifty years after *Brown*.

The aftershocks also had a huge impact on the state's political structure. Over time the all-white Democratic Party integrated, even as the Republican Party became practically all white. The solid Democratic South eventually became the solid Republican South. The day that *Brown* was decided, May 17, 1954, there were 16 private secondary schools in South Carolina, 4 in my home town of Charleston. Today there are exactly 362 private secondary schools in the state—most of which came into existence as part of the "white flight" movement.

Even before the ruling, Byrnes had covered all his bases in the event South Carolina lost. He had urged voters in 1952 to support a constitutional amendment to relieve the state of its obligation to provide public education and to give the legislature the power to close schools rather than accept integration. In 1955 the state legislature repealed the compulsory attendance law.[13] The resistance was fueled by Byrnes, who never accepted the decision. He seemed to become even more embittered.

Two years after *Brown*, Byrnes—then a private citizen, having completed his four-year term as Governor—wrote a scathing critique in *U.S. News & World Report*. Because he was the only living former Supreme Court Justice, his words carried plenty of force. "The Court did not interpret the Constitution—the Court amended it," he wrote in the May 18, 1956, issue. "An immediate consequence of the segregation decision is that much of the progress made in the last half century of steadily advancing racial amity has been undone. . . . The races are divided and the breach is widening. The truth is there has not been such tension between the races in the South since the days of Reconstruction."[14]

Throughout this period, I too opposed the *Brown* decision. The ruling threw precedent overboard and invaded states' control over education. After all, under the legal doctrine of *stare decisis,* or respect for precedent, the doctrine of separate but equal had long been the law of the land. It had been on the books for fifty-eight years and supported in numerous Supreme Court decisions. I had been the principal author of the tax measure to put the state in compliance with *Plessy*'s mandate. Now a different Court, without a change in law, had changed the Constitution. Most important of all, South Carolina's Supreme Court authority, Jimmy Byrnes, had said the *Brown* decision was unconstitutional. Of course no politician in South Carolina or anywhere else in the South could survive without criticizing *Brown*.

In the 1950s it was hard for anybody with a breath in his body not to recognize the combustibility in day-to-day life in South Carolina, given the growing racial tensions. But there was a way forward, past all this hostility. It wouldn't be easy. And it took years. Almost a decade later, I had to tell South Carolinians that it was time to accept change. It was in 1963, when I was Governor and parted company with other southern politicians who were waging war against the federal government and whose constituents were shedding blood to defend their "way of life." I said that it was time for citizens in South Carolina to accept the fact that, like it or not, once we had run out of courts, we had to obey the law. As a result the admission of African American student Harvey Gantt to segregated Clemson was achieved peacefully. It showed the naysayers that they were wrong. Government had worked. Change was achieved without violence. The sky didn't fall.

But in the immediate aftermath of the *Brown* decision in 1954, the political climate in South Carolina was unsettled. Having been in the state legislature for six years, I was ready to make a move and began to run for Lieutenant Governor. The number two post in the state obviously was a stepping stone to the Governor's Mansion. The Lieutenant Governor's principal role is to preside over the State Senate. With my experience as Speaker Pro Tem of the House, I knew that I could handle those duties. Also I had been involved in legislative battles, balancing the budget, passing the sales tax, and improving education. I had a reputation for getting things done.

My opponent, State Senator J. Claytor Arrants, was a farmer, teacher, lawyer, and navy veteran. He had won his Senate seat in 1952 and, earlier in his career, had served a term in the House. Campaigning was easy during that period. You didn't have to run around the state raising money because you had no staff. Candidates relied on volunteers. There was no need to spend on media—no TV or radio or direct mail or even yard signs. We went around the state making "stump" speeches.

Typically candidates took out a newspaper ad before Election Day. Of course the *Brown* decision on May 17, 1954, cast a large shadow over the campaign. Every candidate for statewide office in the 1950s and even into the 1960s had to make clear his outrage over the Court's infringement on state prerogatives. I was no different. An ad in the newspapers two days before Election Day cited my work on education, taxes, and law enforcement—as well as my role in the Supreme Court case. What a man will do in public office is best told by what a man has done: "Performance is better than promises." Arrants was making hay against me by using my efforts to get Brawley appointed to the Charleston County School Board as proof that I favored integration.

In reality nobody paid much attention to the Lieutenant Governor's race. Because I didn't have to pay pollsters or consultants and had no focus groups, my race cost a grand total of $11,000! (By contrast a recent race for Lieutenant Governor reportedly cost more than $1.65 million.) Two days after my Sunday ad ran, I won decisively, 182,694 to 93,005. The victors in the Democratic primary faced no GOP opposition in the general election. But just as the primary settled the state's top officeholders, the political world was turned upside down when U.S. Senator Burnet Rhett Maybank died suddenly, apparently as a result of a heart attack, on September 1.

At the Maybank funeral, I was standing at the door of the Byrnes's limousine when I overheard Mrs. Byrnes say, "Jimmy is coming back to Washington." But it was not to be. Jimmy Byrnes would not reprise his role as U.S. Senator. Instead, when the Democratic Executive Committee hurriedly met after the funeral to anoint another nominee, they looked elsewhere. Under state law political parties were required to submit their nominees sixty days before the general election. And time was of the essence. The executive committee turned to sixty-six-year-old Edgar Brown to replace Maybank. Brown's position as chairman of the Finance Committee in the S.C. Senate made him a political powerhouse, but he had run twice before for the U.S. Senate and lost.

Strom Thurmond had been nominated. But, when he got only eleven votes, Charlie Plowden of Summerton said, "We need to go out of here with a solid front," and moved that Brown be elected unanimously. This was about twelve noon. The meeting had lasted for only about three hours. Governor Byrnes got on the phone with his friends, the editors of the main dailies in South Carolina, and started the write-in for Thurmond. He pilloried the executive committee for not ordering a primary, for depriving the voters of having their say. There wasn't time, but people believed Byrnes. Governor Byrnes had been the best man at Senator Brown's wedding many years earlier but now felt ill will toward the Senator. Byrnes had backed Eisenhower in 1952 while Brown stayed within the Democratic Party fold and supported Adlai Stevenson.

Thurmond jumped into the race, and before long, front-page editorials touting the Thurmond write-in candidacy sprang up, along with pictures of voting machines that highlighted the place to write-in Thurmond's name. The rest is history. Thurmond was the only write-in candidate ever to be elected to the United States Senate. He owed that victory to Jimmy Byrnes.

Of course in the general election, I was running on the Democratic slate with Edgar. I backed him. I got a nice—and revealing—note from him a few weeks after Election Day. He was still nursing his wounds. "Your loyalty to me and to the Democratic Party will always remain as one of the bright memories of the campaign," Brown wrote in the letter dated November 22, 1954. "We fought a good fight but the

Republican segment of the press abused the power of the free press to distort the truth and mislead the people by building up the false issue, to wit: the disfranchisement [sic] of the people, and kept the same alive by feeding it on lies and prejudice. The news columns were closed to our side. The disappointment, of course, was keen but I am grateful to say that I came through in good health and fine spirits and am prepared to carry on as usual."

Once in office as Lieutenant Governor, I made the most of it. Having friends in both chambers of the legislature put me in the catbird seat to act as a go-between to settle differences between the bodies. In assuming the role of the conciliator, I made even more friends. Of course I raced around the state and was a Rotary Club speaker in all forty-six counties. The new Governor, George Bell Timmerman, thought it undignified to hustle for industry. He thought if an industry was interested in South Carolina, he would be glad to give them an appointment. I was always on call to fill in for him. Often Colonel Bob Cooper, the head of the Development Board, let me know I was needed to pinch hit for the Governor at some business function. I would rush to these gatherings and explain, "Governor Timmerman wanted to welcome you. But a highly important matter came up."

These efforts gave me very good experience in lobbying for businesses to locate in the Palmetto State. As I wooed new industries, I also was meeting supporters all over the state. In fact I was really beginning my campaign for Governor. My efforts also led to my campaign slogan later in the Governor's race: "Have experience, will travel." I was ready to tell South Carolina's story: that our government was receptive to new business and that our workers were ready to give "a day's work for a day's pay."

Even as I became the state's top cheerleader for business, I also had to be right on hot political issues. I made clear in a speech in 1956 that, yes, I had been elected as a Democrat, but "not one of the national-minded, swallow-it-all Democrats." Still I noted that I would nonetheless support the national party ticket, Adlai Stevenson and Estes Kefauver, against Dwight Eisenhower and Richard Nixon. I added, "I certainly am bitterly opposed to a Republican administration which has brought us face-to-face with integration in our schools and which has, through unfair administrative policies, among other discriminations against the South, promoted disastrous competition for our textile industry." I closed the speech saying, "We must do what it takes to preserve this way of life, especially to insure segregated schools which will provide equal opportunities with peace and good will."

I noted that South Carolinians had constructed more than eight thousand classrooms and increased teachers' pay for blacks and whites. "Our system of separate but equal facilities comes as a matter of history, culture, and economic background," I observed. "We believe that public schools are intended for education, not integration, and, for my part, schools will always remain segregated in South Carolina."

Six months later, shortly after Donald Russell, the president of the University of South Carolina, announced that he was a candidate for Governor, I tossed my hat in the ring too. In my announcement on January 29, 1958, I noted that I had ten years of public service, including presiding over both the State House and Senate. I knew the legislators and how to make government work. A few weeks later, William Johnston, the Mayor of Anderson and brother of veteran U.S. Senator Olin D. Johnston, also jumped into the race. Like Russell and I, Johnston promised to support segregation in education. He especially sought support from rural voters. Russell went after me for my supposed ties to the so-called Barnwell Ring, a group of powerful rural legislators that included Edgar Brown and House Speaker Solomon Blatt. Russell, who was very wealthy and poured money into the race, produced political advertisements in newspapers that highlighted my youth—I was only thirty-six—and portrayed me as the "Bottle Baby of the Barnwell Ring." The ads featured a baby in diapers, holding a bottle of liquor. He hit a target. In those days Charleston and the lowcountry served liquor, but the Piedmont Bible Belt was "blue-nose" dry. Even today, while they drink up in Greenville, the state's politics is still divided: upcountry versus lowcountry.

I ran on my record—"performance is better than promises"—and emphasized the need to attract more industry to the state. I took issue with the charge that I was connected to the Barnwell Ring and questioned the large deficit that had been amassed under Russell's leadership at the university. Russell was highly intelligent but also somewhat remote and not a natural politician. He spent lots of money, won the endorsement of most newspapers, and had the backing of Byrnes. He and the former Governor had worked side by side for years as law partners, and Russell had been Assistant Secretary of State when Byrnes was running the State Department during the Truman administration.

Political cartoon published during the 1958 Hollings gubernatorial campaign. Hollings Collection, South Carolina Political Collections, University of South Carolina

When voters went to the polls in June, I led, while Russell was second. Johnston, who finished third, was knocked out of the race. Russell and I then went head-to-head in a two-week runoff. On June 24 I prevailed. In many ways, I simply out-hustled Russell. I enjoyed mixing it up with voters, and I am not certain that Russell did. My victory in the primary assured that I would be Governor since the Republicans did not field an opponent against me in November. It would be one of the last times in South Carolina that the GOP would fail to field candidates to run competitive statewide races.

South Carolina was changing. I would have to walk a tightrope. On the one hand, I would hustle for industry and push our citizens to learn the skills that would make the state attractive to new businesses. On the other hand, I needed to keep the peace, especially on the racial front, even as turmoil and violence exploded elsewhere. It was time for South Carolina to shake off its lethargy and become competitive with other states in the Old Confederacy and in the nation as a whole. South Carolinians were about to learn that a disciplined government could make a positive difference in their lives.

I can't write this without thinking of the Summerton 60—individuals who made a difference in the lives of us all—simple citizens who believed and had faith in America and its government. Years later there was a great celebration in the Rotunda of the nation's Capitol in Washington as Congress presented Rosa Parks the Congressional Gold Medal. There was no doubt she deserved the honor. But the Summerton 60 deserved it even more. The picture showing Rosa Parks refusing to give up her seat was taken on December 21, 1956, a month after the U.S. Supreme Court had ruled Montgomery's segregated bus system illegal and two and a half years after the May 17, 1954, *Brown v. Board of Education* decision, finding the "separate but equal" doctrine unconstitutional. When Mrs. Parks refused to give up her seat, she had the Supreme Court on her side. But the Supreme Court was not on the side of the Summerton 60 during their five years of hell. Instead of keeping their seats, they lost their jobs, their homes, their church, and their leader, Reverend DeLaine, who was forced to escape lynching by fleeing his home in South Carolina—never to return. At the time of DeLaine's flight, his son Joseph A. DeLaine Jr. was with the U.S. Army defending the security of the United States in Korea. For five years before Rosa Parks refused to give up her seat, the Summerton 60 withstood every pressure from those trying to get them to drop the case of *Briggs v. Elliott*. But as a result of their indomitable courage, perseverance, and undying faith in America, the words "all men are created equal" in the Declaration of Independence were finally enshrined into the Constitution of the United States. The climate changed. The country changed. Now Rosa Parks could keep her seat, the Freedom Riders could ride, and Martin Luther King could march. At the sixtieth anniversary of the *Brown* decision, the Congress of the United States awarded the Congressional Gold Medal to the leaders of the Summerton 60: Levi Pearson, Harry and Eliza Briggs, and Joseph A. DeLaine.

2

Taking Charge as Governor

Minutes after being sworn in as Governor and delivering my inaugural address on January 20, 1959, I charged up the steps to my office to change clothes for the parade and luncheon. Even in my excitement, I couldn't miss a special-delivery green envelope with gold edges lying on my desk. Its contents provided a preview of one of the most difficult challenges that I confronted over the next four years.

The envelope came courtesy of the grand dragon of the Ku Klux Klan. The Klan was doing its bit to associate with the new Governor by offering a lifetime membership in their hateful group. I immediately returned that letter, not certified but return receipt requested. I knew that this issue wasn't going away easily. Here, on my first day as Governor, the Klan made their presence known. I knew what the racist group was about, but my only contact with them was back in 1951 when, as a state legislator, I sponsored the antilynching bill. As members cast their votes to pass the measure, the grand dragon glared down from the gallery of the Statehouse. After that I figured I would make their enemies' list, and they would have nothing to do with me. Obviously I was wrong.

Swift action was imperative. J. P. "Pete" Strom, the resourceful head of the South Carolina Law Enforcement Division (SLED), was an invaluable ally. I asked him to come to the office after the parade. When I quizzed him about the Klan's membership, Strom gave a surprising answer.

Governor Hollings in his inaugural parade, 1959. Greenville
News-Piedmont, *Hollings Collection, South Carolina Political Collections,*
University of South Carolina

"We have exactly 1,687 members that we know about," he said.
"You keep records?" I asked.

"Yeah, we watch them closely," Strom said. Then, he added, "I'd be glad to get rid of them but no Governor would help me."

"How can you get rid of them?" I persisted.

"I need a little money to infiltrate the [Klan's] order," the chief responded. "That way we can watch them closely at their meetings. They are a dangerous group and don't mind taking the law into their own hands."

"Well, I'll help you," I told him. "We have to get rid of them as quick as we can."

But it wasn't quick enough. Just a few weeks later, I received a call from Sister Anthony Monaghan, a nun in Charleston's Sisters of Charity of Our Lady of Mercy, whom I admired greatly for her tireless efforts to help the needy. She told me to expect a visit from Roman Catholic bishop Paul Hallinan, who would ask for help with some trouble in Williamsburg County, a rural, very poor area southeast of Columbia. The bishop was a revered figure in Charleston, where he resided and where 25 percent of the Catholic population in the state lived. Like Sister Anthony, the bishop always responded to needs in the community, and his selflessness was quickly apparent to all who encountered him.

I met him some days after Sister Anthony had given me the heads-up. Rushing past the reception room on the way to my office, I saw the bishop in the reception room. Having served on the St. Francis Hospital board, I immediately recognized him. Hallinan was the most popular bishop who ever served in the state. Betty Bargmann, my secretary, said he had been waiting for two hours. We shook hands, and, after he was ushered into the office, the bishop got right to the point.

"Governor, do you believe in burning up the Sisters of the Church?" he asked.

Stunned at such a question, I asked, "What in the world are you talking about?"

Bishop Hallinan then described the work of the Sisters of Mercy in feeding the hungry and distributing clothing in Williamsburg County. Two of the nuns, who were white, stopped at lunchtime to break bread in an African American leader's home. For whites to eat with black people in 1959 meant trouble. The Klan quickly moved in. Later that evening thugs went to the small home where the sisters stayed outside of the town of Kingstree, threatened them, and, after darkness set in, burned a cross in the front yard of their home. The cross fell on the porch and set it afire. The sisters extinguished the flames, but they were terrified.[1]

As usual there was no account of the incident in the newspapers. I had known nothing of the violence and was astounded to learn of the Klan's boldness. As he recounted the story, Bishop Hallinan was deliberately tactful and reticent. After all, Roman Catholicism was not very popular in South Carolina. In fact, in several of my campaigns, ward heelers at a number of polling places politicked against me by saying I was "Catholic."

So it was understandable that the Catholic bishop was concerned about how a Lutheran Governor would react to his worries. I put his concerns to rest. I was angry. I sent for Chief Strom so that the bishop could relate the exact details. I then sent three teams of investigators to scour Kingstree. We didn't catch the culprits, but the taunts and threats stopped.[2] The Klan knew the Governor was their enemy, and Sister Anthony knew that she had an ally. She never forgot the attention I gave this problem. Over the years I continued to learn much from her. I admired her and defended her against those, even in Catholic circles, who charged that she was a "meddler" and a "troublemaker."

I knew in taking office that my biggest enemy would be time. In South Carolina in those days a Governor was limited to one term of four years. In order to accomplish anything, he had to move fast. An activist Governor would have to overcome a slew of disadvantages institutionally. South Carolina was essentially a state in which the legislature held all the cards. The Governor's office was weak, and there was no time to make changes. I determined to work closely with the legislature. While serving as Lieutenant Governor for four years and in the State House of Representatives for six years, I had learned how to stroke the key lawmakers to get them to go along. I didn't want the legislators to conclude that my youth—I was thirty-seven—would make me reticent. This was no time for reticence. We had a great deal to do to get the state moving.

To succeed in jumpstarting the economy, I had to have allies in the legislature. I started my efforts by selecting a small group of lawmakers on whom I knew I could rely. In the State Senate, I worked closely with John West, who would later be elected Governor himself, Marshall Parker, and William C. "Billy" Goldberg, an affable, quiet man who got along with everybody and was very popular. Over in the House, my key allies included future Governor Robert E. McNair and future South Carolina House Speaker Rex Carter. Another confidant, Floyd Spence, switched parties to become a Republican in 1962 and later served as chairman of the Armed Services Committee in the U.S. House of Representatives.

Collaborating closely with these half-dozen legislators, I would hammer out my proposals and have a final draft introduced as either "the House plan" or "the Senate plan." One of my allies would introduce it, but everyone knew those measures had the Governor's blessing. I learned long ago that if you give the other fellow the credit, you can get far more accomplished in politics and government. Using this approach, I was able to navigate the legislative process without ever having a veto overridden during my four-year term as Governor.

Much of the country had experienced an economic renaissance after World War II. Personal incomes across the United States were growing rapidly. Consumer spending exploded. This prosperity translated into a boom. Thirteen million new homes were bought in the decade after 1948; TVs became a common household item; and the number of two-car families doubled from 1951 to 1958.[3] The Palmetto State had not shared in this growth. We had made some progress, but economically South Carolina was still very much in the ditch.

I moved quickly to reverse the state's fortunes. First I decided to reorganize the Governor's Office so that South Carolina could actively recruit new businesses as a top priority. Without an all-out push to get our economy moving, we would continue to be mired at the bottom of the heap. It would take a lot of sweat, but by systematically hiring the people with know-how and reorganizing the structure of the Governor's Office, I was certain we could turn things around.

The first order of business was to relocate the office so that the Governor could receive industrial prospects and sell our state to them. When I arrived, the Governor's Office was in the State Capitol. House members and Senators were constantly escorting school classes into the Governor's Office, where the kids could get a picture with the state's chief executive. This was good politics for both the lawmaker and the Governor, but it made it difficult to get any business done. To address this issue, I moved the Governor's Office out of the State Capitol to the Wade Hampton Office Building, where it would be next to the Development Board. An industry executive could be ushered in to see me, and

I could provide him firsthand with my assurances that his concerns would be addressed.

I also hired Ernie Wright as the first Industrial Secretary ever to serve a Governor of South Carolina. He knew all about making a pitch to industry honchos, having headed up the "prospective industry section" of the Orangeburg Chamber of Commerce. Ernie was as eager and upbeat as I was. We also reorganized the Development Board. The existing five-member State Development Board had done little. Bob Cooper, the director, was also president of the board of trustees at Clemson College. Bob was talented, but he had a staff of only five and was stretched thin. We needed a director to devote himself solely to attracting industry. To that end I increased the board from five to one member for each of the fourteen judicial circuits and one at large as chairman, Francis M. Hipp, a prominent businessman who was chairman of the board of Liberty Life Insurance Company. Having a successful corporate leader working with me provided instant credibility—an invaluable asset for a young Governor who was not supposed to know anything about business. Instead of lawyers looking for clients, I gave him an outstanding group of business leaders who were ready, willing, and able to work for new industry.[4]

The board's mission was to make local business executives a part of our team. That was no cliché or political ploy. We wanted everyone to be rowing together to make South Carolina attractive to prospects looking to relocate or to expand. The clout and connections of the businessmen on the board would make a huge difference in turning the state's fortunes around.

As we put our team together, we were lucky to induce Walter Harper to sign up. Walter had been instrumental in the development of the famous research triangle in North Carolina. He was close to North Carolina Governor Luther Hodges, but after hearing our plans, he agreed to come to the Palmetto State as the new director of the Development Board. As soon as the North Carolina folks received his resignation, they pulled out all stops to keep him. They even offered to double his salary. But Harper had given his word to us. And we made a $600 typographical error that put his salary at $15,600—a little more than I was making as Governor![5] He proved to be a great asset.

At the same time, we opened an office in Manhattan. We meant business! And I quietly started making the case for an airplane to allow us to fly business prospects to see South Carolina for themselves. Hipp was able to procure a used twin-engine Beechcraft for $50,000. Quietly Hipp's Liberty Life paid $25,000. The aircraft was used solely to seek industry, but I still took plenty of grief politically as it sounded like a luxury to some of my critics.

The next order of business was to repair the state's image of operating in the red. No industry was going to invest in "Podunk." To improve the state's credit rating, we had to raise taxes. Not surprisingly the state's business community opposed a tax hike. My proposal raised the corporate tax to 7 percent, removed the sales-tax exemptions on coal, gas, and electricity, and imposed higher "sin" taxes on cigarettes, beer, and liquor. It even took away tax exemptions on funeral homes. Talk about stirring a hornet's nest! Business was united in its determination to shoot down these revenue raisers.

On March 31 I went before a joint session of the General Assembly, part salesman and part cheerleader. I wanted to impress upon the lawmakers the urgent need for tax increases. If we were going to compete with other southern states for new industrial plants and jobs, we had to get our fiscal house in order. At the same time, I celebrated the South as a region with "boundless opportunities" that was poised to outdistance the rest of the country.

"The next half of the twentieth century belongs to the South," I told the legislators. "Thirty years ago, the South may have been the nation's number one economic problem, but when the history of America for the twentieth century is written, emblazoned therein will be the story of the region which pulled itself up from the depths and startled the world with a searing record of growth and development." Then I added, "South Carolina, moving as one great team, mobilizing our human strengths and abundant natural resources, can become the symbol of a resurgent new South. But there is no time to lose. . . . We can only lead this parade of progress by acting now."

Despite the sense of urgency that I tried to create, I was up against it. Powerful textile executives wanted no part of a plan that would make electric rates go up. The industry had one of the best lobbyists in the state, my old friend John K. Cauthen, the executive director of the South Carolina Textile Manufacturers Association. He had lots of clout in the legislature, having devoted much time to courting and schmoozing lawmakers over the years.

I also worked the legislature hard. I started bringing in members of the House and Senate for breakfast at the Governor's Mansion each morning to make my case. House Speaker Solomon Blatt was just as eager for new industry as I was. Even though Cauthen was a close friend, I managed to get Blatt to help us pass the measure in the House.

Over in the Senate, I thought I could count on powerful Finance Committee chairman Edgar Brown to help push the hike because he knew well the needs of the state. But before I knew it, the plan was in trouble. Brown had steered it out of the Finance Committee, but a number of Senators, led by influential L. Marion Gressette, proposed an amendment to eliminate my sin tax proposals. West saw that the Gressette amendment was going to pass and used some parliamentary tactics to give us another shot at it. He switched his vote from "no" to "aye" so that he could then move to reconsider the proposal. Before the legislators cast another vote that would decide the fate of the proposal, my executive assistant, Muller Kreps, summoned Brown and West to the Governor's office.

I was not happy. Everything that I wanted for the next four years depended on getting the state's fiscal house in order. I looked at my friend Senator Brown and asked, "Well, Colonel, what happened?"

He said, "Well, Governor, we didn't get enough votes."

I knew that Cauthen had been working his magic in the Senate. I recited the names of some of Senator Brown's cronies who had abandoned us on the earlier vote. I concluded that if Senator Brown, as powerful a Senator as there was, couldn't get their support, then "you are lyin' or you ain't tryin'. Which is it?" I demanded. Senators Brown and West returned to the chamber and leaned hard on some of the holdouts. In the end the proposal, including the sin taxes, passed the Senate. Goodwill for a new Governor and the clout of Senators Brown and West made all the difference.[6]

Without that tax hike, South Carolina's transition from an agricultural to an industrial economy would have been put off. To get out of the ditch, we had to demonstrate that government was fiscally responsible. This would be a recurring theme in my career: the government, whether at the state or the federal level, must not spend more than it has in revenues. My aversion to red ink is rooted in my having grown up during the Great Depression. And I had learned early on in my political career, as a member of the Ways and Means Committee, about balancing budgets.

Having prevailed at getting our fiscal house in order, I then traveled to the big New York financial houses Moody's and Standard & Poor's.

I hoped to convince them to give us a high credit rating. Even with the just-passed tax hike in hand, the Yankee executives remained skeptical.

"Yes, with your measure you've got a balanced budget," they said. "But how can we count on it staying balanced?"

"We have a rule in our House of Representatives whereby any spending bill that comes before the House must include a certificate from the comptroller that the expenditures proposed are within the expected revenues, or else the bill is automatically referred back to the Ways and Means Committee," I explained.

The New Yorkers had never heard of this. Both firms said they would have to study it. It wasn't long before they agreed that we had demonstrated that the state would not fall back into a sea of red ink. They rewarded South Carolina with a triple-A credit rating—the first state in the South to receive one. That rating gave us instant credibility as we met with industry leaders.

We were now positioned to make an effective pitch. Once we had persuaded executives to move to the state, they had to decide where in the state to put down roots. It was not uncommon for an industry decision on a location to be changed at the last minute because of concerns that the town selected didn't offer high-caliber schools. In fact, after fifty years of encouraging industries to locate in the Palmetto State, I'm convinced that a favorable tax structure, good roads and transportation, and a skilled labor market all take a backseat to outstanding public schools as the most important factor in inducing industry to choose one town over another. The topflight supervisory personnel that make a new industry profitable will not come if there are no good schools for their children. My first conference brought together the states' Mayors to tell them to beef up their school systems.

To help get other state leaders on board, I convened the first Governor's Conference on Business, Industry, Agriculture and Education. My hope was that these business leaders would stop whining about tax increases for education and understand that our economy's fortunes depend on good schools. Since South Carolina was always rated at or near the bottom of every national survey, I kicked off a program to take us from "50th to 1st." I called for the reorganization of the State Department of Education to launch a system of educational research and to improve the high-school industrial arts. These moves changed the mindset of our citizens. In fact, Archibald L. M. Wiggins, former

Undersecretary of Treasury under President Harry Truman and a native of Hartsville, South Carolina, observed, "In my opinion, the spark that set off the new interest in education was the Governor's Conference called by Governor Hollings in 1959 at which the educational needs of the State were made clear to the large group of representative citizens who attended this conference."

I was very excited and enthusiastic about the "50th to 1st" initiative. But when I returned to my office after making that pitch, my staff, always looking to prick the young Governor's balloon, had pasted a newspaper clipping on cardboard and put it on my desk. The headline said: "South Carolina #1—in venereal disease." Written at the top of the clipping were the words "Congratulations, Governor, you already made it."

In 1958, even before becoming Governor, I had worked with textile lobbyist John Cauthen to get educational TV launched. The initiative was opposed in the State Senate by former South Carolina Governor Richard M. Jefferies, who was now Colleton County's Senator. Jefferies raised objections based on the cost of the program. I knew how to appease him and make his objections disappear. I appointed Richard M. Jefferies Jr., his son, chairman of the first Educational Television Commission. After that South Carolina educational TV was launched!

As Governor I made sure that educational TV was used as a way to spread limited teaching talent into classrooms all over the state. SCETV was the nation's first closed-circuit educational television network and a pioneer in programming with popular shows such as William F. Buckley's *Firing Line*. What began as a modest initiative quickly grew. Within a decade SCETV would reach hundreds of thousands of students and win many national awards.

As much of a fiscal conservative as I have been throughout my career, I never thought it good policy to scrimp on education programs. We had such a long way to go that I figured most of our citizens would support my efforts. One initiative that has made a big difference in South Carolina involved workers who had long since been out of school. They wanted to prosper as the economy began to grow, but many simply did not have industrial skills. I had become aware of this need toward the end of my term as Lieutenant Governor. And I got lucky.

I was attending a Lutheran Church conference in Dayton, Ohio, where I got religion on technical training. As the Reverend Dr. Heyward

Epting and I were coming out of late services, I spotted a funny looking industry all lit up. "Heyward, let's go over there and see what they're making," I said. The answer? Skilled laborers! Classes in mechanical drawing, welding, punch drills, and all sorts of trades were going full blast at eleven o'clock at night. The rich were getting richer, and the poor in South Carolina stayed poor. I said to myself, "If I get elected, I'm going to get one of these programs."

I didn't forget that experience after taking the oath of office. I called my friend Governor Michael DiSalle of Ohio. I knew he would let us learn the ins and outs of Ohio's training program. Sure enough, he didn't hesitate. "Send your team up here," he said. "I'll take care of them. They'll learn everything we know." Off went our joint Senate-House committee, led by John West and Robert McNair.

Like the battle over the tax increase, the effort to boost industrial training set off plenty of fireworks. The textile industry again put up the biggest fight against funding a training program. It was a replay of sorts. Cauthen, the industry's assiduous lobbyist, who had tried to shoot down the tax hike in 1959, now trained his attacks on this new proposal. Textile companies felt such training would be a threat to their workforce. The industry operated in peaks and valleys. During the peaks, work was spread over three shifts a day, around the clock, six days a week. But during the valleys, only one shift, three days a week was needed. Workers were supposed to stay without jobs during periods when the industry was in its slow phases and be ready to return to their jobs at the start-up. The employees had no leverage. If they tried to shake up the system, it would cost them dearly. Management admonished them not to join unions. The workers were reminded that the boss rewarded loyalty. In short these workers had no options. They owed their souls to the company store.

Given those advantages, the textile industry wasn't about to pay taxes for schools that would impart skills to enable the workers to find better jobs. Pay more taxes, only to lose their workers—no way! The Chamber of Commerce also opposed technical training. Educators who wanted to close their schools in the afternoon rather than staying open in the evenings to provide adults with technical skills also joined the opposition.

Despite all these obstacles, I did some cajoling and lined up enough support in the House to get the measure through. I figured that once the measure passed the House, Senators Brown and West would navigate it to passage in their chamber. But, to my amazement, my executive assistant Muller Kreps delivered unexpected news late one afternoon. He ducked in the door and told me, "Your technical training is dead."

Shocked at that news, I asked, "How's that?"

"The legislature is about to adjourn," Kreps said. "The one remaining bill is the Deficiency Appropriations Bill. It was supposed to have the technical-training measure attached to it. But Cauthen has fixed things. Even Senator Brown is committed to make sure technical training is killed."

"Go down to Walter Brown quick and get a bottle of bourbon," I said. I knew what it would take to soften up the chairman of the Finance Committee. The two Browns had one thing in common. Walter, the Sinking Fund commissioner, was on the other end of the Hampton Office Building. He always kept spirits on hand. I was not about to keep any liquor near the Governor's office. Reporters were always sneaking in to look in the drawers and behind the books on the shelves. They were certain that the Governor, like any good Charlestonian, would keep some booze stashed somewhere close at hand. I was not about to supply my critics with ammunition by having liquor anywhere near the office.

Once Kreps delivered the whiskey in a brown bag, I hurried across the street, up the back elevator to the third floor, and threw open the door of the conference committee. "My, my," exclaimed Senator Brown. "Here's the big Governor." He rose to his feet.

"Let's have a little touch, Colonel," I said, putting the bottle on the table in front of the chairman.

"Now, what do you want," Senator Brown smiled.

"You know what I want—let's have a little touch," I replied.

Paper cups were passed around. Everybody had a swig. "Now," Senator Brown said, "tell the committee."

"I've got to have my technical training," I insisted.

"Oh, you don't want that," he responded. "That program is for the dummies. We've already closed those area trade schools, and we're not going to start them up again."

An argument ensued. I laid it out, describing how awful it was, time and again, to lose business prospects for the state because of our workers' lack of skills. Finally in frustration I stated, "Well you're going to make me out a liar."

"How's that," asked Senator Brown, who seemed somewhat mellowed.

"I've promised Jacobs Chuck Company [which designs precision tools] and Jeffries Manufacturing that I would pay for their training if they would locate in the state. Now I don't know what to do," I said, referring to my pledge to help the two firms if they would set up shop in South Carolina.

After some discussion, Brown finally said, "Well, we can't make the Governor a liar. How much do you want?"

"$364,000," I said.

"I'll give you $250,000 but that's all," Brown replied.

I knew that with that appropriation as a start, I could somehow make it work, but Brown was thinking along the same lines. "Don't come back next year thinking you've started some program," he said. "We've given you this so that you can keep your promise. You dictate it to Isabelle [Wells, his secretary]. The committee is going to cook a rockfish. We've finalized about everything else. Your section has got to go to the printer so that we can move it in the morning."

I thanked the committee members profusely. When they left, I started dictating from memory the provisions for technical training. Jim Smith, the state auditor, suggested that we use the same language in the bill that had passed the House. I immediately agreed that he had a good idea. By making sure that there was no difference between the House and Senate versions we could immediately take a vote on it. I learned later that the House version never set a term of office for members of the Technical Training Committee, so the first appointees would wind up serving for more than a decade. But we were in a rush.

The next morning the legislature passed the measure to make the technical-training program a reality. I was ecstatic because I knew that it would give me a huge advantage as I tried to attract new industry. I quickly appointed a Blue Ribbon Committee to develop a program.[7] The legislation contained a mere pittance of what was needed. It was obvious that we would have to depend on local financing—and I am happy to say that it came through. I broke ground at Greenville for the first technical center. I still remember that cold, blustery morning as I stood with civic leaders Avery Fonda, Pete Marchant, Louie Williams,

Leon Campbell, and Sapp Funderburk, on a desolate, barren hill. Authorities there allowed a garbage dump to be used as the site for Greenville Tech! "Don't dig too deep—we'll get to the garbage," I cautioned.

We shoveled a bit of dirt, and that started Greenville Tech. Our idea was to have one of these facilities within an easy drive for any citizen in the state who wanted to learn new skills. Years later *U.S. News & World Report* did a survey of technical schools and rated ours number one!

The reason we were number one is that we had outstanding local directors such as Tom Barton of Greenville Tech. Barton had earned the nickname "Black Cat" as a tackle in the Clemson line. As his moniker suggests, if Barton ever put that paw on you, you were down for good! He worked around the clock, and it was that kind of tenacity and attention to detail that made the program a success. And the program made a tangible difference. Using their new skills, workers could double or triple their pay.

At one time or another, it seemed that almost every Governor came by to study our technical-training program—and to emulate it. The best compliment of all came years later, in 1996, when Navy played Notre Dame in Ireland. At that time, I was a U.S. Senator, traveling with the Navy Secretary. My interests extended beyond the pigskin. I wanted to check out an Intel plant located just outside Dublin. I had tried to persuade Andy Grove, Intel's chairman, to locate the billion-dollar facility in South Carolina.

As I came into the plant, I was greeted with the words "Hi, Governor, glad to see you again." Surprised to be greeted as "Governor," I immediately recognized Frank McCabe, who used to be at a General Electric plant at Irmo, which is near Columbia.

"I thought you were still with GE," I said, shaking McCabe's hand.

"No, I've been with Intel for ten years now," he replied. "I want to show you the plant. You're in for a surprise."

Putting on head and shoe coverings, I toured the facility for about an hour and a half. Then McCabe turned to me and said, "Get in the car— I want to take you somewhere." About a mile down the road I recognized a facility that was a duplicate of Midlands Tech back in Columbia.

"I sent two teams to study your plant so that we could duplicate your technical-training program," McCabe said. "I got it up and operating in the black in short order with your program. Now I'm a hero at Intel."

I really celebrated that night. Jean Kennedy Smith, the U.S. Ambassador, hosted both the Navy and Notre Dame football teams at the embassy. When I was called on to introduce Lou Holtz, it was obvious that Lou had no idea that I remembered he had coached at Carolina. I recalled that years ago, Carolina's head coach, Paul Deitzel, told Holtz, "Lou, you'll never make it in football. Look for something else." I then introduced Holtz as the National Championship coach of Notre Dame and reminded everyone that Deitzel was selling real-estate lots in North Carolina.

Having launched the technical-educational program, we were better positioned to compete head-on with North Carolina and other southern states. We could attract businesses by talking about South Carolina's ability to provide workers with skills tailored to their needs. Wade Martin was the genius that made it work. He had been the coordinator for the North Carolina system of industrial-education centers until I lured him to work with us.

I can see Martin now with those spreadsheets that outlined the hours of training on that particular industry's equipment and the pay per hour, and the number of skilled workers available in a certain number of days. He would say, "You furnish your equipment and instructors—we'll pay for them," or "we'll do the training for you." He would add the promise that in "so many days you'll be up and operating in the black." Technical training would prove decisive in the intense battle for new industries.

In the push to expand our industrial base, I put into practice a lesson that I had learned some years before becoming Governor. At that time I flew with my friend Andy Griffith (a wealthy businessman who is not related to the actor) to the National Livestock Show in Phoenix, Arizona. Andy was showing his prize bull, Zato Aristocrat. The Valley National Bank held a reception for the ranchers on the third floor of its headquarters building. Walter Bimson, the chairman of the board, was host.

I've never seen such a spread. It was hundreds of miles from any ocean; yet the bank served boiled shrimp and crab cakes, not to mention Haig & Haig Pinch Scotch. That kind of reception, with liquor, would have been totally out of character for our banks in South Carolina back then. Mr. Bimson told me how the bank developed new business.

"We do surveys of community needs and of traffic patterns. If we find an intersection that will support a filling station, we build it and turn it over to a bright Jaycee to own and operate. All he has to do is make his payments and do his banking with us. Last year we started eighty-one new businesses," Mr. Bimson said. "Banks back East ought to have three gold balls over the front door. They're just pawn shops. If you prove that you don't need a loan, that's when they'll give you one."

I related Mr. Bimson's observations to Bob Cooper, and in 1958 we emulated Valley National by creating the Business Development Corporation. I'll never forget Buck Edwards, the chairman, coming to the Governor's office to tell me about the corporation's loan of $367,000 to Bill Detyens to obtain a mobile dry dock to provide ship repairs. Today that little dry-dock operation has expanded into Detyens Shipyards, Inc., and taken over the dry dock of the Charleston Navy Yard, where it refits destroyers for Taiwan and cruise ships for the tourist trade.

I began to hustle for industry during my first year in office by delivering what came to be known as the "No Magnolias" speech, before the New York Municipal Forum. I listed corporations that had put plants in South Carolina—Union Camp Paper, DuPont, Westinghouse, W. R. Grace, and many more. The point was to let those Yankees know that the South was no longer a drag on the national economy.

"In today's South, the magnolia has been replaced by the machine and the country's former number one economic problem is now a throbbing dynamo of progress which promises to be the country's number one economic showcase," I said in the speech, delivered on May 21, 1959. Then came my hard sell. I touted South Carolina's advances in education, its expanded highway system, the growth of the port of Charleston, the state's fiscal responsibility and its pay-as-you-go government, the individual's right to work, and our conservative spirit that championed individual responsibility. We didn't have revenue bonds. I told every prospect that the state didn't have anything to give that it didn't take—and I didn't want to tax him later to bring in a competitor.

As part of my routine, I urged business prospects not to listen to me but rather to follow the widely known slogan for Packard automobiles: "Ask the man who owns one." In other words I suggested that they talk to folks who had moved to South Carolina to hear their stories firsthand. Highly reputed businessmen such as multimillionaire industrialist Peter Grace and Lowell Weicker, president of Bigelow-Sanford, a carpet manufacturing firm, were delighted to talk up the state's virtues.

Between their testimonials and my nonstop salesmanship, I was having some luck. It didn't take much arm twisting to get Standard Oil Company chairman John E. Swearingen to invest in the state. He had grown up in South Carolina, and his father, who was blind, had made a name for himself as state superintendent of education. John was happy to help. He urged his friend Croswell Croft, the son of the Judge of probate for Aiken County, also to set up shop in the state. Croft agreed to have his firm, Pyle National Company, put down stakes. He now has a large new manufacturing facility in Aiken, a beautiful little town not far from Augusta, Georgia.

I found that I was devoting lots of time on whirlwind tours across the country to press South Carolina's case. On one of these tours, I accepted an invitation to address the American Bar Association in San Francisco. I asked Ernie Wright to get me the names of some prospects I might call on in California. Ernie came through, and after my remarks to the ABA, I traveled south to San Leandro, California, where a Friden Calculator plant was located.

When I arrived, it so happened that the company's board of directors was meeting. Surprised to see a Governor, the board members invited me in to introduce myself and say a few words. After I gave my industrial pitch, they said they appreciated my comments, but I was too late. Weeks before they had decided to expand to Holland.

Still, they were gracious. They insisted that I take a tour of the facilities. I thought at that moment that was the last thing I wanted to see. I wanted to make my next call on Smith Corona. Instead I took the tour and learned some very useful information. Friden's plant had been hampered in its California operations. Its labor pact required that the machine operators operate only three punch drills at one time. In Holland, I was told, an operator was permitted to handle six punch-drill machines. Operating punch drills was 85 percent of the cost of their production. By cutting that 85 percent in half, Friden executives figured the company would have a leg up on the competition. That difference prompted the board to vote with their feet and relocate in Holland. I shook the tour guide's hand, thanked him profusely, got in the car, and hurried down to Smith Corona.

Governor Hollings leaving on a trip to recruit new business for South Carolina, c. 1959–62. Hollings Collection, South Carolina Political Collections, University of South Carolina

When I arrived and sat down with managers there, I started into the song and dance about how a California operator in the factory was limited to operating three punch drills at one time but that back in South Carolina, we could operate seven.

"Where did you learn about our industry," the Smith Corona chairman asked.

"I'm just a politician," I replied. "I don't know anything about industry, but my industrial analysts back in Columbia told me to make sure to call on Smith Corona and to describe our productivity."

"Well, if half of what you say is true, Governor, we'll locate a plant in South Carolina," the chairman responded.

Weeks later, after my return to South Carolina, a Smith Corona representative called on me, and I took him to Orangeburg. I outlined my plan: If they would send three instructors to teach about their punch-drill machines, I would pay for the instructors and guarantee one hundred skilled workers in one hundred days, as well as the construction of a plant. I knew Charles E. Daniel, the energetic leader of Daniel International Construction Company, would help me make good on those promises. Smith Corona decided on Orangeburg that afternoon.

One other story shows the team effort of South Carolina's elected leaders back then. John West was finishing his second four-year term in the State Senate and wanted to try for a third. But his constituents in Kershaw County had a history of "throwing the bums out" after two terms. Nobody had served a third term. Though he was well liked, West was getting heat from some constituents for not doing more to attract industry to Kershaw County, which is just northeast of Richland County, where Columbia is located.

He came to me and said, "Fritz, I need an industry, and I need one bad."

I told him I'd see what I could do. I got back to him a few days later. "I've got the ideal industry for you," I said. "The Elgin Watch Company wants to move to South Carolina. It's the kind of industry that you ought to have."[8]

West jumped at the opportunity. He met with the Elgin Watch folks and showed them sites all over the county. As always, when a company considered picking up stakes and moving here, a key concern was the adequacy of the labor supply. They zeroed in on a little town called Blaney, close to Columbia, from which they could draw workers for a nearby factory. The big interstate, I-20, was just opening during that period in the early 1960s.

The Elgin folks wondered if they might put up a sign on the new highway that said, "Blaney: Home of Elgin Watch." The Highway Department rejected that idea as against regulations. Then, just as the Elgin people were ready to look elsewhere, West asked how they would feel if Blaney's name were changed to Elgin. After all Blaney was named for a vice president of a railroad that came through town. The name really had no historical significance.

When West talked about the idea with the Mayor of Blaney, E. C. Potter, he was amenable. They put the issue on the ballot. The name change was supported by a large majority of the town's 109 registered voters. So South Carolina suddenly had a town named Elgin, and we had a watch company by the same name based there. I was happy and so was West. In fact he became the first State Senator in history in that area to run without opposition for a third term.

I also pushed another button to bring new businesses to the state. South Carolina is famous for its plantations. Over many years wealthy folks invested in large tracts of land in South Carolina and converted old plantations into hunting preserves. The owners would gather at a different plantation for Sunday brunch during the fall and winter hunting season. From time to time, I would arrange to be invited.

I figured that I could use those get-togethers to build face-to-face relationships with captains of industry. One thing I learned is that the rich are incestuous, each serving on the other's board of directors. On my desk I kept a Dun and Bradstreet reference book on businesses in which the names of corporate boards across the country are listed. I constantly cross-referenced the boards and was successful at having one board member friend call another to set up appointments for me.

During one of these brunches at a plantation, I met David Luke, chairman of the board of West Virginia Pulp & Paper. He was a member of the Irving Trust Company board. I was talking up the virtues of South Carolina when he invited me to New York to tell my story. Not long after that, I found myself having breakfast on the thirty-second floor of the Irving Trust Building at 1 Wall Street in New York. The board members were gathered around an octagonal table with a spectacular view of New York and the harbor. After hearing my pitch, they began their cross-examination. I told them of our state's triple-A credit rating and described how our technical-training program matched our labor force's skills to the needs of new businesses. And I pointed out that South Carolina was a right-to-work state so that unions were not an issue.

"I don't know anything about industry, but your friends have invested in South Carolina and find that we have a friendly government and a good business environment," I told them. In those days we did not have hundreds of millions of dollars in tax exemptions and other goodies to offer. "All we can promise is a day's work for a day's pay,"

I concluded. From that one breakfast, I was able to entice seven industries to put plants in South Carolina.

The battle for business consumed a great deal of my time. And during my first couple of years as Governor, my friend Luther Hodges of North Carolina kept me going. Luther, like me, had been Lieutenant Governor, but he had become his state's chief executive when Governor William B. Umstead died in office in 1954. Luther was both a friend and a formidable competitor, always hustling and trying to entice industrial magnates to locate in the Tar Heel State. I always found myself trying to one-up Hodges. Once, I remember, he had made a splashy announcement that he would be making calls in Europe to seek out partners for industrial development. To counter his move, I decided to announce that I would be traveling to Latin America for business prospects.

In preparation for the trip, I learned that my hometown of Charleston was on the same longitude as the Panama Canal and was 350 miles closer to Caracas, Venezuela, than was New Orleans. I saw an opportunity. Why should South America's production go through New Orleans when it made more sense for it to come through the port of Charleston?

Peter Grace of W. R. Grace & Company was a big help as we planned this expedition to South America. He had a plant in Spartanburg and a herd of white-faced cattle in the town of Eutawville, South Carolina. An aggressive and enormously successful businessman, Peter had extensive industrial interests in South America, and he ran Panagra Airlines on the South American continent. He got me in touch with Jim es' Stebbins, the Latin American vice president of W. R. Grace Company, who became my "seeing-eye dog" in Argentina, Uruguay, Brazil, and Venezuela. I dispatched Ernie Wright, my assistant, to travel with es' Stebbins to set up dinners, industrial calls, and news conferences in advance of my trip.

That preparation made the trip a success. After a lengthy flight, we were honored by the port of Buenos Aires, which held a reception on the deck of a Swedish ship. The Captain, in welcoming me, inquired about "sunset." Since it was winter in Charleston, and summer down there, I started giving him a weather report.

"No, no, Sunset," he said.

I again remarked on how nice and pleasant it was aboard ship there in Buenos Aires, but again he insisted, "Sunset—sixty kilometers from Charleston."

"You don't mean Sunset Lodge, the whorehouse in Georgetown, South Carolina," I asked.

"Ah, yes," he said. "Welcome, welcome."

Imagine that. I'm all set as a Governor to talk industry and port business, and the first thing they want to know about in Buenos Aires is a whorehouse in Georgetown! I had a better go of it the next day at lunch with a sold-out crowd of six hundred at the Grand Hotel ballroom in Buenos Aires. A Spanish professor at Carolina had coached me on a ten-minute Spanish talk with the proper Argentine inflection. I couldn't give you a word of it today, but they listened intently, and I sat down to a standing ovation.

We called on various ports throughout South America and held news conferences. I learned there's a world of difference between their press briefings and ours in the States. Down there, you state your piece or your reason for the press conference in three or four minutes and then stand down for a reception for the next hour or hour and a half. During that period you answer questions informally, but of course on the record. A stimulating libation is provided. These conferences are relaxed and enjoyable. You even end up thinking the reporter is your best friend—something that would never happen in the States! The trip we took resulted in a big boost to our port business as several South American firms located in the state.

We made a similar foray in Europe and also found a receptive audience. We called on Paulino Gerli of LaFrance Industries in Milan. In Dusseldorf, Frankfurt, and Berlin, my Germanic name, Fritz, opened doors. Today we have more than ninety-one German affiliates and two hundred manufacturing plants in South Carolina. Thousands of South Carolina workers are employed by Michelin, the French-based tire manufacturer, which opened four production facilities and their North American headquarters in the state, and Pirelli came to South Carolina.

All these stories show that we were gradually making headway in bringing new business to the state. It took a great deal of a Governor's time, but "recruitment" of new business was critical. I was determined that South Carolina not be viewed as an afterthought by businesses looking south to relocate. By the end of my term, we had crossed a threshold of respectability.

I learned a lesson about our lagging tourism trade when I lost an argument with my press secretary, Roy Harrelson, former editor of the *Myrtle Beach Sun*. We were constantly trying to figure out our next move to boost the state's fortunes. Harrelson suggested that I do something to improve tourism. He said that Myrtle Beach was outgunning Charleston when it came to tourism.

I had been an assistant at the Ocean Forest Hotel in Myrtle Beach, so I thought I was something of an authority on the tourism business. "We have way more tourists than Myrtle Beach," I said, confidently. "Charleston has the first chamber of commerce in the United States."

Roy would have none of that. We argued, but after some checking, it became clear that Roy was right and I was wrong. Charleston, with its rich history, didn't do a good job of selling itself. It looked out for main-street businesses, but did little to promote tourism.

I knew we could do better. Myrtle Beach actively lured Canadians on their way to Florida during bleak winters. These tourists ultimately came to see the advantages of staying put rather than continuing to travel on to the expensive, crowded Sunshine State. With the opportunity to play numerous golf courses, the Canadians could spend a week or a weekend economically and easily get a tee time. Even though that period was well before satellite TV connections, Myrtle Beach even made a point of picking up the six o'clock Canadian news for later airing at the hotels. To top that off, the Canadian flag was flying everywhere along the Strand! I made a special trip to Toronto as the state's Governor to lay out the welcome mat for the Sun Fun Festival.

I called Joe Riley, a friend, neighbor, and civic leader in Charleston, and told him to meet me at the Columbia Hotel. On the spot I told Riley that he was chairman of the Tourism Committee under the auspices of the State Development Board. (His son, Joe Riley Jr., was elected Mayor of Charleston in 1978 and still holds that office.)

That was my modus operandi as Governor. I would appoint a committee rather than waiting around for the legislature to institute a commission. In those days the Governor was only paid $15,000 a year, and South Carolina didn't have any money for new endeavors. So, to get things moving, I would just take the initiative on the fly by creating committees, offering no pay but still persuading folks such as Riley to sign on.

As Riley sought other members to serve on the committee, we looked to North Carolina for talent. North Carolina Governor Hodges had just returned from a trip to Russia, and Riley's committee had determined they wanted to sign up Jerry Albright, an expert in the tourism field in Tar Heel country. But this time our efforts infuriated

Hodges. He watched as we lured Walter Harper to our Development Board, and was disappointed as we persuaded Wade Martin, another North Carolina executive, to lead our technical-education program. Hodges had had enough. He called me and said in no uncertain terms that my conduct disappointed him. We remained fast friends, but I told him, half joking, "Luther, take one more of those trips to Russia and I will move Mrs. Hodges down here. I am going to beat you any way I can."

One of my most satisfying moments in the effort to boost our economy came one afternoon when I got my hands on a list of some sixty-two calls that North Carolina officials were planning to make in New York. Not about to sit idly as my competition was wooing businesses in Manhattan, I alerted Francis Hipp, the Development Board chairman, and Secretary of Industry Ernie Wright. We cancelled our schedules, and by Sunday evening we were in New York, preparing to make our own sixty-two calls.

Hipp and Wright made sure that when I knocked on doors, the firm's chairman or president would be in. No doubt Luther's industry team had confirmed appointments the next week; and, knowing this, I would introduce myself, mumbling, "Governor Hollings from Carolina," in such a way that it was easy for the secretary to think I was Hodges from North Carolina. In the confusion I was ushered in to see the company bigwig. By the end of that week, we had completed the calls. It took every trick in the book, but in that final year of my term, South Carolina attracted more industry than North Carolina.

I made it up to Hodges. In 1960, after Jack Kennedy's election as President and before he took office, I was visiting Kennedy's home in the Georgetown section of Washington for lunch when he told me he was going to appoint Luther Hodges to be chairman of the Democratic Party. I immediately protested: "Hodges is not a politician's politician; he's a businessman's politician. He can serve you best as Secretary of Commerce." Having been vice president of Marshall Field and president of New York City's Rotary Club, Hodges was on a first-name basis with the captains of industry. My argument prevailed. Kennedy appointed Hodges to be Commerce Secretary. Later, when Hodges called to thank me for making a pitch for him, he asked what I wanted. I said, "You could do South Carolina, North Carolina, and the country a favor by establishing a Tourism and Travel Administration." He did it—and it was a success.

I was also determined to get some industry in the lowcountry. Most prospects avoided Charleston with its unionized paper mill and navy yard. But we had an advantage: our potential for farming. I decided to try to sell that potential to top officers at Campbell's Soup during their annual trek to the Santee Gun Club. Every fall the honchos came south for a hunt. I partied with them one evening, and at 5:30 the next morning, I shared a duck blind with Oliver Willits, chairman of the board of Campbell's Soup, and Beverly Murphy, the company president.

As we chatted, I said, "I've been getting all these industries in the Piedmont and the Pee Dee, but here in the lowcountry around Charleston, I've got to do better. We've got all kinds of farms producing tomatoes, cucumbers, corn, okra, cabbage, kale. It seems to me that I could get a vegetable or tomato soup plant here."

Willits promised to see what he could do to help. Next year at the same time, we were in the same duck blind. "I've got good news and bad news," Willits allowed, as we waited in the still of the morning. "The bad news is that South Carolina tomatoes have a core, and you only produce one crop a year, whereas Texas tomatoes don't have that core and we can get two and a half crops. A soup plant requires $35 million in stainless-steel equipment. We can't afford to invest that much for just one crop. But the good news is we might do it on poultry— if you could produce chickens like they do in Georgia and Arkansas."

That's all I needed to hear. I immediately conferred with the poultry expert at Clemson College, and we planned to hold a dozen "poultry progress days" to gin up interest in the business throughout the state. We traveled to Newberry, Sumter, Latta, Florence, and towns all the way down to the coast. Those efforts paid off when Campbell located a plant in Sumter. A Perdue chicken processing plant later put down stakes in Dillon. When I first took office as Governor, the state's poultry sales topped out at about $19 million. Today South Carolina's largest agricultural crop is not tobacco. It's poultry, which employs about 8,200 in processing and production, with a payroll of roughly $1.56 million per year and sales at about $1.5 billion a year.[9]

To attract industry I wanted to be able to tell prospects that we had a businessman's government. As an attorney, I had done legal work for the State Ports Authority when it underwent a survey performed by first-rate management consultants at Cresap, McCormick and Padgett. Impressed with their report, I retained Cresap to perform similar audits of the Insurance Department, the Tax Commission, elementary and secondary education, and the institutions of higher learning, including the Citadel, Clemson, Winthrop, and the University of South Carolina.

Cresap's surveys found that the only section of South Carolina government without waste was the Tax Commission. By contrast the Insurance Department was a basket case. In order to do business in South Carolina, an insurance company was required to file securities with the Insurance Department to cover potential claims. Auditors were shocked when they opened the closet door of the insurance commissioner's office to find $65 million of securities dumped on the floor—bonds that had not been clipped for years. Furthermore, if you had lost your job, been jailed, and hit skid row, there was still one last chance. You could be licensed to sell insurance. New York, with a population of 24 million, licensed 32,000 agents. Little South Carolina with a population of 2.4 million had 34,000 agents.

How had the chief commissioner survived this malfeasance? By playing the legislators! Every Christmas, Pat Murphy gave each member of the General Assembly a necktie—a cheap way to help guarantee his reelection. I put together the Blue Ribbon Commission of James M. Waddell of Beaufort as chairman, William R. Bruce of Columbia, Hugh C. Lane of Charleston, W. W. Pate of Greenville, and J. Wilbert Wood of Anderson. It immediately shut down several companies. Qualifications for agents were required for the first time. And insurance rates were lowered.

We also needed to eliminate the "pork barrel" or wasteful projects as well as the duplication of programs at our institutions of higher learning. I helped smooth the way to accomplish that by taking advantage of a Clemson-Carolina game in Columbia. We had a brunch at the Governor's Mansion before the kickoff. The boards of trustees from both Clemson and Carolina agreed to join me. This informal gathering helped to begin to tear down the walls of jealousy, as the two groups began to talk to each other. Then I appointed the Governor's Advisory Council on Higher Education, with A. L. M. Wiggins of Hartsville as chairman.[10] Findings of the council helped to smooth the way for the college presidents to work together to increase salaries in state-supported colleges by some 30 percent and to eliminate duplication of curriculum.

In fact I had learned from Cresap that the way to improve the quality of education is at the top—not the bottom. By paying the outstanding professor a premium, a school is able to attract other, younger professors at a discount because they will want to teach with a well-known authority. Similarly students will flock to a school that can boast that it has a renowned expert in the field. My friend John West, a future Governor, was skeptical. "You're bustin' your britches on this one," he told me. Still I was able to persuade the legislature to approve salaries greater than that of the Governor—$19,000 for nine months—to be paid to truly exceptional, well-known professors. These efforts helped to gain national recognition for the University of South Carolina's School of International Business, a leader in global business education.

Even as we managed to get the colleges to work cooperatively and boost teachers' pay, I faced a potential headline in the state's penitentiary system. The Governor's Mansion was staffed by honor prisoners, usually life termers, who had never committed an offense in jail but had taken a life—or multiple lives—in domestic disputes. One of these prisoners, Lathan Crisp, was in charge of the detail at the Governor's Mansion. He had been convicted of three murders.

Late one afternoon, as I was rushing to change for an evening occasion, Crisp asked if he could speak with me. "Sure, Lathan, tell me what's on your mind—I'm in a hurry," I said.

"A fellow's going to die in Cuba tomorrow or the next day," he said.

"I'm not involved in Cuba, Lathan," I responded.

"Yes you are," he replied. "Cuba is the hole in the prison yard where they put bad prisoners. It's thirty feet deep and twelve feet across. They dump prisoners down in the hole, starve them with barely a slice of bread and water each day, and when the prisoner gets so sick he can't move they haul him out, take him to the infirmary, and let him die of pneumonia. Sometimes it's too late. They die in the hole, and they say he died in the infirmary."

"Heavens," I exclaimed. "Let's get him out right now." Then I asked, "What's he in for?"

"He beat up a bad prisoner who was a favorite of one of the guards," Crisp said. He described Gene Smalls, the prisoner in trouble, as the most powerful black man in the penitentiary. Then he went on, "When Gene was fourteen years old, his uncle was robbing some bags of sugar from a Charleston business. Gene was driving the truck and the alarm went off. Gene didn't hear it, but his uncle did and took flight. When the cops arrived, they found Gene sitting in the driver's seat of the truck waiting for his uncle. He was charged with two counts of burglary and grand larceny and given ten years consecutively on each count. Gene had a good record. He'd already served the first ten years and four years on the second count. Since he did everything right, some of the prisoners would pick on him. The fellow he beat thought he could take Gene, but Gene beat the hell out of him. The guards lied and said it was all Gene's fault. He won't last past the weekend."

We saved Gene Smalls—and closed down that "Cuba" operation. Gene took care of my children at the Governor's Mansion, and when I left office, he followed me to Charleston. I got him a good job, and when I won my Senate race in 1966, he followed me to Washington. I helped get him a slot on the night shift at the Senate Post Office. He married a nurse and lived a good life. I still am proud to have been able to make a difference in this man's life and call him my friend.

Another well-known inmate, Emma Lee, was the cook at the Governor's Mansion. She was famous for her pecan pie. Emma Lee had already gotten rid of two husbands with strychnine in a pecan pie. But I still swore by it. "It's the best pecan pie I've ever had," I said on many occasions.

We didn't think anything about it until Robert F. Kennedy visited me one evening. We got to the dessert, and Bob said, "This is the best pecan pie I have ever had."

"Yes," I replied. I immediately began telling Bob about Emma Lee's background. The story left an impression. Bob put down his fork, turned white, and was dead serious the rest of the evening.

When I left the Governor's office, I got Emma Lee paroled. But some years later, when I returned to have dinner with Governor Dick Riley, I couldn't believe my eyes. There was Emma Lee. "What are you back here for," I asked.

"The same thing," she said.

"You mean the pecan pie?" I asked.

"Ya," said Emma Lee. "That third husband, he was trifling. I had to get rid of him."

Even as work at the Governor's Mansion provided a way for some prisoners to work their way back into society, I became increasingly concerned about serious issues at the penitentiary. Drugs were rampant; guards were quick to accept bribes for favors; and stories were circulating that the superintendent was using inmates on his personal farm.

When Wyndham Manning retired as the superintendent of the penitentiary, I appointed Ellis MacDougall, who was doing a good job at the Greenville County Prison. We reorganized the penitentiary. I guess the illiteracy rate of inmates at the time was about 90 percent. None of them had a chance; none had proper schooling. We instituted grade-school classes and put in a high-school course behind the prison walls. Next we installed mammoth laundry facilities for the State Hospital and other state office buildings in Columbia to save money. To impart some skills so that the prisoners could get jobs when they won their freedom, we instituted a furniture-repair shop, and my friend Eugene Stone of Stonesware added a textile facility. During this period we allowed a prisoner to train as a boxer and compete in Golden Gloves tournaments and even added a chapter of the Jaycees behind the walls.

The toughest job for a Governor is deciding when to commute a death sentence. Even in those days, the word was that many inmates were convicted of crimes that they really hadn't committed. The last clear chance for life remained with the Governor. I will never forget the Britt-Westbury case, nor would Mrs. Westbury let me forget. Britt and Westbury robbed a motor court on the edge of Greenwood one dark night. They were speeding away when South Carolina patrolman Harold Ray of Chester stopped them.

Ray knew nothing of the robbery and thought he was dealing only with a speeding violation. He approached the vehicle by the driver's window. Britt, who was driving, just rested the pistol on the edge of the window, pumped two bullets into the defenseless Ray, and sped off as fast as he could. According to Westbury, Britt began wondering whether he had really killed the officer. To make sure, Britt turned the vehicle around and headed back to the spot where Ray lay bleeding to death. Britt took Ray's pistol from the officer's holster and blew his brains out. Again, they took off down the road.

They didn't get far. They were caught and convicted of murder in two trials. Both were sentenced to death. But the story didn't end there. The details will always be fresh in my mind because of Mrs. Westbury. I first learned of the case late one afternoon, when I saw a lady in a print dress sitting in the reception room. I asked my secretary who she was. "Mrs. Westbury," was the reply. "She's been here since early this morning."

"Well, get rid of her," I said.

"Her son has been convicted of murder and is to be electrocuted at six tomorrow morning," she replied.

"Well, bring her in and call the house. Tell them I'll be late because I've got to hear her out," I said.

Mrs. Westbury was calm and determined. She had grown up in awful circumstances but was articulate and obviously intelligent. She described Westbury's father as a drunk who would take the boy out of school time and again and sit him up on the bar while he drank. She did everything she could to keep him in school, but the father would come by at recess and take him away.

"His daddy ruined him," said Mrs. Westbury. Then she proceeded into "lawyer's talk," describing what had occurred in the first trial. I sent for the Attorney General to bring the trial record around. We reviewed the transcripts with Mrs. Westbury until past eleven that night. Westbury had not received a proper trial in the first case, and, as a result, the guilty verdict had been set aside.

He had been given excellent representation in the second trial. Mrs. Westbury finally realized that she had only heard about the first defective trial. I explained to her that as the chief law enforcement officer of the state, it was my duty to uphold the law. In a heinous crime like this, a cold-blooded murder, I had to enforce the law. I had to protect my police officers. If I commuted this death sentence, then the law on murder was repealed, and I ought to leave office, I told her.

She cried and cried, but then she stood up, looked me straight in the eye, and said, "You do your job. I tried to do mine." She repeated that she had tried to do right by her boy, but nobody had listened. Now we had listened. It was past eleven at night. She thanked us for spending all that time with her. Then reaching over, she gave me a big hug and left. I received a Christmas card from her every year until she died. As John Kennedy said, "Life is unfair."

Nearing the end of my four years as Governor, I was feeling bullish. With a triple-A credit rating, the technical-training program under way, and a slew of industries opening offices in South Carolina, we were on a roll.[11] By 1962, my last year in office, South Carolina's economy had begun to undergo a transformation from a primarily agricultural basis to an industrial basis. And President Kennedy's seven-point textile policy, unveiled in 1961 to help U.S. companies, had provided predictability and stability to our state's largest industry.

The state was on the upswing economically. And it had not suffered the bloody, racial violence that had beset some other southern states. I decided that I had a record that would enable me to take on three-term Senator Olin Johnston in the Democratic primary. Indeed I was confident that I could ride my record to victory. Even as I was ready to launch a campaign, however, I learned that the people weren't ready for me! As it turned out, I really wasn't ready either. I should have paid more attention to politics. I misjudged Johnston's strong organization and the power of incumbency of a veteran Senator who had spent years handing out goodies to win constituents' favor.

For fourteen years I had run for public office without a political poll. But then I met Louis Harris, the prominent pollster who worked for John Kennedy during the 1960 presidential campaign. Harris offered to conduct a statewide poll for me. When I saw the numbers, I knew he was wrong. The results showed that Johnston had a substantial lead in his race for reelection. I knew this couldn't be. I had been working the state for four years, and in all candor I hadn't seen Johnston making the rounds. Nor were there many news reports of his activities. I threw the poll away.

But on election night, I learned that Lou Harris was right. I had thought that my work with Mayors and the chambers of commerce, my regular announcements about the arrival of some new industry, and my travels on weekends to New York and elsewhere in search of still more industry, would make me a winner. I was wrong. I hadn't been speaking to the American Legions and the Rotary Clubs around the state. I thought the people knew the wonderful good I was doing! Of course, I also was doomed because of my efforts for Kennedy in the 1960 presidential campaign. South Carolinians had apparently decided that their smart-ass young Governor had sold out the state to an un-popular President Kennedy. In their view I was spending too much time with the "rat pack" and Hollywood big shots and partying with folks whose family had made their money pushing liquor. It just went on and on. Even close friends who were for me could not stomach Kennedy. The young President's unpopularity was so great that a year later, in 1963, when news of his assassination was announced, school children in South Carolina stood up and clapped in the classroom.

By contrast Senator Johnston had the reputation of being the working man's friend. He was born and raised in the Piedmont and had worked in the mills. Johnston was the textile workers' hero. That organization of his ran like a well-oiled machine. Johnston knew how to face down challengers, having done it before. In 1950 he had knocked off then-Governor Strom Thurmond, who had just carried the state as a presidential candidate on the Dixiecrat ticket in 1948. The Johnston-Thurmond battle has been called one of South Carolina's "bitterest campaigns"—a showdown that is said to have been like "a rolling heavyweight bare-knuckle boxing match."[12] Johnston ran a populist campaign and picked up the overwhelming majority of the newly enfranchised black voters who had been turned off by Thurmond's Dixiecrat affiliation. Twelve years later, in 1962, the Senator still knew how to connect with ordinary voters.

I was determined to out-hustle Johnston. I started crisscrossing the state to begin to make my case well before Election Day. In a December 1961 dispatch to *Life* magazine regional editor Dick Billings, South Carolina journalist Charles Wickenberg wrote: "Both Johnston and Hollings act like the election is tomorrow. Both are beating the bushes, talking at the drop of an invitation. South Carolina has never seen anything like this before."[13]

I was eager to go head-to-head with Johnston. I challenged him to a debate, and when he failed to show, I debated an empty chair. I had placed in the TV studio lawn mowers, fishing rods, and other equipment that had been manufactured in South Carolina by companies that had located in the state since I had been elected Governor. Despite that effort, at the end of the "debate," the empty chair won! I tried to paint him as a tool of the Yankee labor bosses and a Washington liberal who had done little to create any jobs in the state. In the end it was all for naught. Johnston just flat-out trounced me. I carried only one county—Calhoun.

On election night I went by the Wade Hampton Hotel to congratulate Senator Johnston. The ballroom was a mob scene. A small stand with a microphone was set up at the edge of the crowd. Mayor Bill Johnston of Anderson was coaching his brother the Senator. Brother Bill had a high-pitched voice. The Senator had a sonorous tone and spoke slow as molasses in January. "Remember Olin, you were a senior member of the agriculture committee, and the farmers were a big help," squeaked Bill.

"Good, good," roared Johnston. "The farmers were a B-I-I-G help."

"And you were on the Judiciary Committee, and the lawyers were a big help," squeaked brother Bill.

"Good, good," Johnston explained in a guttural tone. "The lawyers were a B-I-I-G help."

"And remember you were chairman of the Postal Committee, and the postal workers were a B-I-I-G help," Bill continued.

"Good, good," Johnston repeated. "The postal workers were a B-I-I-G help."

And, then, seeing me edging to the front of the crowd, he pointed ' and said, "There's old Fritz. Remember he was a B-I-I-G help, too."

As despondent as I was about losing, I had to laugh. For the first time, I really liked the fellow. I never knew that Johnston had a sense of humor. Even as I stood there laughing, I should have remembered a lesson I had learned many years before: Never look for gratitude in politics. During World War II, I was a Lieutenant in the army in Le Havre, France, preparing to go to Japan. I was in charge of two German prison camps—Camp Lucky Strike and Camp Chesterfield. I always awoke at five and turned on BBC Radio at six. May 8, 1945, was V-E Day, unconditional surrender day in Europe. On July 25, 1945, I was shocked to listen to an interview with British Prime Minister Winston Churchill. In Britain, if the Prime Minister loses an election, he must vacate 10 Downing Street by six the next morning. Beaten by pissant Clement Attlee, Churchill was on the sidewalk with his rack of clothes and chest of drawers. "What is your comment," the reporter asked.

"The British people are a funny lot," Churchill said. "They show their gratitude for a job well done by promptly voting you out of office." The interview ended. Here was the hero who had just ended a great war, and less than three months after the historic victory, the voters had kicked him out of office. No gratitude whatever!

The 1962 Senate contest was noteworthy for something else as well. After Johnston defeated me, the Senator was not out of the woods. For the first time in about a century, the Republicans mounted a serious statewide campaign. Veteran journalist William D. Workman had decided to run against Johnston as a Republican. Bill Workman's decision was ironic in that he had personally encouraged me to challenge Johnston. But within a few days of my announcement that I was running, he followed suit. I, of course, worked for Johnston in the general election. Workman's respectable showing, about 43 percent of the vote, was a prelude to the political transformation of South Carolina. Long a Democratic bastion, the state was undergoing a rapid change.

Republicans had become respectable. In a stunning turnaround South Carolina would eventually become one of the most reliably Republican states in the union. That those changes were coming was obvious when Governor Byrnes went Republican in 1952, 1956, and 1960, and in 1964, when Strom Thurmond switched parties. He campaigned for Barry Goldwater, the GOP presidential nominee that year. Goldwater became the first Republican to carry the state in a presidential race in the twentieth century—by a bigger vote than in his home state of Arizona.

Democrats could no longer be confident about winning simply by prevailing in the party primary. In 1958, for example, after I defeated Donald Russell in the June primary runoff, I had no Republican opposition. Indeed the Democratic nominee for Lieutenant Governor, Burnet R. Maybank Jr., and our six Democratic Congressmen also were home free. Republicans did not offer any candidates against them. Now, as Thurmond and other Democrats began switching their party labels, the political atmosphere had changed dramatically. The days of one-party dominance were over.

In the 1950s no issue dominated South Carolina politics more than race. These years were marked by the beginning of the so-called walk-ins, sit-ins, lay-ins, and other demonstrations galore. Complicating the situation still more was the competition for headlines within the black community between the NAACP and the Southern Christian Leadership Conference (SCLC). The NAACP would demonstrate in Sumter, even as the SCLC led children to a lunch counter at Woolworth's in Rock Hill in 1960. The atmosphere was thick with tension. The NAACP quickly followed with dramatic marches into the Silver's Five and Dime in Charleston, while another group of protesters marched in front of the Trinity Church in Columbia. Meanwhile, students in Orangeburg were demonstrating. On and on it went.

My phone was ringing off the hook. Invariably the voice on the other end of the line, often one of the state's local officials, all of whom were white, was importuning me: "Governor, you're the chief law enforcement officer. You have the responsibility, but you're letting 'them' take over the streets."

These explosive crosscurrents were evident throughout much of my term as Governor. I was "Mister In-Between." The Governor had to appear to be in charge; yet the realities were not on his side. Again, I returned to my basic precept, *salus populi suprema lex*—the safety of the people is the supreme law. I was determined to keep the peace and avoid bloodshed. I explained my position on handling the lunch counter sit-ins in Rock Hill to the Reverend I. DeQuincey Newman, the prominent, veteran NAACP field secretary in South Carolina.

I told him that I was allowing fourteen customers into the store as fourteen customers left—and no more![14] It was a matter of crowd control. I didn't want the little minority kids at the stools to be crowded by the white punks with peg-legged britches and ducktail haircuts who were waiting to dive and grab a seat as soon as the little black child got up to go to the bathroom. Often there would be physical contact. A fight could erupt at any moment. I knew of similar face-offs in Nashville, where thirteen had been seriously hurt. A couple of people were even killed in Greensboro, North Carolina.

"I know I can't control private property," I said, as I looked at Newman, "but I can control the sidewalks."[15]

Newman, a wiry fellow from Darlington County who was a persistent critic of just about everything the state did when it came to civil rights, made plenty of waves over the years. He never seemed daunted. His constant potshots inevitably attracted press attention. At just about every news conference, I was asked to respond to some new charge that he had made. I had known I.D. for years, having met him when I was in the legislature. I had come to appreciate I.D.'s brilliance, which was on full display when he came to the Governor's office one day with a large group. Each of the African American leaders tried to outdo the others, giving me hell. But I.D. hung back. He let them talk. I was fascinated watching him. He was like Leonard Bernstein, directing with his eyes every overture, every high note, every woe and wail. After listening for some time, he called a pause in the onslaught to let me have a chance to respond.[16] (In 1983 he became the first African American State Senator since 1887.)

I said I was the Governor of all the people, blacks as well as whites. I knew that they didn't believe it, but I was going to be their Governor whether they believed it or liked it. Also I wanted them to understand that I recognized their feelings of being second-class citizens, but I said their recourse was in the courts. Of course, when they left, I knew I hadn't convinced them. They were dissatisfied, but at least Newman knew that he did have a Governor who would hear him out. Before long we even began to appreciate each other's role—and we got to a point where we could enjoy a laugh together. When I wrote a book on hunger in 1970, I specifically cited I.D. in the acknowledgments, noting that he "made me realize that this was a problem that must be solved."

But during this tense period, the outset of the civil rights movement, Newman and I butted heads. When I explained my approach to Woolworth's situation in Rock Hill, he was not at all impressed. He told me that a New York lawyer advised him that I couldn't do this. They were prepared to sue me and might even take me to the Supreme Court. I responded that the police power was vested in the state. I told him to go ahead and send Chief Justice Earl Warren, himself, down to Rock Hill. I would lock him up too.

Meanwhile the news media was picking up on this dramatic story. South Carolina native Frank Blair of *NBC News* reported on the Reverend Martin Luther King Jr.'s preparations to begin the marches for the SCLC in South Carolina. The black demonstrators could stay at a hotel that permitted integration across the line in Charlotte, North Carolina. Refreshed, they planned to start their marches across the state line in Rock Hill. On hearing this news, I immediately went to work.

I replaced the white city police force from Rock Hill with black officers from the city forces in Charleston, Columbia, and South Carolina State University in Orangeburg, an African American school that had a long and distinguished history as the state's sole public college for black youth.

When the marchers got out of hand, black officers would apprehend them. The TV networks' hoped-for clash between black demonstrators and white officers never materialized. When reporters saw blacks being arrested by blacks, the impact was lost. Before long, the marching stopped. The cameramen packed up their equipment and headed for Montgomery, Alabama. There, they got what they wanted—Sheriff "Bull" Connor, fire hoses, and police dogs. I learned the important lesson that black officers are often better able to defuse tensions than white officers. I moved immediately to integrate SLED. I appointed two black officers, Cambridge Jenkins and William Wong of the Charleston Police Department, to SLED. These appointments prompted a number of county sheriffs, my strongest support in law enforcement, to object. A representative group called on me, raging that my move wasn't going to work. But the next week, when a young white woman was raped in a Florence motor court, Jenkins and Wong had apprehended the suspect by six o'clock the next afternoon. Now every sheriff wanted some black deputies.

My strategy of keeping the peace at all costs worked—with the occasional exception. Once, for example, in Orangeburg in 1960, demonstrators were acting up in front of a drugstore where the town powerbrokers gathered for breakfast. Before I could get there, the fire chief, Fisher, had hosed them down. They were herded into a theater to get them out of the cold and get their names for charging them. Among the demonstrators was James E. Clyburn, today the third-ranking Democratic leader in the House of Representatives. Clyburn needles me about that episode; he says I hosed him down but didn't kill him. But he admits it turned into a happy occasion. By the time the police herded the demonstrators into the courtroom, the arrest "had made heroes of us," Clyburn recalled years later. "The whole place erupted in applause," he said, referring to his fellow students who had come to the courthouse to voice their support. Most important, a young woman walked up to Clyburn with some of her friends. He told them he was famished. They walked away. When she later came back with a hamburger, she wound up breaking it in half and sharing it with him.[17] He went on to marry that young girl, Emily, and he has been eating out of her hand ever since.

I closed out four years in office as a southern Governor through this period without one person being killed in demonstrations and marches. My main goal was to keep the lid on everything. All my efforts to bring prosperity to the state would have been for naught if businesses were constantly worried that racial strife was right around the corner.

These concerns informed my actions on more than one occasion. One day I got a call from Dan Beckman, the deputy chief of SLED. "We got him. We got him," he exclaimed.

"Got who?" I asked.

"Martin Luther King," he responded.

"What for?" I asked.

"He had a half pint of liquor on him."

"You're crazy," I said. "Let him go. If we lock up everybody with a half pint, we'd have to lock up most of the General Assembly!"

About this time, trouble was brewing elsewhere. Governor Ross Barnett of Mississippi was defying a court order to admit the first black student, James Meredith, to the University of Mississippi. Barnett vowed to go to jail, if need be, to preserve the status quo. President John F. Kennedy activated the National Guard for action at Oxford and made clear that Barnett must obey the law.

I knew I couldn't go along with Barnett when he called and said, "Hollings, you lead a motorcade from South Carolina. If you lead one, George Wallace says he will lead one from Alabama, and we'll show that Washington crowd how to enforce the law."

"Ross," I responded, "every redneck in South Carolina would get in behind me and when I got to Oxford, I couldn't stop them. There would be no chance of enforcing law and order."

Instead I turned to Chief Pete Strom of SLED and asked him to travel quietly to Oxford. I wanted him to watch closely and learn whatever he could from this clash between federal and state authorities.

What Strom saw wasn't pretty. Even as law enforcement officials were deployed around campus to protect Meredith, a mob rushed in, pelting the guards with all kinds of objects. The authorities responded with tear gas. The mob retreated as federal troops arrived, but the final casualty list was grim: 2 were dead and scores were injured, including 160 federal marshals.[18]

When Strom returned, we knew how to avoid a replay of Mississippi. As civil rights marches were picking up in Rock Hill, Orangeburg, and other hot spots in South Carolina, he and I were determined to keep that lid on. Instead of relying on federal marshals, we decided to use highway patrolmen to keep the peace. We also tried our best to restrict movement of reporters eager for provocative stories and hoping to exploit photo opportunities.

The issue reached a flash point when Charlestonian Harvey Gantt, a black architecture student at Iowa State University, wanted to transfer to Clemson College, which was segregated. Gantt had gone to federal court to try to win a ruling that would mandate his admission to the venerable South Carolina college.

There's an old axiom in politics: "When in doubt do nothing. And stay in doubt all the time." Many of my confidants and advisers told me to end my term without acting on this explosive issue. The litigation was ongoing. Nobody would have objected if I simply had punted. After all, even if Gantt prevailed, he would not actually enter Clemson until a few days after my term ended. "Let your successor, Donald Russell, handle it," they said. "He has the office. It's his responsibility."

My longtime political supporters still couldn't stand Russell. Their resentment stemmed from the tough battle I had waged against him to become Governor four years earlier. Now, as he was about to succeed me, my friends reminded me, "That Russell crowd was against you, why help him now? Let him handle the hot potato. You can't tell what will happen up at Clemson."

It was late 1962, and I had just been defeated as a candidate for the United States Senate. I was angry. "You can take this job and shove it," was my attitude. But I knew I had had plenty of successes during my four years in office. And I wasn't going to end my time in office by ducking or dodging. I thought back to the saying of General Robert E. Lee posted in the Citadel barracks: "Duty is the sublimest word in the English language."

It was my duty to do the right thing. Russell had been the cloistered president of the University of South Carolina. He didn't know law enforcement. He didn't know the troublemakers. He wouldn't have a chance to take charge properly before having to deal with this potential explosion. I was better positioned to handle it. I knew the law enforcement officers. They trusted me. I also knew all the potential troublemakers. I had them in mind when I refused to lead that motorcade to Oxford, Mississippi. And I knew the press. They like to create a story. So the first order of business was to keep the Clemson campus calm before Gantt's entry.

To that end I took steps to avoid violent encounters. I put out the word that the press was not to step onto the Clemson campus until Harvey Gantt was admitted. I compared the situation to the way reporters were treated at Cape Canaveral, Florida. Space officials allowed that their primary function was the safety of the mission. They would keep open their communications and periodically update reporters. Reporters were kept a mile away from the site at blastoff.

I told the press the primary role of Clemson was education, not demonstrations. We couldn't permit reporters corralling students, getting hysterical comments, and precipitating trouble. They could have Harvey Gantt the morning he reached campus and all day long until he went to his room at night. We had the ballroom at the Clemson House for reporters to use as the base from which to file their stories. The Clemson House was an eight-story hotel not far from the dormitory to which Gantt was assigned. The press went along with the arrangement. Later we'd have cocktails for the reporters. I had learned in South America about the importance of the care and feeding of the press corps.

I was able to sell that plan because leading newspaper editors such as Wayne Freeman of the *Greenville News* and business leaders such as John Cauthen of the textile industry were just as worried as I was. They helped to create a climate conducive to maintaining law and order. I also worked with Robert C. Edwards, Clemson's president, and members of Clemson's board, including Edgar Brown, my ally from the State Senate, who was the board chairman. We all had the same goal: keeping the peace.

Meanwhile I was blunt in telling newspaper editors that, while the state would pursue its legal appeals to resist desegregation as far as we could, the courts would ultimately reject our arguments. A full year before Gantt won admission to Clemson in 1963, I told reporters our legal defenses would fall like a house of cards. "You might as well start preparing your readers for the inevitable," I told them. "We are not going to secede."[19]

As the time for my valedictory address to the state legislature approached, Gantt's case was wending its way through the legal system. As the chief law enforcement officer of the state, I was confident that I could steer my fellow citizens in the right direction. Southerners always have been skeptical of anything that smacks of government intrusion in their lives, but I strongly believed that South Carolinians would respond to an appeal based on respect for the law.

No doubt change was coming. The battle for justice and for constitutional rights of our black citizens had precipitated bitter clashes between the races that already had stained the streets in other states. Barnett was not alone in leading in the wrong direction. After losing his bid for Governor in 1958, Alabama's George Wallace was widely quoted as vowing that "no other son-of-a-bitch will ever out-nigger me again." His fierce resistance to integration struck a chord with Alabama voters, who elected him Governor in 1962.

Given these tensions, I checked with Pete Strom again to make sure that all potential troublemakers were covered. Strom had a tab on the Klan. But others were also itching for a fight. For example, A. W. "Red" Bethea, a State Representative, a Clemson graduate, and an unsuccessful gubernatorial candidate in 1962, was a fiery orator and a fierce proponent of resistance. He had declared during his gubernatorial campaign that, if federal courts ordered the admission of a black into a state-supported South Carolina school, he would "close it so tight you can't get a crowbar in it."[20] I was worried about him leading a march to keep Clemson "pure." We watched him closely.

Senator Strom Thurmond didn't help matters. Thurmond, the most famous Clemson alumnus, took a defiant stance. He told a reporter for the *News and Courier* newspaper at the end of December 1962, "I am opposed to Gantt's admission to Clemson. The admission of students is a responsibility for the trustees, and any other action in connection therewith would have to be taken by the executive or the legislative branch of the state government."[21] And in his weekly newsletter, Thurmond decried what he called the "glaring stupidity" of the court's decision ordering the immediate admission of Gantt.

In this combustible atmosphere, I had to deal with the legislature. Some newspapers editorialized for interposition—a stance that contended that the state's sovereignty trumped that of the federal government. I had already sent word to Attorney General Bob Kennedy that we didn't want any federal marshals or troops in South Carolina. I would keep law and order.

Having covered the bases to keep the media and potential rabble-rousers at bay, I was ready to deliver my final speech before the General Assembly. I was ending fourteen years of government service, in which I had begun as a House member and gone on to serve as Speaker Pro Tem, Lieutenant Governor, and Governor. My firm decision was that I could not end my service without publicly addressing this explosive issue. Long after the Civil War had ended, the South was still being torn apart. It had been too long. Lives had been lost, and blood had been shed over and over again as our black citizens fought for their rights and as many whites tried to preserve their "way of life." It was past time to move on.

In my valedictory address to the state legislators, on January 9, 1963, I spoke plainly.

"As we meet, South Carolina is running out of courts. If and when every legal remedy has been exhausted, this General Assembly must make clear South Carolina's choice, a government of laws rather than a government of men. As determined as we are, we of today must realize the lesson of 100 years ago and move on for the good of South Carolina and our United States. This should be done with dignity. It must be done with law and order."

On Monday, January 28, thirteen days after I left office, Harvey Gantt arrived at Clemson to register. He was surrounded by a horde of reporters, who took pictures of him unpacking and getting settled in his room. There was no picketing or jeering.

Change and the resistance to it are dominant themes in southern history. People forget we live in a state that was defeated in war. No region has been more transformed by the powerful forces of change—racially, politically, and economically—over the past six decades than South Carolina and the other ten states of the Old Confederacy.

That valedictory speech reflected what I had learned over fourteen years of service in state government. It was a moment that shows that government *can* work. State law enforcement eased us through this potentially traumatic transition. Calm was maintained at a time when plenty of folks were poised to make trouble.

Gantt's peaceful enrollment in Clemson disappointed some reporters, who were looking for a bloody clash. A New York reporter even observed, "I expected blood. All I got was a cream puff."[22] Not surprisingly, by breaking the color barrier at Clemson, Gantt attracted national attention, including a splashy spread in the *Saturday Evening Post* headlined "Integration with Dignity." That moment in history had far-reaching implications for South Carolina.

I was proud to leave office on a high note. We *had* kept the lid on. Government can work, and in this case it worked for the good of the citizens. South Carolina had not succumbed to the open warfare that was keeping the streets bloodied in Alabama, Arkansas, and Mississippi. On my last day, I left the Governor's Mansion satisfied that I had helped to move South Carolina in the right direction and enthused that I would be returning to my first love, the courtroom, to make a living as a trial lawyer.

3

Getting to Know the Kennedys

I first met Robert F. Kennedy when we were both being honored as two of the Junior Chamber of Commerce's Ten Outstanding Young Men of 1954. We became fast friends. I admired his energy, his concern for others, and his zeal for doing the right thing as he saw it. But plenty of people found him to be brusque. He knew what he wanted and often came on like a bulldozer to get it.

Even as he put some people off, Bob had qualities that I saw time and again in the extended Kennedy family: a seemingly boundless energy and devotion to public service. They did not have to put themselves in the midst of the often personal and acrimonious political battles of the day, but they never shied away from them. As I got to know Bob and his brother Jack, I was struck by how easily they connected with people. Having served with two Presidents as Governor and eight Presidents as Senator, I rate President Kennedy as one of our country's finest leaders. He inspired people—attracted the best and brightest to government, Republican and Democrat.

My relationship with the Kennedys brought me more personal satisfaction and more political grief than any other friendship I have ever had. Opponents in all eight of my campaigns for the Senate—and in my gubernatorial campaign in 1958—tried to make some hay by tying me to the Kennedys. During those Senate campaigns, I was linked either to JFK and Bob or later to their younger brother, Teddy, or to other "liberal" Democrats, from Hubert Humphrey to Howard Metzenbaum to Paul Wellstone to Bill Clinton. They wanted to paint me as a "national Democrat," out of touch with South Carolinians. The Kennedy name was especially poisonous in South Carolina.

I was so sensitive to the political fallout from my friendship with the Kennedys that when Teddy offered a $5,000 contribution to my 1998 campaign for reelection to the Senate, I refused it. As I told him, it would cost me $500,000 in TV time to explain it.

But make no mistake; I am a great admirer of Teddy. After he lost one brother in World War II and two others as a result of assassins' bullets, one might think he would be turned off by public service. Instead he valiantly takes up the torch for labor and the poor and disadvantaged, works daily until late in the evening, and is always prepared for hearings and appearances on the Senate floor. He has become the patriarch of the family and carries the torch.

It may surprise some to learn that Teddy Kennedy, whom Republicans love to use as a whipping boy in campaigns, is actually popular on both sides of the aisle. He is a pragmatist who looks for ways to get things done rather than a polemicist interested in scoring political points. The notion that he is just a tax-and-spend liberal is not true. For example, as labor unions castigated him in 1985, Kennedy voted for the so-called Gramm-Rudman-Hollings bill that forced across-the-board reductions in spending if budget targets were not met. He is without doubt the most effective legislator with whom I served during my thirty-eight years in the Senate.

Of course Teddy and I had our differences. When Boston had its civil rights difficulty in South Boston in the 1970s, I took the floor. "Where is Mrs. Peabody?" I thundered. I reminded everyone that Peabody was the mother of the Massachusetts Governor. She had participated in civil rights marches in Florida, but you didn't hear a peep from her about civil rights problems up North.

"Why isn't she leading the movement in her own backyard?" I thundered. In his booming voice Teddy responded with equal force. There we were, standing side by side bellowing at each other. But these and other disputes didn't affect our friendship. Teddy has a terrific sense of humor, and we often exchanged laughs.

My introduction to the Kennedys really came at that awards banquet the Junior Chamber of Commerce put on for the outstanding young men in January 1955. The ceremony was held in the cavernous Jefferson County Armory in Louisville, Kentucky. In addition to Bob Kennedy and me, the honorees included a number of folks who had made headlines, including Chuck Yeager, the famous test pilot who was the first person to break the sound barrier; Notre Dame football coach Terry Brennan; and Hamilton Richardson, a diabetic and an outstanding tennis player who had been on the winning 1954 Davis Cup squad.

The seating arrangements were elaborate, as the various dignitaries were seated in tiers on stage in front of the large armory. About one hundred were on the bottom row of the platform, while another fifty or so were on seats that had been elevated several feet, and then the ten honorees were elevated still further. The proceedings went smoothly until CBS newsman Edward R. Murrow, the guest speaker, rose and moved toward the microphone.

Immediately Bob, who was seated next to me, clambered down the construction latticework and quickly maneuvered his way like a monkey to the floor. I waved down to ask if he was okay, and he waved back that all was well. Then, when Murrow completed his remarks, Kennedy, quite the athlete, climbed all the way back up. Reports that he had walked out were not accurate, as I distinctly recall how shocked I was at Kennedy's maneuvers—a reaction shared by the other honorees.[1]

When he returned to his seat, he turned to me and said, "I wouldn't be caught on the same platform with that SOB."

It seemed that his gripe went back to 1953, when he served as assistant counsel to the Permanent Subcommittee on Investigations, which was headed by the notorious Senator Joseph McCarthy of Wisconsin. McCarthy and his chief aide, Roy Cohn, were on a reckless hunt to find Communists in the State Department. It was only a matter of months before Kennedy resigned in protest of the tactics that McCarthy and Cohn employed. Murrow had anchored a searing documentary on McCarthy that contributed to the Wisconsin Senator's downfall. Even though he had resigned from his job with McCarthy, Kennedy still had some loyalty for the Senator as a person and was quick to anger at those whom he felt were unfair. Listening to Bob as he let loose his scorn at Murrow, I learned then that he could be unforgiving.

Bob was very firm in his opinions. He was impatient to learn about someone. Anytime you talked to him about someone he should see, his immediate question was, "Is he good?" You had to vouch for the individual before he would spend any time listening. Later, as Senator, I also spent time with the extended Kennedy clan. Bob's wife, Ethel, included me on the weekend tennis and movies at the pool house of the Hickory Hill estate in McLean, Virginia. I invariably came away with renewed admiration for the family. I had to walk a fine line. The Kennedy name was radioactive politically in South Carolina. But I thoroughly enjoyed every minute with the Kennedys.

I'll never forget when Bob and Ethel Kennedy and I flew in late to the Raleigh airport for the inauguration of Terry Sanford as Governor of North Carolina. Evidently the driver who had been arranged for us had given up, so I called a taxi. We piled in and headed down the highway. The driver, making time, was weaving in and out to get ahead of traffic. Ethel, the finest person you'll ever know, called to the driver: "Be careful. Be careful." Without slowing down or even looking toward Ethel, who was seated in the front seat, the driver exclaimed: "You have nine children and telling me to be careful!"

Bob was an outstanding leader. At the 1956 Democratic National Convention, when he asked me to work on South Carolina delegates to get them to support Jack in his bid to be Adlai Stevenson's running mate, I quickly agreed. By that time I had been reading everything I could about Jack Kennedy, about how he'd won the Navy and Marine Corps Medal for heroism in World War II with his PT 109 exploits. He was literate, having written *Why England Slept* and *Profiles in Courage*. And he was, far and away, the most attractive, charismatic politician of my time.

Selling Kennedy to southerners was not easy. He was hurt by his religion. Anti-Catholicism was still quite rampant. The rap against him went on and on: he was too young and wet behind the ears, a Yankee, and a Harvard graduate (meaning an elitist); his daddy was trying to buy public office for him; and he was just "too damned rich" to appeal to the poor and working class. Nonetheless—in order to demonstrate that he had support in the South—I went around doing my best to pick up some votes for him during the convention's roll call for Vice President. Kennedy was helped in his quest for southern support because the contest ultimately came down to him and Senator Estes Kefauver of Tennessee after Senator Albert Gore, also of Tennessee, had withdrawn from consideration.

Senators Kefauver and Gore were anathema to many southerners because they were two of the only three southerners in the Senate who had refused to sign the so-called Southern Manifesto in 1956. Written by South Carolina Senator Strom Thurmond and several other southerners, the manifesto was essentially a declaration of war against the Supreme Court's *Brown v. Board of Education* ruling that separate but equal school facilities were unconstitutional. The manifesto said the Court had no "legal basis" for its decision, that the ruling constituted a "clear abuse of judicial power," and that the Justices had "substituted their personal political and social ideas for the established law of the land." The signers included some of the most influential southern lawmakers in Washington, including Democratic Senators Dick Russell of Georgia, Sam Ervin of North Carolina, J. William Fulbright of Arkansas, and John Stennis of Mississippi. South Carolina's other Senator, Olin Johnston, also signed it, as did all six of the state's Congressmen.

Given those anti-Kefauver dynamics, I was successful in rounding up support for Kennedy. In fact Kennedy made inroads throughout the South in the battle against Kefauver, gaining more support from delegates from Dixie than his southern opponent. But at the call of the roll I ran into trouble when the convention chairman, House Speaker Sam Rayburn of Texas, refused to recognize me. There I was, standing on the back of a chair, Frank Epps of Greenville holding my legs, and I was waving the South Carolina standard way above the rest. I did everything I could to be seen, but my effort was to no avail. I learned later that House Majority Leader John McCormack of Massachusetts had no love for the Kennedys and took advantage of a chance to stick it to them. He urged Rayburn to recognize the Missouri delegation, which had switched from backing Gore to backing Kefauver. Other states followed suit in throwing their support to Kefauver. Rayburn called on me only after Kefauver had gained enough votes on the third ballot to have sewn up the nomination as the vice-presidential candidate.

Kennedy gave a gracious concession speech in which he asked that Kefauver be nominated by acclamation. In fact this setback had a silver lining for Kennedy. The Massachusetts Senator had gained a great deal of national exposure.[2] He couldn't be blamed when Republican Eisenhower clobbered Stevenson in the fall. Ultimately the events of 1956 actually helped to position Kennedy for a presidential run in 1960.

In addition to watching as Kennedy failed to secure the vice-presidential nomination, I had another disappointment at the convention. I had the role of seconding the nomination of South Carolina Governor George Bell Timmerman Jr. for President as a "favorite son" candidate. I wanted to show support beyond South Carolina. As I talked around the hall, someone suggested that I see George Wallace from Alabama.

I introduced myself to George and casually asked where he was from in Alabama. He said "Clayton." That struck a chord with me. At the end of the North African campaign in World War II, I had been sent back to Iran to help an outfit get situated—and that outfit happened to be headed by Colonel Clayton, from Clayton, Alabama. I asked George if he knew of a Colonel Clayton.

"Yes," he said. "That's my cousin."

From that moment George and I were off to becoming good friends. After a brief discussion, I told George I would give him five minutes of my ten minutes on national television in exchange for five votes from Alabama delegates. He said it was a deal. Alabama was to be the first state recognized, beginning at eight the next morning. We were told to be behind the stage and ready no later than seven. We had gotten all gussied up and memorized our speeches for our first appearance on national TV.

Remember this was more than fifty years ago. Five minutes on national television was gold for a young politician. But then to our dismay Alabama yielded to Illinois for the nomination of Adlai Stevenson. That's the way it went the entire day. When the convention broke at six for everybody to catch a quick dinner and come back for the evening session, George and I were finally recognized.

"I'm sure we both made stirring speeches but not a soul in America heard us," I have often recalled of that moment. "I was blanked out by Betty Furness selling refrigerators." Furness, a film actress, had become a highly recognized pitchwoman for Westinghouse appliances on television. Back then, commercials were live productions. She became a fixture in TV commercials, touting the company's products, always ending her sales pitches with the line, "You can be sure if it's Westinghouse."

In the end, whether I was blanked out or not, Timmerman wound up with only a handful of delegates. Stevenson secured the nomination on the first ballot. Years later, I did get the last laugh. Imagine my glee, when after becoming a Senator on the Commerce Committee, I was at a 1967 hearing at which Furness was to testify as President Johnson's special assistant for consumer affairs. When she appeared before the committee, I said, "I've been looking for you Miss Furness." I explained that she had upstaged me on my first opportunity to be on national television. We both laughed. And she went on to do a very effective job as a consumer advocate.

It didn't take long for me to recognize just how much grief my friendship with the Kennedys would cause me back home. I always found myself explaining them away. In my race for Governor in 1958, I got hit with charges that I was running with Kennedy money. I responded that if anyone could show I had gotten a red cent from any of the Kennedys, I would immediately withdraw from the race. Ultimately the potshots missed their mark. I won that contest, but I knew my relationship with "the Kennedys" would always create an opening for my political opponents.

As Governor and head of the state party in 1960, I led the support for Jack in his presidential race. During that fierce battle against Republican Richard Nixon, I had plenty of dealings with Bob, who was then his brother's tough-as-nails, take-no-prisoners campaign manager. Throughout that campaign, when Bob called on you, it wasn't to persuade or to engage in a love-in or to schmooze. He was harsh, curt, and demanding. He was absolutely relentless in advancing Jack's cause. He seemed to move at full speed all the time. Heaven help anybody who got in his way.

That relentless energy and ruthlessness on behalf of his brother became legendary. Of course his abrupt management style didn't go over well with some politicians. Still the toughest part of selling Jack Kennedy to southerners was his religion. I had the worst time on that score.

All the other charges that I cited earlier also continued to be raised: he was a rich Yankee, trying to buy the election. But in the end it was his Catholicism that stung in the South. No Roman Catholic ever had been elected President. There was great suspicion and concern among many southerners about what the religion would mean for the way the nation's commander in chief approached the job of the presidency.

I'll never forget a story that I heard in one little town in South Carolina. It reflects the intense fear and the widespread ignorance about Catholicism that prevailed at the time as anti-Catholic fervor ran so deep that politicians were hard-pressed to overcome it. Two friends were having a conversation about what would happen if Kennedy were elected:

> Beasley turned to his friend Phillips and said, "Phillips, did you hear what I heard?"
> "No, what's that, Beasley?"
> "They say this fellow Kennedy, when he is elected, is going to move the pope into the White House."

Senator John F. Kennedy at the Columbia airport with Senator Olin Johnston and Governor Hollings during Kennedy's 1960 presidential campaign. Greenville News-Piedmont, *courtesy of the Kennedy Presidential Library (Px76–80\SC\6–NP:3)*

"No," exclaimed Phillips. "He's not going to do that."

"Yes, and that ain't all," said Beasley. "They tell me he's going to put holy water in the commodes."

"What's a commode?" asked Phillips.

"Hell, I don't know," said Beasley. "I ain't no Catholic."

I had the worst time trying to reassure voters that Kennedy's religion was not disqualifying. I did get good help from friends such as Tom Pope, the former Speaker of the South Carolina House and grandmaster of Masonry for South Carolina, who went around the state saying the Catholics weren't going to kill all the Protestants.

But the best help I got was from Kennedy himself. First, during the campaign to win the nomination, Kennedy encountered fierce resistance to the notion of a Catholic in the White House as he tried to win over voters in the all-important West Virginia primary. Kennedy decided to address the issue of religion head-on. As Theodore H. White explained in his highly acclaimed book *The Making of the President 1960,* on the Sunday before the primary, Kennedy sponsored a paid telecast in which he took questions from Franklin D. Roosevelt Jr.

A few minutes into the broadcast, Roosevelt asked a planted question about religion, and Kennedy devoted a good chunk of the show to answering it. Relying on his scribbled notes about the show, since there was no transcript or tape recording, White recalled that Kennedy looked into the camera and addressed the citizens directly, saying that "when any man stands on the steps of the Capitol and takes the oath of office of President, he is swearing to support the separation of church and state; he puts one hand on the Bible and raises the other hand to God as he takes the oath. And if he breaks his oath, he is not only committing a crime against the Constitution, for which the Congress can impeach him—and should impeach him—but he is committing a sin against God."

How does an opponent respond to such a powerful appeal? Senator Hubert Humphrey of Minnesota, at that point Kennedy's chief rival for the presidential nomination, was in the unenviable position of having to come up with a compelling response. He couldn't. Kennedy thrashed him. Humphrey's presidential campaign was over. At a press conference Kennedy said, prematurely as it turned out, "We have now buried the religious issue once and for all."

After winning West Virginia and Nebraska on May 10, Kennedy carried Maryland and Oregon and went into the National Convention in Los Angeles as the front-runner. The overriding goal was for JFK to win on the first ballot. As chairman of the South Carolina delegation, I was trying hard to find votes for the Massachusetts Senator. Senate Majority Leader Lyndon B. Johnson of Texas had at that point emerged as JFK's main obstacle to the nomination.

When I heard that Kennedy had been invited to appear before the Texas delegation but had declined, I immediately tried to get him to reverse course. I called one of Kennedy's closet confidants, Kenneth O'Donnell, who had first met Bob when they were teammates on Harvard's football squad. I told O'Donnell in no uncertain terms that if Kennedy couldn't handle the Texas delegation then he couldn't handle the country. He must appear. Fortunately Kennedy did accept the invitation. His appearance was dramatic. He told the Texas delegates that Lyndon was doing a wonderful job as Majority Leader and, for the good of the country, he ought to stay put! The Texas crowd took his comments in good spirits. The appearance helped to cement the youthful Senator's standing. He was a hit. The following day, out of gratitude for my advice, Kennedy sent me a crystal box in which a PT 109 pin was embedded.

Meanwhile I was still working on South Carolina delegates. As we readied for the roll-call vote at the convention, a poll of the delegation showed Johnson had the lead among our delegates. A motion was made for the "unit rule," which required that all votes in the state delegation be cast for the majority candidate, Lyndon Johnson. As Governor and chairman of the delegation, I was sidelined. The unit rule made me useless. So I turned the delegation over to Olin Johnston, the state's senior Senator, and went outside to join the Kennedy crowd as they followed the proceedings from the trailers and "spotted" delegates to keep track of JFK's supporters. I knew all the Governors and I was especially close to Jim Blair of Missouri. I said, "Recognize Jim. Recognize Jim." They did. Blair moved that Kennedy be nominated by acclamation. "Acclamation" differs from "unanimity" in that it requires a majority rather than every one of the votes.

But Olin Johnston, standing with the South Carolina delegates at the back of the hall, mistook "acclamation" for "unanimity." He thought it meant there had to be unanimous support for Kennedy. "I object, I object," Johnston shouted. But in the enthusiasm for bringing the long proceedings to a close, the chairman didn't hear him. Johnston then tried to use the phone to get the chair's attention—to no avail. Finally, he decided to move up to the rostrum. A large and powerful man, Johnston was still gripping the phone and ripped it out as he marched to the front, all the while shouting, "I object!" By this time he had the attention of the media, and cameras followed him. When he reached the front of the hall, it was disastrous. The rostrum was elevated, of course, with a hedge and a picket fence below it. As Johnston arrived at the front, he was pushed along by the crowd and they wouldn't let him stop. Over the fence, he went, falling into a decorative hedge. When I saw this, I was the happiest man in Los Angeles. I had fought for Kennedy and encountered lots of resistance. I even lost my vote when our delegates adopted the unit rule. But now my candidate had won. I could celebrate.

The morning after Kennedy secured the presidential nomination, I was invited to join him and Bob in a suite at the Biltmore Hotel in Los

Angeles. When I arrived, labor leader Walter Reuther, the head of the United Auto Workers, and just about every other leader of some interest or another was trying to elbow his way into the room. Reuther didn't make it in, but I inched my way forward with several other Governors, including G. Mennen "Soapy" Williams of Michigan and Abraham Ribicoff of Connecticut, and a number of other political leaders. Kennedy explained that in order to win he had offered to put Johnson, the Senate Majority Leader, on the ticket. When the name *Johnson* came off of Kennedy's lips, there was a gasp in the room. The hard-charging Texas Senator had thrown plenty of elbows over the years and had mounted a challenge to Kennedy for the nomination. So it's no wonder that Kennedy's decision created plenty of heartburn! Soapy exploded, "LBJ! Hell, I can get more votes for Fritz Hollings in Michigan that I can get for Johnson. They have never heard of Fritz in Michigan but they sure know Lyndon."

Others also objected. Some argued that LBJ's presence on the ticket would send the black vote fleeing to the Republicans. But Kennedy was firm. He motioned to me and asked that I get Bob and meet with Johnson's righthand man, Bobby Baker. "Get the two Bobbys together," he said. "We've got to cut out their wrangling."

So I went with Bob to Johnson's suite. On opening the door in the parlor, I saw Bobby Baker, Lady Bird Johnson, and House Speaker Sam Rayburn. Phil Graham, publisher of the *Washington Post,* and Johnson were in the bedroom. Rayburn was bitching that taking the vice presidency would be the biggest mistake Johnson could make. Rayburn contended that Johnson had a lot more influence as Majority Leader. The Speaker then invoked the famous saying of Franklin Roosevelt's Vice President John Nance Garner, that being Vice President "isn't worth a bucket of warm spit."

Although Kennedy had feared that Bobby Baker would be unhappy to see his boss give up the prestige and power of his Senate post, it did not turn out to require a lot of sweat. I urged them to relax and face the fact that the only shot for Kennedy to carry the South was if we all pulled together. The two Bobbys were both professionals and wanted to win. The fact is that the South and its 128 electoral votes would be crucial in the upcoming election, and they knew it. Then Johnson and Phil Graham came out of the bedroom with everything settled.

After Kennedy and Johnson's nominations, I was invited to the coliseum for Jack's acceptance speech. Kennedy invited me to bring along others from the delegation, but nobody would join me. My delegates were all packing up, returning home in disgust. Most felt it was a mistake for Johnson to accept the vice presidency. They all felt that Kennedy was doomed in the South, particularly South Carolina. I sat with Bob and Ethel and Steve and Jean Kennedy Smith (the candidate's sister) that evening as Kennedy made a dynamic talk, and the country got a glimpse of what an appealing, attractive, and charismatic candidate he was.

After the convention I returned home and went to work in South Carolina to do everything I could to carry the state for JFK. It was non-stop work. Tom Pope, as I mentioned, helped enormously as did former Congressman Dick Richards and Ted Riley, the chairman of the South Carolina Democratic Party. Senator Olin Johnston made a few talks without giving me a heads-up on his plans. He didn't coordinate at all. Meanwhile Senator Strom Thurmond kept complaining that "the Democratic platform was a communist manifesto." And the only Congressman I could get for Kennedy was Bob Hemphill.

I faced an uphill battle in promoting Kennedy's candidacy. The newspaper coverage in South Carolina was dreadful, portraying Kennedy in the worst possible light. And of course Kennedy's Catholicism was still a red flag in the Baptist Piedmont. Kennedy was the best help I had in defusing the issue of religion. Just as he had done in the West Virginia primary, Kennedy hit the issue directly. In a speech before the Greater Houston Ministerial Association, on September 12, Kennedy made clear that he was not about to lose the election because of his religion.

"I believe in an America where the separation of church and state is absolute—where no Catholic prelate would tell the President (should he be Catholic) how to act, and no Protestant minister would tell his parishioners for whom to vote . . . and where no man is denied public office merely because his religion differs from the President who might appoint him or the people who might elect him," he said.

Kennedy was eloquent and reassuring. The speech took the steam out of those trying to make his Catholicism a defining issue of the campaign. Near the conclusion of his remarks, the Democratic presidential candidate suggested that the stakes were sky-high in the election in that it would affect not only how our country would be seen in the rest of the world but also how our own citizens see themselves.

"If this election is decided on the basis that forty million Americans lost their chance of being President on the day they were baptized, then it is the whole nation that will be the loser, in the eyes of Catholics and non-Catholics around the world, in the eyes of history, and in the eyes of our own people," Kennedy said.

I was so impressed by the power of that speech that I obtained a tape of it and crisscrossed the state to get various TV stations to run it. We didn't have the money for the telephone lines to have a statewide telecast. It made a big difference in how South Carolinians saw the young Senator.

Of course Johnson came to South Carolina to campaign, reassuring southerners that even though Kennedy was a Yankee, Johnson was a Texan who would stand up for the South. Even so, when Johnson arrived, we had to be careful about where he would appear. The state's political establishment wanted no part of Kennedy or Johnson. We decided the only place to bring him was the town of Anderson, South Carolina. Johnson was not about to be panned. He appeared with an honor guard at a fairground area. I gathered all the dignitaries I could find, including Senator George Smathers of Florida, Governor Ernie Vandiver of Georgia, Governor Luther Hodges of North Carolina, Governor John Patterson of Alabama, and several Congressmen. Strom Thurmond did not appear. We then went to Rocky Bottom, where Bobby Baker and Frank McCaulay put on an evening barbecue.

I'll never forget Johnson's closing remarks: "I awaken in the morning to open my eyes, and the first countenance I see is that of Robert Baker of Pickens, South Carolina. After my daily toil, late at night I never rest my head on the pillow ready to close my eyes until I see my best friend Bobby Baker, of Pickens, South Carolina." The crowd went wild. When Bobby Baker subsequently got into trouble and was indicted for engaging in fraud and tax evasion, Johnson was nowhere to be found. As Harry Truman said, if you want a friend in Washington, get a dog.

I took off for an industry trip to South America in September, two months before Election Day. Upon my return I attended the Governors' conference in Little Rock, Arkansas. At the request of the press, Cecil Underwood, the Republican Governor of West Virginia, and I critiqued the Nixon-Kennedy television debate. My job was easy. I was all set to make favorable comments—and I did make a few extemporaneous observations. But it was no contest. Kennedy appeared firm and friendly with a twinkle in his eye from time to time. Nixon emerged as a dark figure with his heavy beard and a countenance that made him appear to be as nervous as the proverbial deer in headlights.

As the campaign heated up, both Nixon and Kennedy had scheduled trips to South Carolina. Vice President Nixon announced that he was coming on October 3. Kennedy announced that he would be in the Palmetto State a week later. Hearing that news, Nixon cancelled his October 3 meeting. Obviously he wanted to make his appearance after Kennedy had made his visit to the state.

Kennedy arrived two hours late for a rally in front of the Capitol in Columbia. I thought we had attracted maybe thirty thousand at the beginning. We did everything to entertain them. But half of the crowd had left by lunchtime. Senator Johnston was with me to meet Kennedy at the airport even as Thurmond and the South Carolina press continued to complain about the Democrats' campaign platform. Kennedy gave an upbeat talk. Of course, ever-sensitive to his audience, the young Senator referred to John C. Calhoun and the proud South Carolina heritage. The enthusiasm in the crowd was obvious.

When Nixon finally arrived for his visit, I thought that, as a courtesy, I would greet him at the airport. But I was told that I was not invited. So I stayed away. Nixon arrived on November 3, five days before Election Day. He flew into Shaw Air Force Base in Sumter and was motored in. Attorney General William Rogers was on that airplane, but he never got off it. As the nation's chief law enforcement officer in charge of making sure that southern states abide by the *Brown v. Board of Education* school-integration decision, Rogers was about as popular as pond scum throughout Dixie.[3]

As Nixon spoke on the Statehouse steps in Columbia, I got in the Governor's Cadillac and drove up to Greenville. I asked Bob Jolley of WFBC, the local TV station there, if I could have some time that evening. He gave me a half hour at seven. Imagine pulling off such a stunt today. A half hour of airtime just like that! I got my Citadel friend Jimmy Mann, who was then Solicitor of the Thirteenth Judicial Circuit and would later be a Congressman, to introduce me. As the camera light came on, I appeared behind the desk, talking like a Governor, and then I walked around and sat on the desk speaking informally. I first emphasized that in all good conscience I thought that I was acting in the best interest of the State of South Carolina by backing Kennedy.

I explained that I had gone to Washington with influential industrialist Charles E. Daniel earlier in the year to testify before the International Tariff Commission. I had tangled with Tom Dewey, the former GOP presidential candidate, who represented the Japanese in a textile case. He had kept me busy all morning. Then, when we broke, Charlie, who, as chairman of Daniel Construction Corporation, a Greenville-based behemoth, was a cheerleader for South Carolina's industrial growth, said let's go over and see the chief. I had no idea the chief was President Eisenhower!

We were ushered right in to see the President. He couldn't have been more hospitable. I told him about the case before the Tariff Commission. He said not to worry, that we would win that case. Later in May, when the commission had ruled against us, I called my friend Mike Feldman, Senator Kennedy's aide, to see if the Senator would help us on textiles. The Senator was totally sympathetic. He knew the issue well. We agreed to exchange letters in which he pledged to do everything possible to help boost the textile industry.

I then read the letter from Kennedy to the TV audience. I added: "You heard the talk that Nixon made earlier today. He didn't tell you how his Tariff Commission had found against us."

I was confident that my pitch on television made an impression on voters. Come Election Day, I was overjoyed. Kennedy eked out a narrow victory in South Carolina, winning by fewer than ten thousand votes, with 51.2 percent. That edge was similar to the very close national vote. Kennedy defeated Nixon by the razor-thin margin of one tenth of 1 percent.

One legacy of that campaign was that it marked the emergence of the pollster as an influential figure not only in shaping campaign strategy but also in having a voice in policy making after the election. The contrast to everything I had experienced in politics could not have been more striking. Throughout my fourteen years as a state legislator, Lieutenant Governor, and Governor, I had run campaigns without radio, TV, pollsters, or consultants.

But then I met Lou Harris, Kennedy's official pollster in the presidential race. Throughout the battle JFK waged against Nixon, Harris was constantly writing memos and offering advice. He always had the ear of the presidential candidate. For example, during the primary campaign, Kennedy was stumping with black voters in Wisconsin, a key state. They were backing Humphrey in increasing numbers, according to Harris, who offered the following advice to Kennedy in a memorandum: "Perhaps a late campaign appearance on foot, hand-shaking in the Negro ward of Milwaukee . . . would be in order here," he wrote. "There is a strong strain among Wisconsins [*sic*] that civil rights should be granted to Negroes."[4]

A couple of months after Kennedy took office, Harris conducted a secret poll that found "strong hints here that the public is judging the President for his style, manner and approach rather than on the specifics he is proposing or acting upon."[5] Kennedy was being advised how to act—to the point of shaking hands with blacks in Milwaukee—and even being told how voters were more moved by his Camelot image than by any of his policy positions. The 1960 presidential campaign had transformed the electoral process. Consultants and pollsters began to have more and more impact on a candidate's positions, his decisions on where and how to campaign, even whose hands to shake! Voters see this happening as presidential candidates and others seeking federal office often twist themselves into pretzels to avoid offending anyone.

Kennedy's employment of Harris and, of course, his reliance on his father's deep pockets, marked a change in politics that has accelerated over the years. Kennedy's campaign also was the first to make a strategic decision to push for debates on national TV. Those debates against Nixon had a huge impact on the outcome of the election. His charm and appeal leapt out to the viewers. The Kennedy-Nixon debates also made TV the principal means of political warfare—and the most expensive. Nothing would be the same in future elections. Now the constant pursuit of money to get on the tube and to wage endless campaigns has reached a point where it has corrupted our government.

But a candidate learns from campaigning. Kennedy told me of the best lesson he learned in Madison, Wisconsin. While he was working the streets in the bitter cold, hardly any of the voters would stop to talk. On the third day of campaigning, it was so cold Kennedy ducked into a school and was warming his hands just inside by the radiator. Walking by, the principal asked, "Aren't you Senator Kennedy from Massachusetts?" Kennedy smiled and, recognizing the principal's accent, responded: "Yes, but you must be from Massachusetts too." They shook hands and exchanged pleasantries until the principal, looking at his watch, said: "We're having an assembly in a few minutes. Will you talk to the students?" "I'll be glad to," responded Kennedy. He told the assembly why he was running and what the country needed the next

President to do and then took questions at length. The next day, instead of avoiding him, voters stopped him in the streets. Many crossed the street to speak to him, saying things such as "My son [or daughter] heard you yesterday. You really made an impression on him. I'm going to vote for you." Kennedy said you do better in politics talking to students rather than grown-ups.

Of course the Kennedy versus Nixon campaign turned out to be the last presidential election in which the notion of a Democratic "Solid South" remained a fact. In the coming years, voters in South Carolina and the rest of the Old Confederacy began to flock to the GOP column. The parties were increasingly split along racial lines. White folks, especially in rural areas, abandoned the Democratic Party, which was associated with civil rights. African Americans—who had either been Republicans or voiceless for generations—developed an allegiance to the Democratic Party. I had to spend most of my career navigating these difficult political currents as a steadfast Southern Democrat, trying to get enough votes—black and white—to prevail.

The idea for one of Kennedy's boldest proposals, which became a signature part of his presidency—the creation of the Peace Corps—was germinated near the end of the campaign. Part of the impetus for this notion came during a conference of Governors and industrialists in Miami. I served as chairman of an Industry-Education Conference. The session in Florida featured a keynote talk by retired General James M. Gavin, president of the Arthur D. Little Company, a Boston research and consulting firm. I was impressed with Gavin's reference to something he called the "Freedom Corps," which essentially would provide an alternative to military service for antimilitary young people, who nevertheless would like to serve their country by helping poor countries in various ways.[6]

Gavin described how his company had taken surveys around the country and found that no college student in his senior year was ready to join the army, but 90 percent of them said they would volunteer for a year's service overseas: engineering students to build roads and bridges, premed students to man the hospitals, education students to teach English, and so on. Gavin had an inspiration. "That's what we ought to be doing to spread the American way the world around," he said. Gavin later recalled the tremendous reception for the idea. "The most applause that I ever received in my life," he said.[7]

That evening up in the Governor's suite of the hotel, I realized for the first time that this four-star General was wearing a PT 109 pin. He was for Kennedy. I told him that I didn't know that he supported the Senator. Gavin replied that he enthusiastically backed Kennedy. It was eleven at night.

I told Gavin that Kennedy should use his idea in the presidential race. We shouldn't wait. It was such a good proposal that Republicans might beat us to the punch. I remember trying to call Jack and Bob, but I couldn't reach either of them. So I called Mike Feldman and told him about Gavin's talk. I described the terrific reception for Gavin's remarks and urged Feldman to pass it along to Kennedy. I noted that there were plenty of Nixon backers in the crowd and we couldn't afford for them to run with the idea before Kennedy did.

A few days after my midnight call to Feldman on October 27, Kennedy gave full-throated voice to the Peace Corps and won a terrific, overwhelming response. He went to the Cow Palace in San Francisco on November 2, less than a week before Election Day, and spoke of "Ambassadors of peace" who would serve "as an alternative or a supplement to peacetime selective service, well qualified through rigorous standards, well trained in the language, skills, and customs they will need to know."[8] The idea was ridiculed by Nixon and Eisenhower, but the Peace Corps has become one of JFK's most lasting legacies.

When Kennedy had settled into office, Feldman asked if I would be interested in heading the Peace Corps. I was quick with a response: "You want to kill the baby in the crib with a segregationist southern Governor?" I said he needed someone with a different reputation. He allowed that both former President Herbert Hoover and FBI director J. Edgar Hoover also had turned it down. I suggested that the President might think about asking the dynamic Sargent Shriver to head the new group. The southern Governors were very positive about Sarge, I told Feldman. "He's the most likable fellow with the most get up and go," I said. Later on, of course, Sarge was selected to be the first Peace Corps director.

But I'm a bit ahead of myself because before Kennedy's inauguration, I was invited to lunch with him at his Georgetown home. After lunch I rode with him to the airport, and he said he would make good on his word on textiles—that the way to follow through would be to act under the mandate of national security. The U.S. economy had lost four hundred thousand textile jobs between 1950 and 1960. Kennedy knew that this approach would be both good policy and good politics. I could work with Feldman on touching all the bases and getting a proposal into shape. Then he told me that he was going to appoint my friend Soapy Williams, the Governor of Michigan, as Assistant Secretary of State for African affairs. Kennedy emphasized how we had to pay more attention to Africa, and garrulous Soapy would make a hit. I responded, "Why didn't you announce that in the campaign? If I could have told my constituents that we were going to send that liberal Soapy Williams to Africa, we could have carried South Carolina by a landslide."

A month or so later, I was at Kennedy's inauguration, and, like many others, I thought I would freeze. As bitterly cold as it was, the new President made up for it with the most heartwarming address. He set the tone for his administration with his famous words "ask not what your country can do for you—ask what you can do for your country." He went on to select a fine team for his cabinet. I applauded his selection of Dean Rusk as Secretary of State, as Rusk had seen earlier service in the State Department and was president of the Rockefeller Foundation. I was equally pleased with the choice of Robert McNamara, president of Ford Motor Company, as Secretary of Defense, and prominent investment banker Douglas Dillon as Secretary of the Treasury. It was quite a contest for Secretary of Agriculture. I had just been on a trip to Latin America with Orville L. Freeman, the Governor of Minnesota. Even as a southerner, I was so impressed with this midwesterner—whom I had first gotten to know when we served as Governors at the same time—that I vouched for him for that post. He was one of the best and wound up being a very good member of the cabinet.

But not everything was rosy between the Kennedys and me. After having all but broken my neck for JFK in 1960, I came to find in 1962 that they were beholden to Senator Olin Johnston. That year marked the end of my term as Governor and my primary race against our state's senior Senator. It just happened that Teddy Kennedy was running for the U.S. Senate that same year. Johnston, as chairman of the Senate's Post Office Committee, had something of value to the Kennedys: postmaster appointments in Massachusetts. None could be cleared without Olin's approval. Word went out from the White House to help Johnston. Not only that, outright fabrications were circulated.

Johnston and I faced off with competing speeches at the Parker High School football field in Greenville during the campaign. I thought I had a secret weapon. South Carolina Representative L. Mendel Rivers, the powerful chairman of the Armed Services Committee, had given me the heads-up that Donaldson Air Force Base was on the list to be closed.

After I noted this in my talk, Olin stood up. I can hear him now. "I just got a telegram, let me read it to you," he said in that slow-as-molasses way of talking that he had. "Donaldson Air Base will remain open," he read and then said the message had been signed by President John F. Kennedy.

The crowd roared. I looked like a fool. Politics is politics. I knew the President had nothing to do with it, and sure enough I found out that Dick Donahue, a White House staffer, had sent the telegram. In that Senate race I went on to carry just one county—Calhoun. I should have known that the Kennedy crowd would not be with me in that Senate race.

After all it wasn't long after the word got out that I was going to run that I was called to the White House to discuss textiles. That was a ruse. Feldman, obviously at the President's direction, wanted to talk me out of launching a campaign. He tried to talk me into agreeing to an appointment to the federal bench. He told me what an important position a Judge had, how it provided security for life, and how he was sure that Senator Johnston would approve. Johnston's approval was necessary because a state's Senators sign off on such appointments. Actually a couple of close friends also encouraged me to grab the position. If that job didn't suit me, how about being Ambassador to Australia, Feldman asked. They didn't get it. I wasn't looking for a secure job. I wanted to continue to serve the people of my state. Of course it would be a while before I got to Capitol Hill, as Johnston clobbered me in that 1962 contest.

A year later, in October 1963, I was invited to speak at the annual Democratic dinner in Asheville, North Carolina. I was out of public office at that point, but I was still a huge fan of President Kennedy's—even after the Kennedy clan had backed Johnston. My talk was designed to boost JFK, who remained unpopular in many parts of Dixie.

It must have made an impression, because three days before Kennedy was assassinated, I was invited to the White House. When I went into the Oval Office, the President thanked me for the talk I had made in North Carolina. As I was leaving to speak to O'Donnell in the outer office, the President called out, "Fritz, come back here. Did you hear about your friend Soapy Williams?"

I said, "No, Mr. President, what was that?"

"The poll that we took of the African chieftains to see how they liked Soapy," he said.

"How'd it come out?" I asked.

"Medium rare," he said, having himself a good chuckle.

I then joined the President outside the West Wing, where piles of boxes were stuffed with food destined for West Virginia. The President said George McGovern, who was his special assistant as director of the Food for Peace, was seeking a boost for that program. But the President had promised himself that before he fed anybody else, he'd first feed the hungry in West Virginia. His experience while campaigning there was searing. He saw up close how pervasive poverty was—to the point where some people were going to bed hungry. So, before he gave food to Food for Peace, the President ordered food for West Virginia.

That afternoon he flew down to Tampa, over to Fort Worth, and then to Dallas. At one that day, I was having lunch with a friend in the Kings Tavern in downtown Charleston. I then heard the stunning news. I couldn't believe it. I guess in some ways I still can't.

"Your friend Kennedy has been shot," I was told. I called my old friend businessman Andy Griffith in Orangeburg and asked if he would fly me to Washington. I'd already received word from Bob Kennedy to pick up my credentials for the funeral at the East Wing. When I got them, I also was given a pass to buck the line so that I would be immediately escorted into the Rotunda to walk past the funeral bier to pay my respects. I wasn't bucking any line. I was no longer a Governor, and it didn't feel right to act as though I was. So I went to the end of the line at the Lincoln Memorial. It was six in the evening, and I thought I'd get to the front by midnight. It was a bitterly cold evening. Grouped six or eight across, the folks in the line shuffled quietly toward the Rotunda in the Capitol. It was six in the morning before I got there.

I then hailed a cab to the Mayflower Hotel. I got in a tub of cold water to thaw out. I know I stayed in that tub for a good forty-five minutes. Then I got up, dressed, and started walking around the corner to St. Matthew's Cathedral. Just as I approached the cathedral, walking up, I saw this dapper African American man dressed in a long-tailed coat, formal wear with a striped vest, striped pants, spats, and a derby hat.

I'd seen that derby many times before and sure enough it was the Reverend Isaiah DeQuincey Newman, the head of South Carolina's NAACP. I was about to call out to him when an usher walked down from the steps and, giving I.D. his arm, said in a distinct voice, "Right this way, Mr. Ambassador," apparently having concluded from Newman's elegant attire that he held ambassadorial rank.

I'll be damned, I thought to myself. It was poetic justice. I.D. was ushered up to the third row. The former Governor, a big-time supporter and friend of the Kennedys, was seated on the thirty-fifth row.

The thousand days of the Kennedy presidency had passed in a flash. The elegant style, the eloquence, the boundless energy, the renewed sense that citizens should give something back to the country—all that spirit and hope were snuffed out on that November 1963 afternoon in Dallas by an assassin's bullet.

After that awful, incomprehensible day, Bob Kennedy changed. His no-nonsense, in-your-face public persona softened. His public face began to look far more like the private Robert Kennedy we knew. At the same time, he was in despair. His grief was obvious to those who saw him up close. About three days after his brother's funeral, we were sitting in his living room. Bob was Attorney General, but he had never liked or even respected Lyndon Johnson, who was now destined to complete John Kennedy's presidency.

Grappling with his own grief and his growing distaste for Johnson, Bob was thinking aloud about stepping out of the public arena, quitting public life. He thought he could make his greatest contribution as a teacher. Of course this change was not to be. What I was hearing really was the pain of a man who had lost a brother tragically and suddenly.

Bob could never leave public service. It was what animated him. And the Kennedy movement needed a leader. He could not drop the mantle. So he decided to stay on at least for a while as Attorney General.

I went back home the next week and I started the John Fitzgerald Kennedy Presidential Library fund in South Carolina. I had the help of I. DeQuincey Newman, who was overjoyed when I told him how far behind him I was seated at the memorial service! I also enlisted the help of McKinley Washington of Charleston. I had set the meeting on this project to be held in a mezzanine parlor room of the Wade Hampton Hotel in Columbia.

I hadn't been in the room long before I heard some shouting downstairs. The bellboy was telling McKinley that blacks were not allowed on the mezzanine. I went down and said the hell they're not. I escorted McKinley and the others up. *Brown v. Board of Education* had made segregation in the schools unconstitutional. But here it was 1963, nine years after that decision, and blacks were not allowed on the mezzanine or to eat in the hotels of South Carolina!

The next year, Bob asked some friends, including me, to meet with him in New York. Prominent Atlanta lawyer Bobby Troutman, former Rhode Island Governor Dennis Roberts, and four or five others met with Bob. The discussion was whether or not he should run for the U.S. Senate against Senator Kenneth Keating of New York.

I never heard of such a thing, moving out of one state, Massachusetts, to run for office in another one. I expressed my skepticism. But the majority thought otherwise. They figured that with Johnson as President, Kennedy wouldn't last long as Attorney General. He ought to run for the job to continue to carry the Kennedy torch, they said. So, just over nine months after the President's death, on September 2, 1964, Bob Kennedy resigned as Attorney General. He was going to launch a remarkable race for a Senate seat from New York.

Later I traveled to New York for a bar mitzvah on Long Island, and I decided to go to a Bob Kennedy rally on Long Island as well. Three old streetcars were lined up as the campaign headquarters, and when Bob saw me, he insisted I speak at the rally. I did. Afterward I was convinced that hearing my lowcountry South Carolina accent convinced the audience that all the white foreigners in New York were for Bob Kennedy. On Election Day Kennedy's vigorous campaign paid off. He defeated Kenneth Keating by more than seven hundred thousand votes.

Two years later, in 1966, I was elected to the Senate. After being sworn in, I found my desk was next to Bob's. I was just learning the ropes and was keeping my mouth shut, but Bob was busy. He and I argued about the war in Vietnam. I had just returned from a trip there, and I contended that rather than no-win, it was a "slow-win." I insisted that we needed to change our strategy by escalating our military force there. But even in 1967, Bob knew it was a loser. He encouraged me to read *Street Without Joy,* by Bernard Fall, a 1961 account of the French defeat in Vietnam. Bob already was talking up a withdrawal. Despite our differences on the war, however, we did find common ground on issues such as education.

It really was a most enjoyable period because I got to know Bob and Ethel well. They constantly included me on weekends at Hickory Hill. We played tennis, and I was invited to these wonderful dinners with all the "sparklies," such as Paul Newman. Ethel made sure we all said something. Everyone had to participate.

Representing New York had a big impact on Bob's outlook. He saw the pervasiveness of poverty and the desolate life in the slums filled with rats, hunger, and hopelessness. He began to respond to the wave of migration to New York City from the impoverished rural South. He was creating a stir—and plenty of resentment—by talking about hunger in Mississippi. Critics saw his moves as little more than crass political opportunism. After all it was an open secret that he was contemplating a future presidential bid.

It was in this context that I hit the ceiling in early 1968, when I learned that Bob planned to have subcommittee field hearings in South Carolina to shine the spotlight on my state's hunger problems. By this point I knew that once the Kennedy name was attached to hunger in the state, everything I had tried to accomplish would go down the drain.

I was also very disturbed by the poverty and hunger in South Carolina, but I was sensitive to how change could be brought about. I knew that I could get results but only after quiet, firm work. National publicity now would only harden the feelings of the local officials—Mayors, council members and others—before I could turn them around. And Robert Kennedy was about as popular in South Carolina as U.S. Chief Justice Earl Warren, who had led the Court to its unanimous decision in *Brown v. Board of Education.*

In addition, if Bob went ahead with his plans, his move would surely resurrect all the old charges from my Senate campaign in 1962—that Hollings was a Kennedy stooge, that Kennedy had gotten labor votes for me and had donated money. It was all false, but it would lead people to believe that my interest in hunger was driven simply to get a political boost.[9]

The picture was also complicated because I had to face the voters again in 1968. I was simply filling out the last two years in the term of the late Senator Johnston, who had died in office. If Kennedy toured

South Carolina, it would surely make my reelection bid all the more difficult. After all I had barely turned back a GOP challenger in 1966, and Republicans were making major inroads in the state.

As soon as I learned of Kennedy's plans, I picked up the telephone and told Kennedy I was working to do something about hunger in South Carolina. He was evasive, claiming that his staff had made the plans and that he might go from Savannah, Georgia, to Jasper County to Columbia.

I insisted that I knew there was hunger and was planning to attack it. "Yes, but there's far more than you think," he replied.

"I will have to take a public stance that I had nothing to do with your coming to South Carolina," I said. "Nobody is going to believe me, and you're only going to hurt the cause of ending hunger and all the things that I've been trying to do." He responded that everything had been arranged. I didn't understand the problem, he added. The subcommittee needed to publicize these facts.

At that point, I had had enough. "Now look here," I shouted. "You go down there, and I'm going to get on the plane and go straight up to Harlem. I'm going to call every TV station, and then I'm going to walk right through Harlem for four or five days, everywhere I can, and find every rat eating every child's eye out. And everywhere I go, I'm going to say why isn't Kennedy here? I'm gonna have a New York hunger exposé at the very time you have yours in South Carolina.[10]

"The minute I find you down there, you can count on my being in Harlem. I'm not kidding one damn bit. You'll be messing up the whole thing and I'll say publicly what I've said right here," I added. "I know we've got to have national leadership and a national program, but it's not going to be solved without local participation, local interest and understanding. When you come, you kill off any chances for local leadership. No Irish transfer Senator from Massachusetts to New York is going to go down to South Carolina and solve the hunger problem for me. You handle your troubles, and I'll handle mine."

When we ended the conversation, he had not yet agreed to change his plans. Apparently upon reflection, however, he decided I had made a persuasive case. Kennedy didn't come to the Palmetto State. I felt sorry that we never got to kid about that whole exchange, just as we had about other things on which we disagreed. Both of us knew we were still friends.

Kennedy wound up going to Kentucky instead of South Carolina. He later announced his presidential candidacy. I wasn't part of that movement. I had my own red wagon, and due to the pressures of my reelection campaign in 1968, we didn't see much of one another.

Sometimes it is odd what you remember. I recall that a couple of days before Bob left for West Coast campaigning in Oregon and California, I had asked his advice on investments. I had just sold an interest in some property for $26,000 and knew nothing about the stock market. "You are rich," I said. "Where should I put my money?"

"All of mine is in trust, but I'll ask the trustees," he replied. Just before he left, Kennedy told me that Kennecott Copper and Eastman Kodak were good prospects.

I went on to win my race for reelection in 1968 far more comfortably than I had two years earlier. That victory gave me the latitude to take that hunger tour the following year. By highlighting the issue, I was able to shake the federal bureaucracy's complacency. My tour helped to pave the way to greater help for the hungry through the passage of federal legislation.

As I show time and again in this book, the antihunger efforts in Washington show that government can work. When elected officials were made aware of the pervasiveness of the hunger problem, they could not look away. Denial of reality was not a policy. Upon learning more about the unbelievable hardships that people were enduring, Congress did do something, starting with passage of the Women, Infants and Children (WIC) nutrition program. The lesson is straightforward: Government does work and can be made to work again.

I was staying at the Holiday Inn in Greenville on June 5, 1968, when I got a call sometime around 1:30 in the morning. "Your friend Bobby has just been shot," the voice said. Kennedy was pronounced dead at 1:44 A.M. on June 6.

Bob was controversial, never ducking the tough calls. He was waging a vigorous, tenacious campaign and, in my judgment, was really headed to the White House when he was killed. But the sad news didn't surprise me. As Attorney General, Bob had gone after organized crime. Organized crime was determined to prevent him from being elected. I believe that both Kennedy assassinations were linked to organized-crime syndicates. At that moment, however, all I could think was first Jack and now Bob. It was a terrible blow for our country.

I was heartsick. I went to the funeral at St. Patrick's Cathedral in New York City. I listened as Andy Williams sang at the end of the services. I was going through the motions in utter shock. When I got on the train with family and friends, Ethel asked if I would sit with Caroline, President Kennedy's daughter. That train trip was a heartbreaker.

People were constantly jumping in front of the train, and time and again we had to clear the tracks to proceed. When we got to the Memorial Bridge, I could not take any more. I got off and walked back to Capitol Hill. I drank about four martinis and still didn't feel it. The era of fun in government and respect for government was passing. As JFK is remembered for bringing class to public service, Robert Kennedy will be remembered for bringing hope and inspiration to the classes.

4

Getting Started in the Senate

When I begin a legal case or other work, I go all out. Call it dogged-ness or single-mindedness or whatever you choose, but after leaving the Governor's Mansion and returning to Charleston, I eagerly jumped back into practicing law. I was not thinking about a political future. I told a reporter a few days after leaving office: "The new Governor has the right to get together with the legislators and be the chief spokesman for the state. I'm just going to tend to my knitting."[1]

The great thing about having a general practice of law is that you find yourself working on a range of cases, from antitrust to criminal matters. But perhaps the most satisfying litigation involves personal-injury cases in which a lawyer can make a tangible difference in someone's life. I represented such a person, Harold Tumbleston, a crane operator, who had suffered brain damage as a result of an automobile accident caused by the negligence of a company doing highway repair work. Tumbleston won a record verdict for that time, some $265,000.

Trial work was very satisfying—and remunerative. And it was just as well that I pursued private practice because Governor Russell was determined to keep me away from the political spotlight. Having lost that tough battle to me in 1958, when I was elected Governor, he clearly wanted me off the public stage. So I plowed ahead in my legal practice with my partner, Falcon Hawkins, an army veteran who had led his class at the Citadel while holding down a job at the Charleston Naval Shipyard. He had worked his way through law school. We became a team, working round the clock and genuinely having a good time.

In September 1963 I agreed to speak at the dedication of the Sumter Area Technical Education Center, and in November I spoke at the annual Vance-Aycock dinner in Asheville, North Carolina. President Kennedy's reelection campaign was beginning to get in gear, and my talk to that gathering of Democrats was designed to boost JFK in the South, where he remained very unpopular. My remarks were a takeoff on Thomas Wolfe's novel *You Can't Go Home Again.* The speech was a hit with the President, who invited me to the White House to thank me. Then, just a few days after that visit came the sudden, awful news out of Dallas. He was gone. It hit me like a punch in the stomach. I just couldn't believe it. Working at seeking financial backing for the Kennedy library helped me through that difficult period.

After Vice President Lyndon B. Johnson was sworn in as President, he quickly became a champion of sweeping civil rights legislation that angered many white southerners. By August the 1964 presidential campaign between Johnson and Republican Barry Goldwater was taking shape. It was obvious to me—and probably to anyone with a lick of political sense at that time—that Johnson was not going to sell in South Carolina. Goldwater had opposed the 1964 Civil Rights Act, and his no-nonsense conservatism was appealing to many who felt that Johnson had betrayed his region.

I surveyed the political landscape and wrote the following analysis, dated August 7, 1964, to a friend in Washington: "The South is going through a political change of life, and any change of life is a traumatic experience: hot flashes, cold chills, and many, many months of frustration. The newspaper still predominates and since they are 95 percent for Goldwater, we are in for a tough time. The great difference this time is enthusiasm. The Goldwater crowd is enthused for Goldwater, but the Johnson crowd is not enthused for Johnson. The only enthusiasm that they have shown is to eliminate the Kennedy friends from participation, and if there is not a marked change in the next couple of weeks, South Carolina will go for Goldwater in November."[2]

Then, just a bit over a month later, on September 16, Strom Thurmond switched parties. He went all out for Goldwater. Because many folks in South Carolina were giving up on the national Democratic Party and disparaging its advocacy of civil rights, the GOP was beginning to make inroads. When it came to politics, I was beginning to feel as though I was living in a foreign country. In this period I was relegated to the political sidelines. The Johnson people, ever-suspicious of anything or anybody connected to the Kennedys, had tossed JFK stalwarts overboard. They apparently decided that they wanted to win the election on their own and not appear at all indebted to the Kennedy crowd.

At the same time, perhaps because Governor Russell was wary of my returning to the political fray, he made sure that the word went out that I was "not invited" to participate when Lady Bird Johnson stopped in South Carolina during her eight-state whistle-stop tour of the South in October. She was trying to help LBJ's presidential campaign in Dixie, but it was increasingly obvious the region was not hospitable turf for the President. In fact the President's popularity had sunk so much in the South, which was roiled over passage of the 1964 Civil Rights Act, that Johnson was not even certain that Lady Bird should embark on the tour. Southern Democrats were pleading to keep the Johnsons out of the region.[3]

But Lady Bird thought she could make a difference. When the First Lady arrived in South Carolina, she got a big dose of reality. The resentment that some folks felt toward the President was palpable. In Columbia on October 7, Mrs. Johnson was greeted with chants of "We Want Barry." She tried to quiet the crowd, saying: "My friends, this is a country of many viewpoints. I respect your right to express your viewpoints. Now it's my time to express mine."[4]

Then it was on to Charleston and things were even more tense. The hostility was evident in the signs: "Johnson Is a Nigger Lover," read one. Another said, "Black Bird Go Home," and a third said, "Johnson Is a Communist."[5] Subtlety was not a strong suit among the folks waiting to give the First Lady a piece of their minds. And the local pols were not eager to provide her a forum either. Usually a dignitary such as the First Lady would speak from the City Hall steps, where we kick off important events including, since 1978, Spoleto, the popular arts festival. But the Charleston County Democratic Party was informed that the City Hall steps were not available for the First Lady!

Even though I was shut out of things, I wanted to help out. I got Ed Kronsberg to allow us to build a little platform at his store at Pinehaven near the North Charleston Railroad Station. The word was circulated that Mrs. Johnson was running late and, therefore, to expedite things she would be speaking at Pinehaven. The rude reception given the First Lady was a harbinger of a bad Election Day in the Palmetto State for Johnson. The President was clobbered in the Deep South, losing five states, including South Carolina, but he did very well elsewhere and defeated Goldwater in a landslide.

I wasn't all that unhappy about being on the political sidelines. Hawkins and I were going great guns in our legal practice, in which we were handling a range of cases that covered the gamut. As we looked for ways to expand our business even more, I decided to try to jump into the lucrative bond business. Having been Governor, I knew all the Mayors and the development projects in South Carolina. That knowledge would help me attract clients in need of a lawyer with know-how in bonds. But to qualify I needed a sponsor. I decided to call an old friend. "Who else but Nelse," I thought to myself, referring to New York Governor Nelson Rockefeller. When I reached him, I said: "Nelson, you're rich. Who does all of that bond work for you in New York?"

He said, "I don't know, but I think it's John Mitchell of Caldwell, Trimble & Mitchell. If you'd like to meet him, I'll set it up."

It was Thursday afternoon, and Nelson called me back and said, "You've got an appointment with John Mitchell at twelve o'clock Monday at the Chase Club on top of the Chase Manhattan Bank tower." Mitchell, president of the Chase Club, was a prominent municipal bond lawyer.

I went up to New York City and had a two-martini lunch with John Mitchell, who became a most delightful friend. He gave me two books on bond practices, as well as the Red Book, a listing of the accepted bond attorneys in the United States. He advised me: "You have to work in the bond business for five years before being listed in the Red Book, but I think I can get you in two years. For now, you get the business and I'll handle it for you. You get one-third of the fee and I get two-thirds."

I said, "It's a deal," and returned to Charleston to get rich.

But as so often happens in life, some bolt-out-of-the-blue event changes everything. That unexpected shocker in South Carolina occurred on April 18, 1965. Senator Olin Johnston, our senior Senator, who had clobbered me in 1962, died.

The next shot out of the blue occurred four days later. Governor Russell resigned as Governor, and Lieutenant Governor Bob McNair succeeded him. One hour after McNair was sworn in, he appointed

Russell to fill Johnston's Senate seat. The move angered Mrs. Johnston, a canny political operative in her own right. She was said to have believed that she or Olin's brother, William, should have gotten the nod. "No member of the Johnston family was consulted on my husband's successor," she said.[6]

The appointment was effective only until the next Election Day in the state, November 8, 1966. After Olin's funeral, various friends back in Charleston suggested that I run for the seat, but I didn't give it serious consideration at that moment. In July 1965 Gordon McCabe, vice president of J. P. Stevens in Greenville, called and said: "You've got to run. We're going up to my place in Flat Rock, North Carolina, with all of your textile friends and we'll get them committed to giving campaign money and get you off and running."

"Well, if that's the case, I'll be there," I replied.

When I left the Governor's office a little more than two years earlier, my textile friends had a farewell banquet and presented me with a Rolex gold watch engraved "To textile's best friend, Fritz Hollings." I thought I was on a roll. But Friday night, when the subject was supposed to come up after a round of golf, nothing happened. Gordon came to me the next morning and said, "Don't worry. Robert Small will bring it up and we'll have an understanding tonight after golf." But again, nothing happened. On Sunday, as I was leaving, Gordon apologized, but he said, "I talked to just about every one and for some reason this crowd is all for Russell."

"Good enough," I replied. "I'm happy making a living." I returned home. Meanwhile, some Republicans were urging me to dump my Democratic affiliation, join the GOP, and run for the Senate on their ticket. I never gave a thought to such a move. I was a Democrat, and nothing was going to change that.

Around this time, near the end of summer, my friend Otis Conklin and I were moving his houseboat to the dock behind the Isle of Palms. On the way over, Otis kept arguing that I should run. I told him that there were a bunch of reasons not to run, but chief among them was that I didn't think I could get the money. Otis allowed as how he could easily get fifty friends in Charleston to pony up a thousand dollars apiece.

I said, "You're crazy. If you can get fifty, I'll run." By Thanksgiving, Otis had eight-two, and I began making calls and moving about the state. I was ready to show that textile crowd with their deep pockets that I could get elected without them. I knew that Donald Russell was brilliant and accomplished, but he was not a very good politician. The former president of the University of South Carolina tended to be remote and professorial. He didn't seem to enjoy mixing it up with voters. By contrast I really enjoyed barnstorming the state. I was on a "Fritzkrieg" as the *New York Times* put it. I really think I out-hustled Russell.

Also there is no denying that the way Russell handled his appointment to the Senate rankled many in the Johnston crowd. He did little to mend fences with them after his arrival in Washington. After Russell joined the Senate, he never had contact with Mrs. Johnston, offered no help to the late Senator's staff, and failed to ask any of them to join his office.[7] Bill Johnston, the Senator's brother, endorsed me a few weeks before the primary.

The contest was something of a replay of my other campaigns in that Russell claimed that I was beholden to the Kennedys and had their financial backing as well as labor-union loot. I made clear that the charges were false. Russell also touted his experience as a Senator and as Assistant Secretary of State, a position from which he said he gained knowledge of world affairs. The Democratic establishment in Washington, including President Johnson, backed Russell. That was no surprise. Russell had strongly supported Johnson's losing campaign in South Carolina in 1964, and the President reportedly had urged him to take Johnston's Senate seat. At the same time the *News and Courier* opined that the main beneficiary of Senator Johnston's death was Thurmond. "Instead of facing either Russell or former Gov. Ernest F. Hollings in the general election, Thurmond can now stand by and watch the deadly enemies battle it out for Johnston's old seat."[8]

When I was asked about Russell's Washington service during World War II as Assistant Secretary of State under Secretary of State Jimmy Byrnes, I had a quick response. "I don't think we need State Department thinking in Congress," I said at a press conference. "That's why we're bogged down in Vietnam. I don't think State Department experience will ever help South Carolina."[9]

In fact one of my themes throughout the campaign was that "we need more South Carolina government in Washington and less Washington government in South Carolina."[10] I also set out my critique of our efforts in Vietnam in various speeches. "My opponent tells us that he agrees with the way the federal government is fighting the war in Vietnam," I said in one of the speeches. "Well, let me tell you right now that Fritz Hollings does not agree—I do not agree with my opponent, and I do not agree with the direction of the war. I agree with the President when he says he doesn't want a wider war, but you and I do insist that if we must fight a war at all—let it be a wise war. Victory will not come from presidential press conferences, nor from Senators' speeches. It can only come, it will only come, when we give that great South Carolina commander of our forces in South Vietnam, General Westmoreland, the authority and resources he needs to win."

On primary election day, June 14, 1966, I won the Democratic nomination by a comfortable margin. But I knew that in the general election, the Republicans were determined to continue pressing the momentum they had gained from Thurmond's party switch and Barry Goldwater's win in the state in 1964. Couple those developments with Bill Workman's respectable showing in the 1962 Senate race, and it was no wonder that the Republicans smelled blood. Capturing the second Senate seat in the state would be a huge coup. Their best avenue of attack was to blister Democrats as the party of Lyndon Johnson, Great Society programs, and civil rights. Angered by the 1964 Civil Rights Act and the 1965 Voting Rights Act, plenty of Democrats were fleeing the party. Appeals to race, whether subtle or overt, boosted the GOP in the state.

Given that perilous political landscape, I knew that I was not out of the woods. The general election pitted me against one of my former close supporters in the Piedmont, Marshall Parker, who was a popular ten-year veteran of the State Senate. Parker had shocked me when he announced that he was switching parties to take me on as a Republican. Parker's entry into the race coincided with some bad developments for me.

Worst of these, the state Democratic Party that I had organized successfully for Kennedy in 1960 had turned anti-Kennedy and thus anti-Hollings. Of course the state was totally turned off to the national Democratic Party under LBJ. Parker, sensing that mood, tried mightily to paint me as little more than a lackey to the Kennedys. He was relentless, and I responded by demanding that he "put up or shut up" with proof of a link between me and Bob Kennedy. Parker had no evidence because there was none.[11] At the same time, Thurmond's presence on the ballot for the first time as a Republican ensured that plenty of folks would be pulling the GOP lever. Our concern was that they would likely be inclined to vote for other Republicans on the ballot as well.

Of course African Americans were beginning to vote in larger numbers as well. Don Fowler, chairman of South Carolina's Young Democrats, became "the main emissary to the African American community." Fowler later recalled the powerful, poisonous racial politics of that period. "Among normal, middle-class white people, it was about as popular to be a Democrat as it was to have bubonic plague. Lyndon Johnson was Satan incarnate. We were right in the middle of the Civil Rights Act of '64 and the Voting Rights Act of '65, and Lyndon Johnson and his Great Society were really cranking up. And in the common vernacular, he was 'doing all these things for the niggers.' I mean that was just the atmosphere. If anybody asked an officeholder about the Democratic Party, they would say, 'I'm a *South Carolina* Democrat.'"[12]

In the end, I won by a whisker—just a bit more than eleven thousand votes. Looking back at the battle against Parker, I think I was lucky to win. The race was such a nail-biter because the Republican Party was gaining strength; there was lingering fallout from my primary contest against Russell; and Parker waged an excellent campaign.

Also I didn't have organization, money, or the support of newspapers. "I guess it was one of the longest nights I have spent in my lifetime, watching the votes come in that November," Crawford Cook, my campaign manager, recalled many years later. "It was three or four in the morning before we were even comfortable that we were going to win the thing."[13] The official declaration didn't come until late Wednesday afternoon.

My victory in the special election enabled me to gain some precious seniority over other newly elected Senators. I immediately made a reservation to fly to Washington on Thursday to be sworn in to complete Johnston's unexpired term. I had set up an appointment that day with Secretary of Defense Robert McNamara, but he was out of town. Instead I met, after the swearing in, with Deputy Secretary of Defense Cyrus Vance. Vietnam was one of the big issues in my Senate race, and I wanted to relate firsthand to the top civilian officers in the Pentagon that General Mark W. Clark, Major General Joseph P. Sullivan (retired), General Hugh Pate Harris, who was president of the Citadel, and all the military officers around Charleston and Fort Jackson were saying that the United States had a "no-win policy" in Vietnam.

Vance countered immediately that we were winning, and he emphasized that the President had just met in Honolulu with General William C. Westmoreland, who had told him that we were winning. "Go see for yourself," Vance said.

"When can I go?" I asked.

"As soon as you're ready," Vance replied. "You've got to get a bunch of shots. How about Sunday morning?"

"I'll be ready," I said.

I left the Pentagon and dropped by the Agriculture Department to see my friend Secretary Orville Freeman that afternoon.[14] I was the only southerner to recommend Orville to John Kennedy to be Agriculture Secretary. Most southerners of course preferred someone from our region—not a midwesterner—for such a key post to our constituents.

Tobacco was our state's largest crop at that time. Unfortunately for South Carolinians, Georgia farmers had an unfair advantage in selling their tobacco. The problem revolved around the way farmers market tobacco. Large tobacco firms strongly prefer tobacco to be delivered to them in neatly tied bundles because it saves labor costs. But individual farmers faced enough struggles to find the hands to pick the tobacco, cure it, and transport it to market. There were no laborers to tie the tobacco in neat bundles for the companies. Feeling pressure from the tobacco firms, the federal government provided a subsidy or support payment to tied tobacco but none for the untied. Georgia received an exception to this policy that enabled its tobacco farmers to receive the full subsidies, whether their tobacco was tied or untied.[15]

That exception led plenty of South Carolina farmers to truck over to neighboring Georgia with their untied tobacco in order to take advantage of the subsidy. In 1966, twenty-three million pounds of South Carolina tobacco was sold in Georgia, where the economy flourished. I made it clear to Orville that this did not comply with "equal justice under law." We should get the same treatment in South Carolina as Georgia got—full federal support for tobacco whether it was tied or not. Three other Senators—Johnston, Thurmond, and Russell—had tried to get this policy changed. My friendship with the Agriculture Secretary made all the difference.[16]

I knew that Orville would help me. I made it clear to him that I wasn't asking for an advantage. All I was seeking was fair and equal treatment. Orville promised that he would do the trick, but it would have to be done in a deliberate manner. His decision to pay full supports for untied tobacco to the South Carolina farmer was announced the following summer.

The other thing I made a priority, right off the bat, was to get a sense of how things worked in the Senate. Who better to ask than the dean of the chamber, Richard Brevard Russell Jr. of Georgia? I got on a plane and made my way to Winder, Georgia, to have lunch with this most powerful, influential Senator. We sat in rocking chairs on his porch. As Dick Russell wheezed from the effects of emphysema, he asked, "Fritz, what committee do you want?"

"Armed Services, Mr. Chairman," I answered.

"Oh, you don't want that," rasped Russell, who was chairman of that powerful committee. "You don't understand. In Columbia, in the legislature, you pass a measure and put the money with it, but in Congress, we have the authorizing committee that, after hearings, authorizes a certain amount. Later, the Appropriations Committee has its own hearings and then can appropriate the amount authorized or twice the amount authorized or nothing at all. What you want is a seat on the Appropriations Committee, where things happen."

I took Dick Russell's advice on committee assignments, but, as a very junior Senator, I wasn't able to get onto the coveted appropriations panel during my first three years. Instead I was assigned to three other committees in January when Congress reconvened: Commerce, Agriculture and Forestry, and Post Office and Civil Service. These three panels provided good perches from which to help my constituents. As I said in a statement in January 1967, about two-thirds of the industrial payroll in South Carolina in the textile industry—leading me to seek a seat on Commerce, which handles much legislation vital to that industry. Similarly, given our vast acreage of forests and our many farmers, the Agriculture slot was a good fit; and, of course, I followed in Johnston's footsteps on the Post Office and Civil Service Committee, of which he had been chairman.

I got off to a quick start after taking up Vance's invitation to go to Vietnam and see the place for myself. The day after I was sworn into office, I was given twenty-one shots at the navy yard followed by nineteen more shots at the air base on Saturday morning. That afternoon I went to a Citadel football game, with a 104-degree fever. But when I left Washington Sunday morning, I felt better. I landed in Hong Kong with my escort, Colonel "Spider" Reed, an all-American basketball player who had graduated from West Point. We had dinner with Republican

Senator Hollings with President Lyndon B. Johnson and General William Westmoreland at the White House in 1968. Collection of the author

Senator Hugh Scott of Pennsylvania, who was visiting the Asian port and who was incidentally an expert on Oriental art. We took off Monday morning on General Westmoreland's aircraft, which he sent from Saigon to pick us up. By Monday evening I was ensconced in General Westmoreland's quarters.

Westmoreland was a hero in South Carolina. He had attended the Citadel for a year, then was appointed to West Point, and had risen to the rank of four-star General in charge of the war in Vietnam. He told me everything was on schedule; we were winning. All he needed was 35,000 more troops. At that time, November 1966, we had some 535,000 troops in a country of 16 million. With those reinforcements, Westmoreland said, he would bring the war to a head. The Vietcong would either give up or suffer in what he referred to as Operation Meat Grinder.

Westmoreland emphasized the body count. They were losing ten troops to our one, and they couldn't stand it much longer, he said. But I was skeptical of announcing body counts as a way to sell the war since those figures were doing little to win more support from the U.S. public. Still Westmoreland could not have been more gracious and helpful. He said he wanted me to see the lay of the land for myself.

I started with the Coast Guard and traveled to Phu Quoc, an island off the southwest coast of Vietnam; then I went to view Operation Market Time, which featured gunboats along the Kong River. I then joined the Second Corps with the Twenty-fifth Infantry; I was briefed at Hue, where a major battle exploded just after I left. I learned later that while I was being briefed, the Vietcong had a tunnel underneath the headquarters and were listening in to my briefing.

In the Third Corps area I went into the bush with the Montagnards along the Cambodian border on the Ho Chi Minh Trail. The Montagnards were fierce warriors, who climbed up in the trees and fought with bows and poisoned arrows, killing the Vietcong as they came down the trail.

I was transported from there on a small plane that landed on the deck of the aircraft carrier *Kitty Hawk*. We landed on the carrier seated backwards in almost a crash landing—quite an experience. I was now in the Gulf of Tonkin, just off of Haiphong, North Vietnam's biggest port, where I attended a debriefing of pilots after they returned from a mission. The pilots had to get up rapidly to ten thousand feet, and fly over good targets in the Gulf of Tonkin and Haiphong Harbor—where the Russian supply vessels were docked after having delivered "POL" (petroleum, oil, and lubricants) that was stacked on the docks and lined along the streets. Instead of attacking the area laden with supplies, the pilots were required to drop down to one thousand feet and tried to bomb the laborer with the five-gallon can of fuel on his back. During these missions the pilot knew certain targets were off limits, even as he maneuvered to avoid the enemies' antiaircraft gunfire. When he returned from a dangerous mission, the pilot might have faced court-martial if he had fired upon any areas that were off limits. Imagine, restricting our pilots from hitting substantial targets. Outrageous nonsense!

I began to learn why we were not winning—or at least I began to change my "no-win" belief to a "slow-win" belief. We were hemorrhaging on the battlefield as casualties mounted, and the costs of war were eating away at our economy. Yet our brave soldiers were fighting with their hands tied behind their backs. It quickly became obvious to me that we needed to knock out military targets in the North. It was the only way to show North Vietnamese leader Ho Chi Minh that we meant business.

I next traveled to the I Corps area near the DMZ (Demilitarized Zone) at Da Nang. As we landed on the runway at Da Nang, Lieutenant Colonel Bob Tanguy, a classmate of "Spider" Reed, was helping a wounded pilot get out of an aircraft about to catch fire. More than a decade later, I saw Tanguy again, after he had been promoted to Lieutenant General in charge of the Southern Command in Panama. He had a profound impact on my thinking during the debate in the Senate over the Panama Canal Treaties.

Tanguy spoke with me off the record in Da Nang, and he complained of the limited air operation. After getting another intelligence briefing and thanking General Westmoreland, "Spider" and I returned to the States via Honolulu, where we had dinner with Admiral Harry Felt, U.S. Commander in Chief Pacific (CINCPAC), and Lieutenant General Joe Moore. Moore's close friendship with Westmoreland dated back to their days as Eagle Scouts in Spartanburg, South Carolina. He took me aside and said, "I understand that you are good friends with President Johnson. Here's a list of seventy-five targets. Ask him to give us permission to hit these targets, and this war will be over in one to two months. But don't tell him, for Lord's sake, where you got the list or it will be the end of my career."

"I'm not close to President Johnson," I replied, "but I'll be glad to try to see him and he'll get the message without revealing where I got the list." I called Marvin Watson, President Johnson's appointments secretary, to see if I could meet with the President when I returned to Washington. Marvin asked what time I was arriving. When I told him I was due at eight o'clock Monday morning, he said that I would have an appointment to see the President at nine. The White House would send a car to pick me up.

That was perfect. At nine o'clock I was in the Oval Office with the President. "Come on in here, Senator," said the President, pointing to a little side room where three TV sets tuned to CBS, ABC, and NBC were going full blast. I'll never forget the President's angry reaction when Bill Moyers, who had just departed as the White House press secretary, came on TV and criticized our policy in Vietnam. "With friends like that, who needs enemies?" Johnson snapped.

Seeing Moyers reminded me of better times. I had met him when I traveled to Washington as Governor to testify before the House Judiciary

Committee on Civil Rights. After I had gone over to the Senate to see then Majority Leader Lyndon Johnson, South Carolinian Bobby Baker, the leader's right-hand man and secretary to the Senate's Democrats, took me in hand. He asked if I minded having lunch with a ministerial student. "Of course not," I said.

"The Senator thinks this little Baptist ministerial student from Texas, Bill Moyers, is a young man of promise and he wanted to try him out on the staff," Baker noted. The three of us had lunch. I saw why Moyers had impressed Johnson, as he seemed earnest and affable.

That meeting seemed light years ago as I stood in the White House that December morning with an embattled President, who was being hammered for his handling of the war. I presented him with the list of seventy-five targets that we should hit. "Where did you get this list," the President asked immediately.

"Now, Mr. President, you know if I told you who gave me this list, that would be the end of his career," I replied.

"Well," Johnson said with some sadness, "victory has many fathers, but defeat is an orphan. I'm sitting here by myself, trying to do the best for the country, and everybody's complaining."

Johnson said that he was bombing as much as public opinion would permit. He wanted to bring enough force to demonstrate to the enemy that it had no chance to win militarily and to induce it to seek a settlement. For the first time, I really felt sorry for the President. As much as I wanted to support him the best I could, his prosecution of the war often left me frustrated. By the next fall, I had reflected on my meeting with the President in one of my regular newsletters to South Carolinians. Saying that we need "a strengthening of national will," I decried the growing number of Senators who were talking about bombing halts in the North without addressing the North's infiltration of the South. Then I vented my frustration with the President's war policy.

"When you couple the high purpose of Johnson strategy with the Johnson penchant for polling and politics, the people are left distraught," I wrote in the newsletter. "Many mistakenly credit Lyndon Johnson with being willful, ignoring advice and forcing his opinion on others. The opposite is true. He compromises with everybody. He never deals directly with the problems but only with the politics of the problems. . . . Every significant decision on Vietnam can be equated with the political needs rather than the military needs."[17]

Of course Vietnam was the central issue when, on January 10, 1967, I took my seat in the Senate. I occupied the next-to-the-last seat way over on the right. I was very happy to be there, but to tell the truth, I had a better seat at *My Fair Lady!* Senator Bill Spong of Virginia was next to me in the last seat, and Bob Kennedy, who had prevailed in his improbable race in 1964 as a Massachusetts native running in New York, was on my right. Kennedy and I immediately got into a heated discussion about Vietnam. Known for his fierce determination and willingness to fight, Bob surprised me when he strongly insisted that we had no chance of winning the war.

I would make two more trips to Vietnam, Cambodia, and Laos, during which I learned a lesson. It is a mistake to try to build and destroy a nation at the same time. You've got to first secure the country and then allow the native population to take charge. The mistake played out in Vietnam, as we went out in the daytime over a ten-year period—with lots of firepower, including helicopters, gunships, and flamethrowers—with the goal of trying to secure the towns. Then our troops returned to camp for a six-pack of beer and a movie. At night the Vietcong moved into the village and took over. All the while the village leader, trying to stay alive, played it both ways. In the daytime he was for the GI—at night he was for "Charlie." We never did secure the country. And all too often as we tried to secure a village, we destroyed it.

Now we are repeating that wrongheaded strategy in Iraq—but I hope not for ten years. After more than five years, the world's superpower has yet to secure Iraq. We have never had realistic expectations for that region. We somehow expected different religious sects to fall in love, form a democracy, and secure the country. Today in Iraq we are faced with the same dilemma as in Vietnam. It would take too many troops to secure the country, and a secure Iraq probably won't last anyway. The best we can do is to secure the borders to keep the insurgents and weaponry out—and hope that the Shia, Sunni, and Kurds finally see it in their own interests to reach a settlement.

I made the comparison between our flawed strategy in Vietnam and our equally reckless approach in Iraq in a column I wrote in November 2003 for the *State*: "Now we have another Vietnam. Just as President Johnson misled us into Vietnam, President Bush has misled us into Iraq. As in Vietnam, they have not met us in the streets hailing democracy.

Thousands of miles away, we are once again 'fighting for the hearts and minds.' Again, we are trying to build and destroy. Again, we are bogged down in a guerrilla war. Again, we are not allowing our troops to fight and win—we do not have enough troops. Again, we can't get in, can't get out."[18]

On domestic policy the first bill I introduced as a Senator, on February 6, 1967, was for revenue sharing for education. Bob Kennedy said he couldn't go along with sending all that money to Albany. It would be just like delivering lettuce by way of a rabbit. He would never get any money back into New York City. So I amended my bill to allow revenue sharing with the municipalities and the states. It passed.

During that period, I was determined to learn the ins and outs of the Senate. One of the unpleasant tasks a junior Senator must take on is to preside over the chamber. But I decided that I would get a feel for the Senate by wielding the gavel—and even earn some chits with colleagues by agreeing to cover for them. Typically the presiding officer just sits there and listens. Sometimes somebody walks in and says three words, then walks out.

But there was one constant during that period. Just about every evening, beginning at five, Wayne Morse of Oregon would rant and rage about the mistake of Vietnam. One evening I was relieved by Danny Brewster of Maryland. I didn't notice it but Danny was feeling no pain. By the time I had returned to my office, the phone was ringing off the hook. Danny had just taken one glance at the Senator from Oregon and promptly hammered the gavel down, adjourning the Senate and walking out. At that point Wayne really was speaking to an empty chamber! Majority Leader Mike Mansfield of Montana was beside himself that Brewster had pulled such a stunt. But such colorful stories were the exception. Usually I presided over the customary business. I wound up putting in so much time in that role that I was twice given the Golden Gavel Award for presiding for more than one hundred hours in a year.

Early on I learned a lesson about the enormous clout of the farm lobby. If a Senator fails to go along with the interests advanced by the agricultural sector, he had better be ready to deal with the wrath of the farmer. I got my baptism on this point as a member of the Agriculture Committee.[19] I had not been in the Senate very long, when one day we went into executive session to debate an extension of the farm program.

I was troubled that our national policy was to fork over high payments to farmers not to produce.

How could we as a nation continue to justify exorbitant payments to individual farmers? It was indefensible.[20] My view was that such transfer payments would wind up hurting agriculture generally because the small farmer would suffer. I freely admitted that I was a new member of the committee and didn't know the solution. Instead of a four-year deal, I supported a one-year extension of the program.

Mind you, we were in executive session—no clerks, staffers, or others were present. Within a half hour of the end of our meeting, I got a call and chalked it up to coincidence that a good friend, a farmer, wanted to talk to me about the issue. I explained that I couldn't discuss what had happened because it was executive session. Then more calls came in, and within an hour a caller recited word for word what I had said in the meeting![21]

I had worked with CIA agents, but this farm spy network made the CIA look like a bunch of amateurs. When I left Washington for the weekend and got home to Charleston, I might as well have gone to sleep in a busy telephone booth. The phone rang off the hook. I became cussing mad.[22]

Angry as I was, my farm friends made it clear that I had to support the program. I had no choice. I shouldn't question it. Yet they provided no good reason or justification for their position. I learned that weekend there is no such thing as confidentiality in an executive session in the Senate.[23] I also learned firsthand about the muscle of the farm lobby on Capitol Hill. Farmers are a very close-knit, well-disciplined group and always ready to follow the dictates of their Washington hired guns.[24] What the small farmer doesn't understand is that the high-falutin' Washington influence peddler is promoting big business and could care less about the needs of the individual farmer. In fact over the years farm conglomerates have survived. The small farmer has by and large disappeared.

Later in 1967 I faced the most difficult decision in my political career: the vote on the nomination of Thurgood Marshall to be an Associate Justice of the United States Supreme Court. As I have mentioned earlier, I met Marshall years before in Washington on the eve of the argument before the Supreme Court in *Briggs v. Elliott*. Back then, in December 1952, when Marshall joined Bob Figg and me for breakfast at the railroad station, I observed that Marshall and Figg clearly had high regard for each other. Later, as I watched Marshall argue before the Supreme Court on the issue of segregated schools, I saw firsthand that he was a highly skilled lawyer.

Indeed my regard for him grew over the years, especially when Martin Luther King Jr. hit the scene. The King approach was to take African Americans' problems to the streets of America, whereas Marshall took them to the courts. On June 13, 1967, President Johnson nominated him to be the first African American to serve on the Supreme Court. Although I respected Marshall as a lawyer, I knew that if I voted to confirm him, my political career would be over.

The South looked upon Johnson's appointment of Marshall as nothing more than a political down payment for the black vote. The cry went up, "How in the world could you vote for that fellow who was causing all the disruption in your state?" So I was part of a bloc of southern Senators who voted against Marshall's confirmation. Ultimately of course the Senate, by a lopsided vote of 69–11, confirmed Marshall on August 30.

In later years Justice Marshall invited me to join him and Justice William Brennan for lunch several times. He'd always insist that I recount the story about when we first met. So I'd tell about our breakfast at the train station and describe how Marshall had told Figg and me the story of his having to intervene to help a black family that was getting grief and even threats for moving into a white neighborhood in Illinois.

No matter how many times I told that story, Marshall always erupted into gales of laughter. It was always good to see him. His son, Thurgood Jr., known as "Goody," served as a staffer on my Commerce Committee and later on became secretary to the cabinet under President Bill Clinton. Everybody likes Goody. I am sure that he and his father understood my vote. As I look back at my years in the Senate, that's the one vote I regret. At the same time, I know that if I had voted for Marshall, I'd be writing in this book about a trial lawyer's life rather than a Senator's.

It was just a few months later that my reelection campaign got rolling. The year 1968 was not exactly the most auspicious time for a Southern Democrat. The political world was changing so fast in Dixie that it was beginning to look as if no time was especially good. But then I really got a break. From the first day I was sworn into the Senate, I had wanted to help protect our textile industry from unfair trade practices of foreign competitors. I had championed the textile cause as Governor, but I confronted different obstacles in the Senate.

The problem was that Senators have an uphill battle in trying to take the initiative on textile issues. The Constitution requires that all revenue measures first be introduced in the House of Representatives. If the Senate tries to encroach in this area, the House, whose members are protective of their turf, is not about to allow it. Given those constraints, I was always on the lookout for a House-passed measure affecting revenue or trade that I might use as a vehicle to boost the textiles. In April 1968 I got my opportunity. I pounced.

A measure that regulated trade in cranberries had passed the House and had just been brought up in the Senate. I quickly introduced a textile amendment that would empower the President to impose import quotas or otherwise limit imports to protect our domestic textile industry. I was determined to get Congress to recognize that textile imports were a national problem. We were getting socked by the unfair practices of foreign manufacturers. The textile industry was spending $2 billion a year upgrading equipment and was very productive, but it was battling other countries' manufacturers that were ignoring our trade agreements. We were treating trade as a part of the Marshall Plan rather than as a straightforward competition for business.

My amendment immediately drew a threat of a presidential veto. As would become an all too familiar pattern during my years in the Senate, this White House, like every future White House I dealt with, resisted. The Johnson administration had a pat response: "You're wasting time. Withdraw the measure and the administration will give its best effort to address your concerns at the next trade negotiation."

I wasn't about to buy that nonsense. So, even then, as a very junior Senator, I persisted and was delighted to get the help of Republican Norris Cotton, the senior Senator from New Hampshire. His state, like others in New England, had long been battered by the import of foreign textiles. He promptly agreed to cosponsor my bill. We then set about getting other cosponsors.

Our bipartisan effort met with great success. Some sixty-eight Senators representing every section of the country ultimately signed on to the textile import-control bill. My colleagues recognized that we had been hemorrhaging jobs because of the failure to adhere to the quota system established by Jack Kennedy's seven-point program.

Members of the Finance Committee, sycophants to big business and blind followers of the corporate mantra about the virtues of "free trade," were caught off guard. But after my amendment passed and was returned to the House to be "conferenced"—the system by which the two chambers iron out the differences between their two versions of a measure—the free trade crowd had an ace in the hole: Representative Wilbur Mills of Arkansas, the powerful chairman of the House Ways and Means Committee. Working with the Finance Committee conferees, Mills promptly dropped my amendment. The conferees then passed the legislation, having killed the textile proposal.

But the business leaders in South Carolina knew they had a fighter for their cause. I made it clear that the battle to protect the textile industry was a top priority and would command my attention as long as I served in the United States Senate. I had shown as Governor and now in my second year in the Senate that I could maneuver to pass important trade-protection measures to secure their industry. No South Carolina legislators had ever done this. And at that time Republicans were just as determined to protect the textile business as they are determined today to cut taxes.

Meanwhile I was ready for a tough reelection campaign. I faced a primary challenge from John Bolt Culbertson, a labor lawyer from Greenville who had gained notoriety for his "radical" views and his representation of African Americans. He had served a term in the S.C. House after being elected in 1948.

As the campaign heated up, the country appeared to be unraveling. First President Johnson surprised everybody when he announced in March 1968 that he would not seek reelection. Then Martin Luther King Jr. and Bob Kennedy were gunned down. The shockwaves from the assassinations of those two leaders reverberated throughout the nation. Violence exploded. Cities burned. On June 6, the same day that Kennedy died, I appeared with Culbertson and Republican Marshall Parker, who was pursuing a rematch against me. I said that Bob's tragic death underscored the need for "domestic tranquility and strict law enforcement." Later that month I defeated Culbertson in the Democratic primary.

Having barely eked out a win in 1966, I knew I would have a fight on my hands against Parker in the general election. Parker was out to avenge that narrow loss. Winning the Democratic primary guaranteed little. At the same time, Thurmond was beating the drums for Republican Richard Nixon's presidential campaign. And Parker was now trying to tie me to Hubert Humphrey, the Democratic presidential nominee who was loathed by many white southerners for his years of activism on civil rights! This time, however, I was ready. My record during those two years in the Senate, from fighting for textile workers to trying to goad President Johnson to change his no-win war strategy, helped me win handily on Election Day—by more than 150,000 votes over Parker.

After the election, I was determined to confront the issue of hunger in South Carolina and the nation. I simply could not turn away from the fact that so many South Carolinians were suffering. But this effort was not going to be a walk in the park. Other political leaders in the state, the business community, and the news media went on the attack. Exposing hunger and doing something about it turned out to be one of the greatest challenges I faced in public life. Ultimately this effort provides a case study in how government can work at the federal level. It shows why the naysayers that blame everything on Washington crowd are just flat wrong.

My myopia about hunger had really lifted in January 1968, when Sister Anthony Monaghan, a tireless advocate for the poor and underprivileged, urged me to come visit her Neighborhood House, located at the very spot that I used to play football as a boy in Charleston.[25] It was an eye-opener.

As I wrote in my book *The Case Against Hunger,* "I began to understand some of the things Sister Anthony had been trying to tell me—that hunger was real, and it existed in hundreds of humans in my own home city. I saw what all America needs to see. The hungry are not able-bodied men, sitting around drunk and lazy on welfare. They are children. They are abandoned women, or the crippled, or the aged. They are the part of America for whom civil rights or first-class citizenship is not a part of their wildest dreams."[26]

Even before I began confronting these painful scenes firsthand, I had gotten a lesson in the bare-knuckle politics of hunger in 1967. I had started to do some arm-twisting for food stamps for my state, which all too often didn't seem to get a fair shake. Virgil Dimery, a black leader in Williamsburg County—with the help of some other civic leaders, including county supervisor Hugh McCutcheon—had raised money to set up a food-stamp office. Under the law almost all the cost of the food-stamp program is borne by Washington, but the federal government required that the local political entity set up, administer, and pay for the distribution of stamps. In Williamsburg the cost of opening up a food-stamp office was $23,000. The county political leaders were not about to help underwrite what they saw as an assault on our free-enterprise system.[27] Apparently it reeked of socialism to them.

By the time the folks who were trying to open the food-stamp office came to my office in Washington, they had raised $6,000. They were hoping that the Office of Economic Opportunity (OEO) would pony up the other $17,000. So you might think OEO would jump at the chance to help folks in a concrete way. But bureaucratic rules got in the way. The food-stamp program was administered by the Agriculture Department. There was no provision for the OEO's participation. Ironically the OEO could spend thousands to study the problem but not a nickel of cash to address it!

I asked my friend Sargent Shriver, by then head of the OEO, to come see me. After having taken so much grief back home for backing JFK's presidential bid, I figured it was time for a little reciprocation. I put on the pressure. I told Shriver, seated in my office, that the trouble with this whole Washington mess was that people could study every ill imaginable but never get anything done.[28]

I reminded him that I had helped start the Peace Corps that he had championed, and I had never asked for a thing. Now I was asking for a measly $17,000. I didn't want him to start reciting the law. I was on a roll. I told him OEO had violated more laws than Al Capone. It had wasted plenty of taxpayer funds. It seemed to me that we could violate one regulation on the right side of the ledger.[29]

Anyone who knew Shriver liked him immensely. He was a straight shooter. But I came on strong to him because it was so frustrating that every time you start to do something in Washington, you're accused of trying to get headlines back home. I was serious. I didn't want a headline. I wanted money for food stamps.[30]

The next morning, Sarge told me that he had adjusted some funds and, on the basis of "studying it," OEO could provide the money. We opened the office in Kingstree, Williamsburg County. There was no formal public announcement, but before long the word was out.

Two weeks after the food-stamp office opened, I traveled to the little town of Timmonsville to check out the tobacco market. What I heard there astonished me. A muscular, red-faced tobacco farmer grabbed me by the shoulder as I walked into the warehouse. "That's the worst thing you've ever done—that damn food-stamp program," he said.

"Oh," I responded. "You've got to help people get something to eat."

"No," he retorted. "If you feed them, they'll never work."[31]

I still am dumbfounded as I think back on his comments. The agricultural set-aside program in this section of the state was paying farmers forty thousand dollars a year not to work, but a forty-cent breakfast for a child to make him strong enough to work was going to ruin his ambition. It didn't hurt the farmers' ambition; they were back every year asking for more. I knew then that it would always be difficult to provide for the hungry. But we couldn't turn our backs on folks who were going to bed with empty bellies in the richest nation on earth. Government could work, and I was determined that it *would* work for those who had nowhere else to turn.

Learning of our hunger problems, Sarge Shriver also helped with our health situation. The poor were not only hungry but also without a hospital. Even the ones nearby would turn them away. Working with Dr. Tom Bryan and Sarge, the OEO instituted the Beaufort-Jasper Comprehensive Health Center, the first such facility in the nation. It could take care of the hungry poor for about a third of the cost of the established hospitals. And when the Beaufort-Jasper success became known, these centers spread—twenty-two in South Carolina and hundreds over the nation. These centers are now the emergency rooms for the Mexican migrants. We have two Spanish-speaking doctors now at Beaufort-Jasper to take care of the need.

Meanwhile, as I visited Sister Anthony's Neighborhood House in Charleston, I saw up close the gravity of the hunger problem. In one house seven small babies were in crates or cardboard boxes. Next door a grandmother was babysitting for nine small children while their mothers worked. The Roman Catholic Church was making sure that the babies and children were properly fed, but there were many other children and grown-ups without food in the same neighborhood.

Senator Hollings during his 1969 hunger tour. Hollings Collection, South Carolina Political Collections, University of South Carolina

Word of this visit reached the Reverend I. DeQuincey Newman, head of the state NAACP, and he told me that hunger was far more widespread and causing far more desperation than I could possibly imagine. "You've got to see it for yourself, Senator," I.D. said. But the only way I would be able to address these issues in a meaningful way was to win reelection in 1968 and then put the spotlight on hunger in a way that Washington simply would not be able to ignore.

By January 1969, after having just been reelected by the largest vote in South Carolina history, I had gone with I.D. on a tour of sixteen counties in South Carolina, across the state from Beaufort to Anderson.

I decided to invite each county's political leaders to join us.[32] I'll never forget the grandmother at "Black Bottom," near the Governor's Mansion in Columbia. It was early morning, and her grandchild had just left smartly dressed for school. But the grandmother obviously hadn't eaten in quite some time. What little money she could earn working, she spent on the grandchild's clothes. She was essentially starving herself to make sure that that little girl would look good in school. I.D. shoved a dollar in her hand and said, "Go get some bread." We went through several other houses, and later on I saw that grandmother again. She was so hungry she was eating plain bread.

Nor will I forget the little fifteen-year-old white girl in Anderson. Her mother was sick; her father a drunk; and she was holding down two jobs even as she took care of herself, her two young siblings, and her parents.

It still stuns me to think that there I was in 1969, in South Carolina's lowcountry, in Beaufort County, standing in another shack that housed fifteen black people. It had no heat, no running water, no bath, no toilet, inside or out. The cracks in the wall were covered by old copies of the *Savannah Morning News*. The total store of food in the shack consisted of a slab of fatback, a half-filled jar of locally harvested oysters, and a stick of margarine. The only heat came from a wood-burning stove. One of the men was suffering from pellagra, a disease that was supposed to occur only in underdeveloped countries. One of the children had rickets, and another had scurvy. They were dressed in rags.[33] Others on the islands of Beaufort County suffered from hunger, kwashiorkor, and marasmus. Kwashiorkor is caused by severe protein and multiple nutrient deficiency. Marasmus develops primarily from lack of food calories. Both are rare except in famine conditions. The then-common belief in the medical community had been that kwashiorkor and marasmus could not be found on the North American continent; yet doctors found both in my little state in the richest country on earth.[34]

Nothing in my thirty-eight years as a U.S. Senator affected me more profoundly than the tour I took of my home state to explore the depth of misery caused by malnutrition and hunger. But I was not pleased when a reporter, Phil Jones of CBS, started focusing on the tour. I had been studiously avoiding the press. I knew that you can't learn anything from hungry people as long as reporters are present. They become embarrassed and won't say anything. If they see a TV camera, they'll make a beeline getting away. That's what happened when Jones showed up with his radio recorder.

Worst of all, the publicity stirred up a hornet's nest. Mendel Rivers, the popular and powerful Congressman who represented the First Congressional District, including Beaufort and Charleston, described me derisively as "Hookworm Hollings." He added, "I have no intention of immortalizing poverty or dishing out food stamps."[35]

Thurmond also was dismissive. When the picture of the NAACP director with me interviewing the hungry at Black Bottom was widely distributed, I was the subject of one put-down after another. The gist of the criticism was that my attention to hunger was driven by political opportunism. "Ol' Hollings wants the Negro vote," was the constant rebuff. My office started getting angry letters from Charlestonians calling me a Communist and cussing me for destroying tourism and ruining the state.[36]

And it wasn't just the folks back home that got on my case. Vice President Spiro Agnew took a potshot too. The man who once famously said, "If you've seen one ghetto area, you've seen them all," admonished me in 1969, saying, "Why does not the Senator go to work on the problems of the people rather than mouthing around on TV and making TV shows?"

Still I had a much bigger problem than dodging those brickbats. In order to convey the profound implications of hunger I had to learn all about it from a medical standpoint. Sure I could see it on the tour, but talking about that experience would not be enough to stir the folks at a Rotary Club. A politician, to be persuasive on this issue, had to know the effect of hunger and its costs. He would have to speak authoritatively. Otherwise Rotarians—and other civic groups—would simply dismiss the issue. It was obvious from the stiff resistance to the food-stamp program in 1967 that all of us determined to do more for the hungry would have to overcome hurdles. For reasons ranging from public complacency to philosophical opposition to "giveaways" to simple racism, many lawmakers were not about to sign on to another social-welfare program.

To get up to speed on the biological impact of malnutrition, I began calling doctor friends, who referred me to such experts as Myron Winick of Cornell University, Nevin Scrimshaw of the Massachusetts Institute of Technology, and Charles Upton Lowe, head of the National

Institute of Child Health and Human Development. Lowe was especially helpful because he could provide insights that would explain why malnutrition is such a profoundly grave problem for infants and children. The human brain weighs about three pounds and consists of 13 billion cells; its equivalent in computerization has yet to be invented. Cut your finger, and the cut heals with new tissue. Break your arm, and the fracture is reknit with new bone matter. But injure the brain, and the damage is permanent. There is no growing back or knitting together, for nerve cells are unique. While recent research indicates they may heal, they cannot reproduce.

The great producer of gray matter is protein. It is the element that synthesizes the chemicals. If there is a shortage of protein, then the synthesizing process is slowed, and in many cases the brain is stunted. If the mother denies the child nutrition or protein or if premature birth diminishes the period for rapid growth, then the baby could enter this world with a permanent handicap. Dr. Lowe testified that a lack of nutrition can often result in as much as a 20 percent loss in brain-cell development. During this process of educating myself, I learned to my surprise that hunger overwhelmingly afflicted whites more than blacks.

Armed with this kind of information, I did my best, along with several colleagues, including Democratic Senator George McGovern of South Dakota, a lifelong champion of this issue, to pass legislation that could provide tangible assistance in reducing the incidence of hunger.

I went before the Senate Select Committee on Nutrition and Human Needs, which McGovern chaired, on February 18, 1969, and I set out the case for taking dramatic steps to attack hunger and malnutrition. I confessed that as Governor, I had known the general problem existed but not the extent to which people were suffering from it. At that time I had not wanted anything to get in the way of my agenda of economic development. I noted that my moves to seek new industries for my state as well as state pride "resulted in the public policy of covering up the problem of hunger. We didn't want the vice president of the plant in New York to know the burdens [of locating in South Carolina]. We told him only of the opportunities."

I had come before the committee to make amends. Action was long overdue. I described bluntly my findings during my tour of my state. "Let me categorically state there is hunger in South Carolina. There is substantial hunger. I have seen it with my own eyes. Starving—that is too dreadful a term, but the result is the same. . . . The hunger and burden of the poor can no longer be ignored."

This was no time for politics as usual—or life as usual. The biases against the poor and hungry had to be put to the side. "Many is the time," I said, "that my friends have pointed a finger and said, 'Look at that dumb Negro.' The charge too often is accurate—he is dumb. But not because of the color of his skin. He is dumb because we have denied him food. Dumb in infancy, he has been blighted for life."

Then I took on the politicians who saw my efforts as nothing more than a quest for black votes. These critics also castigated government efforts to help people whom they often saw as lazy loafers looking for handouts. "My trips to the poverty areas recently have been charged as a cheap Democratic trick for Negro votes," I testified. "Hardly. South Carolina's hunger is both white and black. It was Republican [George] Romney who came to South Carolina last year to see the hungriest county in America. It was the Republican councilman that showed me slums in Greenville. . . . What Republicans see should not be termed Democratic trickery when a Democrat views them."

"Another political fact that must be coped with is the constant rebuff—'jobs but not handouts,'" I continued. "Many poverty programs have aborted because the people will not tolerate 'give-aways.' No one has worked more constantly or successfully on job development than I have. . . . I know the need for jobs, but what I am talking about here to this committee is downright hunger. The people I saw couldn't possibly work."

Finally I challenged the committee to develop policies befitting the richest country in the world. "This committee should set as a national goal the elimination of hunger and slum conditions in America," I said. "Ten years ago we set a national goal for construction of a super highway system and the conquest of space. Now, we have about completed this and there is no reason why in the next ten years hunger and slums cannot be eliminated from the American scene."

Of course, the battle over food programs has been protracted. Much of it has been waged by Republican Presidents as a budgetary matter. The way it happens is as follows: A President instructs his director of the Office of Management and Budget (OMB) to draw up budgets eliminating unnecessary or wasteful activities. "See what programs can be eliminated or cut back," is the typical directive from the White House.

Time and again a Republican OMB director thinks he can please the boss by cutting the food-stamp appropriation. We reached a critical time in this exercise when Senator Robert Dole, a Republican from Kansas, saved us. Dole helped to change the popular impression that Democrats supported food stamps and Republicans opposed the program.

First elected in 1968 and often viewed as a partisan slash-and-burn Republican, Dole championed food stamps and was even an architect of the food-stamp program along with McGovern. He really stuck his neck out when President Ronald Reagan wanted to take his budget ax to the program. Reagan's proposal to eliminate certain work-related expenses from food-stamp and welfare benefits was a nonstarter for Dole.[37]

He said that the committee would probably not approve cuts that hurt the "working poor," those who received government assistance while simultaneously holding jobs. Some 21.7 million people received food stamps in November of 1981. The Agriculture Department estimated that 16 percent of all recipients would be excluded from the program or drop out as a result of cuts proposed by Reagan's budget proposal for fiscal year 1983. And benefits would be reduced to another 68 percent of food-stamp households.[38]

Of course Reagan's idea was to slash the federal budget. His proposals would save some $2.3 billion in a program estimated to cost about $11.1 billion.[39] Indeed Reagan had been elected in 1980 on a platform that attacked Washington and the federal government. It was as if the President of the United States wanted the government over which he presided to disappear. The former actor, who played well to the public, would often joke about the excesses of government and make up colorful anecdotes about the welfare recipient driving a Cadillac. It mattered little that there was no factual basis for such stories. The voters seemed to lap them up. But, as I describe later, that anti-government philosophy—as well as Reagan's adherence to "voodoo economics" of massive tax cuts that resulted in staggering deficits—led me to seek the 1984 Democratic nomination for President.

But in 1969 and 1970, as a member of the Agricultural Committee, I really wanted to develop a program along the lines of what eventually emerged as the Women, Infants and Children (WIC) feeding program. I wasn't getting anywhere until Vice President Hubert Humphrey returned to the Senate, winning back his old Minnesota seat in 1970. He led the way and we were able to pass legislation creating WIC. The program provided for regular examinations of expectant mothers by physicians as well as for food stamps during their pregnancies.

The cost of hunger is obvious. It affects a child's concentration. Early on, he repeats a grade in school, then perhaps another grade, and falls further behind. Then he becomes too big and too old for the class, drops out, and gets into mischief—and into crime. I know. As Governor, I used to run a penitentiary. Rather than incarceration, nutrition for infants is needed.

WIC is an example of government working. It has made the difference in hundreds of thousands of lives. Everyone benefits from such government initiatives. And programs such as WIC put the lie to politicians who have built careers on mindlessly tearing down Washington. Their anti-Washington mantra may be a way to win an election, but it is wrongheaded philosophy for improving lives. An activist government can also be subject to discipline, but that notion seems lost on far too many lawmakers.

Of course much has occurred since I wrote *The Case Against Hunger* nearly forty years ago. Feeding programs, food stamps, and school lunches have been instituted. At the local level, churches and civic groups provide vital help with such programs as Crisis Ministries, Meals on Wheels, and Lowcountry Food Bank.

Politics has changed but not the need. Forty-five years ago 12 million people in the United States suffered from hunger. Today as back then, nobody is terribly eager to highlight the extent of hunger that exists in such a rich country. But the government itself keeps statistics. The numbers tell a depressing story. Data released in the year 2000 reveal that more than 11 million households with more than 33 million people have "limited or uncertain access to sufficient food due to inadequate resources." Nearly 3.3 million of these households reported they suffered from hunger. I am pleased to say that South Carolina was not among the ten states with the "highest levels of food insecurity" or among the ten states with the "highest hunger prevalence."[40]

But as a nation we must do better. The solution of course is to put the country back to work. But America's standard of living is difficult to maintain when competing in a global marketplace against other countries where wages for basic labor continue to be far lower than ours and where people don't have the same safety and other workplace requirements that our employers must provide. We can fight back with the right policies. I will show how to put our country back to work. It is long overdue for our leaders to get us back on the right track.

5

Clement Haynsworth's Nomination to the Supreme Court

The nomination of Clement Haynsworth Jr. of Greenville, South Carolina, to the United States Supreme Court in 1969 came at a time of political turmoil. It had been fifteen years since the Court's decision in *Brown v. Board of Education* had required the integration of the public schools. The South had begun to undergo a political realignment. The longtime southern allegiance to the Democratic Party had been torn apart. The "Solid South" was no more.

The ingredients for this shift are clear. South Carolina Senator Strom Thurmond set the stage by waging a record-setting filibuster in the Senate—more than twenty-four hours of talking against the 1957 Civil Rights Act. Then in 1964 he switched party labels and became a Republican. That same year Barry Goldwater became the first Republican to carry the Palmetto State since Reconstruction. Four years later Richard Nixon, with Thurmond's help, easily carried the state on his way to winning the presidency.

In a relatively short time span following the *Brown* decision in 1954, the established Democratic Party of the Old Confederacy—those rural yellow dog Democrats whose allegiance to the party had been unwavering for so long—had drifted over to become the white Republican Party. Meanwhile the new Democratic Party attracted many blacks but a declining share of the white population. As these political changes were occurring, the South also was experiencing an economic revival. The outsourcing of industry and jobs from the North to the South, where unions were not nearly as prevalent, had political repercussions as well. Big Labor bosses began to worry that their clout was declining.

These political developments were decisive in 1968, when President Lyndon B. Johnson tried to promote Abe Fortas from his seat as an Associate Justice to be Chief Justice of the Supreme Court, replacing Earl Warren, who had announced his decision to retire. Immediately leading the charge against the "liberal" Fortas, Thurmond was not about to acquiesce to the promotion of a liberal Justice by a lame-duck Democratic President. Johnson already had announced that he was not running again and had less than six months remaining in his term.

During Judiciary Committee hearings, Thurmond's zealous prosecutorial questioning of Fortas had left even some of his own staffers shaking their heads. "In my judgment, our strategy in the Fortas hearings has been a disastrous mistake," Thurmond staffer James Lucier wrote in a blunt memo; "the line of questioning did not appear to be a sincere attempt to investigate his views; rather it appeared to be an irrational attempt to delay and harass."[1]

When Fortas's nomination reached the Senate floor, Thurmond joined Republican Robert Griffin of Michigan in a filibuster to try to kill the nomination. Recognizing that his nomination would not be able to attract sufficient votes to end the filibuster, Fortas ultimately withdrew his name—a move that Thurmond said was "the wisest decision" that the Justice had made since being on the Court.

Fortas's setback marked the first time that a modern President failed to win the confirmation of an Associate Justice to be Chief Justice. The acrimonious battle left bitter feelings on both sides of the aisle, especially against Thurmond. A few months later, charges surfaced that Fortas was on retainer to a foundation financed by Louis Wolfson, a shady operator who was later convicted of stock market manipulation. Hammered by negative press about these financial dealings, Fortas stepped down from the Court in May 1969. Suddenly Nixon had two vacancies to fill on the Supreme Court—the very opportunity to reshape the direction of the judiciary that the Republican President had longed for.

The battle over Fortas had repercussions that would be costly for South Carolinians and the nation. Nixon was determined to make good on his promise during the campaign to remake the Court. First the President nominated Warren Burger, a Judge on the federal appeals court in Washington and a critic of Earl Warren, to be Chief Justice. Burger was easily confirmed on June 9, less than three weeks after he had been nominated.

But Nixon also had specific criteria for the other Supreme Court vacancy. He told Attorney General John Mitchell that potential nominees must be white southerners with judicial experience who would interpret the law rather than make the law and who were under sixty years of age.[2] The President was determined to follow through on promises made during the presidential campaign, when he had repeatedly blistered the Warren Court for its expansive rulings. He had argued that the Justices were imposing their personal philosophy in their rulings rather than assuming the limited role of Judges to interpret the law as it exists. He promised to bring "balance" to the Court by nominating "strict constructionists."

We had some fine Judges in South Carolina, but Thurmond at this point was no help in influencing the decision process. His zealousness over the years had alienated even some fellow Republicans. They worried that he was hurting the image of the GOP.

Meanwhile I figured I had the perfect nominee for Nixon in Clement F. Haynsworth Jr. of South Carolina. Judge Haynsworth was fifty-six years of age, a Republican, the Chief Judge of the U.S. Court of Appeals for the Fourth Circuit, and a strict constructionist. On May 28 the South Carolina delegation was in the Oval Office during a ceremony commemorating the three hundredth anniversary of the founding of South Carolina. When it was over, I exited the Oval Office first. I stepped aside for the others to leave and quickly reentered. The President was still standing as I said to him, "I have your next Supreme Court Justice for you, Mr. President."

"Who's that?" the President asked.

"Clement Haynsworth of Greenville, South Carolina," I responded.

"I don't know him," he replied.

"Yes you do," I said. "You attended an Investors Diversified board meeting in Greenville, South Carolina, where you stayed with Alester Furman, and Clement Haynsworth next door gave a cocktail party for you."[3]

"Oh yes, that nice fellow that stuttered," he recalled.

"Yes," I said. "He is Chief Judge of the Fourth Circuit, fifty-six years old, and when I ran Jack Kennedy's campaign against you in 1960, he was strong for you in South Carolina."

"Put that in a letter," the President said, "and get it to me right way."

"Yes sir," I replied, and off I went.

Later that day, I sent the President a letter detailing why I thought Haynsworth would be "an excellent choice" to fill the seat vacated by Fortas on the court. The letter emphasized that he had brought the Fourth Circuit to the highest degree of administrative order and efficiency that it had ever enjoyed. I wrote, "His decisions reflect a thorough understanding of legal principles, and his outstanding analyses of complex legal questions would instill stability in the nation's highest Court."[4]

To counter my recommendation of Haynsworth, Thurmond recommended my old political opponent Democrat Donald Russell, by then a Federal Judge in South Carolina. But Nixon was persuaded to go with Haynsworth. At the same time, the White House recognized that Thurmond had political baggage and that his involvement would complicate its efforts to promote a Judge from South Carolina to the Supreme Court. Administration strategists wanted to make sure that Haynsworth's nomination was not tied to Thurmond. It appeared that they got the message to him to be circumspect, lie low, and essentially confine himself in the Senate to written comments other than a few perfunctory remarks. I would handle the nomination.

Meanwhile Nixon formalized the decision about three months later, on August 18. Attorney General John Mitchell gave me a heads-up, saying, "You've got the Supreme Court Justice. I'm sending Bill Rehnquist to coordinate with you." At that time Rehnquist headed the Justice Department's Office of Legal Counsel. (Later he was nominated by Nixon for the Supreme Court and subsequently became Chief Justice.) It was easy working with Mitchell and Rehnquist. Mitchell and I had become close when he had given me advice about becoming a bond lawyer some years before.

I was confident that Haynsworth would be confirmed. His résumé was topflight. After graduating summa cum laude from Furman University, he went on to Harvard Law School and then returned to Greenville, where he gained vast experience as an attorney. Eisenhower nominated him to a seat on the U.S. Court of Appeals for the Fourth Circuit in 1957. As the caseload increased, Haynsworth distinguished himself as the author of balanced, well-reasoned decisions and became

Chief Judge in 1964. In reviewing his background as a Supreme Court nominee, the American Bar Association gave him its highest rating.

Also history was on our side. No Supreme Court nominee had been rejected by the Senate on a confirmation vote since John J. Parker, another southerner, came up short in 1930.

But I quickly got a wake-up call. Organized labor was not about to let a corporate right-to-work lawyer get a seat on the Supreme Court. Today much of the political debate over Supreme Court nominees revolves around abortion rights. Back then, Big Labor was battling against loss of its members as companies outsourced their jobs to the South, often to escape unions. The interest groups mobilized as soon as they thought Haynsworth would get the nod—even before Nixon had made it official. The AFL-CIO sent investigators across South Carolina, looking for dirt, soliciting rumors as they met with South Carolina leaders of Americans for Democratic Action, the NAACP, and South Carolina labor leaders. George Meany, head of the AFL-CIO, announced his opposition. Journalists who had pooh-poohed the charges against Fortas were not going to be burned again. So vast were the rumors and misinformation about Haynsworth, that when I introduced him to the Judiciary Committee for its hearings, I felt as though I was presenting an indicted defendant rather than the Chief Judge of the U.S. Court of Appeals for the Fourth Circuit.[5]

Shortly after the formal nomination on August 18, 1969, I made sure that the nominee called on each Senator individually. Meanwhile I reassured my Democratic colleagues of Haynsworth's character and went out of my way to make it clear that he was not Thurmond's man. As Haynsworth visited Senate offices, he was making a good impression. Hiram Fong, the Hawaii Republican who was his classmate at Harvard, warmly received the nominee, as did New York Republican Jacob Javits, who swapped stories with him about their collections of Jasper Johns's art. And Senate Minority Leader Everett Dirksen of Illinois was doing everything he could to smooth the way for the nominee among Republicans.

But we suffered a body blow when Dirksen died in September. He was extremely popular with Republicans, and, as their leader, he undoubtedly would have obtained a solid Republican vote to confirm Haynsworth. Instead of an ally, the two new Republican Senate leaders opposed the nomination. Pennsylvanian Hugh Scott, who succeeded

Dirksen as the new Minority Leader, was not a Thurmond supporter and refused to handle the confirmation fight on the Senate floor. Robert Griffin of Michigan, who assumed the number two, or Whip, post, was already looking ahead to his 1972 reelection campaign in a heavily unionized state.

These sudden changes at the top of the Senate GOP leadership ladder were a huge setback for us as we tried to line up supporters. The White House recruited the newly elected Bob Dole of Kansas to handle Haynsworth's nomination on the GOP side of the aisle. Labor enlisted Democrat Birch Bayh of Indiana, a gifted orator and member of the Senate Judiciary Committee, to head the opposition.

The Judiciary Committee approved Haynsworth's nomination by a 10–7 vote on October 9. Bayh's line of questioning of Haynsworth made it obvious that the Indiana Senator was trying to pull off a replay of the battle over Fortas's nomination. Having seen Fortas brought down over questions about his ethics, the Indiana Democrat sought to highlight supposed conflicts of interest in Haynsworth's conduct on the bench. Bayh's argument really was that Haynsworth had fallen short of the highest ethical standards by participating as a Judge in a half-dozen cases involving parties in which he had a financial interest. He even had compiled a nine-page "bill of particulars" against Haynsworth.

One of Bayh's favorite "particulars" was that Haynsworth had an interest in a firm called Carolina Vend-A-Matic and that he had ruled in favor of a company that had a business relationship with Carolina Vend-A-Matic. The suggestion was that the ruling had boosted the value of Haynsworth's investment. Bayh even used a chart that showed Carolina Vend-A-Matic's tremendous growth in gross annual sales during the period after Haynsworth's initial investment.

But, I made the case, along with other supporters of the nominee, that Haynsworth's stock interest was "de minimus," or minimal. Actually, in these circumstances a Judge had an obligation to sit and hear the case because there were a limited number of Federal Judges. Replacing a Judge who disqualified himself is difficult. As John Frank, the leading authority on judicial disqualification—a self-described liberal and a strong supporter of the Warren Court—testified, "The criticism directed to the disqualification or nondisqualification of Judge Haynsworth is a truly unjust criticism which cannot be fairly made."[6]

The federal judicial code at that time devoted only a few lines to disqualification and said that a Judge shall disqualify himself in any case in which he has "a substantial interest." In fact the code had been amended in 1948 to add the word *substantial* before the word *interest*. Haynsworth had followed the letter of the code.[7]

Charles Alan Wright, author of the authoritative *Federal Practice and Procedure* text for attorneys, submitted testimony that strongly endorsed Haynsworth and dismissed critics' effort to raise ethical questions. In fact Haynsworth's supporters noted that he had been sensitive to avoid the appearance of conflicts of interest. For example he had removed himself from cases in which his former law firm represented a party or in which a party was represented by his young cousin, a partner in a law firm.[8] He also had recused himself from cases involving former clients with whom he was particularly close before he became a Judge, such as South Carolina's Daniel Construction Co.

Bayh took advantage of the lingering ill will over Thurmond's filibuster of civil rights legislation and his harsh treatment of Fortas. The Indiana Senator insisted, "The question is not whether Judge Haynsworth is dishonest, but whether he has shown the temperament necessary to sit in the highest judicial council." Such a charge was baseless. But too many of my colleagues were making up their minds without thoroughly analyzing the record.

"Senators are jumping to conclusions," I said on the Senate floor. "Rather than the most deliberative body, I almost have the feeling that we are about the 100 fastest guns in the East, trying to get the headline, rather than trying to get to the point in substance of the Haynsworth nomination—that is, the Judge's qualifications to be an Associate Justice of the U.S. Supreme Court."[9]

The American Bar Association examined Bayh's charges and found no evidence of a conflict of interest. We also took the campaign against Haynsworth to labor. John Bolt Culbertson, a South Carolina civil rights and labor lawyer, testified for him. And Haynsworth responded in great detail to the questions raised. But we found too many Senators not wanting to get involved in a "labor fight." They stayed off the floor. We didn't have TV or C-SPAN coverage back then, and of course there was no Internet.

I was anxious to dispel Bayh's charges and to kill all the rumors being hatched to try to discredit the nominee. But even as I worked to clear the air, Bayh refused to stay on the floor. He would make a charge and leave. I even publicly challenged him to a debate so the Senate could hear us together. But he declined to debate. Meanwhile, the interest groups continued to poison the well against Haynsworth.

It got to the point that they were using everything they could find that might hurt him, regardless of how far-fetched it was. For example, headlines blared that Haynsworth was a friend of South Carolina's Bobby Baker, who had resigned as secretary of the Senate in 1963 and was later convicted of fraud and tax evasion. But the Judge had not seen Baker for more than a decade, had had only three contacts with him in his life, and had never engaged in business deals with him.

Such was the nature of the fight. We were continually responding in the newspaper to all these baseless allegations, but Bayh would never appear one-on-one. He repeatedly ducked. Nixon took note of my challenge at a press conference on October 20. "We wondered why Senator Bayh wouldn't debate Senator Hollings," he said. "Senator Bayh is a very articulate man. But after reading the record, I know why. He was well-advised not to debate."

Moving to the final vote, Rehnquist and I had done up a vote count that showed we had a majority for Haynsworth. But now a new disaster! A few days before the confirmation vote, Haynsworth, who was on his way to meet with Rehnquist and me, was intercepted by reporters. When he was aggressively quizzed about his stock holdings, the usually taciturn Judge volunteered that regardless of the outcome of confirmation, he was going to put his stock in a blind trust. Haynsworth had always contended that he had done nothing wrong, but after being so relentlessly pummeled with questions about his holdings, he had decided to go an extra mile. By putting the stock in a blind trust, Haynsworth assumed the critics would have no further basis to raise questions.

A few days later, Herb Block (better known as Herblock), the well-known cartoonist for the *Washington Post*, ruined us. He depicted the Congress as a high court judge presiding as Attorney General Mitchell pleaded his case. The cartoon portrayed Haynsworth, Mitchell's client, as a little school boy with a book bag that had Carolina Vend-A-Matic stock tapes streaming out of it onto the courtroom floor. "But your honor," Mitchell pleaded, "my client hasn't done anything wrong—and he promises to stop doing it." This powerful cartoon lost us five votes—exactly the number by which we fell short of confirming Haynsworth.

In retrospect certain things are clear. If Dirksen had lived, Haynsworth would have been confirmed. The 55–45 vote on November 21 was payback for Fortas. Even the *Washington Post* concluded in an editorial the day after the vote, "The rejection, despite the speeches and the comments on Capitol Hill to the contrary, seems to have resulted more from ideological and plainly political considerations than from ethical ones."

It is small consolation, but years later Senate Democratic leader Mike Mansfield quietly apologized to me for his vote. Also Democratic Senator Tom Eagleton of Missouri said that the one vote he regretted as a Senator was his vote against Haynsworth. Similarly several other Senators who had opposed the South Carolina jurist told me that they had made a mistake.

I was pleased that in the aftermath of this deeply disappointing moment, Clement decided to stay on the appellate court as Chief Judge. He acquitted himself with dignity and good work for many years after the Senate so ill-treated him. And after a unanimous vote in the House and Senate, we renamed the courthouse in Greenville for him in 1983. But that step—sort of a makeup for his mistreatment—was not nearly enough to right the wrong that had been done to him. The country was denied the services of a first-rate jurist on the Supreme Court. Bare-knuckled politics had triumphed over substance.

I was nettled that Haynsworth was "technically" turned down for obeying the law on conflicts. I wanted to make sure that the confusion in the law was cleared up. And Birch Bayh, who was an outstanding Senator, agreed that we needed to clarify the "de minimus" statute so that a Judge would know when he must recuse himself and when he must hear a case. We led the way to passage of a measure to forbid Judges to sit in any cases in which they had any financial interest, regardless of how small.[10] That standard also was adopted by the American Bar Association and is in its Code of Judicial Conduct.

Battles over judicial nominees, starting with Haynsworth and continuing to the present, provide case studies of how the news media have become a hindrance to government working. In the late 1960s newspapers began to change from reporting the news. Instead they seem more focused on promoting controversy.

But blaming the media won't help. How must we rectify this broken process? Senators need to reclaim the review of judicial nominees from the special interest groups that use propaganda and threats to try to get their way during these fights. What good person wants to put himself and his family through the horrific treatment that has become a routine part of the Senate's "advice and consent" process?

Years after the Haynsworth setback, Senator David Boren from Oklahoma and I were the only Democrats to vote to confirm Judge Robert Bork to the Supreme Court. Bork was a former Solicitor General and a member of the U.S. Court of Appeals for the District of Columbia when President Reagan nominated him. The Senate rejected his confirmation 42–58 in October 1987. Unlike Haynsworth, Judge Bork, unhappy with his treatment, resigned from the bench the following year. During the rancorous debate over Judge Bork's nomination, I expressed on the Senate floor a sentiment that I still believe today: "Somewhere, sometime in this Senate we must stand up to the onrush of contrived threats and pressure. As the world's most deliberative body, we must return to our roots. We must deliberate. . . . We are governing by political poll. The most deliberative body in the world is becoming a rigged jury."[11]

6

The Early Fight to Protect the Environment

Even though I was disappointed to have missed out on joining the Appropriations Committee right off the bat, as Senator Dick Russell had urged, I found a great deal of satisfaction in landing a seat on the Commerce Committee. I remained there for my entire Senate career and found it to be the most interesting and educational committee of all.

Members on the committee tend to have their hands on anything that moves. The areas that we worked on included trade issues, the airlines, highway transportation and safety, the broadcast industry, telecommunications, space, satellites, climate change, coastal development, and oceans. We also kept tabs on the Departments of Commerce and Transportation, the National Aeronautical and Space Administration (NASA), and the National Science Foundation—and on more administrative agencies than you could shake a stick at.

In looking back at that period, I am struck by the amount of work that we tackled. We often collaborated across party lines to address issues such as pollution in the oceans. At that time we legislators were not so fixated on constantly trying to score political points. Republicans and Democrats wanted to legislate, to get something done. It sounds strange today, when at times it seems the overriding goal is to get into a game of one-upmanship and to come up with that all-important sound bite that makes the evening news. I don't want to exaggerate the productivity of the "good old days," but the record is clear. Government worked.

Sure, Democrats, who were in control of Congress, were butting heads more and more with President Nixon, but I had found that I could work with John Mitchell. Having an ally in such a high position in the Republican administration proved to be very helpful, especially in my effort to bring some sense to the federal government's approach to oceans and marine policy in general.

In November 1969 Commerce chairman Warren Magnuson of Washington turned to me and said, "You're chairman of the Oceans and Atmosphere Subcommittee." Just like that; I had my marching orders. Senator Magnuson made clear that my responsibility was to develop legislation based on the findings of the Stratton Commission report. South Carolinian Julius A. Stratton, chairman of the Ford Foundation and retired president of the Massachusetts Institute of Technology, led a cross section of outstanding leaders who were trying to bring rationality to our confusing array of federal marine programs.

Stratton had become involved when Congress recognized the need for action to deal with this vast potential of the oceans that we were neglecting. No President had come to grips with the challenges of developing a coherent policy in this area. Duplication of programs and lack of coordination were a serious problem.

So in 1966 Congress stepped in and passed a law to create an independent Commission on Marine Science, Engineering and Resources—which became known as the Stratton Commission—to study our needs regarding the seas and to develop a plan of government organization to address those needs.[1] That law also forced presidential leadership by creating a cabinet-level National Council on Marine Resources and Engineering Development to be headed by the Vice President. The council was charged with coordinating the federal oceans programs scattered throughout the government.

In January 1969, after about two years of study, the Stratton Commission submitted its report, "Our Nation and the Sea"—a plan for national action on the oceans and atmosphere. The commission's focus on pollution and the impact of urban sprawl made it clear that it was imperative that we act. Among its 120 recommendations, the commission most significantly recommended the establishment of an independent National Oceanic and Atmospheric Administration (NOAA) to bring some order to the chaotic federal system in which marine-science programs were scattered throughout twenty-two departments and agencies.

I had already been involved in this area when, in the fall of 1969, I headed a special Senate study on "United Nations Suboceanic Lands Policy," which dealt with how resources in the ocean that were beyond a nation's jurisdiction could be used peacefully. After I was named chairman of the subcommittee in November, we wasted no time in examining the NOAA proposal. I was convinced of the urgency of the issue. I agreed with the Stratton Commission's finding that we must make a bigger investment in preserving the oceans.

Pollution was a growing problem that we no longer could ignore. I knew it firsthand. Back in the summers of 1939 and 1940 I had worked in the marshes with the Army Corps of Engineers as we made a survey of Charleston Harbor and the Intracoastal Waterway. I was measuring the depths of the currents with what they called a hell stick. That stick was drawn taut by an outboard motor boat, as we measured the depths every ten yards or so. The work was exhausting as I was literally in the marshes, sometimes up to my shoulders. I had to be pulled out. So I had seen the bottles and glass and debris that had been tossed into the harbor. Back then most folks just shrugged it off, but it eventually reached a point where 90 percent of Charleston Harbor was condemned because of bacterial pollution from domestic sewage.

That work with the corps made a lasting impression. I was an environmentalist even before I got out of my teens. So I knew all about the need to take concrete action and not just palaver about the problem. My work on the subcommittee had reinforced what I already knew— that this filth and other pollution were constantly moving from the harbor into the sea. The Stratton Commission report reinforced the urgency of the situation as it concluded "beyond doubt that man-made pollution already has affected the entire ocean."

I knew the difficulty we would face in trying to goad the federal bureaucracy into getting off their collective backsides and moving forward to preserve the marine environment. Our failure to act over the years had put us behind the eight ball. Bureaucratic infighting and turf wars in the executive branch were causing delays in putting together a program. So, within a few months of becoming chairman of the subcommittee, I was getting increasingly annoyed at the Nixon administration's seeming indifference to this need or, even worse, its desire to kill the notion of an independent oceans agency in order to preserve the status quo.

I decided to lay down a marker so the White House would be on notice that if administration officials tried to put the kibosh to this effort, they would have a fight on their hands. I was angered by reports that the President was using his so-called Ash Council on government reorganization to block the NOAA proposal. Word was that the administration wanted to make the agency a backwater, lacking any authority. Roy Ash, the head of the President's Advisory Council on Executive Organization, and other administration witnesses urged us to postpone action until the Ash Council had studied the issue and made recommendations.

To make its case, the White House sent some of its top honchos to Capitol Hill to testify and make their pitch for delay. But in the hearings we learned that neither Transportation Secretary John Volpe nor Navy Secretary (and later Rhode Island Senator) John H. Chafee nor the President's science adviser, Lee A. DuBridge, had even bothered to read "Our Nation and the Sea"! It was infuriating. At the same time Vice President Spiro Agnew had held only two meetings of the National Council on Marine Resources, which he chaired.

I didn't have to be clairvoyant to see through the White House fiddle-faddle. The administration was playing games. I noted that the Ash Council wasn't studying—it already had decided to try to minimize the role of an oceans agency. "I am shocked and dismayed at the White House conspiracy to scuttle a chance for an oceans program for the U.S. Government," I said on the Senate floor on March 5, 1970. "This conspiracy has not been casual nor unintentional. It is insidious and the President is involved."

"President Nixon treats oceanography with slightly more dignity than the Board of Tea Tasters," I added. "The President is giving ocean programs of the United States semicustodial care. He is failing to lead, not only in a national oceanic program, but also internationally. And he is taking every step to thwart leadership where it appears."

We were wasting millions in taxpayer dollars to accomplish nothing. The battles between bureaucrats had produced, I said, "a great dispersion and dissipation of energy, duplication of energy, duplication of effort, and attendant inefficiencies . . . even though the government is spending about $900 million per year on ocean programs."

I was tired of hearing about behind the scenes shenanigans at the White House, where various officials were trying to torpedo our efforts for a new agency. John Ehrlichman, Nixon's top domestic affairs adviser, was a roadblock on certain environmental issues. While Ehrlichman is credited with helping in some areas, such as creation of the Environmental Protection Agency, word was that his background as a pro–land-development lawyer from Seattle might be a problem for the creation of NOAA as well as for my subsequent efforts to pass a new law to encourage the safe and sane development of our coastal areas. Ehrlichman apparently considered our initiatives on Capitol Hill as ruining his drive for a federal plan for land use.

It was at this time that I called on my old friend Attorney General John Mitchell. I gave him our report and recommendations, emphasizing the thoroughness of our study and the fact that we had unanimous bipartisan support. I sold it as a national initiative on which President Nixon could lead. Stratton and Edward Wenk, the former executive secretary of National Council on Marine Resources and Engineering Development, accompanied me to make the pitch for an independent agency, as the Stratton Commission had recommended.[2]

Our ploy worked. Mitchell heard us out. He went around the White House footdraggers and directly to the President. But he let us know that while he could support a new body for the oceans, it would not be an independent agency.[3] It would have to function within a department. Of course the Stratton Commission had recommended an independent agency. But you could tell from the commission's report that if the agency were not independent, then it would be logically put within the Interior Department since that was the agency charged with conservation. However, Mitchell told me that Interior Secretary Walter "Wally" Hickel had angered the President by speaking out against the Vietnam War, and Nixon "wasn't going to give him anything."

Sure enough, on July 9, 1970—a few months after that meeting—Nixon submitted Reorganization Plan Number 4, which called for creation of NOAA as part of the Commerce Department under Secretary Maurice Stans. After some debate that organization plan became law. I was delighted because we were really beginning the environmental movement at the federal level. Finally we had established an agency that would provide us with a better understanding of the oceans and atmosphere.

Months before Reorganization Plan Number 4 became law, Congress also passed the important National Environmental Policy Act. It required federal agencies to issue environmental impact statements before developing or drilling or undertaking other projects. It stopped plenty of hazardous projects in their tracks—projects that in the past would have proceeded routinely.[4]

We were beginning to make real progress on the environmental front. Government was working. My subcommittee was in the middle of the fray. We had high-profile witnesses who delivered dire warnings that, unless we acted quickly, mankind would suffer grievously. Jacques Cousteau, the famed ocean explorer, testified in October 1971 that in perhaps the next thirty to fifty years the oceans will be dead. Based on his own observations, Cousteau said that life in the sea in the last twenty years had diminished as much as 30 to 50 percent. In the beautiful Mediterranean, shore life had practically disappeared. It was rare to see a fish there more than three inches long, he said.

Anthropologist, adventurer, and author Thor Heyerdahl also told our subcommittee in November 1971 about pollution in vast stretches of the ocean. Heyerdahl had gained fame for his *Kon-Tiki* expedition, on which he had made a 4,300 mile journey across the Pacific Ocean on a raft that he and several other adventurers had constructed. In 1947, during that *Kon-Tiki* trip from the western coast of South America to Polynesian islands, Heyerdahl saw that sea life existed everywhere, as the waters were filled with plankton. The ocean was clear.

Yet when he crossed the Atlantic in 1970, much had changed. Almost every day of that voyage, the crew sighted drifting oil clots across some 2,700 nautical miles. Imagine it, a continuous stretch of polluted surface water from Morocco to Barbados. On some days the crew couldn't even dip their toothbrushes into the ocean because of the filth. He made clear that ocean pollution was an international problem and that the United States alone could not end it. "There is no such thing as territorial water," he said. "We shall be forever doomed to share the common water which rotates like soup in a boiling kettle. The spices one nation puts in will be tasted by all consumers."

This powerful testimony left an indelible impression. As I said in a speech in 1972, "The time for study and research is gone. What we need today is a re-thinking of our attitudes toward pollution and pollution control. . . . We are killing the great oceans of this planet, and unless we stop this madness, mankind itself may perish from the face of this earth. And that would be the irony of all ironies—man having evolved from the oceans, only to die because he has killed the very source of all life."

No longer could we think of the ocean as a vast cesspool, I said in the speech. You can't simply throw anything into it and assume it will sink to the bottom where the forces of nature would cleanse and recycle it. "Now we know that the oceans of the world are not one big washing machine," I said. "Pollution dumped into the oceans may last there for thousands and thousands of years."

To try to combat this enormous problem, I authored the Ocean Dumping Act, which easily passed both the House and Senate. The measure set up strong safeguards against dumping sewage and other waste into the oceans. Industrial dumping of wastes into the seas would be allowed only if the Environmental Protection Agency issued a special permit. We felt the tangible benefits of this approach back home when we stopped a Georgia-based company from dumping sulfurous wastes off our South Carolina coast.

And after our subcommittee hearings in 1971, we also passed the Coastal Zone Management Act so that our sprawling population would not demolish our nation's fragile shoreline and its resources. We had found that more than half the U.S. population—53 percent—lived within fifty miles of the Atlantic and Pacific, Gulf of Mexico, or Great Lakes coastlines. This is what I called "people pollution," because we had learned that in the following twenty-five years, 80 percent of the population would be living in the narrow area along our coasts and around the Great Lakes.

All this rapidly encroaching population required that we plan and not just sit idly by while our shoreline was wrecked. We had to make room for our recreation facilities, electric-power generating plants, landing fields for our jet airplanes, and ports for our ships. Up to that time we were operating on a first-come, first-ruin basis. Our increased public awareness was translating into action. As an example, BASF, a large German petrochemical plant that had planned to build a facility on Port Royal Sound in Beaufort, South Carolina, was forced to withdraw when our citizens raised environmental concerns. The firm finally admitted that it would have polluted one of the last remaining clean estuaries on the East Coast. That's what made our new law so vital. It was designed to bring some sanity to the development of our precious coastal areas—our beaches, marshes, and tidelands.

Yet another piece of legislation, the 1972 Marine Mammal Protection Act, also was enacted at this time. It imposed a moratorium on killing most ocean mammals. Without our action some of these creatures were in danger of being wiped out. So, we gave the NOAA administrator the authority to keep a check on the whales, porpoises, dolphins, and sea lions to ensure their preservation. We also created a Marine Mammal Commission that would review the entire range of marine mammals and make recommendations to Congress. No longer would these creatures be killed on an unregulated basis. We could not allow them to become extinct without ever giving it a second thought.

In each of these cases, elected officials were acting to address big problems. We were not kicking problems down the road for future generations to solve. Congress was acting on the environment, across party lines. We recognized that the government could no longer look away from pollution or ignore the real pressures that crowding of our coastlines was causing. Inaction was unacceptable. Looking back at that most productive period on tackling environmental issues, I am proud of what we started.

7

The Supreme Court
Corrupts Congress

As we made progress on environmental issues, I found myself unexpectedly in the middle of the fray when President Nixon sought to strike a deal with the Soviet Union to limit nuclear weapons. I say "unexpectedly" because in August 1971, when I first got drawn into this national security issue, I was on my honeymoon with Peatsy.[1] After getting married in the Citadel chapel, we had gone up to Montreal and planned to sail down the St. Lawrence Seaway.

But we were thrown for a loop when the Captain of the ship got in a big row with his wife, who was supposed to do the cooking. Peatsy took charge in the kitchen, and I ended up handling the lines. I still can see the stern of the boat almost submerged and the bow out of the water while I desperately tried to unhook the bowline from the deck of a lock on the seaway. Then, as we approached Quebec, I got a call from Senate Majority Leader Mike Mansfield. We had developed a good relationship, and the Montana Senator figured that taking Peatsy and me to eight countries in Europe and Morocco would be a wonderful wedding present. Peatsy and I never hesitated. We quickly cancelled the remainder of our "voyage," and before we knew it, we were in Europe. It's easy for me to remember Morocco, the last stop on our journey. We landed in Rabat ahead of schedule, and to kill time we walked around the airport, where at one end outside was this pile of boxes of women's Foot Joy golf shoes. Inquiring when we got to the palace, we heard that the king selected the best-looking daughters of the Governors of various provinces as his golf partners. Apparently the king of Morocco still had a harem.

Mansfield had invited us to travel with him to Europe and Morocco to help explain President Nixon's August 15 announcement of a 10 percent surcharge on imports. The sudden imposition of the surcharge had caused worries in European capitals that the United States was withdrawing from the international stage. Senator Mansfield reassured the leaders across the Atlantic that we were not building fences or retreating into a new period of isolationism.[2]

Now that Europe had emerged as a full competitor, we simply wanted a fair shake. Our role had changed from the 1950s, when we helped to rebuild the world from the ruins of World War II, to the 1960s, when we were the world policeman, to the 1970s, when we no longer could act as "a global Santa Claus."

European countries had low unemployment and were not experiencing the severe economic woes that the United States was facing. "Our task, then, is to put our own house in order," I said. "Until we do that, we will be unable to make our maximum contribution toward the making of a better world."

Even as our focus on that trip was on the shifting economic currents, we also were briefed in Helsinki, Finland, about the ongoing Strategic Arms Limitation Talks (SALT). Gerard Smith, our chief arms-control negotiator, outlined a balanced agreement whereby both the Soviet Union and the United States would limit strategic arms. However, unbeknownst to Smith or even to Secretary of State William Rogers, Nixon had set in motion secret back-channel talks with the Soviets. The "official" negotiating sessions were little more than "elaborate frauds." The "real negotiations" were going on behind the scenes between National Security Adviser Henry Kissinger and Soviet Ambassador Anatoly Dobrynin.[3] The balanced agreement that we were briefed on in August 1971 was different from the SALT I agreement presented in January 1972.

It became obvious to me that in their rush to achieve "détente" with the Soviets, Nixon and Kissinger made too many concessions. That interim agreement allowed the Soviets a numerical advantage in missile launchers. Nixon and Kissinger argued the Soviet advantage would be offset by certain other U.S. advantages. The Joint Chiefs of Staff had not even been briefed on the details of the deal before it was signed. Their dismay, as mine, was obvious.

As I studied the agreement, I conferred frequently with Democratic Senator Henry "Scoop" Jackson of Washington, who was an expert in everything related to defense. Jackson had helped John Kennedy score political points in the presidential campaign against Nixon in 1960 with charges that the Eisenhower administration had looked the other way as "a missile gap" had developed with the Soviets.[4]

Jackson told me on numerous occasions that the changes Kissinger had negotiated on the number of warheads and the missile throw weights under this so-called Interim Agreement were not in our country's best interests. It gave the Soviets the edge in too many categories. Scoop made no secret of his misgivings. He even held up the vote on the agreement until passage of his amendment requiring any future permanent treaty on offensive arms to be based on rough numerical equality in strategic forces for each country. Essentially Jackson was arguing that the deal should be acceptable only if the next agreement, to be reached after this one expired, recaptured what we had negotiated away.

As Jackson publicly raised doubts about the wisdom of striking this deal, Nixon told Kissinger to work with Scoop to see if they could reach an understanding.[5] Sometime later Jackson told me that he had made an accommodation with the White House, and he'd vote to ratify the deal. At the same time, he added that he didn't blame me if I continued to oppose it.

I took to the Senate floor in September 1972 and made the case against the agreement because I was convinced that "this pact accords military superiority—perhaps irreversible military superiority—to the Soviets." I contrasted the interim agreement with the other agreement that we had struck with the Soviets, in which each side was treated alike on limitation of antiballistic missiles.

"The principles of equality and parity prevailed and were incorporated into the [ABM] accord," I said, noting that I had voted for the ABM agreement, which the Senate had approved on an 88–2 vote on August 3. "But the Interim Agreement is a horse of another color. The President walked out on sound negotiating principles, and the result is an unequal agreement that could guarantee inferiority in five years and a permanent second-place status for our country thereafter."

Ultimately, however, I was a lonely voice against the deal. Only Democratic Senator James Allen of Alabama joined me during the roll call. Nixon's interim agreement passed 88–2 on September 14, 1972.

I later explained my "no" vote to constituents in one of my monthly newsletters: "We should not be expected to give up more than the Soviets simply to get an agreement," I wrote. "I continue to work for a strong national defense that will keep America second to none."

Looking back at that debate, I see it as another case in which government worked. Yes, I was on the losing end of that vote, but we legislators diligently carried out our duties. We debated, and Nixon was forced to respond. He did so by negotiating with Senator Jackson and supporting Scoop's amendment, which I hoped would not allow the Soviet advantage to become set in concrete. When we didn't equalize strategic arms in SALT II, I helped lead the opposition to it.

Of course getting that deal just a few months before Election Day was a godsend for Nixon. The politician that the media always loved to hate suddenly was portrayed as a daring peacemaker. After building his political career as a cold warrior, Nixon had reversed course and was reaping big political rewards. By then it already was obvious that the President was headed to an overwhelming reelection.

I mention this because I had assumed the chairmanship of the Democratic Senatorial Campaign Committee (DSCC) for the 1971–72 election cycle. My job was to protect our incumbents on Election Day and to try to pad our majority by picking up some GOP seats. The chairman of the DSCC has two big jobs: recruiting topflight candidates and raising lots of money for Senate races. But my task was complicated because at the top of the Democratic slate, our presidential nominee, Senator George McGovern of South Dakota, was never really competitive. McGovern was a good man, who—as I noted earlier—had been on the forefront of the battle against the scourge of hunger. He was not a weak peacenik as the Republicans tried to portray him. He was a patriot who had won the Distinguished Flying Cross for heroic service in World War II. And George is a straight shooter, as honest as can be.

But the Republicans relentlessly hammered McGovern. He had captured the nomination based on his tenacious opposition to the war in Vietnam, and he favored cuts in defense spending, amnesty for draft dodgers, and a program to give every American one thousand dollars. It was not a platform that had much appeal in the South, where McGovern was seen as a weak-kneed liberal. To make matters worse, his star-crossed campaign really hit a landmine before it got out of the gate.

The "reformers" and upstarts who never made peace with our party's establishment during the primaries were running the Democratic Convention in Miami Beach. These activists, adamantly opposed to the Vietnam War, were disorganized and made a mess of things. They were so insistent on delegate quotas that we even had to beat back a challenge to our South Carolina delegation because it didn't include enough women. Florence County's delegation, responding to our urgings to participate in the caucus, ended up with an all-male, black delegation. We arranged for a black leader, Matthew Perry (who in 1979 became the nation's first African American Federal District Court Judge), to present our case to the convention, and my friend Pierre Salinger, who had served as press secretary to President Kennedy, persuaded Willie Brown, Speaker of the California state assembly and a prominent black leader, to come down on the side of South Carolina. We were finally seated.

Such intramural squabbles went on and on and on. Senator Mike Gravel nominated himself for Vice President, and poor George didn't get to the podium to give his acceptance speech until the wee hours of the morning! Nobody in the country heard our nominee give his big talk. And then, House Speaker Thomas P. "Tip" O'Neill and other Democratic leaders wanted no part of introducing McGovern to the faithful at our breakfast to show "party unity" following the convention. So I did the honors—and caught grief back home from constituents who wrote letters hotly scolding me for cozying up to a man they saw as a leftist radical. Things went from bad to worse when, two weeks after our chaotic convention, the political world was rocked by the disclosure that McGovern's running mate, Missouri Senator Thomas Eagleton, had received electroshock treatment for depression in the 1960s. After famously saying that he was behind Eagleton "1000 percent," McGovern had second thoughts and accepted Eagleton's offer to step aside. As the candidate considered potential replacement running mates, I suggested that he choose Sarge Shriver, who was the late John Kennedy's brother-in-law and the most popular of the Kennedy clan. This would cinch Kennedy support for the campaign. I was delighted when Sarge was added to the ticket, but it didn't matter in the end. Nixon clobbered McGovern, who carried only Massachusetts and the District of Columbia. He even failed to win his home state of South Dakota.

Meanwhile, I was trying to keep Democratic Senate candidates from being dragged down by the undertow of the McGovern campaign. Democrats were in control of the Senate, 55–45, but as Election Day approached, our majority seemed precarious. Of the thirty-three Senate contests in 1972, we did have the numerical advantage, as nineteen Republican-held seats were up, while we had to defend only fourteen Democratic seats. But eight of our seats were in the South, where Republicans were coming on fast. And every Republican was hell-bent on tying our candidates to McGovern. In response our party's candidates were running on their own rather than as part of the national Democratic ticket.

On election night, even as Nixon trounced McGovern, we increased our lead in the Senate by two seats. We upset four Republican incumbents who had been considered safe—Gordon Allott of Colorado, J. Caleb Boggs of Delaware, Jack Miller of Iowa, and Margaret Chase Smith of Maine, the only woman in the Senate. Our pick-ups included Joe Biden in Delaware, who is a very effective lawmaker to this day, as well as Dick Clark in Iowa, Floyd Haskell in Colorado, and William Hathaway in Maine.

We lost only one of our incumbents, William Spong of Virginia. I was disappointed to see my friend Bill defeated in a very close race, but he was betwixt and between, never endorsing either McGovern or Nixon. That indecisiveness cost Spong, a good legislator but not a very adept politician. He managed to alienate both Democrats and Republicans. Furthermore his candidacy was badly hurt by Nixon's landslide, which really had an impact in Virginia. The President carried the state by nearly thirty-eight points and won all but one county.

When I was quizzed by reporters about the results, I described the impact of McGovern's candidacy on others on the Democratic slate. "I thank heaven I wasn't running this time," I said in the November 14, 1972, press briefing. "I traveled to those states and campaigned in North and South Carolina [where Thurmond was reelected], Florida, New Mexico, and Texas and other places, and we were running not for McGovern but from McGovern in all those places. Now that's sad when you can't run with your national ticket. Here's [Alabama Senator] John Sparkman, the vice-presidential candidate in 1952, in effect repudiating the national ticket in order to get reelected in 1972."

One of the first calls I made after election night was to George Meany, the president of the AFL-CIO. I was a right-to-work Democrat and never all that close to the national labor groups, but I had to thank Meany for the huge impact that the unions had in boosting our candidates. I readily acknowledge that we could not have done so well without labor's help.

The 1972 presidential campaign set new records for spending, a trend that had been worrisome to the public for some time. The high price of broadcast advertising—and its increasing importance—had sent spending through the roof. In the 1956 elections, spending for all federal campaigns was on the order of $155 million, of which $9.8 million went for radio and TV advertising. A dozen years later, in 1968, the overall spending figure was about $300 million—nearly twice as much as in 1956—and media expenditures had jumped sixfold, to nearly $59 million.[6]

The 1968 presidential election had set new records for spending, as did the 1970 congressional midterm races. The public was increasingly aware of the role of special interest groups, such as labor unions and the National Rifle Association, that tried to buy influence. Twisting the arms of wealthy corporate honchos for money became a routine practice for party operatives. Various executives of industry complained to me about it. It also is a fact that Republicans outpaced Democrats in raising money. Some old Democratic bulls, who had been reelected time and again and had become "legends" in their home states, barely campaigned at this stage of their careers. But even they became spooked by the possibility that some bright young millionaire like Kennedy or others with loads of personal wealth could knock them off. They had to act—if for no other reason than self-preservation.

As the DSCC chairman, I was sort of on the "hot seat" as the Democrats' point man in helping our candidates raise money. At the same time, like most of my colleagues, I supported moves to change the law so that the public would know who was ponying up all that loot. Our citizens should not be kept in the dark about campaign donors. After holding hearings on this subject, the Senate Commerce Committee unanimously concluded: "The necessity for campaign reform is now beyond question and transcends special or partisan interests."

Until 1971 we were operating for the most part under the Federal Corrupt Practices Act of 1925, an outdated campaign-finance law that had been passed in the wake of the Teapot Dome scandal. Recognizing the need for change, Republicans and Democrats joined in an overwhelmingly bipartisan vote to pass the Federal Election Campaign Act of 1971. For the first time in more than four decades, both the House and Senate had come together to enact major campaign-finance reform. Now candidates were required to report all contributions of one hundred dollars or more on a quarterly basis, and even the amount of money a candidate gave to his own campaign was strictly limited. More important, a spending limit was established on media advertising, the greatest costs of a campaign. As Democratic Senator Russell Long of Louisiana characterized it, "every mother's son" could hope to be President once we established the "check-off" system by which taxpayers could earmark one dollar of their taxes to a presidential campaign fund. Our concern was that without government funding, only the wealthy could afford to run in an expensive presidential race. Our new law also imposed strict public disclosure procedures on federal candidates and political committees.

Our efforts in 1971 showed that government worked in a bipartisan fashion. Perhaps we had acted in part out of shame, knowing that the 1925 campaign law was often ignored, and perhaps we were responding to the public fear that public office was being bought. But we acted without partisan rancor. We were legislators doing our job. Lawmakers had recognized a problem and worked together to address it.

Before the 1971 act could be fully implemented, the Watergate scandal exploded onto the nation's front pages. Suddenly revelations of slush funds and illegal corporate contributions forced us to take more sweeping action to clean up the system. Frankly we had to act after investigations laid bare the tactics of Nixon's henchmen, who put the squeeze on corporate honchos and shamelessly shook down fat cats. The details of those audacious shake-downs stunned everybody. Maurice Stans, who had stepped down as Commerce Secretary in 1972 to assume the post of chairman of the Finance Committee for President Nixon's reelection campaign, had pulled out all the stops to amass an enormous war chest for his boss. Various executives of the South Carolina Textile Manufacturers Association told me they were advised that their "fair share" was $350,000. Ten of them agreed to cough up $35,000 apiece.

So two and a half years after the 1971 law had been enacted, we were back at it, determined to pass a far more comprehensive campaign-reform measure. In October of 1973, by an overwhelming bipartisan vote of 60–16, we imposed limits on both contributions and expenditures in federal elections. We created the Federal Election Commission, an independent agency that came into being in 1974, to enforce the law. Our goal was to close loopholes and to create reforms in such a way as to head off the inevitable efforts to circumvent the spirit of the law. We also furthered the effort to provide full public financing for presidential election campaigns on an optional basis.

But we had little time to pat ourselves on the backs after passing this major reform. New York Senator James Buckley, a member of his state's Conservative Party, sued Frank Valeo, secretary of the U.S. Senate, challenging the constitutionality of the new law. The case made its way to the Supreme Court, and on January 30, 1976, the Court handed down a 137-page opinion that included five separate signed opinions. It was a mess! No layman could fathom what in the world the Justices were trying to tell us, but the bottom line soon became clear. In a remarkably ill-founded conclusion, the Court had tossed overboard key parts of our new law. The decision was stunning. While the Court deemed limits on contributions to be constitutional, it reached the opposite conclusion on restrictions on campaign expenditures. Somehow putting a cap on spending violated the free speech protections of the First Amendment. Does anyone think that James Madison intended free speech only for the rich? The Court had amended the First Amendment!

Rather than putting a lid on the cost of campaigns, the Court made our political system a mad dash for campaign cash. All you have to do is look at what happened to me in South Carolina. In my last race for reelection in 1998, I knew that the campaign would require $8.5 million. That translates into a constant push for money. I had to raise $30,000 a week, every week, for six years. I could have raised $3 million in South Carolina, but to get to $8.5 million, I had to travel across the country, from New York to Boston to Chicago and down to Florida and Texas and across the country to California. During every break we took on Capitol Hill, I had to hustle for money. And even when I was in Washington or back home in Charleston, my mind was on money.

Today the cost of a U.S. Senate race in the Palmetto State tops $10 million. A Democratic Senate candidate has no chance of collecting such a sum in Republican South Carolina. He must travel across the country, just as I did, hat in hand. Every House member is in constant rhythm of paying off debt and collecting for the next election campaign.

The money chase has a corrosive influence on every aspect of legislating. Fortunately we were still able to address big problems during this period, such as passing new environmental laws, but the thirst for campaign funds has simply become worse and worse over the years. It has disrupted our work.

In our efforts to correct the distortions caused by *Buckley v. Valeo,* Congress and the Court have for years engaged in various contortions without much success. I have supported various initiatives to deal with the out-of-control money chase. I have backed the so-called McCain-Feingold legislation and public financing. But those efforts fall short of what we need. Instead we should not allow the First Amendment's clear expression of free speech to be distorted. We need a simple one-sentence amendment to the Constitution that would authorize Congress to set spending limits in federal elections.

I repeatedly proposed such an amendment, which says simply: "Congress shall have power to set reasonable limits on the amount of contributions that may be accepted by, and the amount of expenditures that may be made by, in support of or in opposition to, a candidate for nomination . . . or for election to Federal office." Why go this route? Because it would make candidates less obsessed with fund-raising, curtail the clout of the special interests, and level the playing field for less wealthy candidates.

I introduced such an amendment with bipartisan support almost twenty years ago. In 1988 I got shot down when support for my measure fell seven votes short of the sixty needed to end a filibuster. Five years later, in 1993, I had a majority of fifty-two—forty-six Democrats and six Republicans—who expressed a "sense of the Senate" in favor of my nonbinding resolution that called for a constitutional amendment to limit spending. Unfortunately that was the high-water mark for my proposal. In 1995 I tried again, but my proposal was "tabled," or killed, on a 52–45 vote. I lost subsequent votes in 1997, 2000, and 2001.

The problem of course is that as the parties continue to battle each other in this endless footrace for donations, the country suffers. The infamous Jack Abramoff scandal of 2006 revealed the poisoning of our government. And you don't have to highlight such scandals to see that Senators and House members are so focused on organizing for their campaigns that much of the work on Capitol Hill is shaped by the endless political campaign. The bottom line is that the more our elected officials have to remain on the treadmill for campaign money, the less time they have to confer with each other, with their staffs, and with their constituents, much less perform other activities that a good legislator needs to do to continue to learn and to be effective.

8

Imperial Nixon, Cautious Ford

I hadn't been in the Senate all that long—just six years—when President Nixon signed that first bipartisan campaign-reform measure into law in 1972. It showed once again that we could rise above partisan differences for the greater good—even on such a difficult issue as changing the rules for raising money. Our work on that combustible measure reinforced my early impression of Washington that lawmakers on both sides of the aisle often worked well together, even on tough issues. We were not consumed by minute-to-minute political calculations for the next campaign.

Back then we succeeded in part because we got to know each other on an informal basis. Senators would have get-togethers for a drink or a barbecue or in other social settings. We also got to know each other during the day-to-day business of the Senate. Unlike today, there were no TV cameras fixed on the floor proceedings. If you wanted to know what was happening, you would head for the cloakroom just off the floor and swap stories with colleagues as you kept track of the debate. From time to time, a point needed correction, or a speaker needed support, and you could join the debate.

The Senate was a club. We looked out for each other. Today much of that collegiality has disappeared. Senators no longer have time to talk and listen to each other. Instead there is the constant pressure to get on the telephone to solicit money for the party, for the constant campaign. Fund-raisers that used to be arranged so they didn't conflict with the Senate schedule are now so frequent that the schedule is fixed to accommodate them.

I am not saying public servants were angels during my early years on Capitol Hill. We were not above taking partisan potshots from time to time. In fact during the 1970s, Congress was increasingly challenging Republican President Nixon's extravagant claims of executive power. Democrats led the charge against the White House, but some Republican lawmakers ultimately joined us in asserting our constitutional authority as a coequal branch of government. Ultimately, of course, Nixon's dirty tricks precipitated impeachment proceedings. Still, it is striking that in the first years after my arrival in Washington, we got much done, often on a bipartisan basis.

In fact during the Nixon years, Congress finally took some steps that have had a lasting positive impact on the way government works. By 1973 Nixon had been weakened by the Watergate scandal. As revelations of dirty tricks hit the front pages, Nixon's approval numbers sank. The President's own actions wound up backfiring on his effort to build a powerful executive branch that would dwarf Congress. Nixon's high-handed style was so over the top that we asserted ourselves.

We finally acted like a coequal branch by exercising our power of the purse, as provided for in the Constitution. The President had begun to cut off funding unilaterally for programs for which we had appropriated funds. Nixon was acting as if he were king—the Imperial Presidency!

Our problem was that Congress had no budget process. All we had were the Appropriations Committees. I had been fortunate to get on that important Senate panel in January 1971, with the help of Georgia Senator Dick Russell, who died that same month. Former Vice President Hubert Humphrey, who had returned to the Senate, also sought the seat, but as a southerner following the loss of a strong chairman from Georgia, I had the advantage. Also I was helped because Democratic Leader Mike Mansfield was no fan of Humphrey's. Even after having been on the committee a short time, I knew that each of the thirteen subcommittees focused on its own turf. Nobody in Congress was reviewing the nation's overall budget.

I thought it was irresponsible for us to pass measures without regard to total revenues and expenditures and with no thought about whether our spending would drive us into the red or not. Since my days as

Governor, I had advocated balancing budgets. It requires tough medicine and sacrifice. But here we were in Washington, in the greatest deliberative body in the world, and we weren't deliberating over the budget at all. We had ceded control to the President.

The Office of Management and Budget (OMB), created in 1970 to replace the Bureau of the Budget, quickly became a powerful force within the executive branch. When I was Governor, I cultivated my state lawmakers to get them to pass legislation, but Nixon relied on OMB and gave us the back of his hand. He decided on his own to eliminate or cut programs, including those that benefited the unemployed, farmers, students, veterans, small businessmen, the mentally ill, and people living in federal housing. And he didn't stop there. He also used his ax in such areas as vocational education and slum clearance. He relied on "block grant" programs to send funds to the states to get around the Washington bureaucracy, and he let the states administer the programs.[1] His moves prevented us from performing oversight of the executive branch.

All these shenanigans led Ted Kennedy to file a lawsuit that challenged Nixon's right to stiff-arm us over a program that we had passed to boost the teaching of family medicine in medical schools. In June 1974 Kennedy himself argued in federal appeals court, and compared the executive branch's treatment of Congress to something you'd expect in a banana republic.[2] The court agreed.

Both Democratic and Republican leaders recognized that we had to fulfill our constitutional duties. Our action was not about politics but about making government work as our forefathers intended. We no longer trusted the executive branch's budget numbers. We recognized on a bipartisan basis the need to develop our own data and budget, independent of the White House. As my friend Democratic Senator Sam Ervin of North Carolina, chairman of the Government Operations Committee, put it during hearings in 1973: "The Congress cannot long survive as a viable institution if it does not develop the capacity to gather, retrieve, and analyze budgetary data and to exert control over the budgetary powers."[3]

The story of budget reform is a case study of government working well. After overcoming resistance from various Senate committee chairmen, who were fearful they would lose turf and power, everybody came together to hammer out a measure to make Congress a meaningful player in the crucial number-crunching process. Republican and

Democratic members of Congress realized that Congress had no budget process. The Appropriations Committees of both the House and Senate were broken down into thirteen subcommittees each, but they failed to keep track of how the amounts they appropriated related to the overall budget. Each of the thirteen panels would hold hearings on the President's budget, but later, after debates on the Senate floor, we wound up with rising deficits and no clear accountability for the red ink.

We had to have overall control of this haphazard process. Under the leadership of Senator Edmund Muskie of Maine, who went on to become the first chairman of the Budget Committee, we passed the Congressional Budget and Impoundment Control Act of 1974 by a 75–0 vote. The House was almost as unified in passing the measure, supporting it by a 386–23 margin. On July 12, 1974, less than a month before he resigned from office in disgrace, Nixon signed the sweeping new budget act into law. At that point he was in no position to pick a fight with us.

We had succeeded in creating new Senate and House Budget Committees, with strict timetables to develop a budget. We also created a Congressional Budget Office (CBO) to assist in developing strategy and to serve as a counterweight to the executive branch's OMB. I was excited to be one of nine Democrats, along with six Republicans, to be named a member of the new committee. I remained on that panel for the rest of my Senate career and even served as chairman in 1980. When I retired in 2005, I was the last of the original members.

Ed Muskie, who had been the Democratic vice-presidential nominee in 1968, emerged as a gifted leader in his new role of wielding the gavel on the Budget Committee. Muskie and I had known each other since 1959, when we both served on the Advisory Commission on Intergovernmental Relations. We had become friends, and I admired him. He was tenacious and could work up into "righteous indignation" during Senate debates. The Maine Democrat had failed in his effort to be the party's presidential nominee in 1972, but he had returned to his Senate duties as resolute as ever. I especially enjoyed ending a day with a drink with Muskie and his good friend Democratic Senator Phil Hart of Michigan.

Muskie's hard-nosed approach was perfect for the new Budget Committee. Not all that long after the panel was up and running, he drew a line in the sand to defend the budget process. Muskie acted in August 1975—five months after the fall of Saigon and U.S. withdrawal from Vietnam—while the annual military procurement bill was being debated. The Senate had passed the bill, but when it came back for final approval, the House had added about $750 million to the $25 billion measure. In the scheme of things, that addition was not significant, but it exceeded what we called for in our first budget resolution.[4]

Muskie took on powerful Senate Armed Services chairman John Stennis of Mississippi. Though I favor a strong defense, I stood with Muskie, who also had enlisted the support of some Republicans, including Senator Henry Bellmon of Oklahoma. Bellmon, the ranking Republican on the Budget Committee, would later stand with Muskie on other occasions to defend the process. We shot down the military procurement measure on a 48–42 vote. A keen observer of that battle said at the time, "If Stennis had prevailed, he would have shown Congress that it could safely ignore the dictates of the budget process."[5]

Just a few weeks after my assignment to the committee, Nixon resigned and was replaced in the White House by Gerald Ford. The affable new President had spent his political career in the House, rising to become Minority Leader before Nixon picked him to succeed Vice President Spiro Agnew, who had left office after being caught up in a bribery scheme. Agnew ultimately pleaded nolo contendere to falsifying federal tax returns. In the wake of Watergate and the scandal that forced Agnew's ouster, the new President's first job was to reassure the country that we were putting those dark days behind us.

I was candid in my assessment of Ford. "He is sincere and likable, yes, but predictably and ordinarily political. He refuses to learn that once you become President, the best politics is no politics." Having weathered so many scandals, the country was ready for the truth about the state of the nation. I noted that we had recommended a summit conference on the economy in order to "steel the Congress and the people for the hard times ahead," but Ford refused to call for sacrifice.

The economy was tanking, beset by high inflation and the bulging deficit. We needed a show of presidential leadership, but Ford wasn't providing it. He had instead urged citizens to wear campaign-style buttons with the letters "WIN" on them for "Whip Inflation Now." I thought it was silly and told my constituents just that in a newsletter headlined "The Minority Leader in the White House."

This was the time that the best-of-the-best on government finance, Congressman Wilbur Mills of Arkansas, chairman of the Ways and Means Committee, went into the drink. Wilbur had partied too much with Fannie Foxe, the Argentine Bombshell, at a nightclub. Driving home, Wilbur and Fannie got into a fight—outside the car next to the Tidal Basin of the Jefferson Memorial. The ruckus caused both of them to fall into the water. Passersby called the cops, and Wilbur ended up under arrest. At the police station, when asked where his wife was, Chairman Mills allowed that she couldn't come out this evening with him because she had broken her leg. This caused Wilbur's administrative assistant to knock on the door of Wilbur's apartment, waking up Wilbur's wife. When she came to the door, the administrative assistant said, "Miss Polly, I've got good news and bad news." Asked what was the good news, the assistant responded, "Your husband, drunk, got into a row with the Argentine Bombshell and fell into the drink at the Tidal Basin. He's now at the police station waiting for you to come for him." Then Miss Polly asked, "What's the bad news?" "I'm sorry, Miss Polly, but I've got to break your leg." All in Washington then said that the WIN buttons stood for "Wilbur Is Naughty."

I compared Ford to other recent Presidents, who had seemed to grow in the job and undergo something akin to an "internal combustion" in which there was "an explosion of talent and dedication within the man causing him to summon up resources of greatness." I noted that Harry Truman, a bankrupt haberdasher, made historic decisions—NATO, the Marshall Plan, and the Truman Doctrine. After having defended the South's right to filibuster civil rights legislation early in his Senatorial career, Lyndon Johnson had emerged as a champion of civil rights once he was in the White House.[6] Even Nixon, the Communist baiter, had put diplomacy above politics in his opening gestures to the People's Republic of China.

Not so with Ford. "He refused to distribute the pain necessary to get the country moving again," I wrote in the newsletter. "Instead, he opted for a Madison Avenue approach of 'WIN' buttons that were lost and forgotten in a matter of weeks. . . . We waited, hoping and praying that . . . Jerry Ford would really come down hard on the big questions and lead the way to the solution. But there has been no spark—no rise to greatness. Gerald Ford thinks he is still the Minority Leader."

"Members of the House of Representatives are elected every two years, and they fall into the habit of constant campaigning," I added. "There is little time to reflect and grow. The name of the game is one-upmanship. You announce a program before the other fellow can, you introduce the bill first, you grab the headline. Your identification with a problem equates with its solution. If you can state on the stump that you first proposed this or you first introduced that, then you are a leader."

"The people are fed up with Presidents looking to the next election," I concluded. "Now, more than ever they want one looking to the next generation."

My comments were made after Democrats had been on a roll in the November 1974 elections, picking up forty-eight House seats and three Senate seats. (Later it became four, when John Durkin won a special election in New Hampshire.) I had handily won my reelection bid, with more than 70 percent of the vote. One setback that we Democrats had suffered in South Carolina was in the gubernatorial race. Charleston oral surgeon James Edwards was elected as the first Republican Governor in South Carolina since Reconstruction. Edwards's victory gave new ammunition to the antigovernment theme—that eliminating government functions should be a high priority—that Republicans had been pushing in the Palmetto State since 1964, when Barry Goldwater carried the state.

After my reelection in 1974, I was more determined than ever to throw myself into efforts to combat the rising deficit. I could not abide the government writing more and more "hot checks." So, as the Senate considered funding for various agencies in December 1974, I called for discipline. We had to end our profligate ways and not be halfhearted about it.

In a precursor to what years later was called Gramm-Rudman-Hollings legislation, I was very specific in offering an amendment to reduce spending according to a formula that agencies would be required to follow. We had gotten our fiscal house in order back in South Carolina, why couldn't we do the same in Washington? "We have got to reduce government spending in order to reduce the deficit, which is robbing the capital markets of the very funds American industry needs to recover from this recession, depression or stagflation, or whatever you call it," I said during the debate in the Senate.

Such calls for sacrifice and discipline fell on deaf ears. My good friend Democratic Senator Daniel Inouye of Hawaii said that my approach of an across-the-board reduction in spending was a "very drastic step." He and others blamed many of our problems on our growing energy crisis, which they said was caused by sheikhs in the Middle East and other external factors not in our control.[7] But I stuck to my guns.

We needed to lead by example. Instead we lacked the political will to take the tough steps to bring down the deficit. My proposal was shot down on a 63–31 vote. Still my efforts to attack the deficit were a constant in my career in the Senate. I didn't care how many times I was outvoted.

During this period energy issues were more and more on the front burner. In 1973 we had endured an energy crisis prompted by an oil embargo imposed by OPEC, the Organization of Petroleum Exporting Countries. The Arab-Israeli War of October 1973 showed how dangerous it was to be dependent on countries in the volatile Middle East for our energy supplies. But we had no national strategy. I had begun to hold hearings on the energy problem. I felt strongly that we needed to establish one agency in charge of coordinating our national efforts when it came to energy issues.

The idea of a mega-agency in charge of these issues had the support of Senate leaders whose committees had jurisdiction over energy matters, including Democrats Scoop Jackson of Washington, chairman of the Energy Committee, and Abraham Ribicoff of Connecticut, the Governmental Affairs Committee chairman. After some maneuvering, both chambers in the Congress overwhelmingly backed the creation of a new Department of Energy (DOE) in 1977. The Senate passed its measure by a margin of 74–10, and the House followed suit, passing its version on a 310–20 vote. The new department was the first to be created since we had established the Department of Transportation in 1966. DOE officially opened for business on October 1, 1977. It had taken a while, but in launching this new cabinet-level body, Congress had once again showed that the federal government worked. We had come together to address one of the most pressing issues of the day.

At the same time, I found myself fighting Big Oil on another front. In April 1975 I decided to take on the biggest loophole of all—the oil-depletion allowance that allowed oil behemoths to be exempt from taxes on 22 percent of their revenues. That loophole was put on the books in 1926, and over the years plenty of efforts had been made to eliminate that ridiculous tax break. Even President Truman took a swing at it in 1950, but came up empty.[8] Legislators from the oil patch fought like the devil to preserve this windfall for their constituents.

When I took it up, the always-tough and wily Democratic Senator Russell Long of Louisiana, chairman of the powerful Finance Committee, was poised to win again. First elected to the Senate in 1948, Long openly acknowledged making a boatload of money from investments in the oil industry and unapologetically did all he could to protect Big Oil interests. After all Louisiana was the number two oil-producing state in the country.[9]

The issue emerged as we were debating a major tax-cut bill aimed at jumpstarting the sagging economy. The House, with its big new Democratic majority after the 1974 midterm elections, had voted to eliminate the allowance altogether, but in the Senate nobody wanted to take such a position because it looked like a sure loser that would wind up postponing enactment of a needed tax cut.[10] Long's Finance Committee had taken out the House provision that would have repealed the oil-depletion allowance.

On the Senate floor, I fought to end such corporate welfare for the major oil firms while still allowing small independent producers to use it. Senator Ted Kennedy joined me in the battle. In the end we defeated Long's efforts. We'd been babbling about such tax reform for a decade. Naturally I was proud to have led the fight to eliminate the biggest loophole of them all.

But I caught hell back home for my efforts. I was criticized by business leaders who knew nothing whatever about the oil business, and by my home-state press, which even attacked my motives. One editorial accused me of "unpredictable behavior" and said that my actions were based on a desire to enhance my "liberal reputation within the party."

In fact the oil-depletion allowance has been the biggest rip-off on the tax books for fifty years. Prior to the oil embargo in late 1973, the oil companies had racked up profits of $1.1 billion annually. In October 1973 the Arabs—without any increase in their costs—hiked the price of oil from $3.40 to $11.40 a barrel. The resulting increases in oil and gas prices produced even more stunning profits for the companies, a huge windfall. Even after we eliminated this corporate welfare provision, the companies would be earning six times the profits they had two years before. We had been subsidizing windfall profits. I held hearings in the Commerce Committee for fuel economy in motor vehicles, and in June 1975 we reported a measure to require U.S. automakers to double the average fuel efficiency for cars within a decade.[11] We had to wean ourselves off gas guzzlers, but that was easier said than done. Our Commerce measure mandated an increase from about fourteen miles per gallon in 1975 to about twenty-eight miles per gallon a decade later. By hitting that goal, we would save two million barrels of oil per day. "The people are looking for direction," I said on the Senate floor. "It is incumbent on us to provide them with the leadership they seek." I noted that the automobile was "the largest end user of petroleum, accounting for nearly 40 percent of production," and that conserving fuel would boost tourism and the economy.[12]

Powerful automakers' lobbyists made the case that the measure would further cripple the slumping industry. When the bill went to the floor, these hired guns came at us hard. They argued that the changes would give advantages to foreign carmakers, force domestic companies to abandon manufacture of larger models, and hurt the tourist trade.

The industry case was the same old hogwash I had heard before. As the floor manager, I countered that the auto is the largest user of petroleum. Conservation would reduce gasoline prices. I had no confidence that the industry would follow through on a voluntary commitment to greater fuel efficiency. "The automobile companies are in business to make money, and their credo is, the bigger the car the bigger the profit," I said.[13]

As the debate grew heated on the Senate floor, a Chrysler vice president commented in a hallway of the Capitol that I was a no-good "son of a bitch." However, a few years later, when we were writing legislation to prevent Chrysler from going belly-up, he came by the office and apologized. He added that if Chrysler had only produced more Horizons, a more fuel-efficient car, the company would have survived without needing a bailout.

After we passed the Corporate Average Fuel Economy (CAFE) measure 63–21, President Ford signed it in December. Again we had tackled a big problem by passing bipartisan legislation that was in our national interest. We could not—and would not—sit back and do nothing. It was the right thing to do then, and in recent years Congress has revisited that issue. Finally in 2007 lawmakers passed legislation to raise the CAFE standard.

President Ford signed the measure even though it was a rejection of his push to stem oil consumption by allowing prices to rise. He swallowed hard and went along with the energy measure over the opposition of conservative Republicans and the oil industry.[14] He acknowledged that the legislation marked "the first elements of a comprehensive energy policy." The President had one eye on the calendar. Election Day was less than a year away. He needed some victory laps.

In the end, however, passage of the major energy legislation did not save Ford in the 1976 campaign. The Nixon pardon, a primary challenge by conservative California Governor Ronald Reagan, a poor debate performance against Democratic presidential nominee Jimmy Carter—as well as the continuing economic slump—were enough to send the President to a narrow defeat.

I was delighted at the prospect of a southerner from a neighboring state, former Georgia Governor Jimmy Carter, taking the oath as President. He had campaigned as an outsider, a man intent on cleaning up the mess in Washington and never telling a lie. That approach struck a chord with voters wearied by Nixon's shenanigans and wanting change. Unfortunately, as it turned out, the new President really was such an outsider that he never quite figured out how best to deal with Congress. Though we had some big victories that continued to show how Washington could work for the larger good, we also began to hit some road bumps. The promise of Jimmy Carter proved to be more than he could deliver.

9

The Carter Years

A Time of Big Battles

When Jimmy Carter arrived in Washington, he was all about being the anti-Nixon. He promised to bring truth telling back to the White House and put an end to the imperial trappings of the presidency. On his inauguration day, instead of riding pompously in a limousine in the parade, the new President and his wife, Rosalynn, walked down Pennsylvania Avenue. Carter later sold off the *Sequoia,* the presidential yacht, and he even carried his own luggage.

Small symbolic steps are one thing, but I really hoped that he also would bring a southern commonsense approach to the nation's problems. After all he had not only won a tough presidential campaign but he had also been a successful businessman, running that famous peanut farm in Georgia. It was quickly apparent, however, that Carter would often be hampered by taking a hands-off approach to lawmakers. He didn't realize that a President must do some wheeling and dealing in order to get proposals enacted.

Though he had some major successes on Capitol Hill, he could have done far better. A graduate of Annapolis, the President tried to run the government as he had captained his nuclear submarine. Once a policy was set, like a command onboard ship, there was not much follow-through with personal calls or conferences to cajole lawmakers to vote with the President. Carter just didn't hobnob with Senators or Congressmen. He didn't cultivate confidants on Capitol Hill. Plenty of

Rosalynn Carter, Joan Mondale, and Peatsy Hollings at a 1977 Ladies of the Senate luncheon. Hollings Collection, South Carolina Political Collections, University of South Carolina

Democratic lawmakers were privately frustrated at the distance they felt from the White House.

Despite those serious shortcomings, Carter was willing to take some big risks politically. The best example of course was the President's unwavering stance during the protracted fight in 1978 over the Panama Canal Treaties. The Panama Canal had assumed great importance in the United States over the years, both strategically and symbolically. On September 7, 1977, Carter and Panamanian leader Brigadier General Omar Torrijos Herrera signed treaties in which the United States agreed to relinquish control over the canal in the year 2000. Everybody knew that an enormous clash would follow as soon as the debate over ratification began on Capitol Hill.

I still remember the heated correspondence that some constituents sent me. Forget subtlety. Much of it in fact was vitriolic in a personal way—calling me a sellout and a communist sympathizer and such—while other South Carolinians heaped scorn on what they saw as capitulation by the President. Other Senators were bombarded with similar messages. Treaty opponents often were emotional. They saw the transfer of control of the canal as a sign of U.S. weakness.

Carter's agreement with Torrijos came after years of negotiation over the status of the canal. Other Presidents had also supported negotiating a new treaty. President Ford took a beating for backing a new deal when Ronald Reagan unleashed a barrage against him during the battle for the GOP presidential nomination in 1976. The former California Governor made the handling of the canal a key issue. His view, shared by many conservatives, was that we built it; we paid for it; and we should keep it. Such debates over control of the canal went back to the Eisenhower administration, when the President agreed to fly the Panama flag alongside the American flag in the Canal Zone, despite the fact that the House had overwhelmingly passed a resolution condemning such a move.

Initially I was very much opposed to the treaties. As early as 1973, in one of my periodic messages to constituents, I made clear my unhappiness about the way we were giving everything away. "I believe America's position should be one of complete sovereignty over the Panama Canal," I wrote. "The Panamanians want a Panama Canal operated by Panamanians, for Panamanians to benefit Panamanians. We cannot afford such a giveaway. From a military standpoint, the Panama Canal is of the utmost importance. It is vital to our safety and well-being. The Canal is essential to our trade and commerce. To relinquish control over the Canal is to allow others to dictate America's destiny."

Then after a trip in August 1977 with a Senate delegation to the Panama Canal, I changed my mind. I had read David McCullough's *The Path between the Seas,* which recounts our actions in building the canal. It tells of the sweetheart deal that we struck with the new Panamanian government to give us control. Ever since we signed that treaty in 1903, there had been disputes about sovereignty over the canal.[1] On my trip to the canal, I was greeted on the tarmac by Lieutenant General Bob Tanguy, head of the Southern Command. When I first met him twelve years earlier at the DMZ in Vietnam, Tanguy was a Lieutenant Colonel. A West Point graduate, a realist, and a "blood and guts" fighter, he was, I knew, dedicated to the best interests of our country. I asked for his thoughts about the treaty.

"In this day and time you can't own the middle of another man's country," Tanguy allowed. "We just lost fifty-eight thousand GIs fighting for self-determination [for Vietnam], and we've got to work out a solution whereby we can defend the canal. The Panamanians must control their own country."

Bob Tanguy's counsel was powerful. I also had heard similar messages from others in the command as well as from U.S. business leaders who had spent years living in Panama City. I talked at length with Admiral James L. Holloway III, the chief of naval operations and a South Carolina native. Holloway and others, with very few exceptions, agreed that ratification of the treaties was in our best interest. Everything I was hearing convinced me that it was time to revise that treaty and not be seen as an "occupier."

I explained in my regular newsletter to constituents why I had changed my mind. "After looking at this question from every angle, listening to both sides over the years and visiting Panama for another firsthand look, I join all our recent Presidents, the Joint Chiefs of Staff, and a bipartisan group of political leaders in supporting Senate ratification of the treaties," I wrote.[2]

The treaties, I added, "are the best safeguards for an open canal, and they guarantee America's continued access and continued freedom of transit permanently. If this treaty prevented our ability to use or defend the canal, it would be different. But it does no such thing. On the contrary, the United States continues to operate and defend the canal until the year 2000. After 2000 we retain the right to intervene to guarantee the canal's accessibility to U.S. shipping."

Anticipating the uproar back home, where passions were running very high against the treaties, I tried to put the debate in perspective by noting that we needed to learn the lessons of Vietnam. People do not like foreigners in their country. The Vietnamese didn't like it, and the Panamanians were no different. I wrote: "The Republic of Panama has developed a nationalism of its own. The people are proud; they are patriotic. They have learned the cardinal principle of government—the right of the people to determine their destiny. The ten-mile strip of foreign occupation in the heart of their country is viewed the same way as if the French had retained a five-mile zone on either side of the Mississippi."

At the same time I recognized the growing frustration in our country. The cry was going up that we had lost Vietnam and were pulling back from Korea. Many Americans feared that we were in retreat. But, I said, the Panama Canal Treaties underscore our moral strength. And I frequently noted that the treaties had the backing of much of the military brass and had been endorsed by every President from Eisenhower to Carter.

In this period, back on Capitol Hill, I was impressed that Minority Leader Howard Baker of Tennessee was working on rounding up Republican votes for ratification. I got together with Baker, told him how I'd changed my mind, and said I was sure I could persuade other Democrats to back the treaties. We went to work. Of course South Carolina's senior Senator, Strom Thurmond, and the press back in the state had not changed their minds. They were totally against the "giveaway." I made numerous appearances in South Carolina, and the battle lines were drawn when I debated Major General George L. Mabry Jr., a native of Sumter, South Carolina, and a Congressional Medal of Honor winner. We faced off at an American Legion post, and the Major General wasted no time in emphasizing the giveaway. I responded by quoting Admiral Holloway, a native of Sullivan's Island in South Carolina. I also cited the words of Lieutenant General Dennis P. McAuliffe, the U.S. commander of the Canal Zone.

Mabry and I were neck and neck, point followed by counterpoint, with the Legion building so packed that some of the onlookers had to stand. The climax came when Mabry referred to the Chinese embassy in Panama. "If we ratify this treaty," he contended, "it won't be long before the Communists from the People's Republic of China will control the Canal." I knew that the Republic of Panama had recognized Taiwan and refused to recognize the People's Republic of China. I immediately responded that if the Major General could prove that the Red Chinese had an embassy in Panama, I would withdraw from the Senate. Of course, you don't win an argument with a Medal of Honor winner before a crowd at an American Legion post. At least his mistake let me get out of that meeting alive.

Opposition to the treaties was manufactured by a small group of determined Senators, who were buttressed by lobbying organizations such as the American Conservative Union. They hired a direct-mail expert who bragged about using a machine that spewed out more than eighty million letters a year. He was churning out messages on Panama so that Senators, when asked, invariably reported that their correspondence was running ten to one against ratification of the treaties. In my message to constituents, I made the case that leaders do not make decisions by putting their finger to the wind. Edmund Burke put it best when he said, "Your representative owes you, not his industry only, but his judgment; and he betrays, instead of serving you, if he sacrifices it to your opinion." Sometimes in public service, you act despite the fact that your efforts are not supported by your mail. I suggested to the critics that they ask Admiral Holloway, a straight shooter who stated: "I'm strong for these treaties as being in the national interest."

As I was making my case back home, Carter was deploying every bit of lobbying help that he could muster. Heavy hitters from the defense and foreign-policy worlds, both Republicans and Democrats, were deployed. Treaty opponents were spending millions on radio and TV spots. They had even produced a documentary. Carter put everything on the line by making it clear that his ability to conduct foreign policy would be undermined if the treaties were defeated. I worked with Robert Beckel, who was handling this issue for the White House congressional-relations office. I told him that, if we just explained the issue clearly, we could sell it to the public. Beckel was convinced that my support for the treaty provided political cover for some other southern Senators and moderates who had been hesitant to back the deal.[3]

After more than a month of debate, there was much anticipation and anxiety as we finally came to the vote. Nobody was certain of the outcome. The first vote, on March 16, 1978, was on the so-called neutrality treaty, which guaranteed that Panama would be permanently neutral and keep the canal open to all nations' vessels. Carter had agreed to two conditions: the United States had the permanent right to defend the canal against any threat to its neutrality, and U.S. vessels could go to the head of the line during emergencies. In a rarity in the Senate, every member voted from his desk rather than following the usual informal style of walking in and voting. After all one hundred names had been called, the treaty passed 68–32—one more "aye" than was needed for ratification.

A month later, on April 18, the Senate, by the same margin, ratified the basic treaty to give Panama "full responsibility" for operating the waterway on December 31, 1999. Thurmond opposed both treaties. But we had won. I was delighted to celebrate that victory at the Panamanian embassy. I was the only U.S. politician there, having been invited by Ambassador Gabriel Lewis, to join the jubilant Panamanians.

Beckel tells a hilarious story about that period of high political tension as Senators fretted about the fallout from their votes. Democratic Senator James Abourezk of South Dakota had been threatening the White House that he would oppose the treaty unless a gripe of his on some unrelated issue was taken care of. As the vote was about to occur, Abourezk retreated to a phone booth in the back of the cloakroom just off the Senate floor. Democrat John Culver of Iowa made it his mission to get Abourezk to vote. "Get your ass out of the phone booth and come out here and vote," Culver said. Then he took some paper towels and shoved them under the phone booth door and lit them. "He had literally burned Abourezk out of the phone booth," Beckel recalled.[4] When he emerged and went to the floor, Abourezk was the last Senator to speak before the vote. He voted "aye."

The ratification of the Panama Canal Treaties is another case in which government worked. The effort had to be bipartisan in the Senate because only fifty-two of the sixty-two Democrats voted for the treaties. Sixteen Republicans also supported ratification—a testament to Howard Baker's persuasiveness. Despite the heated rhetoric and intensive lobbying by the right wing against the treaties, sixteen of the twenty-nine Senators who were seeking reelection in 1978 supported the agreements.[5] Such a hard-fought victory comes at a price. In 1998, during my last campaign for the Senate, my opponents still used my support for the Panama Canal Treaties against me.

On April 19, 1978, the day after the vote on the Panama Canal, the Senate took on another controversial issue. We overwhelmingly passed a measure to deregulate the airline industry. Looking back on it, I wish I had paid more attention to the debate. I had been preoccupied with the high-stakes battle over the Panama Canal Treaties. Carter was all for deregulation, and had appointed Alfred E. Kahn, chairman of the New York Public Service Commission, to head the Civil Aeronautics Board (CAB). Kahn, who was a true believer in deregulation as some sort of economic panacea, led the charge for ending controls on airline prices and routing on the theory that the carriers would jump into new routes that the CAB had kept closed. My friend Howard Cannon of Nevada, chairman of the Senate Commerce Aviation Subcommittee, championed the bill, as did Ted Kennedy.

I joined eighty-two of my colleagues in supporting airline deregulation, but I wish I had listened more closely to arguments made by George McGovern. George worried that small communities, such as those in his state of South Dakota, would be left out in the cold if the measure passed. He foresaw poorer service and higher fares for such towns. George was right. Airlines concentrated on serving major markets, leaving folks in South Dakota, South Carolina, and other rural, less populated states to suffer. I tried to make amends two years later when I led the charge against trucking deregulation in the Commerce Committee. As I told my colleagues then, I had become a born-again regulator. I lost the debate on trucking, but this notion that government regulation is bad and that the market always knows best is shortsighted. The fervor for deregulation, championed by Carter, was simply not justified. Government must not off-load its responsibilities to protect citizens from rapacious pricing schemes and indifferent service. Even Kahn acknowledged at a Commerce Committee hearing in 1987 that communities served by just one carrier face higher fares and less frequent service. As I listened to Kahn and other Transportation Department officials talk up airline deregulation in that hearing, I let them hear the perspective of those living in smaller, rural states. "My service has gone down, my price has quadrupled; yet I'm hearing an expert administrator say everything's working just fine," I said.[6] The embrace of deregulation marked the beginning of a new direction in Washington that would shortly be driven by a new President, Ronald Reagan.

Not long after the debates over Panama and aviation deregulation, the Senate became embroiled in a protracted, knockdown, gloves-off war over something called labor-law "reform." It pitted the nation's union movement—pressing full tilt for a change in labor laws, their number one priority—against those of us who saw this "reform" as little more than a power grab by unions. Big Labor was desperately trying to regain its declining clout. The debate consumed five weeks of time on the Senate floor, as opponents of the effort tenaciously filibustered the measure. We had to withstand an extraordinary six separate votes to end the filibuster, or, in Senate parlance, "invoke cloture."

"What they are really trying to do is change the rules and change the balance because the union movement is losing momentum," I told South Carolinians in May 1978 during one of the short taped interviews that we called "Straight Talk from Washington," an effort to keep constituents informed of my thinking. This legislation, I said, was aimed at the South, and I was not about to let it pass without a fight.

But the odds were stacked against us. First the measure had passed overwhelmingly in the House, 257–163, in 1977 with the support of

33 Republicans. In the Senate, Democrats outnumbered Republicans 62 to 38 and most Democrats, of course, were very close to organized labor. We had just reduced the number of votes needed to cut off a filibuster from 67 to 60. And Carter was itching to sign the bill to win credit with labor—an important constituency for him to cultivate. Unions of course were lavish in doling out campaign contributions. Meanwhile, labor bosses geared up to throw their considerable lobbying muscle behind this bill. When it came to the Senate floor, the legislation had plenty of momentum, as the Labor and Human Resources Committee had passed it 16–2.

I saw the measure as a radical step that would force unions on businesses large and small. It set strict time limits on votes by workers about whether they wanted to belong to a union. An election would have to be held within a few weeks after a petition was filed by a union. This provision for quickie elections would prevent employers from having enough time to make the case against the union. If an employer stopped production to tell the employees of the disadvantages of organizing, then union organizers could come on company grounds during working time to make their case for union membership. In short it was a ticket to enforced unionization. "These are dangerous type precedents," I said in one of my "Straight Talk" segments. "It would prey on small businesses."

When I was Governor, one of my selling points in attracting firms to relocate was to talk up the fact that South Carolina is a "right-to-work" state. Union membership is not compulsory. Most of our workers choose not to belong to unions.

The battle over labor-law reform was fierce. My office, like others, was inundated with postcards and other correspondence from constituents. It seemed that everybody had an opinion. In Washington the lobbying campaign on both sides was going full throttle. Hired guns for businesses and for unions stalked the hallways to buttonhole Senators and make their case.

Those of us who opposed the bill knew that a majority of Senators were for it. The only way to stop "labor-law reform" was by filibustering it. Senate Majority Leader Robert Byrd decided to apply as much pressure as he could to pass the measure. He opted not to use the usual "two-track" system, in which part of the day is devoted to a filibustered measure and part of the time to other business. That meant opponents of the bill had to be on the floor constantly. Byrd was trying to wear out the Senators who had joined in the filibuster by refusing to move to other business. We had to talk the bill to death—that's what a filibuster is.

We easily turned back the first several votes to end the filibuster. After those attempts, Byrd tried to make the legislation more palatable by amending it. The new measure would limit the access of union organizers to a company's premises, and it included other technical changes. I saw these moves as doing little to revise the substance of a very bad bill. "The garment of shield and sham should be removed from this hypocrisy and nonsense," I said.[7]

But Byrd's move made the margin closer. Those of us trying to kill the bill were sweating bullets because our own vote count showed that Byrd was close to rounding up the sixty votes needed to invoke the cloture rule. The Majority Leader was working overtime to coax reluctant Senators to join him. Knowing these dynamics, I figured I might try a little persuasion of my own behind the scenes.

We knew that Democrat Ed Zorinsky of Nebraska was one of the key uncommitted Senators. Both sides were working to get his vote. Unbeknownst to anyone else, I tried to lean on him through one of my old supporters down in Greenville, Freddy Collins. Collins's dad and Zorinsky's dad had been in business together for years in Nebraska and were good friends. I called Freddy and asked if he might have his dad put a word in to Ed's dad on this labor bill. Freddy readily agreed.

Meanwhile, as the roll call had started and we headed toward another in a series of close cloture votes, I cast my vote and then raced over to the fourth floor of the Russell Senate Building. I was headed to Ed's office, but I took a remote elevator so nobody would see me. When I reached the fourth floor, I spotted Ed walking down the hall. I said, "Ed, I really need your help on this one. This is a big issue back home and if you can vote my way, then I'll be your man on something you need." He just gave me a high sign.

I hurried back to the Senate floor. Tension was building, as the vote was very close. Zorinsky was one of the last to enter the chamber to cast his vote. I'm not sure that any other Senator besides me knew how he would vote. The suspense was broken when he voted against ending the debate. We had prevailed. I was determined to kill the bill for good, so when Byrd tried to send it back to the Labor and Human Resources Committee to be redrafted, I objected. I was trying to force yet another cloture vote that would clearly spell doom for labor-law reform.

Finally, after some parliamentary maneuvering, we recognized that even if the bill was sent back to the committee, the chances for a return to the floor were remote.[8] The debate over labor-law reform already had consumed much floor time and Senators were ready to move on. So we all agreed to let the Majority Leader send the bill back to the committee. "If and when" it was reported out again by the panel, it would be taken up by the Senate again. Managers of the bill insisted that they could recraft it in such a way as to win passage. But those of us opposed to it knew we could stop it again. Byrd never did bring it up again.

Just a couple of months after that debate over labor law ended, in August 1978, I jumped into a battle over the appropriate role of government in education. At stake was nothing less than the preservation of our public school system. I was up against Democratic Senator Daniel Patrick Moynihan of New York, a witty former Harvard professor who, along with Republican Senator Robert Packwood of Oregon, had cooked up a proposal to provide tax credits for private elementary and secondary education. The Senate had approved tax credits for college tuition a number of times in the past. By including elementary and secondary schools, the Moynihan-Packwood proposal struck an emotional chord in those of us who had long supported the public-school system. At the heart of their bill was the wrongheaded notion that the government has the same obligations to private schools as it has to public schools. I saw their proposal as nothing less than an assault on public education that would benefit the few at the expense of the many.

Moynihan was formidable. Having served in Republican and Democratic administrations as Ambassador to India and the United Nations, he was greatly respected by his colleagues. Still I was not about to let him get by with saying that education was never mentioned in the Constitution and that it originated in the United States with the Boston Latin School, though no doubt many could argue the latter. John Adams had stated in our country's early days, "The whole people must take upon themselves the education of the whole people and bear the expense of it."

This notion of tax credits for private education was simply repugnant to my view that our government's duty is to provide only public education. Its duty toward private schools is to leave them alone. I started in public service by leading the fight to fund public education. I championed South Carolina's first sales tax to help fund repairing and refurbishing public schools that served minority students. But to this day we have never appropriated enough for public schools. The first bill I introduced when I arrived on Capitol Hill in 1967 was for federal revenue sharing for public education. Too many states with large minority populations, such as South Carolina, had inadequate funds.

The Moynihan-Packwood proposal was bad news in the South. In 1954, when the Supreme Court ordered the public schools to be integrated, there were exactly 16 private secondary schools in South Carolina—4 in the City of Charleston: Bishop England High School, Ashley Hall, Porter Military Academy, and Gaud School for Boys. Today, we have 362 "white flight" academies. This tax-cut proposal would actually encourage the development of more such academies. As I said at the time, "You might as well call it a segregation subsidy." The result would surely be that public schools would never get adequately funded. Rich folks who send their children to private schools in New York would be the chief beneficiaries of this scheme.

I made it a priority to shoot down this bill. I teamed up with the brilliant Senator from Arkansas Kaneaster Hodges Jr. We were helped by expert lobbyists from the National Education Association, who knew this issue inside out. From the get-go, we knew that Moynihan's credibility on education would be a huge hurdle. He and Packwood seemed to have a clear majority at the outset of the debate. To reverse that advantage, we worked day and night and used a series of arguments to make our case. Historically public education was at the very heart of this country's beginnings, we noted. Anything that would reduce its role in society would turn our backs on our past. We also highlighted the constitutional prohibition against such aid. Many private schools were operated by the Catholic Church, so providing them with tax relief violated the First Amendment prohibition against government establishment of religion.[9]

Our arguments were straightforward and powerful: the proposed tax credits would benefit the few at the expense of the many, encourage the formation of substandard segregation academies, destroy the diversity of our system of public education, add to our country's sea of red ink, and violate the mandate of the First Amendment. Throughout the debate President Carter made clear that he would veto any tax bill that included tuition credits for private schools.

After the debate had been fully aired, Moynihan moved to table or kill my amendment to remove the tax-credit provision from the legislation. We defeated that move 57–40. Then when the vote on the merits of my amendment followed, we prevailed on a 56–41 vote. We still weren't totally in the clear. A House-Senate conference committee was taking up a compromise version of the education bill without the tax credits. But Bob Packwood was not ready to give up on his proposal.

Instead of trying to put their original proposal in the legislation, Packwood pushed a "pilot program"—a limited version of the tax credits whose constitutionality could be quickly ruled on by the Supreme Court. A number of Senators had opposed the measure because of their concerns that it was unconstitutional. Obviously Packwood hoped that, if the Justices decided it was constitutional, then he and Moynihan would have new ammunition to renew their efforts to win over skeptical Senators.

There was no chance that either Hodges or I would accept such an approach. I told Russell Long, the Finance Committee chairman, that I would filibuster the pilot-program proposal, and I then conveyed the same message to all the conferees. They were not about to spend more time on this issue at the end of the session when they had other priorities. So the pilot program idea was dropped. I have always believed that public education is the best investment a state—and a nation—can make. I was heartened to see that belief sustained in the Senate.

The defeat of the tuition tax proposal may well have helped to create some momentum for the creation of a separate Department of Education. We had shown that the federal government has a vital role in protecting public schools. President Carter's proposal for the new department passed the Senate in 1979 by a lopsided 72–21 vote. The margin was much closer in the House, 210–206. Despite plenty of GOP opposition to the new department, a majority of lawmakers had demonstrated a conviction that the best defense of our country is an educated citizen. Government worked. A separate department designation gave education the stature that it should have. Of course, from the moment it was born, the Education Department was a favorite target of Republicans, who repeatedly promised to eliminate it.

During this period I also was hopeful that Congress and the President would come together to pass needed legislation on one of my top priorities—trade. I figured that this southern President would recognize the need for government to change its course. In fact I wrote Carter during the presidential campaign to remind him of President Kennedy's pledge to keep textile imports at a level that would not endanger our existing textile jobs.[10] Carter was already on record as saying that, if elected, his administration would continue trade policies consistent with preserving U.S. jobs. My concern was that the platform committee at the 1976 Democratic National Convention didn't even refer to the issue, despite my having raised it, along with other delegates. Meanwhile the Republican Party platform had made clear that the GOP favored "bilateral agreements to protect our domestic textile industry."

Carter responded to me on October 2, 1976, and was reassuring. He wrote that he supported renewing our trade agreement, which was due to expire in 1977, because it provided access to our markets "while at the same time protecting American industry and jobs from a sharp and disruptive flow of imports." But later, when I tried to follow up with a bill to protect the textile industry, Carter was no help. I didn't know that he had been seduced by David Rockefeller to the designs of the Trilateral Commission.

My battle with Carter over trade was joined midday on Friday, September 28, 1978, a few months after the debate over the Panama Canal Treaties. The congressional session was about to end. It was a few weeks before Election Day, and the Senate chamber was just about empty as most members had left for the weekend to campaign. The Export-Import Bank Bill came up for consideration. I was hoping for a bill that I could use as a vehicle to push my proposal to protect the textile industry.

Trade bills are considered revenue measures, and all revenue bills must originate in the House. Since I couldn't initiate action in the Senate, I was always on the lookout for such a bill that had come to us from the House. I was not about to let one move without pouncing. That Friday afternoon, I had a clear shot. I pounced with my textile amendment. The timing was perfect. The Multilateral Trade Negotiations were taking place, and it appeared that we were about to agree to reduce tariffs imposed on foreign textiles entering the United States.

Why should foreign products come into our market free of such tariffs while our products are at a disadvantage when they enter foreign markets where governments subsidize their domestic industries? My amendment would prevent a reduction in tariffs on textiles coming into the United States. The Carter White House howled that my approach would torpedo the entire Multilateral Trade Negotiations. They cried that one industry should not get such a carve out and that European negotiators would retaliate against our farm products.

My friend Senator Abe Ribicoff of Connecticut, chairman of the Finance Subcommittee on International Trade, did his best to coax me to withdraw the amendment. He argued it would be defeated in the Senate or later in the House, and in any case would certainly be vetoed by the President. "We would be foolish to risk losing all the work and all the possible benefits of an improved international trading system just because one sector wants to be treated differently from any other sector of our economy," he declared during the debate.[11]

But I was unyielding as a matter of principle. This was not an issue on which I was about to engage in horse trading one favor for another. That Ribicoff would do his best to get me to reverse my position was no surprise: Finance Committee members are ardent free traders who generally are in lockstep with big business, the oil industry, and agricultural interests. Despite my affection for Ribicoff, I was not about to step aside.

Resisting Ribicoff's pleas, I noted that our textile trade deficit exceeded $5 billion, and we had lost about four hundred thousand textile jobs as a result of imports over the past decade. "At the Tokyo round of tariff negotiations, we do not want to cut another vein while we are hemorrhaging in this fashion," I said. Meanwhile I got a colleague to hold the floor as I raced to the cloakroom to start making calls to alert textile executives and round up support. I called Jim Self of Greenwood Mills; he was playing golf. I called Robert Small of Dan River Mills; he was playing golf. I called Bill Close of Spring Mills; he was on a trip. I called Bubby McKissick of Alice Manufacturing; he was playing golf. I called other friends to no avail. I knew that there could still be one textile executive working Friday afternoon—Roger Milliken, or "Big Red" as they called him. He and I were political adversaries. Later I came to admire him as the best corporate leader in South Carolina. But when Vice President Nixon made a campaign visit to Columbia in 1960, I intended as Governor to go to the airport and welcome him. Of course I wasn't for Nixon personally, but the people expect their governor to be courteous when the Vice President visits. I was told in no uncertain terms that Roger Milliken didn't want me at the airport. Roger and I had not spoken in years. But now the state and the country's interest was at stake. When I called Milliken, he answered the phone. I quickly told him what I had done and the predicament I was in; unless I got support for the amendment, I couldn't hold the floor beyond the next morning. I didn't mind going all night because nobody much cared, but by morning we had to show that there was a strong movement in support of textiles, or we'd lose our credibility. Roger "stayed on ready" when it came to international trade. He's the one corporate executive who supports American production. "Don't worry," he said. He went to work, and I went to filibuster. Meanwhile the administration turned up the heat to shoot down my efforts. Illinois Senator Adlai Stevenson III, the bank bill's floor manager, said that Special Trade Representative Robert Strauss, a Washington insider close to big business, had told him that he would urge President Carter to veto the bill if my amendment was attached to it. Roger spread the word. Before long calls were coming in from not just the textile manufacturers but the National Association of Manufacturers, the U.S. Chamber of Commerce, the farmers, the Wool Growers Association, the American Cotton Council, and the American Farm Bureau. When it was apparent that the blooming thing could pass, Ribicoff surprised me. He moved to table my amendment, which would kill it. We turned it back on a 56–21 vote. Then the textile amendment on the Export-Import Bank Bill was adopted by a voice vote.

Now that the bill had passed the Senate, the free traders and Carter White House dug in on the House side. My amendment was stripped from the Export-Import Bank Bill and put on the Carson City Silver Dollar Bill in the Banking Committee. Henry Reuss of Wisconsin was chairman. Reuss was a free trader, and the strategy was not even to have a quorum of the Banking Committee to meet and act. We were about to adjourn, but Congressman Kenny Holland (a South Carolina Democrat), Milliken, and corporate America overpowered Reuss. We secured a quorum of the Banking Committee, and the bill was reported to the House. As in the "perils of Pauline," at the very last minute, just before adjournment on Saturday afternoon, October 14, 1978, the Carson City Silver Dollar Conference Report was passed by the House. We amended it, and it passed the Senate by a vote of 48–13. Now we had to get a final vote on the House side. Speaker Tip

O'Neill had promised me a vote. But my problem was to get a quorum in the House. Finally on Sunday afternoon we obtained a quorum and passed the conference report. All to no avail. President Carter vetoed textiles.

There is no question that corporate America in 1978 was against free trade. It was 100 percent for protecting its production and its workers. And corporate America was the principal entity in developing markets overseas. U.S. Ambassadors the world around were trying to make friends with the host countries and weren't much help. There was a general undercurrent that the striped-pants crowd was selling out the interests of the nation. Government was working on all cylinders. Even though President Carter vetoed the bill, Senator Bill Roth of the Finance Committee persuaded the President to have the commercial counselors report directly to the Secretary of Commerce, as agricultural counselors reported directly to the Secretary of Agriculture—not the Ambassador. Now corporate America would work with the Secretary of Commerce to develop markets overseas.

At that time Carter was letting our defense needs down. The President and Secretary of State Cyrus Vance were moving headlong to negotiating a new Strategic Arms Limitation Treaty with the Soviet Union: SALT II. In June 1979 the President and Soviet President Leonid Brezhnev signed the deal. Carter addressed a joint session of Congress to try to win congressional support.

Having been one of two Senators to oppose the first SALT deal, I had little stomach for another treaty that furthered the Soviets' advantage. Although in 1972 my friend Scoop Jackson of Washington had added to the earlier treaty a provision that required future strategic-arms deals to be based on rough numerical equality in weapons, SALT II failed that test. As I often say, there's no education in the second kick of a mule. So, this time around, Jackson and I both refused to sign on to the deal—a blow to the White House.

The treaty only underscored my larger concerns about the state of our sagging national defense even as the Soviets were going full steam ahead. To address this disparity, Senator Pete Domenici of New Mexico and I proposed to boost our defense budget by 5 percent—and Scoop was with us. As I said during the debate, "It is time to wake up to the fact that we are engaged—whether we like it or not—in a serious competition with the Soviet Union, in which military strength inevitably plays a role. It is time to take our defense needs seriously. . . . While the Soviets build toward superiority, we allow our own strength, and consequently our own credibility, to ebb."

Budget Committee chairman Ed Muskie opposed our proposal because, he said, it would fuel inflation. Even Armed Services Committee chairman John Stennis was against it because he worried that defense lobbyists would use the big jump to justify higher, even reckless hikes in the future. Still, when the vote was tallied on September 18, the 5 percent increase was approved by 55–42 on a bipartisan vote. Thirty-one Republicans joined twenty-four Democrats to show that lawmakers still could come together on a bipartisan basis, identify problems, and address them. Government worked.

I also put the onus on the White House—and Carter. "The country's defenses are so weakened and imperiled that . . . only a President can reawaken it and give the proper leadership," I said. "It is very difficult [to do so] through Senators and amendments."[12]

Why, a reporter asked, did the bill pass despite the opposition of Carter, Stennis, and Muskie? "It shows and demonstrates a very strong feeling and misgiving that the American people have about their defenses sliding over the past ten years," I replied. As it turned out, that vote was one of the last displays of bipartisanship for some time. The coming elections dramatically changed the country's direction. And politicians found that crowds responded when they took potshots at Washington. Government was soon used as the scapegoat, the convenient target for politicians looking for easy applause lines.

As Sam Nunn of Georgia, Scoop Jackson, and I highlighted the need to boost our defenses, it was clear that SALT II was not gaining much traction in the Senate. Then external events really did it in. When Iranian militants seized hostages in our Tehran embassy in November, their audacity reinforced a growing sense of our national weakness. Support for SALT II took a hit. Then the Soviets delivered the coup de grace when they invaded Afghanistan in December. Carter asked Byrd to pull the treaty back from consideration on January 3, 1980.

Even before that setback, Carter was fighting for his own political survival. Three days after the embassy takeover, Ted Kennedy announced that he was a presidential candidate. Reporters had been asking me for some time whether I would back Carter for reelection. It was an easy decision for me. I figured Carter, a fellow southerner who had carried South Carolina in 1976, would keep the South in play. I knew that there was no way that Kennedy would have any shot in the Old Confederacy. I was still getting grief for backing JFK in 1960!

A group of us in the Senate, already anticipating a tough political environment in the 1980 elections, trooped to the White House to give the President our support. Danny Inouye of Hawaii, Dee Huddleston of Kentucky, Dale Bumpers of Arkansas, and I were invited to dine in the family quarters. I had never been to the second floor of the White House, and Carter gave us a tour, including the Lincoln Bedroom. After dinner, he directed us to his private office, where he really did a lot of work without the distractions of the Oval Office. As he chatted, Carter reached inside a desk drawer and removed what looked like pipe cleaners. As the President was talking politics, he occupied himself making "honey bugs," a favorite bait used by fly fishermen. He clipped and twisted the objects and obviously was looking forward to using them as bait.

Meanwhile we were telling him that it was time to kick it into gear. Frank Moore, the President's congressional liaison, and others on his staff had to get off their duffs. We exchanged political intelligence and such. Unbeknownst to us, Carter had been planning a possible rescue attempt to free the hostages in the U.S. embassy.

In April 1980 he launched the mission over the objections of Secretary of State Cyrus Vance, only to abort it when several of the rescue helicopters developed mechanical problems. Vance submitted his resignation as a matter of principle, and Carter picked Ed Muskie to replace him. After the Senate confirmed Ed to be Secretary of State in May 1980, I was suddenly the Budget Committee chairman.

Right out of the gate, I had to battle to maintain budget discipline while also sticking to my guns on the 5 percent defense spending increase. Presidential politics and interest groups' demands were playing havoc with getting a budget resolution passed. Trying to face down Kennedy, Carter pushed for more spending on favorite Democratic domestic programs and less on the Pentagon. We persevered and ultimately prevailed in directing more resources for our military.

President Carter was "smack dab" in his reelection effort. His campaign efforts were blighted by the daily announcement of another day of our hostages held in Iran. The President made a valiant attempt at rescue as suggested by the Pentagon, but it went down in flames. Then Carter was defeated in November 1980 by Reagan with a sweep that ousted six of the best Democratic incumbents: Warren Magnuson of Washington, Frank Church of Idaho, John Culver of Iowa, George McGovern of South Dakota, Gaylord Nelson of Wisconsin, and Birch Bayh of Indiana. Jimmy Carter is a strong person and far and away the nation's best former President, building homes for the needy and settling international disputes. The people denied him a second term because of an impression of weakness. More important, Carter's veto of the textile trade bill sent a definite message to corporate America.

Business is always ahead of the politicians. Business had been trying to protect its investment politically in Washington and through litigation in the courts. It had found the court approach cumbersome and costly. Now that the door had been slammed on them politically by a veto from a former southern textile Governor, corporate America determined to get used to jet lag. It decided to not just import the finished goods, but to outsource—produce offshore and import their own production. I championed three more textile bills through both houses of Congress but only with the help of labor. Carter started the outsourcing trend, and Clinton's North American Free Trade Agreement (NAFTA) turned it into a hemorrhage.

10

The Assault on Government

After the shock of the 1980 elections, we Democrats learned our lesson. We had fiddle-faddled and been complacent when we should have been aggressive. We allowed Ronald Reagan to strike a chord with voters by running against Washington. Although we had lost control of the Senate, there was still time before Reagan took office to show the public that a disciplined government could make a difference in their lives.

As chairman of the Budget Committee, I started making the rounds the second week after Reagan's election. I went one on one down the roster of senior Democrats who had just been tossed out of office. I buttonholed Birch Bayh, Frank Church, John Culver, Warren Magnuson, George McGovern, and Gaylord Nelson. I told each of them that we could forget about another Democratic President ever getting elected if we didn't show that we could do something about the budget deficit. They all agreed and said they would support me.

Then I went to the White House to see President Carter. I told him that he would be leaving office with a deficit bigger than the one he inherited from President Gerald Ford. I asked him to keep Jim McIntyre, the director of OMB, and Herky Harris of OMB's legislative affairs office off the Senate floor. I would get the votes needed for legislation to reduce the deficit. McIntyre and Harris had spent the year taking care of various Senators' needs in order to assure a favorable vote for Carter. I had already obtained commitments from the leadership and important Senators for spending cuts, and I didn't want Senators holding up their votes for something from the White House. When the

Republicans saw we were cutting spending, they joined in, and we reduced the deficit projected by CBO to less than what Carter inherited from President Ford.

That clear bipartisan determination was evident on December 3, 1980, a month and a half before Reagan was sworn in, when the Senate passed a budget "reconciliation" measure that cut spending by $4.6 billion and raised $3.6 billion in additional revenues. The 83–4 vote marked the first time in the six-year history of the budget process that we had trimmed the deficit.[1] The House also passed the legislation that same day, on a 334–45 vote. Our action meant that for fiscal year 1981 we had chopped more than $8.2 billion from the deficit.

As the outgoing Budget Committee chairman, I briefed Reagan before his inauguration in January 1981. He was ensconced in Blair House, across the street from the White House, when Alan Greenspan and I delivered a dose of reality about the state of the budget. The President-elect did not realize the extent to which the country was swimming in red ink—from spiraling inflation, the actions of the Organization of the Petroleum Exporting Countries (OPEC), and the energy crisis. Reagan had promised to balance the budget in one year, and it was obvious that he was shocked by our assessment. "Oops, it'll take three years to get it in balance," he said. We agreed that the target date for balancing the budget should be no later than 1984.

I told the President-elect that he could count on me to support spending cuts and business tax cuts to stimulate jobs and productivity. But I cautioned against across-the-board personal-income-tax cuts. They could create an inflationary spiral.[2] I wasn't alone in that assessment, as a number of leading economists warned that business tax cuts should come before personal-income-tax cuts. Tax cuts for individuals would force the government to write checks with more red ink—and the rising deficit in turn would cause higher interest rates. As always my pitch was to make balancing the budget a priority.

But Reagan would not buy my approach. He had campaigned for the so-called Kemp-Roth proposal that called for three annual 10 percent tax cuts for individuals. Reagan was not about to reverse course after making clear at the GOP Convention in July 1980 that it was a key part of his economic agenda. I thought it was ludicrous, and during the budget debate in November 1980 I said that this "Kemp-Roth, Mickey Mouse, across-the-board, free lunch, get-the-government-off-your-back" tax cut was not sound policy.[3] Even George H. W. Bush, before signing on to be Reagan's running mate, had derided supply-side fiscal plans as "voodoo economics." GOP Senate leader Howard Baker of Tennessee also had called it "a riverboat gamble."

President Reagan was an affable, likable character, but he was wedded to an ideology premised not just on a desire for smaller government but on a visceral contempt for government. His rhetoric went beyond the usual cheap politics of whipping up on Washington. The President's message was that government was the source of our problems. His irresponsible formulation translated into a policy of indiscriminately slashing government programs, contracting out programs, providing enormous tax cuts for the wealthy, and increasing the defense budget while cutting the revenue to pay for it. It was a recipe for disaster. By the time his second term ended in 1989, President Reagan left the country heavily leveraged, with a staggering debt. He had steered government far off track.

Early skirmishes between the Reagan administration and Congress foreshadowed all the problems to come in the next eight years. The Budget Committee, under new Republican chairman Pete Domenici of New Mexico, had begun its work, and our early inclination was to give the new President's economic game plan a chance. Still, we had a window, a moment, with a popular, newly elected President, to take some bold action to reduce the deficit. To take advantage of this, I went to Domenici and promised to get bipartisan support for my proposal to freeze the annual cost-of-living adjustment (COLA) for Social Security. "We shouldn't be borrowing the money to give anyone a raise," I said.

I knew we could sell my plan because of the reception I got when I described it to seniors during a debate at Council Bluffs, Iowa, with Democratic Congressman Claude Pepper of Florida. When I asked for a show of hands from seniors who would forego a COLA rather than increasing their grandchildren's debt, a majority of the crowd raised their hands. That plan would save $38 billion over three years. Senator Domenici thought well of my suggestion and made the case to Reagan in March 1981, when the President came to Capitol Hill. He got nowhere. The President said he wouldn't reverse his campaign promise not to reduce Social Security benefits.[4] Domenici responded that the President wouldn't be reversing himself because the cost-of-living increase was not a reduction of benefits. The President wouldn't budge. We needed the go-ahead from Reagan to show that the government really could be disciplined. Had he gone for it, I was confident that we could win the debate for making such a sacrifice. The Senate would pass it. But sacrifice was not the message the Reagan White House wanted to sound.

David Stockman, Reagan's OMB director, was a hard-charging former two-term Congressman from Michigan, who was driving the show. He was a true believer in supply-side economic nonsense. This youthful, thirty-four-year-old former divinity student failed to encourage the President to go with a serious, straightforward way to attack the rising deficit by dealing with Social Security costs, which accounted for a bit under one-third of domestic spending.

In those heady days, the Reagan team was wedded to the theology of cutting taxes. Some of these ideological warriors believed that, if we just reduced taxes in a big way, the economy would grow so much that it would produce sufficient revenues to balance the budget. It was pure Alice-in-Wonderland. Soon enough it was obvious that their plan was deeply flawed.

Despite his failure to get Reagan to tackle Social Security costs, Domenici continued to press ahead on the President's budget to get it out of the Budget Committee and onto the Senate floor. Like other Republican leaders, Domenici recognized that, notwithstanding his reservations, he was not about to spoil the President's honeymoon. After all, Reagan's smashing victory on Election Day had coattails that carried in enough new Senators to put the GOP in the driver's seat. The newly empowered Republicans felt indebted to the President.

It was a new experience for Democrats to write a budget as members of the minority party, and the press was quick to report our "squabbling."[5] I was blunt in critiquing some of my colleagues' efforts to open up our national pocketbook and spend more. Democrats were getting pegged as the party that lacks discipline when it comes to spending, I said. Our failure in that area was one of the reasons we had lost control of the Senate. The public, I told them, wants a leaner budget. "I don't see how we can become a real majority party if we don't represent the majority."[6]

At the same time even the Republicans who were concerned that we were headed toward more deficit spending recognized that this was no time to make trouble for the administration, especially in the wake of John Hinckley Jr.'s attempt to assassinate President Reagan on March 30, 1981. As the President recuperated from gunshot wounds, his popularity soared. Lawmakers gave Reagan a heroic reception when he delivered a nationally televised address before a joint session of Congress on April 28. He called for us to work as a team and to ratify his program to solve the nation's economic woes. It was good theater and great politics. That performance gave new impetus to his agenda.[7]

Reagan led the charge to enact his sweeping tax-cut proposal by personally lobbying members of Congress. He again turned to his strong suit—a nationally televised appeal on July 27, just a couple of days before we voted. Constituents responded by bombarding Capitol Hill with phone calls and telegrams urging us to vote for his plan.[8] Even some of my skeptical colleagues couldn't resist the tide.

I couldn't buy Reagan's program. During an early debate in the Budget Committee, I set out my concern that it was a bunch of hocus-pocus. It's time, I said, "to get back into the land of realism. There is no way to inflate the economy with tax cuts the size of the President's and move to balancing the budget by 1984."[9] It just didn't add up. Reagan, Stockman, and the others were dreaming and sending the country into the ditch.

Reagan's program guaranteed continued deficits. My solution was to reduce the Reagan tax cut from 25 percent to 15 percent, eliminate various additions to the tax legislation that Reagan had not sought, and cut out defense increases. The President could continue to eliminate regulations, retain his business tax cuts, and simply scale back the personal-income-tax cut, from 10 percent to 5 percent in 1983 and 1984. "This would give Reaganomics a chance to get off the ground," I wrote in my monthly newsletter to constituents in October 1981. "If the economy bounces back, interest rates go down, and revenues go up, then we can easily increase the 5 percent back to 10 percent."

But I didn't have much company. The Senate overwhelmingly backed Reagan's proposal to slash individual tax rates by 25 percent over three years. On July 29, only ten other Senators joined me in opposing the tax cuts—including one Republican, Mac Mathias of Maryland. By an 89–11 margin, the Senate had bought into the fantasy that somehow huge tax cuts and a big defense buildup could be accomplished without creating enormous deficits.[10] Thirty-seven of forty-seven Democrats voted for Reagan's proposal. House members also overwhelmingly gave their stamp of approval to the President.

I made no apologies for opposing the tax cuts. I critiqued Reagan's program in a message to my constituents and used a hypothetical to drive my point home. Suppose, I wrote in my monthly newsletter in

October 1981, that the Governor of South Carolina went before the General Assembly and proclaimed that we would start supply-side economics in the state. The Governor would make the pitch that we would attract industry and jobs and rejuvenate the economy by reducing revenues by 15 percent over five years. Given a budget of $2 billion, that plan would cost the state $300 million in lost tax revenue each year. The budget would be written in red ink, and we would fall into a deficit for the first time in twenty years. We'd lose our triple-A credit rating; industry would no longer come to the state; and the Governor, I wrote, "rightly, would probably be run out of the state."

Then I drew parallels to the federal government. Wall Street already had concluded that the Reagan administration's arithmetic "didn't add up." Without a course correction, investors were jittery. They saw mountains of debt in our future. We couldn't reduce the deficit by spending cuts alone. In the 1984 budget, three items would cost the government $750 billion: entitlements, such as Social Security, at $400 billion, which Reagan had pledged not to reduce; defense at $250 billion; and interest on the debt at a cost of $100 billion. Given the fact that revenues for 1984 would amount to only $750 billion, Reagan's plan left nothing for other government services, from agriculture to the judiciary to the FBI to the national parks!

By failing to recognize the reality of these stark numbers, Reagan wound up looking bad when he finally admitted a miscalculation. On November 6, the President acknowledged that he was not going to be able to balance the budget by 1984. Then Washington was rocked when the December 1981 issue of the *Atlantic Monthly* magazine hit the newsstands with a cover story headlined "The Education of David Stockman." In the story, the OMB director told William Greider, a columnist and assistant managing editor at the *Washington Post*, the truth about the fallacies of the Reagan economic agenda.

Stockman's confessions confirmed what I had been saying. Supply-side economics was an illusion to conceal the standard business-Republican economic doctrine of giving the wealthiest citizens the biggest tax breaks. "Kemp-Roth was always a Trojan horse to bring down the top rate," Stockman told Greider. "It's kind of hard to sell 'trickle-down,' so the supply-side formula was the only way to get a tax policy that was really 'trickle down.'"[11] It became increasingly apparent that the real aim of the Reagan plan was to run up deficits in order to eliminate government programs. By forcing the government to pay rising interest costs on its debt, the crew at the White House hoped to deprive Democrats of the opportunity to spend money to start new social programs. They even hoped to starve existing ones.

We now know that Stockman was beginning to sweat bullets over the budget even months before his confession to Greider. On August 3, just five days after we passed the tax bill, Stockman told the President at a lunch meeting of the administration's top economists that the deficit would continue to grow.[12] He even pondered whether the White House should keep its goal of balancing the budget by 1984. The President, according to one (unidentified) participant at the meeting, "looked stunned." Reagan decided to stick to his guns on that promise.[13] And even though he had rebuffed my proposal on Social Security, Reagan knew he had to do something.

Our problem in Social Security could be traced back to more than a decade earlier when political one-upmanship created havoc with the program. In 1972 Arkansas Congressman Wilbur Mills, the powerful chairman of the Ways and Means Committee, made reckless promises after launching a presidential campaign. In a bid for the senior citizens' votes, Mills said that, if elected, he would boost their Social Security benefits by 10 percent. President Nixon, who was seeking reelection, one-upped him to 15 percent. Nixon signed the enormous increase into law on July 1—in plenty of time for recipients to receive their checks with a hefty hike before they went to the polls. In addition Nixon approved automatic cost-of-living increases in Social Security when inflation indices rose. Since inflation climbed throughout much of the 1970s, the costs of Social Security skyrocketed. By 1981 the program's costs were going through the roof. Funded by taxes paid by workers for retirees' benefit, the program was taking a hit because fewer workers were supporting more retirees. Stockman saw the problems in Social Security as an opportunity for the President to take a whack out of the welfare state.[14] The OMB director decided it was no time for baby steps. President Reagan, who had opposed Senator Domenici's suggestion to hold the line on Social Security, now reversed himself and signed off on sweeping reductions, including large cuts for folks who opt for early retirement and big rollbacks in disability payments. As soon as the administration's proposal was unveiled, the President was pilloried for going back on his word not to touch Social Security. House Speaker

Tip O'Neill called the proposal "despicable" and a "rotten thing to do."[15] Critics charged that the administration was trying to balance the budget on the backs of Social Security recipients.

The popular President knew he had gone too far. He beat a hasty retreat. In a nationwide address on September 24, Reagan said that in order "to remove Social Security once and for all from politics," he would create a bipartisan task force to review all options and develop a plan to restore Social Security's "fiscal integrity." The goal was to get sufficient reserves in the trust fund to be able to meet the large obligations that would materialize when the baby boom generation began to retire. It came to be known as the Greenspan Commission for Alan Greenspan, the Republican economist who served as chairman. When the commission eventually issued its report in January 1983, it recommended a large hike in payroll taxes. It also called for a tax on benefits of high-income recipients—a change that had never occurred in the history of the program. And it recommended a six-month delay in the retirees' cost-of-living adjustment as well as a change in retirement age from sixty-five to sixty-seven by the year 2027.

After we had quadrupled the Social Security tax in the 1970s—a move that was supposed to fix the program into the next century—here we were following the same script all over again just a few years later. The legislation meant that the average worker would be paying more in Social Security taxes than in federal income taxes. At the same time, economists told me that these tax increases would result in the loss of perhaps one hundred thousand to two hundred thousand jobs in the next several years. I advocated a temporary freeze on cost-of-living increases. This approach was more efficient and fairer than the administration's approach. It would ensure the survival of the system. If enacted, my proposal would show that our government could deliver on its promises to retirees. My arguments fell on deaf ears. After a bunch of maneuvering, the Senate passed the administration-backed bill 58–14 on March 25, 1983. The House had passed it the day before by a vote of 243–102.

When Reagan signed it in a well-attended ceremony on April 20, he said the legislation would "allow Social Security to age as gracefully as all of us hope to do ourselves, without becoming an overwhelming burden on generations to come."[16] Those were fine sentiments, but lawmakers and Presidents never can keep their hands off the trust fund. They use it for any and every program but Social Security.

Indeed the history of the period from the time Reagan took office through the enactment of the Greenspan Commission's recommendations shows the President's actions didn't match his rhetoric. One earlier moment was especially telling. Reagan went on a campaign road trip in February 1982 to rally support for his budget and dared lawmakers to challenge him. "To the paid political complainers, let me say as politely as I can, 'Put up or shut up,'" he chortled.[17]

I took the dare. I went to Senate Majority Leader Howard Baker and to Pete Domenici and outlined a proposal that essentially called for a freeze on domestic spending, elimination of the July 1982 tax cut, reduction of the 1983 tax cut to 5 percent instead of 10 percent, a freeze on defense spending in 1983, and a 3 percent cap on future annual increases. The two GOP leaders urged me to put my plan out to the public.[18]

I predicted that my alternative would lower the deficit to $42 billion from Reagan's own forecast of $91.5 billion. By fiscal 1985, I said, we'd even have a $4 billion surplus. "Truly, the ox is in the ditch," I said, adding that both parties "have to pull together" to get it out. The administration wasted no time in taking potshots at what became known as the "Fritz Freeze." Treasury Secretary Donald Regan led the charge, calling it "absolutely ridiculous." But Howard Baker, who was looking for an alternative at a time when even Republicans on Capitol Hill were criticizing the White House budget, called it "intriguing."[19] My proposal didn't pass, but Republican lawmakers were clearly beginning to recognize that they had better do something about the deteriorating budget numbers. They knew the public was increasingly uneasy about the growing deficits.

Before the Senate addressed that issue, I became embroiled in a red-hot debate over the renewal of the 1965 Voting Rights Act in June 1982. It was the only time in our long careers that Senator Strom Thurmond and I faced off in a showdown on the Senate floor. I strongly favored renewal of the law while Strom never had much use for it. In fact, seven years earlier, in 1975, when the Voting Rights Act had been renewed, he had said it was "unfortunate that the Congress ever enacted such an unconstitutional piece of legislation."[20]

I had gone to the floor to give a feel for voting conditions in South Carolina over the years. Were it not for the law, literacy tests that were still on the books in the state would be used to block citizens from voting. "I am pleading on the floor to recognize the history and the background where the states themselves treated black voters differently," I said.[21]

"It is not easy or a happy thing to get up and tell of this particular history, but unless we can speak honestly and realistically and objectively of what we have learned from our experiences, then we are not going to be able to vote intelligently," I added.[22] This was no time to remove the federal government from ensuring that every citizen's right to vote was guaranteed. "The fundamental rationale [of the law] was to put an end to all forms of racial discrimination in voting once and for all," I noted. "This job is not done."[23]

I added some comments because I anticipated that my remarks might be mangled by reporters and misrepresented by critics. "I do not want the media to say that Senator Hollings ran down his state of South Carolina in order to garner the black vote, and all he is doing up there is just putting on a show for the black vote," I told my colleagues.[24] "We are doing way better, but there is still discrimination. And I do not know whether we will be dead and gone when all discrimination is removed. Hopefully, this act will help remove any that persists still today."[25]

The following day Thurmond all but accused me of attacking South Carolinians. "Yesterday's statement by my distinguished colleague from South Carolina regrettably focused almost entirely on the negative aspects of our state," he said. Clearly angry, Thurmond continued: "The implication that we in South Carolina are dealing with the issue of voting rights in any way other than a proper manner is simply inaccurate and without foundation. It ignores the efforts of thousands of our citizens to achieve a peaceful and harmonious society in which citizens of all races can participate in our democratic society. It is irresponsible to overlook these efforts and must be frustrating to our citizens who have worked so hard for the common good."

"There was no evidence that anyone in my state is being denied the right to register or vote," he insisted.[26]

"No evidence," I said incredulously when I returned to the Senate floor later that day; "I take marked exception to that and its accuracy." I cited violations in the senior Senator's own backyard—Edgefield County—where a voting-rights case had been brought by Thomas C. McCain, an African American and thirty-year resident of the county. The *McCain* ruling was written by Federal District Court Judge Robert Chapman, whose nomination had been suggested by Thurmond.

Judge Chapman, a former chairman of the Republican Party in South Carolina, found that in Edgefield, where Thurmond was born, "there is still a long history of racial discrimination in all areas of life. There is bloc voting by the whites on a scale that this Court has never before observed and all advances made by the blacks have been under some type of court order." Chapman's withering characterization of Edgefield's voting practices continued, "The law requires that black voters and black candidates have a fair chance of being successful in elections, and the record in this case definitely supports the proposition and finding that they do not have this chance in Edgefield County. . . . [There] is ample proof in this case that the black candidates tend to lose not on their merits but solely because of their race."[27]

Those findings led Chapman to the "inevitable conclusion that the rights of the blacks to due process and equal protection of the laws in connection with their voting rights have been and continue to be constitutionally infringed and the present system must be changed."[28] McCain appeared before the Judiciary Committee when Thurmond was chairman and provided copies of this 1980 ruling that detailed the history of egregious treatment of African Americans at the voting booth in Edgefield. Yet Thurmond was saying "no evidence" even though the evidence had been presented to him. Chapman had been appointed by President Nixon, and I reminded my colleagues that he was "a pedigree Republican, not a white-flight Republican."[29]

My comments were not designed to indict the people of Edgefield County, as Thurmond charged. Instead my goal was to fill a vacuum in the debate by describing how voting conditions over the years made it imperative to renew the Voting Rights Act. Responding to Thurmond's effort to downplay the need, I said this issue was so clear that I was "impatient" and had "a feeling of frustration as to why we are even debating it."

As the debate came to a close, Thurmond clearly still had misgivings about the bill. He offered an amendment to weaken the law, but it was defeated.[30] Ultimately the senior Senator capitulated. On the final roll call on the legislation, he voted with me. On June 18, the Senate passed the bill 85–8. President Reagan signed it on June 29. At a time when the government had gone off course on so many issues, it had worked, in this case, to make a difference in citizens' lives.

Meanwhile Reagan was determined in his first term to make good on his campaign promises of chopping away at government programs.

He seemed to take great delight in making Washington the bogeyman for all things wrong. On campaign trips around the country, the President pretended that he wasn't a part of the government. Somehow he was an "outsider" trying to straighten things out in what he called the "puzzle palace on the Potomac."

Consistent with that theme, in 1982 he appointed Peter Grace, the head of the multibillion-dollar W. R. Grace & Company, to lead a commission to identify waste, fraud, and abuse in government. I was a member of the commission, along with more than 150 corporate honchos and others who shared the desire to eliminate needless programs. We thoroughly reviewed all the agencies and departments and functions. The President seemed to be saying that if only leaders could get a handle on the monstrosity that was our government, we could make life better for the people. He was still looking for a magic bullet.

The fact was we needed to pull together as a people and sacrifice, not wait for others to find answers. When the Grace Commission eventually released its report in January 1984, we had come up with 2,478 recommendations that would save more than $420 billion. But many were in dispute, including post exchanges and commissaries on military bases. I contended they were part of the soldier's pay. Others thought them waste. The report showed that "waste" is in the eye of the beholder. Stockman, again in a confessional mode, told *Fortune* magazine in early 1984, "Some still think there are vast pockets of fraud, waste, and abuse out there. In fact, nearly every stone has been turned over."[31]

Even before the Grace Commission came forth with its recommendations, I saw the need for a change in direction in Washington. I felt the country needed someone who would be straight about the big problems that we had to tackle. No one offering sugarcoating or palaver or glib answers, but someone who would call for hard work and sacrifice. I know everyone in the Senate looks in the mirror and sees a future President, but I felt I had something to offer. Reagan's policies had been disastrous. Having served as chairman of the Budget Committee, I had been in the center of the debates over the deficit. I knew where we had gone off course and how to get the country back on track. Former President Herbert Hoover had appointed me to the task force on the nation's Intelligence in 1954. I knew all about foreign threats and national defense having served ten years on the Defense Appropriations Committee. I had the experience as an executive, as a Governor who had done the unpopular and raised taxes to bring my state's budget into balance and to get a triple-A credit rating. I could bring similar discipline to the national stage. We could do better. On April 18, 1983, I announced my candidacy for the White House and unveiled an agenda that was all about making government work.

11

Attacking the Excesses of Reaganomics

"We're in trouble, deep trouble," I said in kicking off my presidential campaign on April 18, 1983. "We've got work to do, lots of it. In the last few years, we have stalled, lost our unity, lost our purpose, and stopped pulling together for the common good. We have become a nation of single issues and special interests."

I decided to jump into the race because our government was failing the people. Rising deficits, reckless spending on defense, spiraling unemployment, and, perhaps worst of all, the failure of President Reagan to appeal to the common good made it obvious we needed a call to sacrifice.

My campaign platform was built around the notion that it was time to pay our bills and to restore the people's confidence in government. No more spending willy-nilly with no thought to the consequences for the nation's bottom line. Of course that approach would require discipline. Plenty of my friends thought that my running for public office as a conservative was ludicrous. How did I expect to win on a call for sacrifice? But I was not about to change my tune. My theme was consistent, starting with my first election in 1948. When government fails to pay for itself, citizens grow cynical about their elected officials, and problems compound. Even though President Reagan was well liked personally, the public was growing worried about his seeming indifference to the growing ocean of red ink that his policies had caused.

Instead of asking whether our citizens as individuals were better off now than four years ago—Reagan's famous question that helped defeat Jimmy Carter—I said in my campaign kickoff speech that we should be asking, "Are we as a nation better off?" That distinction really was important. Rather than appealing to self-interest, our leaders should appeal to the common interest. We should follow President Kennedy's challenge in 1961 to "ask not what your country can do for you—ask what you can do for your country."

"My campaign," I said, "offers little in the way of comfort. It rejects the politics of supply-side gimmickry. It rejects the politics of special-interest conservatism and interest-group liberalism. It disdains the politics of neo-this and neo-that. My campaign offers the politics of work. Share the work. Share the sacrifice. Share the benefit."

I ran to reverse Reagan's policies that had put us in such a deep hole. Even Reagan's own budget director recognized that the President was driving us over the cliff. After he left his job in 1985, David Stockman wrote in *The Triumph of Politics* that "the Reagan Revolution ended up as an unintended exercise in free lunch economics."[1] In that confessional book, Stockman belatedly acknowledged, "The records will show that within the span of a few short years the United States flung itself into massive hock with the rest of the world. And it occurred so swiftly that it was hardly debated or remarked upon until it was too late."[2]

Leaders in Congress, both Republicans and Democrats, knew that Reagan's economic policies were hogwash. Senator Robert Dole of Kansas, the Republican chairman of the Finance Committee, ridiculed the supply-side notion that cutting taxes would generate more revenues. Dole liked to tell the story of the good news and the bad news. Asked the good news, he would respond, "A busload of supply-siders just drove over the cliff." Then, he followed with the bad news, saying: "There was one empty seat." His friends thought he was talking about Jack Kemp!

I addressed those economic concerns in my campaign kickoff speech. "We're stalled for two basic reasons: Our leaders managed to sleep through important shifts in the world economy; and we allowed the Reagan administration to carry out fundamental changes that will eventually bankrupt our treasury, destroy our government and subvert our morale," I said. "We can no longer afford self-indulgence, and we can no longer afford Ronald Reagan."

My prescription for getting out of the ditch was nothing like those dreamed up by ad agencies for Reagan to make voters feel that it was "morning again, in America." Instead I appealed to citizens to look beyond themselves to a larger national good. We should freeze spending, I said, without cutting programs or reducing taxes. We had to address the budget deficit. My plan would save $700 billion over five years. The campaign boiled down to a debate about the role of government. Reagan, I observed, blamed government for our problems. Even as companies outsourced jobs and relocated plants overseas, Reagan chalked those job losses up to the "free market" at work. He saw no role for Washington as workers in hard-hit industries such as textiles suffered. "Imagine that," I said. "The world is going to hell in a handbasket made in Taiwan, and the President of the United States says our government is the problem."

To this day I think my campaign message was on target. But I ran out of money and had to withdraw from the Iowa caucuses. As a Democrat from a small Republican state, I couldn't raise sufficient funds. Most of the general public is not particularly interested in the election process and feels that there is plenty of time to make up its mind before the November elections. Those who do participate in the primaries are interested either in politics or in some special interest. The special interests need money to get out the vote—the more money, the more getting out the vote. I targeted New Hampshire to try to spring a surprise on the front-runner, Senator Walter Mondale of Minnesota. Mondale had the best organization and lots of money. As it turned out, I had too little of both. Money really is the mother's milk of politics. And I had nothing to offer but an appeal to fiscal discipline, common sense, and generosity. When I received 4 percent of the vote in New Hampshire, I observed that the results "got me back to a hard reality." (I took Dixville Notch, famous as the first New Hampshire town to announce its primary results)

I withdrew from the race on March 1. The hard political reality that you have to have boatloads of money to win had sunk in. I also faced another obstacle. Every time I "scored" at a particular event, my staff would report: "Yes, but they say you sound like Jimmy Carter." In the aftermath of Carter's presidency, voters were not going to take a chance on another southerner. I do not regret having given it a try. The country is strong. As I said in ending the campaign, "It was one of the best educations I've ever had." You learn by traveling the country that people are the same in all regions.

"The usual statement is 'a funny thing happened to me on the way to the White House,'" I said in withdrawing. "Nothing happened to me on the way to the White House." I endorsed Senator Gary Hart of Colorado, whom I felt had the best chance against Reagan. Meanwhile I returned to the Senate. Ultimately Mondale won the nomination and was crushed in Reagan's landslide.

During Reagan's second term, I resumed my attacks on the rising budget deficit, our misguided trade policies, and the intensifying effort of the U.S. Chamber of Commerce and big business to limit the rights of people injured by defective products to receive a fair recovery. Each of these fights has a common thread: Our government had gone off course and was no longer protecting our citizens. Our workers were losing jobs because our leaders had gone AWOL, refusing to engage even though we were in the midst of a trade war. And even the sanctity of jury trials was under assault by the hired guns for business and industry.

I was heartened in this period that my colleagues in the Senate had seen that we were being eviscerated by Japan's trade policies. Having been labeled a protectionist for so many years, I felt it was long overdue that Japan was viewed for what it is: a model of protectionism. The Japanese government had closed its market to U.S. goods. Its goal was not profits but market share. In its pursuit of that goal, it would sell for cost in international trade and make the profit in the domestic market. The imbalance in trade between the two countries had jumped from $19.3 billion to $33.6 billion—the largest disparity to that time that we had ever had with any other country.[3]

This gap was not lost on the public. Suddenly, more than a year before the 1986 congressional elections, Republicans already were concerned about the political fallout from our misdirected trade policies. Reagan, however, seemed detached from the plight of so many of our citizens tossed out of work by this stacked competition.[4] By late March 1985, the Senate had passed by a vote of 92–0 a resolution that castigated "unfair Japanese trade practices" and called for retaliation unless Japan opened its market to our products. A similar resolution passed in the House.[5]

A few months later, the House passed a trade bill to reduce textile imports from Taiwan, South Korea, and Hong Kong—three textile producers that were making huge inroads in our market.[6] The bill also helped the U.S. shoe industry, which was hard-hit by rising imports. When I tried to move that bill in the Senate, I was stymied by the free traders on the Finance Committee, such as Bob Packwood of Oregon, the chairman. At the same time, Republican Senators Daniel Evans of Washington and Phil Gramm of Texas, fierce critics of my proposal, were poised to shoot it down by launching a filibuster.[7] Reacting to their moves, I wound up sticking the textile legislation on the reconciliation bill, which could not under Senate rules be filibustered. My strategy was attacked by Russell Long of Louisiana, the senior Democrat on the Finance Committee, who argued that it would invite others to use future reconciliation bills for controversial proposals. Still I stood fast and led the way to defeat several efforts to kill the bill. I wasn't about to let the Finance Committee doom this measure. I circumvented the committee and began attaching it to other legislation.[8]

Seeing that my bill was not going to be shot down, Bob Dole, who had become Majority Leader in 1985, had no choice but to cut a deal. I agreed to remove the textile legislation from the reconciliation process in return for his promise to allow an up-or-down vote on the bill without a filibuster. On November 13, 1985, the Senate passed it 60–39. Several weeks later, the House accepted the Senate version by a vote of 255–161.[9] Lawmakers, on a bipartisan basis, had recognized that it was past time to engage in trade battles and not simply be spectators as our jobs disappeared.

I didn't think Reagan would veto the bill because of the political fallout it would cause.[10] Public opinion was with us, as reflected in increasing concern about the plight of workers being thrown into unemployment lines as a result of our trade policies. I felt a veto would be devastating to Republicans in the 1986 congressional races.

To further turn up the heat on the White House, we had textile- and apparel-company executives call on the President.[11] I was confident that we would finally enact textile legislation based on Reagan's own words. The President had told folks attending a fund-raising dinner in South Carolina on September 21, 1983, that, "recognizing the importance of [the textile] industry to the national economy, an employer of nearly two million people . . . our administration [will] seek to relate imports to growth in the domestic market."[12] Reagan added that while his administration believed the marketplace should sort out competition, "we know there are times when exceptions must be made due to special circumstances to support the Multi-Fiber Arrangement, which gives us the ability to protect our domestic textile and apparel manufacturers within the international system."[13] Those words echoed Reagan's promise during his presidential campaign in 1980.

But we weren't satisfied with promises. Business leaders from Virginia, North Carolina, South Carolina, Georgia, Alabama, and Mississippi lined up to make the case in Washington for this protection. Meanwhile I responded to the false charges that our industry was not productive or competitive. In fact the textile industry was spending $2 billion a year to modernize and downsize its operations. I pointed out that they were getting the job done with fewer workers. Where there used to be 20 in the card room, now none. Where there used to be 115 in a weave room, there were now 15. Our textile industry in the South was far and away the most productive industry in the world. Our companies could compete with other companies but not with other countries.

President Reagan, however, reneged on his pledge to support textiles. His reversal meant that U.S. companies would get no help from the government. After Reagan vetoed the legislation in December, textile companies accelerated their flight to more-accommodating off-shore locations. Their goal was to find places where wages were low, and health and retirement benefits were not required—and where governments subsidized and protected their businesses.

Reagan tried to make his action seem less offensive to those of us who had fought this battle with soothing words in his veto message. "I am well aware of the difficulties of the apparel, textile, copper, and shoe industries," he said, "and deeply sympathetic about the job layoffs and plant closings that have affected many workers in these industries."[14] The rhetoric could not disguise the fact that, just as Carter and Nixon had done before him, Reagan had turned his back on our nation's workers. One White House after another had refused to acknowledge the obvious: we were in a trade war. Instead of attacking, they disarmed.

Reagan's "sympathy" included a directive to Treasury Secretary James Baker to study textile and apparel imports to determine if they exceeded levels established in previous negotiations. He also would provide $100 million more to retrain workers who lost jobs because of imports. All that palaver was too little, too late. Who needs a study? The facts were clear. Our trade deficit was going through the roof. It was approaching $150 billion. Why? Our "partners"—other countries seeking the upper hand—were winning the trade war by paying sub-standard wages and doing everything else they could to gain an advantage. I said at the time, "Our industry stands helpless against an 18 cent an hour wage, child labor, polluted environments, trade cartels, and tricky government protectionism. With the Reagan Act of all talk and no policy, America's industry will be forced to locate overseas. The worker can say good-bye to his job."

Even as the trade battle played out, I was also fighting on another front. By the fall of 1985, a couple of my colleagues and I had decided to try to do something dramatic to stop the budget from sinking further into the red. Five years of the Reagan administration had proved that neither Congress nor the White House had the self-discipline to apply the brakes even as we headed toward an economic train wreck. It was obvious that government was not working. We were dangerously off course. You didn't have to be a "deficit hawk" to be seriously concerned about our fiscal sanity. It had taken us 205 years and thirty-eight Presidents to get to the $1 trillion national debt mark, and in less than four years we were closing in on a $2 trillion debt.

To do something about this alarming situation, I joined two freshmen Republican Senators, Phil Gramm of Texas and Warren Rudman of New Hampshire, to propose a sweeping change in the way we dealt with the budget. Our bill called for automatic reductions in the deficit over a five-year period until the budget was balanced by October 1990. The rationale for the bill, which came to be known as Gramm-Rudman-Hollings, was crystal clear. If government was ever going to work again, lawmakers and the President could no longer ignore the deficit. The legislation was consistent with everything I had been saying and proposing for years. It was my effort to bring South Carolina values to Washington. In fact it took a page from the way we had run things for years in the Palmetto State. When I first became a state legislator, almost four decades earlier, the South Carolina House of Representatives required that, upon a second reading of an appropriations measure, the comptroller must issue a certificate that the spending in the legislation could be paid out of the state's revenues. If it couldn't, the measure was automatically referred back to the Appropriations Committee. In that same spirit, Gramm-Rudman-Hollings required across-the-board cuts to comply with the agreed-on budget ceiling.

In order to avoid any shenanigans to circumvent the legislation, we had designed it to work mechanically. If Congress and the President

Senators Hollings, Phil Gramm, and Warren Rudman, January 9, 1986, at the time of the Gramm-Rudman-Hollings Act. Hollings Collection, South Carolina Political Collections, University of South Carolina

failed to write a budget that hit the deficit target for the coming fiscal year, the Gramm-Rudman-Hollings law would impose automatic, across-the-board cuts in federal spending to meet the target.[15] We used a fancy word, "sequester," to describe how the President would be required to withhold a chunk of congressionally approved spending if we had failed to meet our budget targets. We exempted Social Security from the automatic cuts in order to get the votes to pass the legislation. Essentially our proposal mandated a cut of $36 billion a year for five years to get to a balanced budget.

Gramm, a cocky, hard-charging former economics professor, was strongly wedded to the ideology that government was the enemy and must be chopped. Many years before, as an economist at Texas A&M University, he had said his research centered on "how to get rid of government."[16] He was fiercely partisan and had a habit of rubbing people the wrong way. The most dangerous place in Washington was between Phil and a television camera. Rudman was also a proponent of smaller government, although he did not share Gramm's fervor or ideological drive to eliminate broad swaths of government. Rudman was so put off by rising deficits that he was seriously thinking about not seeking reelection in 1986. He detailed his unhappiness in his *Combat: Twelve Years in the U.S. Senate.* "By 1985 I was disgusted," he wrote. "I agreed with Thomas Jefferson that for one generation to incur a public debt and pass it along to the next generation is a violation of natural and moral laws. I felt betrayed by Reagan and his advisers."[17]

I knew that my decision to join two Republicans on legislation that would literally force automatic budget cuts would alienate some of my Democratic friends. Sure enough, Lawton Chiles, a senior Democrat on the Budget Committee, was put off by the proposal. Chiles and I and our wives had socialized regularly over the years, but the Florida Democrat cooled toward me as I pushed legislation that, with its automatic spending cuts, seemed to take a bite out of the Budget Committee's authority. Chiles took umbrage. We no longer got together after work.

The unhappiness went beyond Chiles. Other Democrats worried that I had provided a bipartisan cover to what they saw as a radical Republican proposal. During the debate on the Senate floor, Democratic leader Robert Byrd of West Virginia threatened to filibuster the bill, as did Senators J. Bennett Johnston of Louisiana and Gary Hart of Colorado.[18] Plenty of Democratic constituencies hated the measure, as they feared it would result in massive cuts to their favorite social programs.

As the bill was hammered by some Democrats, President Reagan also had reservations about the measure. His concern was that it would take aim at the Pentagon, which would be subject to the automatic budget cuts the same way domestic programs were. Reagan eventually went along with the bill, as his advisers figured it would never pass. The President, apparently not fully understanding the way Gramm-Rudman-Hollings would work, continued to insist he would still be able to pour more money into the defense budget.[19] His Defense Secretary, Caspar Weinberger, did understand the implications of the bill for his department and strongly objected to mandated reductions in the Pentagon budget if the deficit target was not met. But the inclusion of the Defense Department within the law's purview was a big attraction to a number of lawmakers who felt it was past time for the Pentagon's belt to be tightened.

As Democratic leaders took potshots, I reflected that, if my spending freeze had been adopted several years earlier, we wouldn't have been in such dire straits to require such a dramatic step. I said, "If we could have gotten that deficit monkey off our back in 1982 with a simple freeze, you would never have heard of Gramm-Rudman-Hollings, and we would be near a balanced budget today."[20]

The sales pitch was truth in budgeting. Once both houses of Congress agreed on a budget resolution, all appropriations had to come within the budget. Despite all the vitriol aimed at us and at the legislation, we had some leverage. Nobody was happy about having to vote to raise the debt limit to $2 trillion. Our pitch to colleagues was that, by supporting Gramm-Rudman-Hollings, their votes would show that they were serious about doing something about all that red ink.

The Senate debate over the legislation in October 1985 occurred on a seat-of-the-pants basis. The proposal had not gone through the usual committee process, and formal economic and procedural analyses had not been done. "We're buying a pig in a poke," Byrd argued. "We're not prepared to bring the sword of Damocles down on the poor, the young, the old, on all the defense and domestic programs." Senator Johnston was just as adamant, calling the measure "legislative Armageddon" and "the most damaging to the constitutional process, the most extreme piece of legislation I have seen in the Senate in twelve years."[21]

In the end, however, Gramm-Rudman-Hollings was attached to the debt-ceiling increase. When the vote was tallied on October 9, it passed overwhelmingly, 75–24. We had fourteen up-and-down votes on amendments and carried the majority of Democrats against the opposition of the Democratic leadership: Budget chairman Chiles, leader Byrd, and Whip Alan Cranston of California. Our supporters included Ted Kennedy and John Kerry of Massachusetts and Chris Dodd of Connecticut. A majority of both Democrats and Republicans had joined together to do something dramatic to excise this cancer of debt that was eating away at our government.

After the Senate had acted, it took about two more months for the House and the Senate to reach an agreement on the precise contours of Gramm-Rudman-Hollings. Both bodies agreed that, should automatic cuts be necessitated, they would be drawn equally from defense and the domestic programs that had not been exempted. We had taken a first step toward responsible governing. At a White House ceremony on December 18, the President said: "From now on, when the public hears the names Gramm, Rudman, or Hollings, they'll think of deficit reduction." As he continued, Reagan essentially took defense cuts and tax increases off the table! He pledged to meet the targets in the legislation by "cutting or eliminating wasteful and unnecessary programs."

We had anticipated that Gramm-Rudman-Hollings would be challenged in court. Democratic Congressman Mike Synar of Oklahoma did not disappoint us. Before the ink was dry, he had gone to federal court to attack the constitutionality of the new law. On February 7, 1986, a special three-judge federal court panel found that our decision to empower the General Accounting Office (GAO) to order cuts in spending was unconstitutional. The GAO, the panel found, could not exercise authority reserved for the executive branch. The Supreme Court affirmed that ruling on July 7, holding that since the Comptroller General, who heads the GAO, is subject to removal by Congress, he cannot exercise executive branch powers such as ordering departments to cut their budgets.

To fix this problem we gave the OMB, in the executive branch, the power to pull the trigger on automatic cuts if the deficit target was not met. Stockman had moved on, but his performance at OMB had left plenty of us skeptical about whether we could trust the agency with cutting both defense and domestic programs. So we were very specific about how it had to administer the cuts. In order to pass the new legislation, we agreed to move the deadline for reaching a balanced budget from 1991 to 1993 and to put a limit on the automatic budget cuts for fiscal years 1988 and 1989.

Gramm-Rudman-Hollings worked for a "blissful two-year honeymoon. Congress and the White House stopped cheating and fibbing and settled down to cut the budget deficit from $221 billion in 1986 to $150 billion in 1987."[22] But we began to backslide. In short order the budget process was failing once again. OMB's estimates of the deficit began to be an exercise in wishful thinking. Its rosy estimates meant that we would avoid the automatic cuts called for in the law. We were back to playing games and tricks and dodges. The deficit began to grow again. Gramm-Rudman-Hollings was intended as a sword to prompt fiscal responsibility. Now Congress was using it as a shield to protect wasteful spending. I decided to divorce myself from the sham.

As the battles on the deficit played out in the 1980s, I found myself trying to prevent bad legislation from emerging from the Commerce Committee. Corporate America had retained plenty of hired guns to

*Senators Frank Lautenberg, Hollings, and James Exon during Budget
Committee hearings, c. 1987. Hollings Collection, South Carolina Political
Collections, University of South Carolina*

make the case for limiting court awards to victims of unsafe products.
Starting in the 1970s, various forms of product-liability legislation had
bubbled to the surface. Momentum for a product-liability bill seemed
to be growing. The effort to take away the basic right of citizens to
have their day in court is another example of government going astray.
Why? Citizens seeking compensation for injuries they suffered as a
result of defective products should not be impeded from a just recovery.
Yet powerful business lobbyists were constantly trying to change the
rules to stack the deck against these innocent victims.

A parade of business executives swarmed like bees around Capitol
Hill with stories about how they had been hit hard by skyrocketing
premiums for liability insurance. Something had to be done, they cried.
They blamed their rising insurance costs on runaway jury verdicts that,
they said, were being regularly awarded to plaintiffs. These tales of

reckless verdicts and such were exaggerated. The tort system was not out of control. I put the blame for their rising premiums where it belonged—on the insurance industry, which was looking to increase its profits. The State of Florida passed a products liability measure on the promise of reduced insurance rates, and after passage the rates went up.

Many Republicans who had long advocated states' rights suddenly sought to pass legislation to federalize this area of the law and override state laws in order to limit victims' recoveries. There was no good reason to set aside state law—except that businesses figured they would find more sympathetic Judges and juries in federal courts than in state courts. In late June 1986 Republican Commerce chairman John Danforth of Missouri decided to move a product liability bill that included a $250,000 cap on court awards for pain and suffering. His move was met with sharp resistance.

None of my colleagues was more moving on this issue than my good friend Daniel Inouye of Hawaii. Danny is highly respected, and his heroism in World War II, during which he lost his right arm, is well-known. "It is easy for those who have not been the victims to be setting the caps," he said. "It is difficult to put yourself in the position of the woman [who lost fertility]. She may not get married because of that disability. I do not know how much that is worth. The guy who loses an arm, because he is not as strong as the rest of us, may become gun shy and not date women, so he is a bachelor for the rest of his life. What do you do? What price tag do you put on that?"23

Though the committee did pass legislation to limit court awards and to set federal standards for product liability lawsuits on a 10–7 vote, I made clear that I would filibuster it. It did not reach the floor until late September, and at that point my threat was enough to convince Majority Leader Dole to pull it from consideration and allow more pressing matters to be taken up. This fight against product liability would consume considerable time over the years. I recall that one of the top lawyers pushing for "tort reform," Victor E. Schwartz, who was counsel to the Product Liability Alliance, a large group of businesses, thanked me profusely at Christmas for "another great year." Indeed lobbyists on both sides of this contentious fight were feathering their nests quite nicely as our battle went on and on and on.

On Election Day 1986 Democrats won big. We retook control of the Senate, picking up eight seats for a 55–45 majority. It was the largest net pickup since 1958. I took the reins of the Commerce Committee from Danforth. That perch put me in a good position to influence some of the major measures that were so hard fought between industries, such as overhauling the nation's communications laws.

In the last two years of the Reagan administration, I was involved in several contentious battles, including one over campaign-finance reform. The debate over imposing limits on the massive spending on political campaigns periodically reached the Senate floor, and in 1987 and 1988 it grew especially acrimonious. Majority Leader Byrd never wavered in his efforts to try to win enough votes to end a filibuster and allow a vote on sweeping legislation that he and Senator David Boren of Oklahoma were championing. Invoking cloture requires sixty votes. Their proposal would limit spending on a state-by-state basis. Republicans wanted no part of the legislation, which they saw as an effort to limit their fund-raising and keep them in the minority. GOP Senators also opposed another feature of the Byrd-Boren proposal, which provided for public financing for candidates who agreed to abide by spending limits. Critics also took aim at the legislation's reduction in broadcasting and postal rates for candidates who agreed to stay within certain spending limits and at the bill's limits on political action committees.[24]

I also opposed my Democratic colleagues' bill, which I saw as a convoluted solution when a far more straightforward approach made more sense. My proposed constitutional amendment to allow Congress to limit campaign spending is the cleanest way to repair the broken system, which the Supreme Court created with its ill-advised, poorly reasoned decision in *Buckley v. Valeo* in 1976. In its ruling the Court illogically decided that Congress could impose limits on contributions but that it could not similarly restrict campaign spending because such restrictions violated the First Amendment. Ever since the decision was handed down, I have highlighted its absurdity and tried to pass legislation to undo its pernicious effects.

During the titanic battle over campaign finance reform in 1988, I was well positioned to get a vote on my proposal because Byrd was in a deal-making mood. He agreed to put my measure on the Senate floor in return for my support of his cloture motion to allow an up-or-down vote on his bill. I was happy to agree to make that deal even though I strongly opposed his legislation as the wrong approach.

The Byrd-Boren legislation provided a cure worse than the ailment it sought to remedy. "For heaven's sake," I said on the Senate floor, "amidst the carnage and wreckage of the deficits, let's not pile on yet another open-ended spending program in order to entice candidates into [agreeing to] limits. Instead, go right to the source. Score a bull's eye by reversing the error of *Buckley v. Valeo*. Let us pass a constitutional amendment that empowers Congress to legislate campaign spending limits."[25]

The richer you were, the more "free speech" you had! Meanwhile, for those who were not wealthy enough to finance their campaigns out of their own pocket, the endless chase for dollars was polluting Capitol Hill. "To a distressing degree, elections are determined not in the political marketplace but in the financial marketplace," I said during the debate in 1988. "Our elections are supposed to be contests of ideas, but too often they degenerate into mega-dollar derbies, paper chases through the board rooms of corporations and special interests."[26] My amendment would empower Congress to control spending in federal elections. We didn't need the "contortions and complexities" that the Byrd-Boren bill contained, with its "piecemeal, shot-gun approach," I said.[27] Ultimately, after a series of cloture votes that had begun in 1987, Byrd removed the bill from the Senate floor when it lost yet another such vote on February 26, 1988.

As he promised, Byrd allowed a vote on my proposal. Republican Senator Mitch McConnell of Kentucky led the charge against it, arguing that it violated the First Amendment. On the contrary, I said, I was trying to overcome the Court's absurd *Buckley* ruling and level the playing field so that a candidate's speech is not enhanced or limited based on his wealth. Ultimately I sought to invoke cloture in order to end the filibuster and get a vote on the amendment. On April 21 my proposal received a majority—fifty-two votes—eight short of the sixty votes needed for cloture. A bipartisan majority of the Senate in 1988 had voted again to limit campaign expenditures.

At the end of Reagan's term, my actions on two very different trade measures underscored that I am not reflexively opposed to all such deals. I support those that allow us to compete on a level playing field. An example of such a pact involved Canada. Reagan and Canadian Prime Minister Brian Mulroney had negotiated a deal that was taken up by Congress in 1988. The agreement with our northern neighbor, which is our largest trading partner, was aimed at ending tariffs and other restrictions on trade between us over a ten-year period.[28] As a conservative Democrat from South Carolina, I believed in free markets such as Canada's. That nation also enjoyed relatively the same standard of living as the United States. On September 19, 1988, the day on which I joined eighty-two other Senators in voting for the U.S.-Canada Free Trade Agreement, I explained on the Senate floor, "I believe the bill will benefit U.S. companies and U.S. workers. Given a fair chance to compete, they are the most productive in the world."[29]

I always have favored promoting free markets as opposed to the oxymoronic concept of "free trade." Trade is a negotiation, a deal. There is nothing free about it. Just look at the European Union (EU). To join the EU, a country must have respect for human rights and the rule of law and an economy that satisfies the indicia of a free market, including property ownership protected by a respected judiciary, labor rights, and so forth. In other words, the EU requires a level playing field among its various members. The agreement with Canada was in that spirit. Precisely because of that, I embraced it. It went into effect on January 1, 1989, but a few years later, in January 1994, it was superseded by the North American Free Trade Agreement (NAFTA) when Canada decided to be a part of that deal.

On the very same day that Reagan signed the U.S.-Canada Free Trade Agreement, September 28, 1988, he vetoed another trade bill that would have addressed the woes of the textile industry. The President rejected a measure that I was championing to impose a comprehensive system of quotas to protect textile workers rather than relying on a bunch of negotiated trade limits. As I made the case that the government must stop bleeding the textile industry, the usual suspects in the free-trade camp in the Senate came out swinging. Republicans Daniel Evans of Washington and Bob Packwood of Oregon threatened a filibuster. Gramm later joined them in attacking the bill. They contended that in taking unilateral action to protect the textile industry, the United States would violate international treaties and invite retaliation.

Their arguments didn't prevail, as those of us worried about the unfair loss of more textile jobs carried the day yet again. The Senate passed the bill on September 15 with a 59–36 vote. The House followed suit eight days later. After Reagan vetoed the measure, the House, on October 4, fell eleven votes short of overriding that veto. The textile industry was now convinced that it wasn't going to get help from either a Democratic or a Republican President. Textile executives who had long taken pride in making products that were "crafted with pride in the

U.S.A." were now talking about outsourcing. I had been wrong to think the President wouldn't have the gall to veto a second measure in the face of this despair.

Ending the Reagan era with a discussion of that veto is fitting. He had gone back on his word. The textile industry was getting clobbered by increasing imports. The President had looked the other way. Just as he had been in denial as the deficit exploded, he had failed us again. His failures were further magnified in the final two years of his administration as the stock market took a precipitous drop on October 19, 1987, and the country was rocked by revelations of illegal arms sales in the so-called Iran-Contra affair.

When George H. W. Bush was elected President in 1988, I thought perhaps the country could right itself from the disastrous policies of the previous eight years. Sure, Bush had been Reagan's Vice President, but he also had spoken the truth when he called supply-side economics "voodoo." Though he had been a loyal member of the Reagan administration, I hoped he could change our direction and get the country back on the right track.

12

Missed Opportunities

When George Bush took the oath as President in 1989, everybody on Capitol Hill knew something had to be done about the soaring deficit. Ronald Reagan's profligacy had put the country in a deep hole. For more than two hundred years in which thirty-nine Presidents had served before Reagan, our combined national debt was less than a trillion dollars—exactly $909 billion. After eight years of Reagan, the debt had tripled to $2.6 trillion, with interest costs topping $255 billion a year. Reagan, who had pledged to end the "tax and spend government," instead had brought about "all spend and no tax government." Tax cuts for growth had produced growth in the debt—not the economy.

It was time to take away the punch bowl and go to work. I offered to help the new President. When Dick Darman, the incoming director of OMB, came to my office as he was making the rounds on Capitol Hill, I told him, "If the President is ready to impose a budget freeze and a 5 percent VAT [Value Added Tax], I will take the Budget chairmanship rather than Commerce." As the senior Democrat on both committees, I had that option. And I promised to round up the votes to report the legislation out of the committee to get it to the Senate floor.

I had worked with Dick's father, Morton, when he was president of the American Wool Growers Institute. Dick, like his dad, knew how Washington worked, having served in various high positions, including Deputy Treasury Secretary in the Reagan administration. As head of OMB, Darman was in a position to drive the new administration in the right direction. If we were really serious in wanting to set the economy right, my proposal would do the trick because it would generate revenues that would ultimately lead to the elimination of the deficit.[1]

A VAT is essentially a national tax on goods and services that adds a levy to a product at each stage of its assembly. I figured it would take about a year for the IRS to initiate the new tax and for the business community to implement it. But, once we imposed it, I estimated it would generate as much as $70 billion a year in additional revenue. If we went with it, the federal deficit—at just over $155 billion in fiscal 1988—would be eliminated in three years. As I made clear to reporters, it was "total folly" to think the deficit could be reduced without increased taxes.[2]

Darman later reported back that the President appreciated my offer, but he was not starting his administration with a tax increase. I was disappointed. The country was terribly off course. If Bush planned to change our direction, he had to do it at the beginning of his term when "the honeymoon" was on. No politician wants to raise taxes. President Bush obviously felt especially constrained after making his misguided promise at the Republican National Convention: "Read my lips, no new taxes."

Still, as I told reporters a few days after Bush's inauguration, the spirit of harmony between the President and the new Congress was fine, but it shouldn't be allowed to obscure the facts of life. "We're in a real crisis situation in this country economically," I said.[3] I didn't want to sound like Chicken Little, but the sky really was falling in on us, and nobody was doing much of anything about it.

Despite the cold shoulder from the White House and the resistance of Democratic congressional leaders, I decided to push for a VAT anyway. I saw it as the most sensible way to help deal with our budgetary woes. As I made my case in Washington, I also was blunt in letting my constituents know my views. I hoped to win them over. "Wake up, America," I wrote in one of my periodic newsletters in 1989. "We have a deficit and debt of astronomical proportions, and, if we don't act now, the slightest glitch in the economy will turn into a vast gulch."

Although the political forces were not aligned with me in 1989 or later, I continued to beat the drums for the VAT for the rest of my political career. Despite its popularity in many countries around the world, there has never been enough political will in the United States to enact it.[4] More than fifty countries—including Canada, Japan, and

China—have adopted the tax. As a result, they have an advantage over the United States in international trade. The VAT is an indirect tax. Direct and indirect taxes are treated differently under the rules of international trade. A country with a VAT gets a rebate on its exports while there is no rebate for countries with a direct tax. Also, imports into the United States are not taxed at the border, but when our products are sold in a country with a VAT, they are taxed at the border. In short U.S. exports are taxed twice while exports from countries with the VAT escape such double taxation. I've been trying to remove this disadvantage to U.S. manufactured goods for years, but to no avail. My colleagues know the need, but many have been elected on a promise not to raise taxes.

By late February 1989, I had begun talking up the virtues of the VAT, coupled with a spending freeze. My proposed 5 percent VAT exempted food, housing, and health care, and it was—as I said at the time—"our best bet for reining in our self-destructive borrowing binge." I made clear that to avoid any shenanigans, the revenues generated by the VAT should go to a special account—a Deficit and Debt Reduction Trust Fund at the Treasury Department that could be used only to reduce the deficit and debt and not to "stoke up the federal gravy train."[5]

My friend Democratic Senator Lloyd Bentsen of Texas gave me a hearing before the Finance Committee, which he chaired. One of my witnesses, Dr. Sijbren Cnossen, was an expert on the value added tax, having drafted it for the Netherlands, the United Kingdom, and elsewhere. He explained the mechanics and merits of the tax. After hearing us out, it was obvious that the Finance Committee members were sympathetic. Republican Senator John Chafee of Rhode Island even remarked quietly as the committee filed out of the hearing room that if they had a secret ballot, the panel members would unanimously support a VAT.

Of course, once the White House put the word out that it was opposed to the tax, no one was about to stick his neck out for it. The failure to take decisive action—often out of fear of TV attack ads in the next campaign—is one reason that nothing gets done in the Congress. Lawmakers are very sensitive to how they will look in their next campaign with these TV shorts running against them. Given those concerns, most of them were not about to support a tax that the President opposed.

My message then was the same as it is today. We had to take action and not just sit back and watch as other countries ate our lunch. After the Democrats retook control of the Senate, I used my perch as chairman of the Commerce Committee to focus on our industrial competitiveness. Our standard of living was at stake. The hands-off, laissez-faire attitude started by Reagan and continued by Bush put our workers and industries at a disadvantage around the world. Nobody was sounding the alarm.

One of Reagan's favorite lines was that his administration would "get government off our backs." Bush picked up that theme before he became President, when he headed the Reagan administration's task force on deregulation. One catastrophic result of removing government as a watchdog was the collapse of the savings-and-loan industry. We wound up devoting much of 1989 to debating legislation to bail out the thrift industry. Many hundreds of savings and loans had gone belly up after deregulation had enabled them to engage in reckless, speculative activities. Those failures ultimately cost the government in the neighborhood of $150 billion.

This love affair with deregulation and the hands-off approach of government to trade was taking a heavy toll on the economy. Other countries were actively assisting their industries and manufacturers. They were picking winners and taking over world markets. By failing to set an industrial policy, we were slow to translate many of our breakthroughs in technology into successes in the marketplace. Worst of all, Japan, with its domestic market closed to competition, engaged in long-range planning. By contrast Corporate America was and is preoccupied with short-term results. Executives nervously seek to make their quarterly reports as attractive as possible because they know these performance reports affect decisions of investors, which in turn affect the price at which the company stock is traded. Forget long-range planning—it's all about tomorrow's profits!

Already, the U.S. share of the market in televisions, machine tools, automobiles, steel, and textiles was in steep decline. We would celebrate some breakthrough in technology only to see other countries exploit it by rapidly making it a commercial success. As I said back then, "We get the Nobel Prizes, and the Japanese get the profits."

In these circumstances government can make a difference. In 1989, to address this issue, I focused on the reauthorization of the National Institute of Standards and Technology (NIST) within the Commerce

Department. As chairman of the Subcommittee on Commerce Appropriations, I earmarked funds to institute the Advanced Technology Program. It provides government funding, matched by the private sector, for various consortia of universities, private sector researchers, and others to speed development of generic technologies that can be developed for industry. The goal was to put U.S. industry on the same footing as our foreign competitors. NIST had been created at the end of the Reagan administration despite resistance from the White House. Now, as I was seeking to boost its funding, we were hearing the same arguments about the perils of "industrial policy." We had an "industrial policy" for private aircraft production—the government funding its research and financing its bills with the Export-Import Bank of the United States. But clichés—such as "the government shouldn't pick winners and losers"—were coughed up. It was as if all the top officials in the executive branch had collectively stuck their heads in the sand. They simply refused to see—or were in denial—about what was happening in the worldwide marketplace. Other countries were doing for their domestic industries precisely what my critics said we should not do. As a result we were falling farther and farther behind.

Why not step in and offer inducements for companies to invest in research and development essential to our country's competitiveness? Craig Fields, who was a whiz at the Defense Advanced Research Projects Agency (DARPA) in the Pentagon, told us that we were losing ground in part because such technological advances were stuck in the bureaucracy awaiting development. Corporate America wouldn't invest in long-range development unless assisted by government.

So I took the issue up in 1989 because I saw that reauthorizing NIST would help our industries develop cutting-edge technology and speed the commercialization of these new products. At the same time, I had seen our smaller companies having difficulty in mastering new manufacturing equipment. The Japanese and the Germans were going great guns in helping their businesses. And I had seen firsthand—many years before when I was Governor—what a difference agricultural research and extension services meant to farmers. So I proposed a new network of Manufacturing Technology Centers to provide advice and help to small manufacturers so that they could take advantage of technological breakthroughs that NIST had helped to bring about. This Manufacturing Extension Partnership Program was launched in 1989 and since then has grown to serve all fifty states and Puerto Rico. If we could become more competitive, it would close our trade gap, put people back to work, and generate more revenues. The White House remained wedded to a hands-off philosophy. When the Commerce Committee had hearings on the program in 1989, we heard from Deputy Commerce Secretary Thomas J. Murrin that the administration had not yet decided on the "degree of government involvement" it favored to promote emerging technology.[6]

What was more telling about the administration's lack of commitment was that it did not include any funds in its budget request for NIST's Advanced Technology Program (ATP),[7] but I kept the program alive in the Appropriations Committee. As chairman of the panel's State, Justice, Commerce Subcommittee, I made sure the Advanced Technology Program was funded. By 1990 I had directed $35.9 million for ATP and $11.9 million for the Manufacturing Technology Centers. These centers have made a real difference to so many small manufacturers, often located in heavily rural states such as South Carolina.

It was always a battle to keep the funds flowing for these programs. To protect ATP from the usual criticisms that it was "pork" and such, Senator John Danforth of Missouri, the ranking Republican on the Commerce Committee, and I worked to report an authorization bill. After extensive hearings and negotiations in 1991, we fenced off ATP to prevent "pork" from being included in its budget. We didn't want it larded up with wasteful or undeserving projects. We required that the technology for a grant had to be certified as unique by the National Academy of Engineering and that the applicant's industry had to put up 50 percent for the project. Finally awards could be made only by a group of professionals in the Commerce Department—not by the President, the Secretary, or a Senator or Congressman. With this breakthrough in January 1992, the House passed the bill 392–1. The Senate already had approved it at the end of the 1991 session. President Bush signed it on February 12, 1992.

Despite the progress on Capitol Hill in passing such legislation to boost our competitiveness, Darman and other top White House staffers never stopped pushing a hands-off approach by government. They even reportedly engineered a move to oust Craig Fields.[8] He was "reassigned" in the spring of 1990. After sixteen years at DARPA, he resigned rather than accept the "reassignment." Call it a triumph of ideology over common sense. One would think that our economic competitiveness would be a phrase on every politician's lips, but Fields's ouster showed otherwise. President Bush simply did not seem to be able to empathize with the economic insecurity that so many of our citizens were feeling. In the end his seeming detachment was very costly to him politically.

It was in this vein of protecting our workers and economy that I tried again to get a trade bill enacted. Having failed to overcome a veto by Carter and two vetoes by Reagan, I knew that the White House was the biggest impediment to getting a bill enacted. I redoubled my efforts to get a big enough vote to override a Presidential veto for this desperately needed legislation. Our case was straightforward: the textile industry employed two million workers—making it the largest manufacturing sector in the United States. If we did nothing, the industry would eventually be obliterated, and thousands of workers would be tossed into unemployment lines.[9] An industry that President John F. Kennedy found vital to our national security would be gone.

Foreign manufacturers were exporting textile and apparel products to the United States in record numbers. Imports of foreign textiles had tripled between 1980 and 1989—a huge jump that had resulted in a textile and clothing trade deficit of $26 billion in 1989.[10] Similarly imported shoes were gaining a dominant position in the U.S. footwear market—increasing from 50 percent in 1980 to 80 percent by 1989. Plant closings were becoming a common occurrence. We were getting the stuffing kicked out of us by low-wage workers in the Third World.

So in April 1990 I introduced a new quota measure that would, among other things, impose a ceiling of 1 percent growth annually on textile and apparel imports and leave the nonrubber footwear at 1989 levels. I had drafted the bill to get the support of Senators who represented farmers in the Midwest and others whose constituents included shoe producers. It worked. Both Senate party leaders—Majority Leader George Mitchell from Maine, a shoe-producing state, and Republican Bob Dole, the Minority Leader from farm country in Kansas—endorsed the measure. We made our case before the Finance Committee. I was not going to pull punches. The future of our domestic textile industry was on the line. This measure, I told the Finance Committee on June 7, 1990, was designed to "prevent the outright extinction of the U.S. textile, apparel and nonrubber footwear industry."

Two weeks later the committee, by voice vote, reported the measure out without recommendation. That vote enabled us to continue to make our case on the Senate floor. We faced determined opposition, led by Senator Bob Packwood of Oregon. "I can't think of a single, justifiable smidgen of comment to say in favor of this bill," said Packwood.[11]

The White House wasted little time in informing us that, if the bill passed, Bush would veto it. Following the tired script used by Reagan, Bush said the bill would harm consumers by forcing them to pay higher prices, violate our international agreements, and undermine ongoing trade negotiations. Packwood and fellow free trader Senator Slade Gorton of Washington also argued the bill would torpedo our trade negotiations and invite retaliation. I responded that such criticisms were off the mark. "This strengthens our negotiators' hand," I said. "They can say: 'Watch out for what they're doing up there in Congress.'"[12]

We defeated one amendment after another designed to water down or kill the textile legislation. After the Senate finally voted on the bill on July 17, we had put together the largest margin ever to back a textile measure. We racked up sixty-eight votes—eight more than we garnered in 1985 and eleven more than in 1988.[13] That number, sixty-eight, was one more than we needed to override Bush's veto. Republican Senators who supported our broad, bipartisan bill included William Cohen of Maine, Jim Jeffords of Vermont, Warren Rudman of New Hampshire, and both Republican Senators from Pennsylvania: John Heinz and Arlen Specter. In fact Bush barely hung on to a majority of Republicans in the Senate, 23–22.

The House took the measure up in September and overwhelmingly backed it, 271–149. Bush made good on the White House threat, trotting out the usual rationale for turning his back on textile workers. Besides arguing that the legislation would undermine ongoing negotiations, Bush said in his veto message on October 5 that the textile industry was doing quite nicely. "Economic indicators illustrate that the problems this bill is intended to address do not exist," he said. Five days later, the House fell ten votes short of the two-thirds vote needed to override the veto. President Kennedy had saved the industry in 1961, but now four Presidents—Johnson, Carter, Reagan, and Bush—had thwarted efforts to protect our nation's textile industry even after substantial majorities of lawmakers had backed our legislation.

Too bad President Bush didn't take the time or trouble to travel outside his bubble of economic advisers with their "economic indicators." If he had gone on the road to South Carolina and elsewhere around the

*President and Mrs. George H. W. Bush with Senator and Mrs. Hollings
at Ford's Theater, March 10, 1989. Peatsy Hollings was an active member
of the theater's board of trustees and for many years helped chair the annual
gala salute to the President and First Lady. Official White House photograph, Hollings Collection, South Carolina Political Collections, University
of South Carolina*

country and talked to people who once held jobs in textile factories,
Bush surely would have reached a different conclusion. The President's
indifference reinforced the impression that growing numbers of Americans had of him—detached, out of touch, and uncaring when it came
to the needs of ordinary, hardworking citizens. That image eventually
did him in when voters came to decide whether he should be "rehired"
for a second term.

During this period Texas Senator Phil Gramm and I had agreed to
appear on ABC's *This Week with David Brinkley* on September 16,
1990. As members of the Budget Committee—and authors of the

Gramm-Rudman-Hollings legislation—we had been invited to discuss the summit on the budget deficit that had been convened between senior administration officials and congressional leaders at Andrews Air Force Base. Sam Donaldson was up to his usual tricks when in the middle of the budget discussions, he veered off the subject.

"Senator," Donaldson asked me, "you're from the great textile-producing state of South Carolina. Is it true you have a Korean tailor?"

Before I could respond, Donaldson interjected: "Let's see the label in there. What is the label in there?"

"I bought it," I replied, "the same place right down the street where, if you want to personalize this thing, where you got that wig, Sam."

"Well," said Donaldson, now himself off guard, "I just want to ask you because it's [the story of my imported suit] out there."

"Well," I responded, "I've got to give it back to you, if you want to personalize it. That's the trouble. We play games with this thing. It's too serious a problem to be playing."

"I'm not playing a game," Donaldson said. "I'm asking you a question."

The recording room burst into an uproar. David Brinkley, the show's host, immediately gave a "time-out" signal to Gramm and me to get off the set. Phil and I ducked off to wait in the side hospitality room for Sam to come. The cameramen crowded in crying, "You got him. You got him. You've got to have a drink with him." I waited for an hour, but Sam didn't come off the set. As I left the studio, I knew this encounter would generate hard feelings. "Take a long look around this studio," I advised my press secretary, "we won't be invited back here any time soon." I had been on the very first *This Week with David Brinkley* show in 1981 and usually appeared four or five times during the year. Not any more. I was never invited back.

That episode shows another reason that Washington doesn't work these days. It's not just a reflection of lawmakers' constant preoccupation with chasing campaign dollars. We also are failing people because journalists too often are in the business of pursuing sideshows and not looking at the big picture.

For example the media could do a better job of reporting on Social Security. The inordinately high tax agreed to as part of the adoption of the Greenspan Commission's recommendations in 1983 produced surpluses in the Social Security trust funds. The President and Congress were using those surpluses to pay for increased spending on other programs. We would report a deficit, minus the Social Security surplus, in order to try to give the appearance of fiscal responsibility. I resented this deception.

Consequently I proposed an amendment to exclude the Social Security trust funds from all budgets. We should have truth in budgeting. That proposal passed the Budget Committee 20–1. I was shocked that Senator Gramm of Texas had voted "no." The two of us had spent countless hours to push Gramm-Rudman-Hollings, and we had succeeded by selling it as a surefire way to reduce the deficit and to guarantee that our budget numbers were accurate. Now Gramm had reversed course. He apparently opposed the public knowing the truth about our raiding Social Security trust funds to pay our other bills.

Republican John Heinz teamed up with me to make the case on the Senate floor that we must not continue to misuse Social Security. Our provision, Section 13301, ensured that taxpayers' money sent to Washington for the Social Security trust fund would not be siphoned off and used so the government could lie about the true size of the deficit. The logic of our argument was so powerful that the Senate passed our proposal 98–2 on October 18, 1990. Even Gramm reversed course again and supported it. Only Republicans Bill Armstrong of Colorado and Malcolm Wallop of Wyoming opposed it. For the first time, a law was on the books that prohibited Social Security from being abused.[14] It was straightforward. Presidents and Congressmen could not use Social Security funds for anything other than Social Security. We had walled off the program for retirees from raids.

I thought enactment of that law would end the deception. But, to my astonishment, it did not matter a whit that we had made it illegal to stick Social Security funds in the government's general-operating accounts. In the years since President Bush signed the Budget Enforcement Act of 1990 (formally known as Omnibus Budget Reconciliation Act of 1990) on November 5, he and Presidents Bill Clinton and George W. Bush, along with members of Congress, have brazenly violated the law.[15] They continue to use Social Security as a piggybank to be shaken for funds to mask the magnitude of the deficit. Meanwhile, as I had said in 1989, those government-issued IOUs to the trust fund that supposedly keep account of that money illegally drawn out of Social Security might as well be secured by Confederate banknotes.[16]

Is it too much to ask our elected officials to follow the law? Nothing inspires public cynicism more than when their representatives act as if the laws somehow don't apply to them. I would return to this battle several times before I retired. Politicians in Washington should have recognized that the Social Security trust fund must not be diverted to other programs or used to offset tax cuts. South Carolinians and taxpayers from every other state deserve to be assured that the dollars they pay into the system for Social Security will be used solely for Social Security.

Just a few months after we had passed the provision to cordon off Social Security, Congress became deeply embroiled in a debate over whether to authorize war against Iraq, which had invaded Kuwait on August 2, 1990. The Senate lived up to its billing as the world's greatest deliberative body as we engaged in a sober discussion over whether to authorize the President to use military force against Iraq if its troops were not withdrawn from Kuwait.

One must remember that we had supported Iraqi leader Saddam Hussein for eight years in Iraq's war against Iran. Back then we had pursued a policy of wooing Saddam with subsidized wheat sales to the tune of more than $5 billion. With the savings from our generosity, Saddam had been able to build a huge military. As the run-up to war accelerated, it was particularly stunning that only a week before the invasion, April Glaspie, our Ambassador to Iraq, seemed to reassure Saddam when he sought to find out the U.S. position as he prepared to invade Kuwait over a territorial dispute.

"We have no opinion on the Arab-Arab conflicts, like your border disagreement with Kuwait," Glaspie said, according to a transcript of the exchange. "James Baker [the Secretary of State] has directed our official spokesmen to emphasize this instruction. . . . All that we hope is that these issues are solved quickly."[17] The testimony in the Intelligence Committee was "we don't have a dog in this fight."

With the assurance that we would stay out of this war, Saddam invaded. We had no bases in Kuwait. We had a tremendous military base in Saudi Arabia. Bush suggested that the Saudis could be next on Saddam's hit list. But we knew that the Iraqi leader had no intention of provoking us by attacking Saudi Arabia.

British Prime Minister Margaret Thatcher was adamant that the United States must respond to the Iraqis' action. Days after the invasion, she lit a fire under the President, admonishing the commander in chief to be "'Churchillian' in handling Saddam." One of her senior advisers observed, "The Prime Minister performed a successful backbone transplant."[18] Within months of Glaspie's meeting with Saddam, Bush had assembled and launched a massive military deployment to the region in Operation Desert Storm.

I faulted the mixed signals that the administration had sent to Saddam. I said at the time, "Given this indifference or ambivalence prior to August 2, Saddam must have been surprised when, after the invasion, President Bush belatedly declared Kuwait's integrity to be a vital national interest of the United States, justifying war and the loss of American lives. If it is now U.S. policy to militarily oppose naked aggression anywhere in the world, then the 82nd Airborne is going to be a very busy group of men and women for years to come."[19]

Prior to the debate on the Senate floor, the Armed Services Committee held hearings. Democratic chairman Sam Nunn of Georgia urged the continuation of economic sanctions that had been imposed in August against Iraq rather than precipitously resorting to military action before the sanctions had a chance to work. Former chairmen of the Joint Chiefs of Staff also testified that they preferred a gradual buildup before resorting to force. Our best ally in the Arab world, Jordan, sided with Saddam. As a member of the Intelligence Committee, I was informed of all the ramifications of this effort. I concluded that invading Kuwait wasn't worth the life of a single GI. In retrospect I feel just as strongly that we should not have gone to war. Kuwait had rebuffed the United States when we needed an airstrip to land our aircraft during the Iran-Iraq war. Kuwaiti representatives had repeatedly voted against our interests in the United Nations. "They have not been our friend. They are certainly not a friend of democracy and human rights," I noted.[20]

When the debate reached a crescendo, many of us in the Senate were confident that President Bush would be rebuffed. But the President had a "come to Jesus" meeting with Republicans in the Senate and twisted enough arms to prevail. Nunn and I and other longtime supporters of a strong defense opposed the use-of-force resolution. On January 12, 1991, a closely divided Senate voted 52–47 to support the use of force if Iraq failed to withdraw from Kuwait and failed to comply with UN resolutions. The House followed suit by a 250–183 vote. When Iraq had not withdrawn from Kuwait after a January 15 UN deadline had passed, Bush gave the order to commence an aerial attack on January 17. After some thirty-eight days of such bombing, we launched a successful ground campaign and had liberated Kuwait by February 27.

Bush announced a cease-fire in what had been a six-week war. We had not sustained the large number of casualties that so many of us had feared.

The success of Operation Desert Storm, of course, had a political dimension. Bush's approval numbers shot up, and Republicans looked to capitalize on their good fortune. Senator Phil Gramm, the hard-nosed, aggressive Texan, was chairman of the National Republican Senatorial Committee during the 1992 election cycle. Although we had worked together on Gramm-Rudman-Hollings, he was looking to defeat me and others who had opposed the war. But the GOP effort to paint me as a peacenik would not wash with the folks who knew me best, South Carolinians. As a Citadel graduate, a veteran of three years of combat in World War II, and one of the Senate's foremost "hawks," I was not about to be pigeonholed as weak on military matters.

My critics' cacophony was deafening. I knew I had a battle on my hands as I faced the voters in 1992. As South Carolina was increasingly a Republican state, the national Republican Party smelled blood. Former Congressman—and a former supporter—Tommy Hartnett was the GOP nominee. He brought up all the old charges against me, from my association with the Kennedys to my support for the Panama Canal Treaties and my opposition to the Gulf War. He charged that I had lost touch with South Carolina. During one of my debates with Hartnett, I had just had it. I told Hartnett, "You're full of prunes."

Hartnett even used the racial preference ad that reelected Jesse Helms in North Carolina. This TV ad showed a white worker trying to get a promotion who learns that an African American was chosen instead so that his company could comply with affirmative action. Hartnett's TV ad was on homosexuals instead of African Americans. Senator Paul Tsongas of Massachusetts had come to me one day with a proposed bill to eliminate prejudice against homosexuals. He said he wanted a southern cosponsor, and I agreed to cosponsor. This bill was to prevent discrimination, not to give preference, but Hartnett's ad indicated that I favored homosexuality. It caused a "tempest in a teapot" in the Charleston area, where friends knew Hartnett and me, and the homosexual ad was pulled in the lowcountry, but Hartnett kept it running in the Piedmont. I prevailed in the election narrowly—by just three points—but it was a sweet victory. I had taken some tough hits as a result of my vote against the war. But as I said on the campaign trail, I had no regrets. The people had sent me to Washington to use my best judgment. I had been scorned time and again for stances that I had taken over the years, from telling our citizens that we must allow Harvey Gantt to integrate Clemson, to going on the hunger tour in South Carolina to highlight the urgent need to address malnutrition, to supporting the Panama Canal Treaties. My vote on the Gulf War was cast in that same spirit. Of course no vote is more difficult than one that results in putting our young servicemen and servicewomen in harm's way. Once the troops are committed, I always support them.

On Election Day 1992, in addition to my victory, voters across the country had elected the most diverse freshman class in Senate history. Four women and a Native American were joining the "club."[21] Those changes, while significant, were trumped by Bill Clinton's defeat of George H. W. Bush in the presidential race. I was hopeful that a southerner in the White House would tackle the tough issues of the deficit and trade and that government would really work, once again, as our forefathers intended.

13

The Early 1990s

From Budget Battles to Trade Wars

It quickly became apparent that President-elect Clinton was serious about taking the country in a new direction. He was saying all the right things about economic priorities, especially his determination to take an ax to the budget deficit. He had promised in the campaign to cut the deficit in half by the end of his first term. That stance was reinforced a month or so before he was sworn in as President, when Clinton, who had just stepped down as Governor of Arkansas, convened an economic summit in Little Rock. A broad range of folks, from Fortune 500 CEOs to shop owners and academics, reached what Clinton has described as "an overwhelming consensus" that he should make deficit reduction his top priority even if it meant cutting his promised middle-class tax relief or eliminating it altogether.[1]

After twelve years of Reagan and Bush, I was reassured that the President would not be buying into some ideological magic wand to get us out of the economic doldrums. It would take strong medicine. I had confidence in Clinton's economic team, led by my old friend Lloyd Bentsen of Texas, who agreed to leave his post as chairman of the Senate Finance Committee to be Treasury Secretary, and Leon Panetta, the California Congressman who departed as chairman of the House Budget Committee to be director of the OMB. They were "deficit hawks" and made the case to Clinton that reducing the deficit was the most important thing he could do to jumpstart the sluggish economy.[2] Their presence was an antidote to David Stockman, Kemp-Roth, supply side, and trickle down!

The Clinton team got a jolt when Richard Darman, President Bush's OMB director, admitted that he had considerably underestimated the deficit projections for the coming year. There was plenty of suspicion in the Clinton camp that the Bush folks had deliberately withheld this information during the campaign, but that really was irrelevant. All that mattered was that the White House and Congress take decisive action. On February 17, 1993, in his first address to a joint session of Congress, the President called for the kind of shared sacrifice that showed his views to be in accord with those of Bentsen and Panetta. Not only was Clinton dropping the tax cuts, but he also did the politically difficult thing of proposing to boost taxes.

It was a straight-up proposal without ducking or bobbing and weaving. Clinton had a realistic plan to stop the country from sinking further into debt. His five-year plan was designed to raise $357 billion from new taxes while saving $375 billion with spending cuts. He also called for an economic stimulus program that included a permanent investment tax credit for small businesses and more spending on housing, education, job training, infrastructure, child care, and subsidies for the working poor.[3] As he painted a picture of the slumping economy in his address, Clinton specifically said he was not assigning blame. "There's plenty of blame to go around—in both branches of government and in both parties." But if that was an effort to reach across the aisle, Republicans were in no mood to accept the olive branch. Having attacked their trickle-down theory in the campaign, Clinton was not about to get a break from them. But Democrats were going to do everything we could to push his proposal forward. Even Alan Greenspan, the Federal Reserve Board chairman, a conservative Republican, gave the President the thumbs-up. He told the Senate Banking Committee two days after the speech that the budget-deficit plan was "a serious proposal" and that deficits were "corrosive forces slowly undermining the vitality of our free-market system."[4] He was not so enthusiastic about the other part of the Clinton proposal—the spending program to stimulate the economy.

I knew that Clinton would have a very tough fight on his hands. I sensed that the President wanted to show how a Democrat in the White House could be responsible in dealing with our budget crisis and at the same time remind the American people that government could make a positive difference in their lives. These first days of his presidency were a repudiation of the Republican notion that government was the problem. The new President had started in the right direction.

The GOP critics were worked up into a lather because of the proposed tax increases and because they felt the President should have called for more spending cuts. They decried the ratio of about three dollars in tax hikes for every one dollar in spending reductions. Senator Pete Domenici, the senior Republican on the budget panel, said simply, "it isn't going to work." Republican Senator Don Nickles of Oklahoma was more scathing. He blasted the proposed tax increases as "grossly, totally, completely irresponsible" and said the hikes threatened to blunt economic growth and add hundreds of thousands of people to the unemployment rolls. When the Republicans came out shooting at the Clinton proposal, I responded in kind in the Budget Committee. It was "grossly irresponsible" for Republican Senators to blister the Clinton proposal when they had refused to support a spending freeze in the past, I countered. They had watched passively and twiddled their thumbs as Presidents Reagan and Bush quadrupled the size of the deficit from $1 trillion to $4 trillion. Republican policies had "wrecked the economy" and "dug us a real deep hole." "We don't have the luxury of worrying about the ratio of tax increases to spending cuts," I added. "There is a difference in what is desirable and what is necessary. Our task is to do what is necessary. Let's turn the tide and have freezes, spending cuts and tax increases."[5]

We were a superpower that was superbroke. Clinton was trying to turn things around. Yet we were hearing the same old song from Republicans, who were so wedded to tax cuts that they didn't even acknowledge the facts. Reagan and Bush had recklessly increased the debt by $3 trillion.

As the debate intensified, President Clinton lost some steam when he got hammered in the press over the withdrawal of two cabinet nominees for Attorney General, Zoë Baird and Kimba Wood, for employing illegal immigrants as nannies. The Republicans redoubled their attacks against the President's economic program, charging that his $16 billion stimulus package was chockablock full with pork and that the deficit-reduction proposal was all about higher taxes. The bad patch pulled Clinton off message. In the Los Angeles Times, I noted that Clinton could draw on the experiences of the "New South" past and the "New Democrat" present. As Governor I had faced the necessity of cleaning up my state's fiscal mess before I could entice new industries to South Carolina. Clinton knew this drill from his own experience. He had balanced ten budgets as Governor of Arkansas. He needed to proceed in the same fashion as President by dealing with the deficit first. "First serve the spinach, then the sundae," I wrote. "Let's be blunt about Democrats: Most Americans don't trust us to spend their tax dollars frugally. Reagan and Bush could kite $3 trillion in hot checks on defense while quadrupling the national debt, and the public still perceived them as fiscal tightwads. But if a Democratic President presumes to ask for $16 billion in economic stimulus, he is savaged as 'just another tax-and-spend Democrat.' The antidote for this poison is patience."[6]

The focus should have been on the deficit first and then on investment. From June to August, when we voted on the budget, we engaged in some fierce debates on the Senate floor. Everybody knew the vote would be a nail-biter, and I was not going to shrink from pointing out that the Republicans were guilty of more than a tad of hypocrisy. The only way to solve the budget mess was with new taxes, and I quoted none other than Stockman, Reagan's budget director, for support. On the Senate floor, I quoted from his mea culpa in the June 1993 issue of *New Perspective* magazine, in which he wrote that Republicans' "frenzy of excessive and imprudent tax cutting [in July 1981] . . . shattered the nation's fiscal stability." And he added: "A noisy faction of Republicans has willfully denied this giant miscalculation of fiscal governance and their own culpability in it ever since. Instead they have incessantly poisoned the political debate with a mindless stream of anti-tax venom while pretending that economic growth and spending cuts alone could cut the deficit."[7]

Who better to reveal the hoax of Reagan's supply-side policies than one of its architects? Stockman also made my central point throughout the Senate debate, when he wrote, "There is no way out of the elephantine budget deficits which have plagued the nation since 1981 without major tax increases." As Republicans kept calling for a "tax-free 1993" and other such poll-driven gibberish, I said, "They have no shame. They have no embarrassment."[8]

When the House voted on the final measure on August 5, the margin could not have been closer, 218–216 to support the proposal. The five-year plan—which had been adjusted over the summer to include about $254 billion in spending cuts and $250 billion in tax increases—

was not supported by a single Republican. Forty-one Democrats also opposed the measure. In the end Democratic Congresswoman Marjorie Margolies-Mezvinsky of Pennsylvania, who represented a Republican-leaning suburban district, bravely cast the decisive vote for the legislation even though she had promised to oppose tax increases. She lost her reelection bid in 1994, but—as later became evident with the economic good times that followed passage of the measure—she had done the right thing.

When the Senate commenced consideration of the Clinton plan, Democratic Senator David Boren of Oklahoma and the Midwest farm crowd led an organized opposition to the plan's major provision, an energy tax. Once they had defeated the energy tax, we were in a soup. There had been all this talk of the necessity to increase taxes, but no one was in charge of any particular initiative, leaving a group of us in the Senate cobbling together an increase in any and every tax—income, Social Security, gasoline. By this time the Republicans smelled blood. The new President was on the ropes with his fiscal policy in disarray. And the Republicans in the Senate and House determined not to yield a single vote to help him out of his dilemma. As a member of the Budget Committee, I was wheeling and dealing, trying to secure support. Boren of course was against any tax increase as were several other Democrats, such as Sam Nunn and Bennett Johnston. We were one vote short of a tie, which we knew Vice President Al Gore could end by casting the tiebreaker in his role as President of the Senate.

The fate of the bill ultimately came down to Democratic Senator Bob Kerrey of Nebraska. Bob, a former Governor whose heroic service in the navy in Vietnam was recognized with the rarely awarded Congressional Medal of Honor, is talented, always forthright, and a tough fighter for his principles. Bob had little use for Clinton, whom he had run against in the 1992 presidential campaign. I urged him to put aside his personal feelings because there was a great deal at stake in this vote. Clinton's presidency was riding on passage of the legislation. The administration had put everything on the line for the measure as Clinton intensively lobbied lawmakers. The White House made the case that its whole economic program depended on passing the tax package. Bob came through, although he didn't think the measure went far enough in attacking the deficit. "I could not and should not cast a vote that brings down your presidency," he said on the Senate floor, as if he were talking directly to Clinton, shortly before the vote. That vote made it a 50–50 tie, which was broken when Gore cast the fifty-first vote for the measure.

When President Clinton signed the legislation on August 10, it marked the first step in reversing the tide of deficit spending. Republicans who had predicted that the sky would fall from enactment of this proposal were proved dead wrong. Phil Gramm, the Senate's resident economist, repeatedly castigated the legislation and said with confidence that its passage would make the economy weaker and result in job losses for hundred of thousands, including Clinton.[9] Congressman John Kasich of Ohio, the ranking Republican on the House Budget Committee, predicted that the legislation would lead to "bigger deficits, bigger government and fewer jobs."[10] He even pledged to change parties if the plan worked. And Senator Bob Packwood of Oregon, a former chairman of the Finance Committee, said he would give us his house in Washington if the plan worked. Ultimately Clinton's sober approach led to a robust economy, a soaring stock market, the creation of more jobs, and a declining deficit.

Democrats had shown that we could be fiscally responsible. As pleased as I was at Clinton's serious, tough-minded approach to reducing the deficit, I was just as displeased that he decided to go along with the nonsense of free trade. I was shocked that yet another President bought into the dogma of free trade as an economic panacea. I had tried for many years to stop the outflow—initially of textile jobs and then of all jobs—as "free" trade took its toll. Now I was fighting a policy that started when President George H. W. Bush signed the North American Free Trade Agreement (NAFTA) in December 1992. He had left it up to Clinton to get it through Congress.[11] I figured that a southern Governor, knowledgeable about creating jobs and about the toll that free trade had taken, would stop the hemorrhaging. Certainly not NAFTA! But the President went gung ho for NAFTA.

I don't reflexively oppose all trade agreements. I backed the U.S.-Canada Free Trade Agreement, but it was between two countries with similar standards of living and comparable free markets with worker rights. I backed free trade with Jordan even though we have different standards of living because Jordan is strategically important in one of the world's most volatile regions.

The NAFTA agreement with Mexico did not make sense. U.S. companies face a mountain of mandated costs such as providing safe working conditions, parental leave, clean air and water, Social Security, and on and on. Every one of these requirements adds costs to U.S. goods. Mexico by contrast had no labor rights or exacting environmental regulations. As we approach negotiations with Mexico or with any other country our leaders often seem to forget that trade is a competition. We cannot afford to act like Goody Two-shoes as we lose our shirts in manufacturing. Our workers can compete with any other companies around the world, but they cannot compete with other countries that subsidize their workforce and protect their markets.

Clinton had been elected President with the indispensable help of organized labor, but when he got to the White House he abandoned the unions. He lined up with the Fortune 500 and Business Roundtable and Wall Street crowd, and fiercely lobbied for the pact. He even put up two giant white tents on the South Lawn, where the titans of business and industry gathered to talk up the benefits of NAFTA—and make campaign contributions.[12] In campaigns, instead of the votes, go first for the money.

I traveled to Tijuana, Mexico, and saw the squalid conditions of the working-class neighborhoods surrounding the foreign-owned assembly plants, known as *maquiladoras*. The poverty and wretched foulness was far worse than what I had seen on my hunger tours in South Carolina in the late 1960s. In the Tijuana valley, scarcely half the living quarters had plumbing and only one-third had fresh water. Thousands lived in makeshift structures, resorting to doing things such as putting five garage doors together and calling it home. Forget about sewage treatment. Human waste was flowing in the streets. One electric line ran through many houses to provide light. To get TV reception folks had to rely on improvised efforts such as hooking up two car batteries. As I noted during the debate on the Senate floor, foreign companies had settled in the valley and made false promises to get the go-ahead to build their plants.

"They have said, let us build our plants in your city, let us pockmark your landscape with toxic-waste dumps, let us hire your people for disgracefully low wages, and in return we will give you jobs and, in time, a middle class and the basis for democratic government," I said on October 14, as the debate in the Senate became more intense. "Far from rising, wages in the maquiladoras are significantly lower than they were a decade ago. The sprawling slums of Tijuana, Ciudad Juarez, and Nogales make a mockery of this promise of middle-class prosperity. Yet now the North American Free Trade Agreement dares to peddle the very same false promises, only on a broader scale. Again there is the promise of a growing middle class and democratic reform. But it is a lie. In truth what NAFTA would accomplish—at best—is to turn all of Mexico into one big duty-free maquiladora zone. It would produce the same exploitation of Mexican labor, the same environmental rape, the same cementing of the corrupt political status quo in Mexico."[13]

There were no labor rights in the plants in Mexico. When I visited there during the Memorial Day recess in 1993, my guide was a young lady from a prominent family who owned one of the best jewelry stores in downtown Tijuana. She was trying to help the workers. "Senator, the Mayor of Tijuana has a group of twelve workers. He wants you to hear their story," she said.

"I would be glad to," I replied.

The Mayor had the twelve workers assembled in a tent that we visited. Several months before, heavy rains had hit hard in the San Diego–Tijuana area. The rain persisted so long that it wreaked havoc in the Tijuana settlement. The bay in Coronado was discolored from the silt that had flowed from the settlement, where the encrusted earth had turned to mud. Houses were crumbling or sliding. The residents worked day and night to try to keep their homes together. The relentless rains had caused the workers to lose three days on the job. Under Mexican work rules, they were docked an additional day for each day lost.

Then in February a worker in the plastic-coat-hanger plant had lost an eye because there was no eye protection. Finally, around the first of May, a popular supervisor told the bosses that she was pregnant and felt sick and had to go home. They told her she couldn't leave. "Get back out on the floor," they said. She returned to her job and later suffered a miscarriage. As a result of such treatment, twelve workers agreed to pool their resources and travel to Los Angeles, California, to retain a lawyer and organize a union. But they ran into a problem. When their factory had moved to Mexico from Santa Ana, California, the company's attorneys had signed some papers organizing a mock union for the Tijuana plant. Of course, when they arrived in Mexico, the workers never saw a shop foreman. No one there had ever heard of a union. The company had engaged in some shenanigans involving an exchange of money that made the mock papers have the force of law. So it appeared that they had a union when they really didn't. Under

Mexican law, if you attempt to organize a union while you already have one, you are fired. Later, when I received five hundred dollars for an article for *Foreign Policy* magazine in which I advocated a "common market" approach rather than the one envisioned by NAFTA, I sent that money to my guide in Tijuana and urged her to use the money to organize. Here I was, a "right-to-work" politician, encouraging the workers to organize a union! I'm still enraged today as I write about this mistreatment of the workers. I told this story time and again to my colleagues in the Senate and did my best to defeat NAFTA.

NAFTA would bolster the Mexican oligarchy and legitimize oppression, I argued in that Winter 1993–94 article. "Instead of rushing pell-mell to integrate an underdeveloped economy with a developed economy, the United States should follow the example set by the European Community," I wrote. I noted that there were years of intense negotiations before Spain, Portugal, and Greece were allowed to be integrated into the European Community. The community members taxed themselves $5 billion over five years to fund economic reforms in those three countries. This provided a development fund to boost their economies, and in return for these funds, Greece, Portugal, and Spain instituted democratic reforms.

"A North American Common Market would require the nations of North America to enter into a social compact to establish minimum standards for labor rights and environmental protection as well as a common commitment to protect the individual liberties that are a foundation of a democracy," I wrote. "A North American Common Market, with a common external tariff, could be an effective vehicle for competing with the emerging trade blocs in Europe and Asia."

A President has a tremendous advantage when it comes to a battle for votes on Capitol Hill, and Bill Clinton was highly effective in using that advantage on NAFTA. Clinton played a round of golf with a particular Congressman, who just happened to be undecided. A Texas Congressman got two C-17's approved to help his district, and yet another Lone Star Representative got a cultural center. The *New York Times* listed a slew of "freebies" that led to changed votes. How can you fight such blandishments? Those goodies helped to fix the vote. There was nothing that I or any of my similarly disposed colleagues could do about it. The icing on the cake occurred when Vice President Gore went on CNN's *Larry King Live* show and got the best of Ross Perot, a third-party candidate in the 1992 presidential race and a fierce critic of NAFTA. Perot was doing extremely well in the debate until Gore mentioned that we didn't want to return to the protectionism of Smoot-Hawley, a 1930 law that raised tariffs to record levels. Perot lost his cool. I had spent two hours briefing him the morning of the debate. Perot already had been talking about the "sucking sound" of lost jobs should NAFTA pass, and he wanted to get a fix on all facets of the federal budget. We had not discussed Smoot-Hawley, but that 1930 law did not cause the Depression. It was passed eight months after the market crash in 1929, and the measure affected one-third of our trade at a time when foreign trade amounted to just 1.3 percent of our gross national product. Moreover, Secretary of State Cordell Hull's *reciprocal* trade program in 1934 had returned the nation to a positive balance of trade.

The Perot debate hurt, and Clinton's mastery as a speaker and a backroom dealer was too much for those of us opposed to NAFTA. On November 17, 1993, the House approved the deal, 234–200, and three days later, the Senate also endorsed it, 61–38. Most of Clinton's support came from the GOP. Thirty-four of forty-four Republican Senators backed NAFTA, but only twenty-seven of the fifty-five Democrats did so.[14]

It is beyond dispute that NAFTA and other free-trade deals have come at a cost. Since NAFTA's enactment, the U.S. trade deficit has taken off. In 2006 it hit a record high of $763.6 billion. Instead of creating two hundred thousand jobs, we've lost two hundred thousand–plus. Instead of solving the immigration problem, we exacerbated it. Two million Mexican small farmers were inundated with subsidized U.S. farm imports and headed over the border to find work.

After the pitched battle over NAFTA, President Clinton turned his energies to renewing the General Agreement on Tariffs and Trade (GATT). GATT was an agreement among more than one hundred countries to reduce tariffs and other barriers on manufactured products, agriculture, and services. It created and empowered the World Trade Organization (WTO) to referee members' disputes over trade—a feature that I and other critics cited as a threat to U.S. sovereignty. Congress began consideration of GATT in late September 1994—less than two months before the midterm elections—under so-called fast-track rules that require each chamber in Congress to act with only an up-or-down vote and no amendments. I am adamantly opposed to this "fast track," in which Congress rolls over to the executive branch.

The Hollingses observing the fiftieth anniversary of the Normandy invasion with Sally Howie McDevitt at the gravesite of McDevitt's father, Abbeville native Thomas D. Howie, "The Major of St. Lo," June 1994. Collection of the author

By agreeing to that procedure, we relinquished our role as legislators as expressly set out in Article 1, Section 8, of the Constitution, which provides that Congress shall regulate commerce with foreign nations. Under fast track, it was all or nothing. I decided to take advantage of another aspect of the fast-track rules that empowered each committee chairman with jurisdiction to take as long as forty-five days to consider the bill.

As chairman of the Commerce Committee, I was going to take all forty-five days. But in making that decision, I knew we had to have meaningful hearings. After all, this was the opportunity that I had been yearning for. A real review of the issues raised by GATT was needed because the Senate Finance Committee, which has primary jurisdiction over trade, historically has had a mindset of the more trade deals, the better. It is callous toward workers and casual on trade. I wanted to take that month and a half and conduct a comprehensive bipartisan examination of what free trade entails, its costs and its benefits. Such a review, I hoped, would educate my colleagues that free trade had us heading over the cliff.

Of course, by deciding to use all forty-five days, I would take the battle over GATT past the midterm elections. My intentions infuriated the White House and angered congressional Democratic leaders who were eager for a big victory on Capitol Hill that might boost their prospects in what looked like difficult upcoming elections for the party. Having seen his sweeping health-care reform proposal (which Hillary Clinton had developed) go up in smoke, the President also was desperate for a victory lap.

The White House tried everything to mollify me and to get me to back off from using the full forty-five days. I met with the President on September 26, and Clinton made the pitch that he needed ratification of the deal quickly so he would be well-positioned heading into meetings in December with Asian and Latin American leaders. The White House also tried to win me over by making some concessions, including imposing more restrictions on Chinese apparel imports. That move provoked some yelps from retailers. They also toughened U.S. sanctions against dumping of imports.[15]

I was pleased by those moves, but I was not about to budge from my opposition to GATT and my incredulity at the creation of WTO. Initially Senate Republican leader Bob Dole shared my skepticism. But as time passed, it became clear that Dole was really more interested in cutting a deal than in drawing a line in the sand. All the while I knew my efforts to torpedo GATT were a long shot, but this issue was so important that I was not going to be deterred by long odds. As always critics were all over me, blasting my "protectionist stance" as a bid to save textile jobs in South Carolina. At a news conference on September 28, 1994, I explained that my position went beyond my state's interest to the fact that "so-called free-trade policies" had resulted in a loss of our manufacturing capacity. "I'm not shilling for a particular industry," I said. "I'm shilling for the United States of America."

The only reason to renew GATT would be if it had worked and we were creating jobs and strengthening the economy with free trade. But I knew firsthand that the textile industry was hemorrhaging jobs to overseas factories and that "hard" manufactured products such as automobiles, steel, and computers were on the ropes. The Finance

Committee passed GATT under fast track with no amendments! We scheduled eight days of hearings and had a lineup of witnesses with wide-ranging views.[16]

As I made my case, the administration was working overtime to line up supporters. I had lunch with Leon Panetta, who, by this time, had been made chief of staff, and he told me that the White House already had some three hundred votes in the House. I was astonished at his fast work considering that Congress had not had time to debate GATT in the two days since Clinton had submitted it. "You ought to be O.J.'s lawyer—you know how to really fix the jury ahead of the debate," I said to Panetta, referring to the acquittal of O. J. Simpson in the trial for murdering his wife and Ronald Goldman.[17]

As I began to set out why this was a bad deal for the United States on multiple levels, President Clinton had put on his salesman's hat and become a cheerleader for how wonderful GATT was. It provides, the President said, greater trade opportunities, and "that is good news for our workers and our future."[18] Once again Clinton was overlooking the fact that our markets would be flooded with imports, but other markets would not be so open to U.S. products. This new dispute-resolution system was not going to change that fact.

I plowed ahead with our hearings. We learned that 4.5 million U.S. workers had lost permanent jobs to outsourcing from 1991 through 1993. Forty-seven percent of those who had returned to full-time jobs often were making far less pay than before. Another 13 percent had given up on the job hunt and left the labor force. In 1980 Europe and the United States both had a deficit in textile trade of $4 billion; but, at the time of the hearings in 1994, Europe's deficit in textile trade had been cut to less than $1 billion, while the U.S. deficit had jumped to $31 billion. The Europeans knew how to compete in the trade wars, in which the Japanese were even more skilled. Japan kept an imported Ford automobile on the docks in Tokyo for four months to be inspected. A Toyota delivered on the docks in Le Havre, France, in 1994 took a year for inspection. In contrast to these nontariff barriers, the United States takes delivery of one thousand Toyotas in Portland, Oregon, inspects ten an hour, and puts them on car carriers to be sold in the eastern United States the next day. We learned that Japan is a living example that you can export without having free trade.

The best evidence came from Sir James Goldsmith, a member of the Foreign Relations Committee of the European Parliament. He spoke of his background in business and his work in various countries well before free trade existed. "I am a free trader on a regional basis and I have always been for free markets and free enterprise," Goldsmith testified.

Then he described two enterprises under GATT, one in the United States and the other in China: "They're both making the same products to be sold in the same markets using the same technology, having access to the same capital. The only element which distinguishes one from the other is that one can employ forty-seven able people for the cost of one person in the developed world. . . . [And] on top of that [China has] no protection and no trade unions and none of the obligations [that are imposed on U.S. companies]."

Goldsmith asked rhetorically which country will be more attractive. "The answer is obvious," he said. "We give a huge reward to the one who leaves [outsources] and we penalize—indeed, bankrupt—the one who stays."

We learned that the purpose of the economy is to serve society and not the other way around. Too frequently in the United States, our only interest is in economic indices. GNP (gross national product) or GDP (gross domestic product) is a measure of economic activity, not a measure of good activity or bad activity—merely activity. As Goldsmith attested, "You can have growth in GNP, while at the same time destroying your community." The purpose of the economy is not just to improve the indices. Rather it is to boost the prosperity of the people and provide social stability. The purpose of GATT is to increase corporate profits and gross national activity. The result is a loss of production and jobs in the United States. Such job losses will destroy the stability of our society and result in "a continued breakdown in family life, a continued increase in crime, impoverishment, and all the other ills that we are now suffering," Goldsmith testified. Goldsmith also described the impact of globalization:

> What we are witnessing is the divorce of the interests of the major corporations and the interests of society as a whole. It used to be said that "what was good for General Motors"—and we all believed it, it probably was true—"was good for the United States." That is no longer true. The transnational corporations . . . now have $4.8 trillion per annum in sales. They account for one-third of global output. The largest one hundred account for one-third of all

foreign direct investment. Now, where do you think the bulk of that investment is going? It is going where it earns the most. There is no other way it can go. What chief executive can invest otherwise, Mr. Chairman?

So if . . . you have freedom of movement of capital, freedom of movement of technology, and you can employ people forty or fifty times cheaper, who are skilled, and you can import their products back anywhere in the world, that is the basis of global free trade. How can those investments, how can these transnational companies who have $4.8 trillion of sales invest anywhere other than where it is cheapest and where their return is greatest?

Analyzing the WTO, Goldsmith stated that he had read about it and had concluded that "the one thing which is certain is, bottom line, this is giving up national sovereignty."

Finally Goldsmith got the attention of members when he stated, "All my business life I have worked to increase profitability. But I believe that when you get to a system whereby so as to get the best corporate profits, you have to leave your own country, you have to say to your own sales force, 'Goodbye, we cannot use you anymore, you are too expensive, you have got unions, you want holidays, you want protection,' so we are going offshore, you destroy your own nation. I think that is short-term thinking. That is the real short-term investment, because that is like making a profit on the deck of the *Titanic* playing cards, and in a clever, as opposed to wise way."

In illuminating the problems with GATT, the WTO, and mindless adherence to free-trade policies, these hearings had an impact. Some witnesses painted a clear picture that—by empowering unelected bureaucrats of small countries to make major, binding decisions—WTO is a threat to U.S. sovereignty. During this period Republican leader Bob Dole said there must be an "escape hatch" from the decisions of these bureaucrats. But the Kansas Senator was not going to put off a vote on GATT and WTO indefinitely. He got together with Majority Leader George Mitchell and agreed to hold a two-day lame-duck session on November 30 and December 1, 1994, at which time we would vote.

Before we returned for the vote, Republicans had clobbered us at the polls. As a result of unhappiness over Clinton's tax hike, the debacle of the White House's failed health-care proposal, and discontent with the President's and Congress's performances, especially the relentless partisanship on Capitol Hill, voters put the GOP in control of both the House and Senate for the first time in forty years. It was a wipeout, pure and simple.

When we returned after that Election Day massacre, Dole shifted into his deal-making mode. As the incoming Senate Majority Leader, he had a chance to cement his role as what one commentator described as a "power broker in the new Washington." On the day before Thanksgiving, Dole announced from a White House podium that he had reached an agreement with the administration that would deal with potential arbitrary decisions rendered by the WTO. He was satisfied that "we've resolved concerns about the WTO."[19] U.S. Trade Representative Mickey Kantor set out the agreement in a letter to Dole on November 23, 1994, in which he acknowledged that "concerns remain, in Congress and around the country, about our sovereignty under the WTO." To address such concerns, Kantor pledged that the Clinton administration would "support legislation next year to establish a WTO Dispute Settlement Review Commission" that would be made up of five Federal Appellate Judges, chosen by the President in consultation with leaders in Congress. The commission would review final WTO dispute-settlement reports adverse to the United States. If it decided three times within any five-year period that the WTO panel had "demonstrably exceeded its authority" and acted "arbitrarily or capriciously," then any lawmaker "would be able to introduce a Joint Resolution" to disapprove further U.S. participation in the organization. "If the resolution is enacted by the Congress and signed by the President, the United States will commence withdrawal from the WTO agreement," Kantor wrote.

Like other critics of this pact, I saw Dole's deal as window dressing. Despite all the reassurances, this proposal was never enacted.[20] It was obvious that once Dole had signed on, the vote itself would be anticlimactic. On November 30 the House overwhelmingly passed the measure, 288–146, and the following day the Senate also easily passed it, 76–24. That lopsided vote was a disappointment. Our workers were going to be hurt by this capitulation to the sirens of free trade.

The following day we elected a new leader. The Democratic leadership post was up for grabs, as Mitchell had announced earlier in the year that he was not seeking reelection. I backed Senator Chris Dodd of Connecticut, a smart, gifted, affable lawmaker whom I felt would be most effective in counterpunching Dole, who would be the new Majority Leader. But the tenacious, youthful Tom Daschle of South Dakota bested Dodd by a single vote. Daschle proved to be a creditable, resourceful leader.

In January 1993 I introduced Senate Bill no. 4 (S4) to transform the Department of Commerce into the Department of Trade and Commerce so we could organize the government to compete in international trade. I also was involved in another battle that centered on boosting government efforts to make U.S. high-tech companies more competitive in the global marketplace through loans and grants. I had done lots of work to build bipartisan support in the House and Senate for a bill to enhance U.S. competitiveness. The measure increased funding for the Commerce Department's National Institute of Standards and Technology (NIST) to assist new civilian technology programs.[21] The program was aimed at providing the country's 360,000 small and midsized manufacturing firms with the wherewithal to pursue cutting-edge, often high-risk technologies. It authorized $2 billion for such cooperative efforts. I saw the legislation as a slam dunk, with obvious benefits and no downside. We had plenty of momentum when the bill, called the National Competitiveness Act, emerged from the Commerce Committee without any objection. But when the measure reached the Senate floor, I got into a heated debate with Senator John Danforth of Missouri, the ranking Republican on the Commerce Committee. Danforth had not opposed the bill during the committee hearings, but during the floor debate he argued that the legislation caused concerns about the "appropriate relationship between the federal government and the private sector." He called it "industrial policy" and added that "it is the picking of winners and losers."[22]

"It is the judgment of this Senator that governmental officials will never be the shrewd venture capitalists that we will find in the marketplace," Danforth continued. "We are politicians and politicians apply grease to the squeaky wheel. . . . I am concerned that government subsidies for research and development in the private sector are going to gravitate toward those parts of the private sector with the most political clout."[23]

I was stunned by Senator Danforth's unexpected potshots. "That is an astounding conclusion," I responded on the Senate floor after he had urged our colleagues to defeat the bill. It was as if the Missouri Senator had amnesia. He and I had conferred several years earlier, when this program was initially developed, and we had drawn up the measure so that it would not be larded up with lawmakers' favorite projects. It would not be business as usual. "We both agreed that this should not be a pork-barrel program, we should not politically make the decisions in Washington," I said, in describing our efforts four years earlier.

"We wanted to make absolutely sure this would not end up in ear-marking in subcommittees—I pick one and you pick one and so on— [and] that we would insist on peer review, and . . . [merit review by] the National Academy of Engineering," I said.[24]

"We are not talking about politicians picking winners," I continued. Private industry must come forward with capital, and the government's contribution would be strictly limited to about 25 percent. As for pick-ing winners and losers, I went down the list of how lawmakers in Wash-ington had "interfered" time and again with market forces. Rather than allowing the market to work its will, we passed legislation setting the minimum wage and establishing requirements for Social Security, Medicare, Medicaid, workplace safety, plant-closing notices, and on and on. Contrary to Senator Danforth's critique, I said, "It is not a major shift in philosophy. Heavens above. We have never left matters strictly to market forces. We already have an industrial policy, and always have." The U.S. industrial policy created the technological revo-lution: the Internet browser from a federal research laboratory at the University of Illinois, the computer mouse from a Stanford University research lab. Aircraft research for the Pentagon developed the nation's dynamic aircraft production, and Danforth and I worked together to introduce Sematech to save the computer industry.

As the debate continued, I reminded Senator Danforth that he had supported comparable initiatives such as the bailout of Chrysler, the development of Sematech, and a government partnership with semi-conductor manufacturers—as well as the earlier version of this com-petitiveness legislation that we had passed overwhelmingly and that President Bush had signed in 1992.

I was dumbfounded that after supporting similar measures in which the government helped to boost private sector initiatives, Sena-tor Danforth had chosen this measure on which to do an about-face. After some heated exchanges, the measure ultimately passed by a vote of 59–40, but we didn't convene a conference of House and Senate members until September 27, 1994. The legislation never emerged from the conference because the session ended. Republicans, sensing that they were going to do well on Election Day, were not going to give us a victory.

It was disappointing because this legislation would have helped U.S. companies stay in the lead in cutting-edge technology. We missed an opportunity to expand a very good program that would have made U.S. firms more competitive. The Republican obstructionist strategy, as I have noted, paid dividends at the polls as the Republicans romped to take control of both chambers. The just-say-no approach played out in other areas as well, from telecommunications and campaign-finance reform to health care, all of which tanked before Election Day 1994. Republicans played up the notion that Congress was dysfunctional and must undergo radical change. The voters agreed.

During this period and throughout the Clinton administration I was unable to make headway with my simple proposal to end the money chase in campaigns. I repeatedly brought to the Senate floor a constitutional amendment to empower Congress and the states to limit campaign spending. In 1993, 1995, 1997, and again in 2000, I made the case that we had to stop the constant chase for campaign dollars that took up so much of our time. A constitutional amendment would be the surest way to get lawmakers back to doing their jobs rather than devoting so much energy to the hunt for loot to spend on TV advertising.

To correct that craziness, I contended that public financing and other initiatives would never work. The rich would still buy the office, and skilled lawyers would find loopholes. Only a constitutional amendment permitting Congress to control spending would stop the chase. Consequently I continued to press for a bipartisan Joint Resolution to amend the Constitution. In 1993 I put forward a sense of the Senate resolution that Congress should pass a constitutional amendment to limit campaign expenditures. As in the past, the same cast of characters emerged, with Republican Senator Mitch McConnell of Kentucky making the biggest ruckus on the other side. He made the same tired argument that Senators who voted for my proposal were supporting an amendment of the First Amendment for the first time in two hundred years.

That argument had no merit. It was the Supreme Court and Senator McConnell who were limiting speech—not me. My proposal said nothing about curtailing free and robust discourse during a campaign. Instead, if enacted, it would have stopped equating money with speech, as the Supreme Court had done in 1976 when *Buckley v. Valeo* allowed a ceiling on campaign contributions but not on candidates' spending. The Kentucky Senator had often complained that we spend more on pet food than we do on elections. I responded during the debate in 1993, saying that his "eloquent Kibbles 'n Bits defense" of the status quo was wrongheaded. "Unlike cat food, elections should not be up for sale," I said.[25]

Again, as in 1988, a bipartisan majority backed the proposal— forty-six Democrats and six Republicans, fifteen shy of the number needed for a constitutional amendment. I was not deterred by not picking up more votes. In 1995 I was back at it when I tried to attach the campaign-finance amendment to the Balanced Budget Constitutional Amendment. That effort was turned back when a motion to table (or kill) my proposal was passed by a 52–45 vote on February 14, 1995. Two years later my constitutional amendment failed by a 38–61 vote on March 18, 1997. And on March 28, 2000, my proposal again failed when sixty-seven Senators voted to table it.

Even though support for my proposal slipped over the years, I remain convinced that the outrageous amount of money candidates must raise to participate in politics is a cancer on the body politic. That cancer could be excised by a constitutional amendment to end the out-of-control money chase. I supported the McCain-Feingold reform measure that was signed into law in 2002. But it is only an incremental approach. By contrast my amendment would deal with this issue once and for all. Unless we enact it, the never-ending quest for campaign dollars will continue to undermine our political system and lead plenty of citizens to conclude that the government is up for sale.

14

Protecting the Public Interest

After the political tidal wave that swept Republicans into control of Congress in 1994, the Democrats were on the defensive. Pugnacious Congressman Newt Gingrich of Georgia, the new Speaker of the House, had led the GOP to victory with his campaign blueprint known as the "Contract with America." The contract and Gingrich's other initiatives constituted a Republican assault on government. Their agenda was aimed at attacking Social Security, Medicare, and Medicaid—and abolishing the Departments of Commerce, Education, and Energy. For years Gingrich had reached a national audience by taking advantage of opportunities presented by C-SPAN to disseminate his antigovernment, antitax messages in speeches at the end of each day's proceedings in the House. He promised a Republican majority would downsize government.

His strategy worked. Democrats had grown complacent, and on Election Day voters booted the party from control of both the Senate and House for the first time in forty years. The best Democrats could do now was to fight a rearguard action to save Social Security and the other government programs and departments that the Republicans were attacking. On the positive side, we picked up where we left off and worked on the deregulation of telecommunications in 1995.

It was long past time for Congress to reassert itself in telecommunications policy. We had relinquished our role in telecommunications to the courts following the Justice Department's antitrust litigation against AT&T. That case was settled in 1982 by a consent decree that broke up "Ma Bell." Seven Baby Bells would control the local tele-phone market, and AT&T would provide long-distance service. This arrangement allowed the Bells to sit back and rack up profits for pro-viding local service under regulations written by the Federal Communi-cations Commission (FCC).

Meanwhile technological advances were revolutionizing the tele-communications world, paving the way for the Bells, cable-television firms, and others to offer new services. Voice, video, and data technolo-gies were converging so that the Bells, for example, could offer video services to compete with cable, while cable TV firms could compete to provide telephone service. The Bells argued that it no longer made sense for them to be confined to a single line of business. They should be allowed to compete, to invest, and to provide these new services. They looked to Wall Street for the financing, and Wall Street wanted predictability. The investors favored deregulation of the telecommuni-cations industry. It was up to us to write the new rules for the market-place.

I had seen the costly chaos caused by the deregulation of airlines, trucking, and savings-and-loan industries and had become a "born again regulator." Because I was a senior Democrat on the Commerce Committee, as long as I stood fast there would be no deregulation, no advances in communications. But I also recognized that I could not reflexively oppose deregulation in telecommunications. It was increas-ingly obvious that this marketplace was very dynamic, and I decided it was better to make changes that would bring at least some benefits to the public rather than let deregulation run amok. So in 1994, while I was still chairman of the Commerce Committee, I introduced a mea-sure to deregulate telecommunications gradually while protecting the interests of consumers. One of my overriding goals was not to repeat the mistakes of the past.

Our first problem was to write the rules so that the seven Bell monopolies would not be allowed simply to jump into a new line of business without any conditions. If they were allowed to do that, they could squash any competition before it got started. These powerful Bell companies had access to the calling records of almost all U.S. citizens, and they would be able to use that power because their competitors would have to go through Bell switchboards. It was a technical head-ache to write legislation that would ensure fair competition. Ultimately both the House and Senate and then the Bells agreed on what came to be known as section 271, a fourteen-point checklist that the Bells had to satisfy to show that their markets were open to competition before they would be allowed to offer new services.

Next I made certain that we didn't make the same mistake we had made when we deregulated airlines and trucking. We had abolished the administrative bodies overseeing airlines and trucking operations—the Civil Aeronautics Board in 1984 and the Interstate Commerce Commission in 1995. If we had maintained these agencies, they could have assured the orderly transition to a deregulated market. Instead the airlines competed by going for the profitable long hauls, while limiting service and raising the cost for travel to medium-sized cities. The long-haul competition became so intense that a number of carriers went broke while others wound up merging into mega-airlines. Similarly the sixty-five coast-to-coast long-haul truckers dwindled to eleven.

We had learned our lesson. In drafting legislation to deregulate telecommunications, we maintained the role of the FCC. We empowered it to oversee the Bells' compliance with the fourteen-point checklist and other provisions before allowing the seven companies to jump into new markets. We held eleven days of hearings and heard thirty-eight hours of testimony to make sure that the measure met the concerns of every interest. Then the bill we drafted was reported out of the Commerce Committee by a bipartisan vote of 18–2.

After the Labor Day break in 1994, several of the Bells decided to pull out the stops to shoot down my bill. They saw it as too regulatory. Senator Dole took the lead by presenting my staff with a lengthy amendment that would have gutted the bill's promotion of competition in the Bells' markets. I decided the legislation could not go forward. I announced that we had run out of time in the session to pass the measure, and I also suggested that Dole was acting at the Bells' behest. "We will not be held hostage at the last minute to ultimatums and to the desires of certain parties to substantially rewrite a bill that passed the committee by an overwhelming and bipartisan vote," I said.[1]

The powerful Bells' calculations were obvious. These companies had decided to try to kill the bill. They were betting that Republicans would win control of the Senate in 1995, putting friendlier, more deregulatory-minded lawmakers in charge of the show. Meanwhile Majority Leader George Mitchell knew we had been thorough in our hearings and that the bill had strong bipartisan support. He was confident that the legislation would easily pass before we adjourned for the elections. When

Dole and several others threatened to filibuster the bill, Mitchell hit the roof. He had hoped to enact this major legislation to give Democrats a boost at the polls. Although he had already announced his retirement, Mitchell made it clear that he thought the first order of business when the Senate reconvened in January should be telecommunications deregulation.

After the November 1994 elections wiped out the Democrats, Republican Senator Larry Pressler of South Dakota became chairman of the Commerce Committee. He and I worked together on the sweeping legislation, and after lengthy negotiations we drafted a measure similar to the one from the year before. The Commerce Committee overwhelmingly passed it on March 23, 1995, by a vote of 17–2. Less than three months later, on June 15, the Senate easily passed the legislation by an 81–18 margin.

The House passed a far more deregulatory measure on August 4, by a 305–117 margin. It allowed the Bells to jump into the long-distance business before competition took hold in their own markets. Like our measure, it also lifted price controls on cable service that had been imposed by the 1992 Cable Act.

Our task now was to reconcile the two versions of the measure and retain enough support to pass the legislation and get it to President Clinton's desk. Larry and I negotiated with our House counterparts, Republican Representative Tom Bliley of Virginia, the Commerce Committee chairman, and Michigan Representative John Dingell, the senior Democrat on the committee. I wanted to make sure that we retained a strong role for the FCC to protect the public interest and that we included provisions to protect consumers while freeing the industries to compete. The Bells opposed the requirement that they meet a "public interest" test before being allowed to enter new markets. I insisted that without such a test, there would be no legislation. The House eventually accepted it.

As we negotiated, a partisan meltdown was occurring on Capitol Hill on other issues. Late in 1995 the government was shut down twice. Federal workers were sent home because of bitter disagreements over the budget between President Clinton and the Republicans. It was the longest such shutdown in history. Clinton, to his credit, held firm. The Republicans ultimately capitulated, and the government reopened. Poll numbers showed that the public blamed the GOP for the impasse by an almost two-to-one margin.[2] Gingrich had overreached. The power of public opinion derailed mindless GOP efforts to dismantle important federal programs on which the public depended.

Despite all these fireworks, our negotiations on telecommunications legislation continued. The budget battle helped us because it forced GOP leaders to focus elsewhere. As we hammered out our differences, I found Bliley a pleasure to work with. We stayed in touch with all the various industries that would be affected by this sweeping reform. Jim Cullen, president of Bell Atlantic, negotiated for the seven Baby Bells. Cullen was an honest broker. Looking back at that time, I can say that all of us, regardless of our differences in philosophy, were trying to do our best for the country by drafting legislation that would create a smooth transition to a competitive market. But U.S. West and Bell-South, two of the Baby Bells, were cantankerous. Cullen would agree that an item suited the Bells, and then call back later to say that U.S. West or BellSouth objected. Finally we satisfied U.S. West, but John Clendenin of BellSouth was holding out for some different language. We returned from the Thanksgiving break in November 1995, and finally, on December 20, we agreed on Clendenin's language and the four of us—Bliley, Dingell, Pressler, and I—shook hands on our final compromises.[3]

We had succeeded in retaining the requirement to ensure the Bells faced competition in their own market before being freed to offer other services. The FCC would also oversee the Bells' compliance with the fourteen-point checklist. I also prevailed in retaining a strong role for the FCC, which would have the final say in determining whether it was in the public interest to allow a Bell to offer long-distance services. I felt confident that we had struck a deal providing enough benefits to each of the competing industries so none of them would try to shoot down the bill. Enthused, I called Clendenin, who was already in Florida for the Christmas holidays. Asking about the language, he queried, "Are you sure?" I read it to him, and he said: "I'll support the passage of the bill and BellSouth will be in long distance this time next year."

Man, was I happy! I thought as a courtesy I ought to call Vice President Al Gore. He had not communicated with me about the measure, but he was always talking about the Information Superhighway. Now we had paved the way to bring it about. About four that afternoon, I called the Vice President to give him a heads-up that House and Senate negotiators had agreed on a telecommunications conference report. He thanked me, and I forgot about it.

Later that afternoon, I was in the office listening to Tom Brokaw, the anchor of *NBC Nightly News*. Halfway through the program, Brokaw announced, "Wait a minute, folks, I've got an important announcement from the Vice President of the United States." I thought at first the President had been shot. But I was relieved when Vice President Gore came on saying he was proud to announce that the House and Senate had agreed on deregulating telecommunications. But then he added, "I got everything I wanted." I was aghast! Niceties and jealousies control the Congress. I had no idea what Vice President Gore "wanted," but his statement wouldn't help us in adopting the conference report in either the House or the Senate. In fact there was a violent reaction. Gore's comments infuriated Republicans. He made it sound as if the legislation was his baby. Dole, who had become Senate Majority Leader, said that the jury was out on whether the Republican Congress would support the compromises in the conference report. Gingrich added potshots as well. The measure is "dead as Elvis," said Republican Representative Michael Oxley of Ohio, one of the senior members of the Commerce Committee, who added that Gore's taking credit was "well orchestrated."[4]

Despite all the barbs, I knew we had a good report. My task was to prevent it from being shot down at this late stage. The criticisms made life especially difficult for Bliley, who had agreed to changes that did not make some of the firebrands in the House Republican caucus happy. Critics said that he had signed off on a bill that was so regulatory that it made Al Gore happy. Tom began to waver and wonder whether we should reopen the legislation to mollify the GOP leaders. I insisted that we stick to our guns. During the Christmas holidays and all of January, I stayed in close touch with Tom, who wanted to do the right thing. Despite all the pressure, Bliley held firm. We did face one last-minute snag that threatened to bring the legislation down when Dole, who was running for President, bellyached that broadcasters were getting a multibillion-dollar giveaway because under the legislation they were to be awarded new spectrum for advanced TV signals for High Definition Television (HDTV). Eventually he backed off from his threats to battle the free spectrum "giveaway" and said he'd hold hearings on the issue.[5]

Once that issue was out of the way, our resolve was rewarded. On February 1, 1996, the Senate passed the sweeping telecommunications reform legislation by a vote of 91–5, and on the same day the House

The Hollingses with the Clintons, 1998. Official White House photograph, collection of the author

cleared the measure on a 414–16 vote. President Clinton signed the bill at an elaborate ceremony at the Library of Congress on February 8. Government had worked. The new law spurred development of the Information Superhighway while protecting the public interest, promoting competition, creating jobs, and providing most citizens with access to a wider array of information than anyone could have imagined.

I have always said that there are only two ways to run for public office—scared and unopposed. Trying to be reelected a seventh time, I had plenty of reason to be scared. In 1998 I was a Democrat in a state that had become totally Republican. The Republicans made me a target right out of the gate. My opponent, three-term Congressman Bob Inglis, a thirty-eight-year-old lawyer, was something of an enigma. He had run for Congress on a term-limits pledge. The Congressman was aggressive and smart. As a member of the House Judiciary Committee, Inglis had called for Clinton to step down as a result of the President's lies about an affair with an intern, Monica Lewinsky. He tried to tie me to Clinton, who, as I observed, was "as popular as AIDS in South Carolina."

As Election Day neared, it was obvious that it would be another close race. Industry, my principal support in campaigns, was now opposed to me because of my fight against NAFTA. In 1992 Bob Thompson of Greenville, the president of the U.S. Chamber of Commerce in Washington, had wanted to be sure of my reelection. The big day in Greenville, the most Republican county in South Carolina, is the Fourth of July. They celebrate all day with a colorful parade of hot-air balloons at the air base and the Greenville Symphony Orchestra performing at the baseball stadium in the evening. For the evening highlight in 1992, Thompson had me read Lincoln's Gettysburg Address with the symphony playing in the background. But in 1998, because of my opposition to NAFTA, the U.S. Chamber of Commerce put out thousands of flyers against me in South Carolina. The state's textile executives always met on the first Monday of every month at the Piedmont Club in Spartanburg for an evening of drinks and business talk. As textile's hero, I had been their guest before, but in 1998 I couldn't get invited. For the seventh time I stressed that "performance is better than promises" and made an accounting of my past six years in office. That message worked. I prevailed by a margin of 53 percent to 46 percent. Voters were not kind to the GOP in the 1998 races amid all their noise about impeaching Clinton. Republicans lost five House seats and only broke even in the Senate. Nonetheless, the Republicans pressed on against Clinton, and on December 19, 1998, the House voted to impeach the President.

The impeachment of President Clinton and his trial in the Senate signaled the climax of political partisanship. Of course everyone was shocked and embarrassed at President Clinton's conduct, but it wasn't a high crime or misdemeanor of office, the Constitution's requirement for impeachment. The President's wife, Hillary, was right when she spoke of a "vast right-wing conspiracy." That was obvious from the way the case for impeachment was developed. As I said on the Senate floor, "Locking up witnesses who did not testify to what they [prosecutors] wanted, . . . paying off others and securing them and hiding the witnesses, and on and on, and thereafter subpoenaing [Lewinsky's] mother in tears. . . . And they come up with private sexual misconduct. . . . To make this thing public after all that expense and effort, I would be embarrassed as a prosecutor to bring it."[6]

After four years of this nonsense I was shocked that an independent prosecutor was allowed to explore sexual misconduct that should have been kept off the record. It was outrageous that this salacious material was made public and stunning that an independent prosecutor had made it the crux of his case. I took my Republican friend Lindsey Graham, a Congressman from South Carolina who is now a U.S. Senator, to task on this point.

Graham was a member of the prosecution team from the House of Representatives and was constantly charging the President with "lying under oath," "lying under oath." I called George Duckworth, a Republican and the Solicitor in Lindsey's district, and said, "George, in divorce cases many times one or both parties are charged with adultery. One wins and the loser has lied by signing a 'verification' to the summons and complaint charging adultery. The jury or Judge has found against the verifier. As a result, the verifier could be charged criminally for lying under oath." Then I asked George, "How many times have you taken a loser in a civil case of adultery to the criminal court and charged him criminally with lying under oath?" He told me that he had never done so in seventeen years. Now my friend Lindsey in Washington was making a criminal charge because of a statement that would never have led to such a charge back home.

It was all about political gamesmanship. That's how partisan politics has gotten. Soon somebody will want the Jefferson Memorial razed because President Jefferson engaged in sexual misconduct. As I write this book, some folks are calling for the impeachment of President George W. Bush. Again such charges are nothing more than political partisanship.

The Republicans fell far short of the requisite sixty-seven votes they needed in the Senate to convict the President and send him packing. The whole episode was a fiasco. The Speaker of the House and many other Republicans simply had lost all sense of perspective. They were hell-bent on embarrassing the President. But Gingrich, who later acknowledged that he had had an illicit affair even as he was seeking the impeachment of the President, had no shame. Three days after the disappointing election results in 1998, Gingrich stepped down. Then the Speaker-designate, Republican Bob Livingston of Louisiana, also stepped down after acknowledging that he too had had an extramarital affair. Republicans next turned to little-known Representative Dennis Hastert of Illinois, a likable former high-school wrestling coach who had served a dozen years in Congress, to be the next Speaker.

Having prevailed in the battle over impeachment, Clinton was determined not to fold his tent and be a placeholder until he left office. He decided to resume his work with Republicans on trade. In January 2000, he vowed to make an "all-out effort" to win permanent normal trade relations (PNTR) status with China, a move far more popular on the GOP side of the aisle than it was among Democrats. Again repudiating the support of organized labor, Clinton went on the road to win support for PNTR. He met with business leaders, cajoled wavering lawmakers either in intense meetings at the White House or in phone calls, and regularly made strong public comments about the benefits of the deal. He argued that China had made many concessions and that in ratifying the deal, Congress would pave the way for our products to enter a rich, new market, thereby creating new jobs. The usual array of business groups fell in line behind the agreement, and their lobbyists talked up the great boost its enactment would give to exports. Some of them played hardball, including the irrepressible Thomas Donohue, president of the U.S. Chamber of Commerce, who reportedly threatened to cut off campaign contributions to lawmakers who defied him on this vote. "If somebody's on the margin and they screw up on this vote, they'd better not look to me for money," he reportedly warned.[7]

What these cheerleaders neglected to acknowledge was that PNTR would result in companies making investments in China by moving their plants and other facilities there to take advantage of cheap labor. Our trade deficit would get worse. We would weaken the economy. Also we had no need to pass PNTR since Congress already had approved normal trade relations annually with China. Why make it permanent rather than continue our annual review, especially given China's record on human-rights violations and their own closed markets? Finally the cheerleaders were not about to talk about the concession that we had made: Clinton had agreed to phase out quotas on Chinese textile imports by 2005 and to end our right to impose unilateral trade sanctions on Beijing.[8]

Labor unions tenaciously battled the deal. I took the floor in September 2000 and laid out the facts, including our bankrupt trade policies. Our balance of trade deficit was growing, and our workforce in manufacturing had declined from 41 percent after World War II to 12 percent. Since NAFTA had passed in 1993, some 38,700 jobs had left the little state of South Carolina and had gone to Mexico and China.

Yet we were hearing the same arguments again—that this deal would create jobs. Baloney. My position was not about being against China, but about being for the United States to recognize that trade is not free. It is an exchange of something for something. As long as we kept acting as if it were foreign aid, we would continue our industrial disarmament in the trade war.

The jury was in long before the debate commenced in the Senate. On September 19, the Senate passed the PNTR bill in a vote of 83–15. The House had passed it on May 24 in a vote of 237–197. I had known its passage was a foregone conclusion. Politically, with an election a few months away, it was safer for most of my colleagues to support free trade than to oppose it. But the impact of the deal was obvious to me. Textile jobs would continue to leave South Carolina, and the U.S. manufacturing base would continue to decline.

As the Clinton administration came to an end, public confidence in government was being tested. We had much work to do, and yet we were wasting time on partisan showdowns. Despite our differences on trade and the distraction of the impeachment battle, Clinton had been quite a President. He had the guts to raise taxes and pay the bills. He had brought us from $400 billion in deficits to a nearly balanced budget. As a result, the nation enjoyed eight years of the strongest economy in its history. So-called tax-and-spend Democrats had passed welfare reform and balanced budgets. Clinton had shown that government could work.

Unfortunately, after Clinton left office in 2001, his successor, George W. Bush, steered the country miserably off course and erased the economic gains that Clinton had achieved. Bush took us into a war in Iraq that we had no business being in. He squandered an opportunity to bring the country—and even the world—together after the dreadful attacks of September 11, 2001. The United States became more isolated on the world stage. Our military was weakened, and our deficit got much worse. Bush's failures as President have made it more challenging for future Presidents and policy makers to get the country back on the right track.

15

The George W. Bush Years

Reckless Policies Divide the Country

As the nation focused on the dispute over the Florida vote in the presidential race, we had political drama of our own in the Senate. A month after Election Day we learned that the Democrats, helped by the good economic times under President Clinton, had picked up four seats. Those results translated into an evenly divided Senate—fifty Republicans and fifty Democrats. Of course, when George W. Bush was finally declared the winner, the GOP retained control because Vice President Dick Cheney, in his role as President of the Senate, would cast tie-breaking votes.

My impression of George W. Bush is that he is the perpetual candidate. Good-looking and engaging, he easily connects with voters as he assumes the role of cheerleader that he first played in prep school. Given the ball, he knows how to run it. Unfortunately he was given the "spreading democracy" ball in Iraq but has no idea of how to put a team on the field to win. The heavy burdens of government do not worry him. During his six years as Governor of Texas before becoming President, he didn't develop a feel for government. Under the Texas constitution, the Governor's office is weak. The Texas chief executive doesn't even write the state's budget. Much of the Governor's power is based on his ability to schmooze, backslap, and cultivate state legislators. In Texas the Lieutenant Governor leads the way, and Bush and Democratic Lieutenant Governor Bob Bullock became fast friends.

So in early 2001, as President Bush entered the White House, his main assets were good political instincts and fine skills at campaigning. For his approach to governing, he took a page from President Reagan's playbook: "The government is not the solution. The government is the problem. The government is too big."

Now that we had a Republican President, I looked for Bush to continue the fiscal discipline of the Clinton administration. For eight years the economy had boomed as millions of new jobs were created, the stock market flourished, and good times rolled. Not a single Republican had voted for Clinton's fiscal discipline, but the GOP spin for the last four years of Clinton's term credited their party for the economic boom. Although there was talk of a recession early in 2001, many economists predicted it would be mild and wouldn't last long.[1] To my chagrin Bush used the chatter about an economic slowdown as a rationale to press for a massive tax cut of $1.62 trillion over a ten-year period.

The new President got a big assist in his tax-cut campaign when influential Alan Greenspan, chairman of the Federal Reserve, appeared before the Senate Budget Committee on January 25, 2001. Greenspan's testimony—just a few days after the inauguration—carried great weight. I expected the usually cautious Fed chairman to put a brake on the Bush administration's mantra about the benefits of tax cuts. He had provided support at a critical moment for President Clinton's tax hikes to reduce the deficit. All we needed now was to just hold the line on spending and taxes. Instead, as Greenspan surveyed the economic landscape, the bespectacled economist abandoned his principles and stated, "In today's context where tax reduction appears required in any event over the next several years to assist in forestalling the accumulation of private assets, starting that process sooner rather than later likely would help smooth the transition to longer-term fiscal balance." I almost fell out of my chair.

Greenspan had long said that paying down the debt should be our top priority. And at the moment Greenspan was testifying, the Secretary of the Treasury was reporting in the "Debt to the Penny" that rather than paying down too much debt, the 2001 budget was in deficit $65 billion. Yet with a new President in office cheerleading for tax cuts, the Fed chairman jettisoned good sense and joined in all the happy talk. Papa Bush had blamed Greenspan for his loss in the 1992 race, and Alan didn't want to get on the wrong side of the new President by continuing his drive to cut deficits and opposing tax cuts. And, with his marriage to NBC news correspondent Andrea Mitchell, to support tax cuts would insure the couple's place on the White House invitation list.

"I'm your friend . . . , but in all candor, you shock me with your statement," I told Greenspan at the hearing. "You are going to start a stampede here this morning."[2] I went on to take him to task, but the horse was out of the barn. No one was more respected on fiscal affairs than Alan Greenspan. His testimony set the tone for our debate over the tax-cut proposal on Capitol Hill.

The notion that the treasury was "awash in money," as Republicans argued, was without basis in reality. A careful examination of President Bush's own budget figures showed the public debt would increase in the next ten years from $5.6 trillion to $7.2 trillion. We needed to forget about ten-year projections, which have no reliability. Unforeseeable events—such as war—make such predictions haphazard. "The way to stop Reaganomics II," I wrote, "is with a one-year budget. We survived two hundred years with one-year budgets."[3] I urged a budget freeze just as I had in the 1980s. Just take this year's budget for next year. Such a freeze would delay spending increases and tax-cut proposals until next year, when we know more about the economic slowdown.

Despite my arguments and those of a number of my colleagues, there was no stopping tax-cut fever. We moved ahead on what I described as "Reaganomics II," a tax cut of $1.6 trillion. You didn't have to be an astrologer to know the outcome of this battle. Having raised taxes in 1993 and then been punished by the voters in 1994, when we lost control of the House and Senate, Democrats had learned a lesson. "Mum" was the word on tax cuts. Sure we would modify the President's proposal around the edges, but he was going to wind up with most of what he wanted. On May 26, 2001, a dozen Democrats joined all fifty Republicans to pass a $1.35 trillion tax cut through fiscal year 2011. Though slightly reduced from what Bush initially sought, it still was the largest tax cut since Reagan was in the Oval Office. The tax cut went to the wealthiest Americans, and the economy received little stimulation. The deficit continued to rise.

There wasn't much time to reflect on the tax cut when a turn of events dramatically changed the Senate. Low-key, moderate Republican Senator Jim Jeffords of Vermont, who had become increasingly alienated from President Bush, dumped his party affiliation to become an independent who would caucus with the Democrats. Suddenly the

50–50 Senate was no more. Jeffords's defection gave Democrats a 51–49 edge. I regained the gavel of the Commerce Committee and of the State, Justice, Commerce Subcommittee in the Appropriations Committee. That change became especially significant a few months later —after the attacks on September 11, 2001—when I was tasked with a leadership role in writing legislation on aviation, port, and rail security.

Everybody will always remember where they were on September 11, 2001. I was in the Capitol briefing the leadership on the State, Justice, Commerce Appropriations Bill. All of a sudden out of the window I could see the flames from the Pentagon after the plane had crashed into it. Earlier, in my office, when I saw television coverage of the first aircraft hitting one of the twin towers of the World Trade Center in New York, I thought that the plane had simply been blown off course. Now, as word circulated that a second aircraft had hit the other tower and smoke rose from the Pentagon, it was obvious we were under attack. I returned to my office, passing Senators and staffers who were rushing pell-mell out of the Russell Senate Office Building. I learned later that we were all lucky. Another plane had been heading for the Capitol when its passengers heroically fought the hijackers and sent their aircraft straight into the ground of Pennsylvania.

September 11 was a harrowing day for everyone across the nation. Responding to the crisis, lawmakers accustomed to moving deliberately shifted gears to act quickly. Business as usual was unacceptable. The partisan passions that had been evident in the first nine months of the Bush administration were put aside, at least for a short time, as we scrambled to pass legislation to make our country more secure. This was a test for government. At this critical moment in history, could Congress and the President enact legislation to better protect our country and reassure our citizens that the federal government was working in the broad public interest?

The events of September 11 indicated that we must improve homeland security. We needed better protection for airlines, ports, and rails. Less than two weeks after the attacks, President Bush created the White House Office of Homeland Security. He made an excellent choice in former Governor Tom Ridge of Pennsylvania to head the office. But the White House initially resisted efforts by Congress to make the new post part of the cabinet and thus subject its head to confirmation by the Senate, and Ridge repeatedly refused to testify on Capitol Hill about the administration's agenda.[4] But then Bush reversed course and backed

Senators Hollings and John McCain, during a 2003 Senate hearing on the reauthorization of the FCC and related matters, June 2003. Collection of the author

the creation of the cabinet department. He even blamed Democrats for being obstructionists and resisting his version of the legislation—and used that version of the story on the campaign trail to help Republicans retake control of the Senate in 2002, the year in which Congress voted to create the Department of Homeland Security.

As chairman of the Commerce, Science, and Transportation Committee, I was charged with writing legislation to beef up airline, port, and rail security. The notion that the private workforce provided airport check-in security was laughable. The screeners were paid minimum wage and often couldn't speak English. They were baffled when my wife, Peatsy, tripped the checkpoint alarms because of her "titanium knees." She had had knee-replacement surgery. We knew the alarm bells were going to ring, as I tried to explain, but the screeners were confused. They couldn't communicate. They weren't trained or professional. The government had to take over the responsibility for airport and airline security, but in setting about federalizing the airport screeners, I ran into a brick wall. Nick Calio, President Bush's congressional liaison, told me that federalizing the screeners was "dead on arrival at the White House." "That may be so, but I will continue on course," I told him.

After drafting legislation to federalize screeners and to secure the airports, we turned to securing the airplane. We received the best advice from El Al, the Israeli airline. Meeting with me and Democratic Senators Frank Lautenberg of New Jersey and Jay Rockefeller of West Virginia as well as Republican Senators Conrad Burns of Montana and Ted Stevens of Alaska, the chief pilot of El Al outlined its security system. It required a locked cockpit door. Once closed and made secure, the door was never opened in flight.

The pilot explained that any disturbance in the cabin required the crew to contact the control tower at the nearest airport and land immediately, at which time security would meet the plane. I can see that pilot briefing us now. "They can be assaulting my wife in the cabin, but I don't open the door. I go straight to the ground, to the nearest airport, with law enforcement meeting me on the tarmac. The terrorists know this," he said. "They have no chance of changing a plane into a missile and running it into a skyscraper or nuclear plant. There's no chance of hijacking a plane. If they want to kill a number of people, they can do it easier in the terminal without having to kill themselves." When asked about bathroom facilities, he said each cockpit now contained a small unit. "As a result of this procedure, there has not been an attempted hijacking in thirty-two years," the pilot stated. That was seven years ago.

When told of El Al's security system and a thirty-two-year safety record, the committee unanimously reported a bill to the Senate that provided for federalizing the screeners and for securing cockpit doors and going to the ground for any emergency. When that bill was called for consideration, we had no trouble passing the provision that federalized screeners. But U.S. airline pilots had an amendment presented to allow them to open the cockpit door for any disturbance or to go to the bathroom. They eliminated my "never open the door" provision, and today the prospect of another 9/11 attack looms. A co-conspirator working in the hangar or with the food suppliers could tape a couple of loaded pistols under a seat while cleaning the cabin or loading food. Then the attackers could go through normal security, knowing that once on board they would be armed for a takeover. Congress continues in the gymnastics of requiring air marshals, marksmanship training for the pilot and crew, and restrictions on movement in the cabin. After seven years, we long since could have equipped the cockpit with a secure door and a small bathroom facility and eliminated the chance of a plane being hijacked or turned into a guided missile.

Even before 9/11, Democratic Senator Bob Graham of Florida and I had introduced a measure to enhance port security. We had been concerned about a potential threat, but now the threat was real. Our government had no intelligence whatever on Osama bin Laden's maritime holdings. But Lloyd's of London had issued a report showing that bin Laden owned ten tankers and had an interest in ten more. We also learned that two of his ships delivered the terrorists and explosives to the port of Mombasa, Kenya, to blow up the American embassies at Nairobi and Dar es Salaam, Tanzania, in 1998. Common sense indicated that bin Laden could easily send one of his tankers up the Delaware River in the dark of night and blow up the tanker and tank farm at Philadelphia. Or, instead of going to Arizona for flight training, as some terrorists involved in the September 11 attacks had done, bin Laden's crews could get jobs on an Exxon tanker, throw the Captain overboard at the last minute, and blow up another port city.

U.S. seaports also are vulnerable because of the confusing, overlapping security responsibilities spread among different officials. By law the Coast Guard Captain is in charge of security. But customs officials think they are in charge, and drug-enforcement officials know they are in charge, while immigration officials ask others to step aside because they are in charge. Without a clear, consistent line of authority for security from one seaport to another, we are hard-pressed to coordinate policies to protect our maritime borders. Amid this confusion the federal government treats our ports as if they somehow are exempt from terrorist attacks. While we fund the border patrol to head off illegal entry at our land borders, the government invests nothing of a comparable nature for port security. We simply provide officers from the Coast Guard, Customs Service, and the Immigration and Naturalization Service, but otherwise we rely upon state-controlled port authorities and private marine terminal operators to handle security. Given the magnitude of the cargoes and their delivery to areas close to large populations, we face major vulnerabilities when our seaports are not protected. The constant, frustrating battle for me was to try to get the resources to do the job.

We had to secure not only ships and cargo, but the wharf, perimeter area, and port facilities. A master plan was needed to fix responsibilities. One of our biggest obstacles was that port operators viscerally oppose heightened security. They view it as interfering with commerce. The business operations of seaports are intensely competitive. The operators are concerned primarily with ensuring speedy turnaround time for vessels—from arrival and docking to unloading and departure. Beefed-up port security meant delays and additional costs.

After some quick hearings, I fashioned a comprehensive measure that was reported unanimously out of the Commerce Committee. It also passed the Senate on a unanimous vote in December 2001. The House passed an alterative version six months later, in June 2002. Most important, both measures called for an assessment of the vulnerability of our ports as well as grants to bolster security. But when Senate and House conferees began to negotiate to reconcile the differences in our versions of legislation, I ran into stiff resistance to my approach. I was a strong proponent of the financing in our bill that called for a $15 user fee on each cargo container, which was estimated to raise as much as $850 million a year—revenue that would cover security costs at fifty-five of our principal ports. House conferees attacked the fee as an increase in taxes, which they opposed. Lobbyists for shipping firms and others turned up the heat against it. The House was not about to sign off on a tax. After arguing all summer, I finally got the House parliamentarian to rule the $15 was a user fee—not a tax. Then the House conferees insisted that our bill violated the constitutional requirement that every measure affecting revenue must originate in the House. We agreed and urged our counterparts to introduce the conference report in the House as an original bill. By proceeding in that fashion, they would act on it first, and when they passed it, we would pass it and send it to the President for his signature. No way, they said!

It was obvious that the White House and Republican leaders were all for port security, but they didn't want to pay for it. We salvaged the legislation by withdrawing the user fee. Instead we required the White House to submit its financing plan for the measure within six months. President Bush signed the legislation on November 25, 2002, but the administration didn't follow through. It was disappointing. We had finally enacted legislation that for the first time would create a national system for securing our maritime borders, but we were not funding it.

Despite the obvious vulnerability of our ports, the White House looked the other way. For the three fiscal years following September 11, 2001, President Bush requested zero dollars for port security. Money that he budgeted for port security was folded into the new Department of Homeland Security. Everybody knew that those funds would be spent on traditional Coast Guard activities such as drug interdiction.

The failure to provide funds specifically for the protection of our ports is outrageous. We keep planning as if the terrorists are stuck on one method of attack—air. So we boost aviation security, but neglect other transportation modes. For example every aircraft that approaches the continental limits of the United States is immediately identified by a transponder signal that travels from the plane to a receiving station somewhere along the coast. On 9/11 there was no such identification system for shipping. We required such transponders onboard all ships approaching the coastline. Passing the legislation was not a big sweat, but it has been like pulling teeth to finance. The Coast Guard estimated it would take $110 million for a comprehensive tower system to receive the signals, but we got an appropriation of only $21 million on one try and $27 million on another. As a result no tower system has been installed.

Since 9/11 Senate Republicans have defeated no fewer than five separate Democratic amendments to provide for port-security funding. My last effort to include user fees to generate the funds was stripped out of legislation by the Commerce Committee on April 8, 2004. The Senate later passed the measure to boost port security on September 29, but the House failed to move it. Even the S.C. Ports Authority in South Carolina opposed the $15 container fee. The failure to fund this vital area has left the nation's ports wanting, and it makes our citizens vulnerable.

We had a similar story in rail security. Twice after the attacks on September 11, the Commerce Committee passed legislation, but it went no further. Then, on March 11, 2004, news of the stunning terrorist bombings of four trains on Madrid, Spain's commuter rail system made headlines around the world. The attacks killed close to two hundred people and injured more than eighteen hundred others. In the wake of those bombings, the Commerce Committee unanimously passed sweeping rail-security legislation on April 8.

"We're not waiting for a train to blow up here before we take action," I said at the time. "Rail security is a matter of national security." The legislation required an assessment of security risks to be conducted within 180 days, provided $185 million in grants to upgrade rail security throughout the country by hiring more police and more canine units, and improved our equipment to detect explosive devices. It was a straightforward response to give the public more confidence in the safety of railroads.

The Senate passed our Commerce Committee bill on October 1, 2004, on a voice vote—no dissent—that provided nearly $1.2 billion for passenger rail and freight transportation. Yet that was as far as it got. The House never acted. This is a crying need. We can only hope that we don't suffer the same calamitous attack as was visited upon Madrid. But the fact is that our tunnels and rail system remain exposed. Government fails its people when we don't take obvious steps to protect them. Lawmakers simply opted not to spend the money required to protect thousands of miles of railroad tracks.[5] The failure was a replay of our experience with port security.

I ran into the same problem when I sought increased funding for Amtrak. Without such a boost, critical repairs of the train service's infrastructure would be neglected and the danger of a failure on the system increased, according to a warning by the Transportation Department's Inspector General.[6] Despite the gravity of the situation, our last authorization for the passenger rail service expired in 2002. Since then cries for privatization had grown. Even with the help of the very skilled David Gunn, Amtrak's president and chief executive officer, we could not turn things around. Amtrak clearly provides a public service, but that notion fell on deaf ears on Capitol Hill. We had struggled and struggled. Congress doesn't believe in providing for train travel, much less rail security.

September 11 did not occur because we had a lack of intelligence. We responded quickly, identified the terrorists in Afghanistan, and pursued them. The problem was a failure on the part of the National Security Council (NSC) to coordinate, analyze, and deliver intelligence to the President. How can the President be fully apprised of domestic threats on a timely basis if the NSC does not include the Attorney General or the director of the FBI, I asked during a debate in the Senate.[7]

I learned about intelligence in 1954 as a member of the Hoover Commission Task Force investigating the intelligence activities of the United States. Those were the days when Senator Joseph McCarthy of Wisconsin was traveling the country charging that the Defense Department, the State Department, and the intelligence agencies of the government were infiltrated with Communists. The White House and Congress agreed that a thorough review of the charges be conducted by the Commission on the Reorganization of the Executive Branch, headed by former President Herbert Hoover. The five-man task force appointed by Hoover was headed by General Mark Clark, then president of the Citadel. Clark asked if I would serve as general counsel to the task force, but I begged off because I couldn't give my full time to the job, which was in Washington. Then he asked Hoover to expand the task force to six members, and I was appointed and was able to accept because being a task force member would require less of my time than being counsel.

I traveled with General Clark back and forth from South Carolina to Washington for the work. The ground rule of intelligence is "need to know." That is, officials in intelligence avoid at all costs passing on intelligence findings to anyone other than those who need to know because the less others know, the less chance for leaks. Agents working in the same section of the CIA can be working on different countries and never know or realize it because it is not necessary. I learned that the CIA considered the biggest leakers were members of Congress. The rule then was never tell them anything. When I first got to the Congress in 1966, Senate Majority Leader Mansfield and other congressional leaders didn't want to be briefed on intelligence, positioning themselves to be innocent of any leaks.

Today, following the creation of the House and Senate Intelligence Committees, the two panels must be briefed by the CIA and others involved in the gathering of classified information. But you can bet your boots that members are never told about critical intelligence findings. For example, if the CIA had information that Saddam Hussein was in a certain house in the Anbar province, nobody at the agency would inform the intelligence committees. The important National Intelligence Estimate that everyone refers to as the authority on intelligence would never include such information. Only the President and the team that was hunting Saddam down "needed to know."

In the fall of 2002, as Congress debated a measure to establish a Department of Homeland Security, I had learned enough from my earlier experiences to know there was a far simpler approach to correcting our problems. The NSC had to be reorganized. The real purpose of the NSC is to connect the dots. As Harry Truman had said in 1947, when the NSC was created, "The functioning of the Council shall be to advise the President with respect to the integration of domestic, foreign, and military policies relating to the national security so as to enable the military services and the other departments and agencies of the government to cooperate more effectively in matters involving the national security." But in reality the NSC was created to protect the country against foreign threats, primarily by using information provided by the Departments of Defense and State and the CIA. Today we need to enhance the NSC to protect against domestic threats by also reviewing the data gathered by the Attorney General, the FBI director, and the secretary of Homeland Security.

By adding the Attorney General, the NSC would be privy to the latest information from the Immigration and Naturalization Service, Border Patrol, Drug Enforcement Administration, Bureau of Prisons, and state law enforcement. The President could count on timely, wide-ranging reports on domestic as well as foreign threats.

My proposal was aimed at correcting the problems that we had learned about in investigations into the events leading up to the attacks on September 11. The CIA, FBI, and others in intelligence and law enforcement had failed to "connect the dots" by sharing the results of their work. They simply had not communicated with each other. For example the CIA had been tracking a couple of the terrorists later involved in the attacks, but it never gave the FBI a heads-up. If informed of their presence, the FBI could have conducted a covert investigation to learn of their mission.[8] I set out on the Senate floor why it was so important to correct this communications problem at the heart of our intelligence failures. Expanding the membership of the NSC would go a long way to fixing it. Despite my pleas, my proposal fell short by an eyelash (48–49) on September 12, 2002. Instead we've added another thousand-man bureaucracy in intelligence to oversee and analyze intelligence for the nation. Coordination of intelligence at the NSC is still lacking. We larded on analysis.

This was our deficiency in Desert Storm. One of our famous earmarks in the Senate was when we on the Defense Appropriations Subcommittee kept alive the Central Command in Tampa, Florida. The White House was intent on phasing it out, not providing any appropriation for it. Since we kept the Central Command alive, its commander, General Norman Schwarzkopf, came not to the House or Senate Armed Services Committee to report after his victory but first to our little Senate Defense Appropriations Subcommittee. He allowed that what he got out of the CIA was overanalyzed; that the analysts kept cutting the corners and rounding the edges, defending their work so much that he ended up with "mush." He had to depend on his pilots for intelligence in Desert Storm. This caused me to learn that we have dozens of CIA analysts, who are paid as well as a Senator and receive substantially more for overtime. Senators aren't paid for overtime, and I always thought that, if I stayed in Washington as a retiree, I could easily stay put in my home with a job out at Langley and an increase in pay for just analyzing. Bottom line: Instead of coordination of intelligence at the National Security Council, we've got more analysis, with the intelligence cost to the government soaring to $50 billion.

It's been more than five years since the gargantuan Department of Homeland Security was created. I was one of nine Senators to oppose the legislation creating the new agency. "A new Department of Homeland Security is unnecessary," I said. "The worst case is for the department to be set up and our country lulled into thinking we are all safe and secure. A September 11th could still easily happen." The department's incompetence in responding to the devastation of Hurricane Katrina in 2005 resulted in plenty of unnecessary suffering. It is a case study of how government does not work. We had trouble with the Federal Emergency Management Agency (FEMA) after Hurricane Hugo in 1989. I hounded the agency to improve, and when James Lee Witt from Arkansas took over, he did an outstanding job cleaning up FEMA. After Hurricane Andrew of 1992, we responded. But merging FEMA into the Department of Homeland Security was a disaster. As has been detailed in many accounts, the department, having absorbed FEMA and raided its budget, had undermined the government's ability to respond to natural disasters.

Throughout 2002 Bush's rhetoric for war against Iraq was getting hotter. The President's preoccupation with Iraq was strange. After all, we were hitting Afghanistan in pursuit of those responsible for the attacks on September 11. Iraq had not been connected to the attacks, but you wouldn't know it from the way Bush was talking. As Bush kept up the pressure against Iraq, some lawmakers signaled that he should win congressional support before launching a strike. Bush ultimately agreed, and the White House initially sought a very broad mandate from Congress that would have given the President sweeping authority to "restore international peace and security in the region." Bush was forced to modify that language after enough lawmakers, Republicans and Democrats, saw it as a blank check that they were unwilling to sign.[9] The specific language of the proposed Joint Resolution was limited: "The President is authorized to use the Armed Forces . . . as he determines to be necessary and appropriate in order to: (1) defend the national security of the United States against the continuing threat posed by Iraq; and (2) enforce all relevant United Nations Security Council resolutions regarding Iraq." Saddam certainly posed no threat to our security. We were threatening Saddam. And the United Nations Security Council was in the midst of inspections for weapons of mass destruction (WMD). Attempts to get a second resolution were abandoned by President Bush.

I had learned over the years that the best intelligence in the Mideast came from Mossad, Israeli intelligence. Israel must always be vigilant. It doesn't have time to go to the United Nations or convene a summit on an imminent threat. Israel must strike before that threat becomes a full-blown attack, as the little country demonstrated in 1981, when its warplanes knocked out Iraq's nuclear facilities. Israel launched the strike without warning, and it was harshly criticized.

If there were any chance that Iraq harbored WMD, Israel would surely know. So I asked Defense Secretary Donald Rumsfeld at a briefing: "What about Mossad? What do they report?" When he answered "nothing," I knew that his response was not conclusive because I was not in the "need to know" loop. In the Senate, we never received intelligence briefings that revealed with specificity such highly sensitive matters as whether WMD had been located. There were hints and innuendoes but nothing more. Still, as a member of the Defense Appropriations Subcommittee, I knew all about the $2 billion spent annually for U.S. flights over the Kurdish section in northern Iraq and the Shia section in the south. From time to time, we knocked out radar and gun sites, but I am confident that if something of greater magnitude had been identified during those flights, I would have picked up at least a suggestion of it even if nothing specific. Handling the appropriations for the State Department, I had obtained a document listing the forty-five countries where al-Qaeda was operating on 9/11. The list included seventy cells in the United States, but it did not include Iraq. More important, in "Don't Attack Saddam," a studied analysis published in the August 15, 2002, issue of the Wall Street Journal, Brent Scowcroft, who had been the National Security Adviser for Presidents Gerald Ford and George H. W. Bush, warned, "At minimum, it would stifle any cooperation on terrorism, and could even swell the ranks of the terrorists."[10]

I was prepared to oppose Bush's request for congressional approval to invade. But the President gave a speech that changed my mind. On October 7, 2002, three days before our vote, President Bush stated in Cincinnati, "Facing clear evidence of peril, we cannot wait for the final proof—the smoking gun—that could come in the form of a mushroom cloud." The President, having been apprised of critical intelligence, was clearly saying that we had to act to prevent Saddam from using nuclear weapons. Anytime the Commander in Chief makes such a declaration—be he a Republican or a Democrat—he's got my support. On October 10, I cast my vote, along with seventy-six of my colleagues, for the resolution. The previous day the House had endorsed the resolution by a vote of 296–133. At the time of the vote, I thought that Israel had located WMD and that we were going to knock them out to save Israel the criticism.

Obviously I was misled by the Commander in Chief. I didn't make a mistake. I cast the right vote in light of President Bush's description of the threat facing us. I will assume responsibility when I am wrong, but in this case the fault lies with the President, or the President's lies caused the fault.

It's unfortunate that the President and others in his administration forgot the keen observation of the Spanish American philosopher George Santayana, who said, "Those who cannot remember the past are condemned to repeat it." The lesson of history in the Muslim world is that religion is stronger than freedom and democracy—even life. The Ayatollahs control. It took Saddam, a strong-armed tyrant and secular Sunni, to keep the Kurds, Sunni, and Shia together as a nation. Sixty-five years ago those of us who fought in World War II helped to liberate Morocco, Algeria, and Tunisia; yet none of those countries opted for democracy. We liberated Kuwait seventeen years ago. It too has yet to opt for democracy. It took Kemal Ataturk's bold ideas and initiative in the 1920s to begin the modern Turkish republic and move the Muslim country to embrace democratic ideas.

Before we launched our invasion, we should have known better. The history was clear. After we defeated him in Desert Storm, Saddam, who remained in power, went after the Kurds and Shia because he felt they had not responded vigorously to the U.S. attack. As a consequence, for eleven years the United States had been flying over two-thirds of Iraq and bombing radar and gun sites to protect the Kurds in the north and the Shia in the south from Saddam's Sunni and his Ba'ath Party.

Rather than facing a threat to our security from Saddam, the United States had been threatening Iraq for eleven years.

The one lesson that we know by heart is that democracy comes from within. You can't force-feed it with an invasion. We forget who attacked us on 9/11 and why. Like it or not, Osama bin Laden is a patriot in the Muslim world. In September 2007 Yaroslav Trofimov published *The Siege of Mecca,* telling how Osama bin Laden turned against the House of Saud at the Mecca uprising in 1979. Bin Laden later contended that the U.S. support of Israel was another crusade of the West against Islam. Wealthy and determined, he was angered that U.S. troops were allowed to use Saudi territory from which to attack Iraq in the Gulf War in 1991. He saw that as a desecration because nonbeliever Americans were allowed to occupy the birthplace of Islam. He made so much trouble for the kingdom in Saudi Arabia that he was expelled. He eventually made his way to Sudan, but the Sudanese booted him out to Afghanistan. Billionaire bin Laden did not set up in a castle or mansion but got down on the ground with the troops he trained and plotted his strategy. His followers were made to know that the U.S. presence in Saudi Arabia, Kuwait, Bahrain, Qatar, and the Persian Gulf was proof positive that the United States was on a modern-day crusade against Islam. He blew up the U.S. Air Force barracks in Riyadh, Saudi Arabia. We didn't get the message. Next he was implicated in the 1993 World Trade Center bombing. We didn't pay attention. Then he blew up the embassies in Kenya and Tanzania in 1998. Still, we didn't listen. Then in 2000 he blew up the USS *Cole,* and again we didn't listen. Finally, when he organized the destruction of the twin towers of the World Trade Center and hit the Pentagon on 9/11, we listened. We responded by pursuing him in Afghanistan, defeating al-Qaeda, and forcing Osama into hiding. But then our invasion of Iraq provided bin Laden with propaganda to use against the United States. After five years of war, we've proved to 2.3 million Iraqi refugees and 2 million displaced Iraqis that the United States is worse than Saddam. And with Lebanon, Syria, Iran, Jordan, Saudi Arabia, Pakistan, and the Palestinians more against us than before the invasion, we need to understand that we are creating terrorism rather than eliminating it.

The trouble with our invasion of Iraq is that we as a nation have yet to decide why we invaded. In 1996 Benjamin Netanyahu was elected Prime Minister of Israel. Netanyahu commissioned a think tank in Jerusalem to recommend a course for Israel with Yasir Arafat and the Palestinians. Richard Perle, Douglas Feith, and David Wurmser headed the task force, which submitted the report "Clean Break," recommending that Israel make a clean break from the negotiations with Arafat and the Palestinians. Arafat couldn't be trusted, they said; it was a waste of time. Instead, they said, the way to secure Israel was to democratize the Mideast. The Perle group recommended bombing Lebanon, "rolling back Syria . . . [and] drawing attention to its weapons of mass destruction program," and replacing Saddam with a Hashmite ruler favorable to Israel. After Netanyahu rejected "Clean Break," Perle, Feith, and Wurmser returned to the United States and joined the Project for the New American Century—which also included Dick Cheney, Donald Rumsfeld, Paul Wolfowitz, Scooter Libby, Steve Cambone, Jeb Bush, Elliott Abrams, and William Kristol. Members of this group prevailed on Republican Senator Trent Lott of Mississippi for a resolution for regime change in Iraq, which we adopted unanimously by voice vote on October 7, 1998. At the time Republican Senator Jesse Helms of North Carolina stated, "It will not send in U. S. troops or commit U.S. forces in any way." And Senator Bob Kerrey of Nebraska stated that "this bill is not a device to involve the U.S. militarily in operations in or near Iraq. The Iraqi revolution is for Iraqis, not Americans, to make." The last paragraph of the resolution prohibited any military action. The Senate felt it was supporting internal dissension in Iraq, not an invasion. Opponents of invasion, such as Senator Robert Byrd and Senator Ted Kennedy, let it pass unanimously. Members of the Project for the New American Century beseeched President Clinton in 1998 for regime change in Iraq. In December 1998 Clinton ordered a national air attack known as Desert Fox. As Michael R. Gordon and General Bernard E. Trainor describe it in *Cobra II:* "415 cruise missiles were launched while American and British planes dropped more than 600 bombs. The Pentagon later estimated that it had killed 1,400 members of Iraq's Republican Guard and set back Saddam's supposed weapons program two years."[11]

When George W. Bush was elected President, proponents of "Clean Break" hit pay dirt. Suddenly those who favored striking at Iraq held seats of power. Vice President Dick Cheney—who continually has tried to link the 9/11 attacks to Saddam despite the absence of evidence—is the most influential policy maker in the administration. Richard Perle, one of the authors of "Clean Break," became chairman of the Defense Policy Board, a federal advisory committee to the Defense Department.

The top three positions in the Defense Department were occupied by Rumsfeld, Wolfowitz, and Feith. Steve Cambone of the Project for the New American Century became Undersecretary of Defense for Intelligence. Scooter Libby became Cheney's chief of staff, and David Wurmser became the Vice President's Middle East adviser.

In January 2001, days before Bush's inauguration, the incoming President visited the Pentagon. I asked my friend, Secretary of Defense Bill Cohen why he was at the Pentagon. To everybody's surprise, Bush sought a personal briefing on Iraq arranged by Cheney's office. The fixation on Iraq continued after he took the oath of office. At the first meeting of the NSC, all the discussion revolved around Iraq. It was just ten days after his inauguration, and Bush—in what appeared to some at the meeting to be a "scripted exchange"—asked what was on the agenda. National Security Adviser Condoleezza Rice responded, "how Iraq is destabilizing the region."[12]

At this time Saddam Hussein was defeated and posed no threat. After Saddam had made an assassination attempt on George H. W. Bush when the former President attended a ceremony in Kuwait in 1993, President Clinton had responded by ordering a strike. A missile went down the stack of Saddam's intelligence headquarters in Baghdad. Saddam had gotten the message and was lying low. At the time the United States was overflying, bombing, and destabilizing Iraq. The United States was a threat to Iraq's security, not vice versa. On June 1, Condoleezza Rice chaired a meeting of the Principals Committee to plan four options on Iraq, one planning for a U.S. invasion.[13]

When the 9/11 attacks occurred, the "Clean Break" crowd in the Bush administration saw an opportunity. Within hours of the attacks, Rumsfeld had obtained orders from the President to prepare to go into Iraq. Meanwhile Bush himself was looking for a link between the attacks and Saddam. As recounted by Richard A. Clarke, the NSC counterterrorism director, in his *Against All Enemies*, Bush pulled him and several others aside on September 12 and asked them to see if Saddam was connected to the attacks. Clarke told him that they had looked several times to see if there was state sponsorship of al-Qaeda and found no links to Iraq. The President said he knew that, but he wanted them to examine it again. "Look into Iraq, Saddam," he said testily to the small group. Clarke had similar experiences that day with Wolfowitz and Rumsfeld. Wolfowitz insisted that Iraq must have participated in some fashion. "CIA was explicit now that al-Qaeda was guilty of the attack," Clarke wrote. But he said that Wolfowitz wouldn't accept that finding. "It was too sophisticated and complicated an operation . . . for a terrorist group to have pulled off by itself, without a state sponsor—Iraq must have been helping them." Meanwhile Rumsfeld's comments left Clarke dumbfounded. The Defense Secretary, wrote Clarke, "complained that there were no decent targets for bombing in Afghanistan and that we should consider bombing Iraq, which, he said, had better targets. At first I thought Rumsfeld was joking. But he was serious and the President did not reject out of hand the idea of attacking Iraq."[14]

On September 11, 2001, Lieutenant General Greg Newbold, director of operations at the Pentagon's Joint Staff, was in London briefing the British on the no-fly zones of Iraq. When he returned, he assured Douglas Feith, "We were working hard on Afghanistan." Feith responded, "Why are you working on Afghanistan? You ought to be working on Iraq." On September 15, President Bush held a two-day war council at Camp David. "Rumsfeld encouraged Wolfowitz to raise Iraq at the meeting," and "Wolfowitz, who was sitting in a back row, pressed the case for confronting Iraq during the first round of the administration's new war on terror." Four days later Perle summoned the Defense Policy Board "for two days of meetings, which largely concentrated on Iraq."[15]

A Downing Street memo that describes a meeting between British Prime Minister Tony Blair and his senior national security team on July 23, 2002—months before the March 2003 invasion of Iraq—shows that Bush was intent on invading Iraq regardless of whether Saddam had weapons of mass destruction. The memo refers to classified U.S. policy and states that "Bush wanted to remove Saddam, through military action, justified by the conjunction of terrorism and WMD. But the intelligence and facts were being fixed around the policy." The intelligence was being contrived. Finally, in a leaked transcript of talks at Crawford, Texas, between President George W. Bush and Prime Minister José María Aznar of Spain in February 2003, a month before the invasion, Bush told Aznar, "In two weeks we will be ready militarily. We will be in Baghdad at the end of March." At the time the United States was lobbying the United Nations Security Council for a second resolution authorizing military action. But Bush dropped the effort after it became clear that the resolution would be blocked, and on March 19 he invaded. Bush was determined to invade and democratize Iraq to secure Israel pursuant to Richard Perle's plan of "Clean Break."[16]

I recognize the other reasons put forward for invasion. Many feel that President Bush invaded to finish off Saddam, which Daddy Bush failed to do in Desert Storm. Alan Greenspan has said everyone knows it was for oil. We know several reasons for which we are *not* in Iraq. We are not in Iraq because it had weapons of mass destruction, and we are not in Iraq to protect the security of the United States. When Republican Senator John Warner of Virginia, a former chairman of the Armed Services Committee, asked David Petraeus, the General in command in Iraq, at a hearing on September 11, 2007, six years after the attack, "Does [our strategy] make America safer?" the General didn't have U.S. security in mind. He answered, "I don't know, actually. I have not sat down and sorted out in my own mind." We also didn't invade Iraq to defeat Osama bin Laden or al-Qaeda because Saddam wouldn't allow Osama bin Laden or al-Qaeda to come into Iraq. It was our invasion that opened the door for al-Qaeda to enter that country.

All the retired Generals are now appearing on TV lamenting the fact "that we didn't have a strategic plan for Iraq." False! We went in on Bush's strategic plan of a quick invasion. The Bush administration was greatly influenced by Ahmed Chalabi, a ne'er-do-well Iraqi refugee who had escaped a bank-fraud charge in Jordan and was obviously Bush and Cheney's strategic planner. Without securing the country, the plan was to hold quick elections, allow Ahmed Chalabi's crowd to take over, stabilize the country, and establish democracy in Iraq. In January 2003, as I recognized the drift to war, I proposed a 2 percent VAT to pay for the war and a draft for the necessary troops. The United States had always increased taxes to pay for every war. But the White House put out the word that my tax bill was dead on arrival, and I couldn't get any cosponsors. It was then that Rumsfeld stated publicly that we had enough troops. I know, as the chairman of an Appropriations Subcommittee overseeing the State Department, that they were planning a quick peace because I was objecting to their plans for an elaborate embassy complex in Baghdad. As the last holdout, I let it go forward only because of my respect for Secretary of State Colin Powell. We now know that the administration planned to meet any need for additional troops by "contracting out." President Bush now has more "contract-out" personnel in Iraq than troops.

With Chalabi saying we were going to be met with sweets and flowers, we launched our attack on March 19, 2003, by hitting the outskirts of Baghdad with a barrage of cruise missiles and bunker-penetrating bombs. We followed with ground forces that fought their way toward Baghdad, where they toppled the statute of Saddam Hussein in downtown on April 9. Back home everybody was encouraged by this dramatic picture. President Bush wasted little time in giving the public the impression that the finish line in war was already in sight. On May 1, the President landed aboard the USS *Abraham Lincoln* and spoke to the sailors with a backdrop that displayed a prominent banner reading "Mission Accomplished." As the sailors cheered, Bush declared, "Major combat operations in Iraq have ended. In the battle of Iraq, the United States and our allies have prevailed. And now our coalition is engaged in securing and reconstructing that country." But we never deployed enough troops to secure Iraq. We had no idea of securing Iraq. And we still don't.

I was elected to the United States Senate on Tuesday, November 6, 1966, was sworn in as a U.S. Senator on Thursday, and the following Monday, I was with General William C. Westmoreland in his quarters in Saigon, Vietnam. The first thing General Westmoreland asked for was 35,000 more troops. At the time he had 535,000 in a country of 16 million. Yet Rumsfeld's war plan in Iraq called for 300,000 troops in a country of 26 million. Rumsfeld had no idea of securing the borders, clearing the area of enemy or insurgents, locating caches of weapons, establishing law and order in metropolitan Baghdad, or securing the country. At the moment Bush declared victory on May 1, 2003, we had more than 300,000 troops in Iraq. But Rumsfeld was concerned that we would be considered occupiers, so he decided to "cut and run." We reduced our troop levels from more than 300,000 to only 150,000 by August and fewer than 110,000 in January 2004.

In short we went from war to occupation. We let Saddam's Republican Guards go free with arms. We made the Ba'athists hostile by disenfranchising them. Then we force-fed elections. The Sunni refused to participate; the Kurds voted not for democracy but for autonomy; they also voted to pay no taxes to Baghdad and to keep the oil in Kirkuk. Our man, Chalabi, ran last in the first election. After the second election we rejected democracy by rejecting the winner, and after five months we handpicked Shia leader Nuri al-Maliki as President of Iraq. As one swallow does not a summer make, one or two forced elections did not a democracy make. In the invasion thousands of Iraqis were killed, with Aljazeera TV reporting the daily count as U.S. atrocities. This served as a clarion call: If you want "to get the infidel," come to Baghdad. Al-Qaeda operatives infiltrated and started chaos amid insecurity. Shia, Sunni, and Kurds started protecting themselves. A civil war ensued. As referees in a civil war, we try to unscramble the egg. Two and a half million refugees have fled Iraq. Another two million Iraqis are displaced from their homes to safer areas in-country. Those Iraqis remaining in-country live in terror without the basics of water, lights, or oil. Overall, it is estimated that between two hundred thousand and six hundred thousand Iraqis have been killed. It's no wonder with these results that the United States is now viewed as the enemy rather than the liberator. A poll shows that a majority of Iraqis believe it is good to kill Americans. Instead of eliminating terror, we create it.

And the Arab world has turned against us. This is exactly what President George H. W. Bush warned against. He said to watch out, not to go into that place. In his 1998 book, *A World Transformed*, he said, "I firmly believe that we should not march into Baghdad. To occupy Iraq would instantly shatter our coalition, turning the whole Arab world against us and make a broken tyrant into a latter-day Arab hero. [It would be] assigning young soldiers to a fruitless hunt for a securely entrenched dictator and condemning them to fight in what would be an unwinnable urban guerrilla war." We didn't give Maliki law and order or a democratic government. Now we complain that Maliki doesn't have law and order or a competent government. We expect Maliki to induce the Sunni, who were in control under Saddam, to become a minority faction in a government run by the Shia. We also expect Maliki somehow to persuade the Kurds to embrace the Sunni, who had gassed them. In other words we expect religious sects, who failed in one thousand years to join in democracy, to democratize now. After three years of training Iraqis to defend Iraq, we have produced not a democratic government but soldiers who protect their own sects.

We have failed to learn from the past. We spent ten years in Vietnam pursuing a policy of "Vietnamization," hoping that South Vietnamese troops could take control of their own fate. It cost us 58,000 lives and 153,000 wounded. We still lost. Now we're trying to "Iraqify" Iraq with the same strategy. There is no education in the second kick of a mule.

On October 15, 2003, the U.S. Senate confirmed the "Clean Break" policy for Israel in a resolution by Senator Lindsey Graham of South Carolina "to express the sense of Congress that the removal of the Government of Saddam Hussein has enhanced the security of Israel and other United States allies." Senator Graham said at the time, "I argue that we are much more secure as a nation. . . . But there is one nation where this has made a dramatic difference. This is the State of Israel. This resolution says in very simple and strong terms that disposing of the Saddam Hussein government has made the State of Israel a more secure place." Senator Graham added, "Let it be said that the men and women who sacrificed to make the Iraqi people free have sacrificed in a way to make people in Israel and our own country safer, more secure, and their hopes and dreams maybe will be realized." Senator Mitch McConnell responded, "They [Israelis] are extremely grateful that there is one less terror state in the region to threaten Israel and the United States. In fact, you could argue that Israel benefits every bit as much, if not more so, from the change of regime in Iraq, than we do in the United States."

All of us are for Israel, and I voted for Graham's resolution, which was adopted 95–2. But Prime Minister Netanyahu of Israel, who had rejected "Clean Break," was proven right. We were making Israel less secure, not more. When we went from war to occupation in Iraq in 2003, I knew that invading Iraq was a mistake, and I took the floor of the U.S. Senate to tell my colleagues of my "Cambodian moment." Majority Leader Mike Mansfield had quietly opposed the war in Vietnam for years. He had a practice of writing memos against the war to Presidents Johnson and Nixon while publicly supporting the war on the floor of the Senate. But finally, when Cambodia was invaded under President Nixon, he snapped. Going on television, he said Vietnam was a mistake from the get-go. The next day he received a letter from an admirer who had just lost his son. He said: "I just buried my son to come home and watch you say that the Vietnam War was a mistake from the beginning. Why didn't you speak out sooner?" I reached my Cambodian moment when I realized that we had gone from war to occupation, hoping for democracy to flourish in Iraq. I didn't think our occupation was worth the life of a single additional GI.

Senator Lindsey Graham brought our policy into focus, questioning General Petraeus at the September 2007 hearing on Petraeus's report on the surge, a plan to increase the number of troops in Iraq. Senator Graham asked, "'Put on the table as honestly as we can what lies ahead for the American people and the U.S. military if we continue to stay in Iraq. . . . It's highly likely that a year from now we're going to have at least 100,000 troops in Iraq?"

"That is probably the case," Petraeus said. "Yes, sir."

Graham's follow-up was even more surprising. "How many people are we losing a month, on average, since the surge began, in terms of killed in action?"

"Killed in action is probably in the neighborhood of 60 to 90."

Graham then noted that "we're spending $9 billion a month to stay in Iraq. . . . So you're saying to the Congress that you know that at least 60 soldiers, airmen and marines are likely to be killed every month from now to July, that we're going to spend $9 billion a month of American taxpayer dollars, and when it's all said and done, we'll still have 100,000 people there. You believe it's worth it in terms of our national security interest to pay that price?"

Petraeus said: "Sir, I wouldn't be here, and I wouldn't have made the recommendations that I have made, if I did not believe that."

The General knows better. Moments before, Petraeus had acknowledged that he didn't know if this sacrifice in blood and treasure would make us safer. Then, in response to Senator Graham, he said that a continued occupation of at least 100,000 troops for the next ten months—with 600 killed, thousands casualties (many severely wounded), and a cost of $90 billion—is worthwhile because of the unrealistic goal of turning Iraq into a democracy.

My beef with Iraq is the command. We all know that the troops have performed admirably, but the command is lousy. In World War II, we defeated both Adolf Hitler and Tojo Hideki in a little over three and a half years. In Iraq, a country two-thirds the size of Texas, it seems as though we could have closed off the borders, secured the country, and cleared out any production of Improvised Explosive Devices. After five years of war, 70 percent of the casualties there are not in combat—but in trucks. If GIs are put into Iraq to fight, there are too few. If they are put there to die, there are too many.

We have gone from war to occupation in Iraq only to attain "victory" when a democratic government is established in Baghdad strong enough to control the country. In the meantime we engage in a charade of training enough Iraqis to fight for their country. In World War II we

The Hollings staff in 2004. Many staffers worked for Hollings for extended periods, some more than thirty years. Collection of the author

took raw recruits off the streets of Brooklyn and in six months had them trained and at war in Africa. After five years there are enough Iraqis trained to fight; the trouble is they are ready to fight each other. So the Bush policy is to continue to ask GIs to be killed and spend billions in Iraq until enough Shiites, Kurds, and Sunni stop fighting and join in a political solution of democracy in Iraq. Iraqi Defense Minister Abdul Qadir said in January this would take "until at least 2018." We can't get a political solution in Congress, much less a political solution in Iraq. While we hope for Iran's cooperation, President Bush calls that country "evil." Then he delivers nuclear capabilities to Iran's neighbor India and tells Iran she can't have the same, threatening war if she tries. Now Bush labels Iran's army "terrorists." If we had labeled Hitler's army "terrorists," we would never have had peace. Syria, Iran, Jordan, and other nations of the Middle East are overwhelmed with refugees from U.S.-occupied Iraq. Seeking the assistance of these nations without withdrawing U.S. forces is to ask that they support U.S. occupation. Trends are not in that direction. Stability among the factions in Iraq can be established only after a U.S. withdrawal.

In March 2004 I traveled to Iraq and Afghanistan with Senators Ted Stevens and John Warner. Stevens at the time was chairman of the Senate Appropriations Committee and, of course, in charge of Iraq appropriations. Warner was chairman of the Senate Armed Services Committee. Necessarily we received the "big dog" treatment at every stop. Landing in Jordan, we spent an hour and a half with King Abdullah, who is one of the most able leaders in the region. As a youngster he observed the founding of Israel and the wars involving that nation. In Desert Storm in 1991 his nation supported Saddam and Iraq. Yet he is now our strongest ally in the Mideast. At the conclusion of our conference, King Abdullah directed his remarks to Senators Stevens and Warner. He knew that they had the ear of the President, and he was "talking to President Bush": "Tell the President to get more active to settle the conflict between Israel and the Palestinians. This is the reason for terrorism against the United States."

When we got to Kuwait, the emir, Sheikh Jabir al-Ahmad al-Sabah, counseled: "The United States has to settle the conflict between Israel and the Palestinians." Then in Pakistan we conferred with President Pervez Musharraf for almost two hours. I learned, for example, that he had requested helicopters to search for Osama bin Laden six months earlier but still had not received them. I knew we had State Department helicopters deployed against the opium production in Afghanistan. As the senior Democrat in charge of State Department appropriations, I promised that Secretary of State Colin Powell would gladly allow Musharraf to use the State Department helicopters to search for bin Laden. As we were standing up to leave, Musharraf counseled about the terrorist problem against the United States. He concluded by saying, "Settle the conflict between Israel and the Palestinians and 85 percent of the terrorism in the world will disappear."

In the war on terror, we make the mistake of fighting the symptom rather than the cause. Terror, the symptom, is a weapon, a strategy—not a war. We don't call the Crimean War with its famous "Charge of the Light Brigade" the Cavalry War, or World War II the Blitzkrieg War. And the terror in Israel-Palestine is different from the terror in Ireland—and from the terror in Spain, Algiers, or the Philippines. Musharraf's point is that we fight the symptom and give benign neglect to the cause of the Israel-Palestine conflict. This has been the Bush strategy for six years. Now Condoleezza Rice is finally trying to attack the cause.

But in Afghanistan we create the cause as we fight the symptom. The Taliban gains strength as we fail to make war against bin Laden. If we knew where he was, we would bomb him. The only war we've won since World War II is "Charlie Wilson's War," when the United States and the Mujahideen ousted Russia from Afghanistan. But today much of the Mujahideen has become Taliban, and we now make war on them. The Taliban defeated the Brits; they defeated the Russians; now they're about to oust us. Their cause is against foreigners, not democracy. We've given them seven years, many lives, and much treasure to opt for democracy, but they fight harder against foreigners destroying their way of life. Our way of life, democracy, comes from within and cannot be force-fed by invasion. We need to pull out of Afghanistan and Iraq and provide democracy where they want it— Mexico. We can solve the trade, drug, and immigration problems with Mexico with a five-year Marshall Plan. We don't have any drug, trade, or immigration problems with Canada on our other border. Canada has property ownership, labor rights, antitrust provisions, a respected judiciary, and the apparatus of a free market. For years I worked on the little subcommittee appropriating billions for walls along the Rio Grande, the Border Patrol, the Drug Enforcement Administration, immigration, courts, prosecutors, probation, judges, jails, etc. We could save money and democracy by stopping the waste of a trillion dollars in Iraq and Afghanistan and putting in a Marshall Plan to clean up corruption and drugs in Mexico and to provide our neighbor with a free market and democracy.

16

Making Government Work

As I leave the Senate after thirty-eight years, everyone is complaining about the political standoff in Washington; nothing gets done; the government doesn't work. People don't realize how overorganized the country is; how the country has split into interest groups and how the Congress is simply a reflection of the people and the country. During my years in the Senate, I have watched politics and the Congress become overorganized and fractured too—and the political system become corrupted with money.

In Washington, Jefferson, and Madison's day, there was no Rotary Club to speak to. As Alexis de Tocqueville wrote, people gathered mostly on Sunday for church. Now every community is replete with civic clubs, cancer drives, environmental rallies, walks, runs, and demonstrations for something. One doesn't have time to think. One only plans the next meeting or the next morning. And the free press or media keep us overorganized. In the famous debate in the 1930s over how to organize and maintain a strong democracy, Walter Lippmann contended that what was needed was to gather around the table the experts in the different disciplines—defense, housing, finance, foreign policy, law enforcement, etc.—hammer out the needs of the country, and give the list to the President and Congress to enact. Educator John Dewey countered: "Let the free press report the truth to the American people and the needs of the country would be reflected by their Senators and Congressmen in Congress." This is what Thomas Jefferson had in mind when he observed that, asked to choose "between a free government and a free press," he would opt for the latter. Today the free press no longer reports news; with an eye to profits, it concerns itself with entertaining, polling, and reporting opinion rather than fact. We now read the newspaper not to learn the facts so we can reflect on a policy or need. The newspaper has taken a poll, and the reader inadvertently lines up with opinion rather than reading the facts with reflection.

Politics is overorganized. When I started in politics sixty years ago, the cost of a campaign was a newspaper ad on the weekend before the election on Tuesday. Just volunteers—no paid staff, no radio, no TV, no campaign headquarters, no pollster, no consultants, no negative polls, no push polls, no focus groups, no fund-raisers, no Internet, no billboards, no yard signs, no airplanes, no mailings, no state party to worry about, no national party to worry about. World War II was over. You and a few friends decided on your running. Today the national party comes from Washington and picks the candidate. If you're not its candidate, the party leaders will tell you that they're going to raise money against you in the primary, so you'd better not waste your time. And if you are their candidate, they'll want to pick your pollster, consultant, and campaign manager. And the one thing I've learned is that business is way ahead of the politician. I had just been elected in November 1966, when Claude Wild, the lobbyist for Gulf Oil, invited me to the Carlton Club on the second floor of the Sheraton-Carlton Hotel on the corner of Sixteenth and K Streets in Washington. As a lawyer I had searched the title for Gulf Oil's refinery on the Cooper River in Charleston, and Archie Gray, general counsel for Gulf, thought I should get to know the Gulf people in Washington. On my second visit with Claude at the Carlton Club, he mentioned how they were going "to get rid of Ralph Yarborough," then the Democratic Senator from Texas. I had not met Senator Yarborough, but Claude told how they had this young, bright Lloyd Bentsen in mind, and the oil crowd was going to elect him to better represent their interests. Of course that's exactly what happened. Bentsen became Senator, and he looked out for oil interests just as I would look out for South Carolina textiles. The oil crowd in Texas planned years ahead for their representation in Washington. When I ran for Governor in 1958 and U.S. Senator in 1966, no textile or business interest asked me to run. Most business wasn't organized. But today all businesses are like oil, seeking out a likely winner for their interest, financing him or her, and spreading the word. They make sure that all candidates, whether theirs or not, are favorable to their interest should they be elected. For example a candidate for the U.S. Senate or House of Representatives can barely announce his or her intention to run before a member of the local Chamber of Commerce is knocking on the door asking his or her support for "tort reform." Tort reform is explained in such a way as to sound like "reform," a right thing to support. Later, when an issue arises in Congress to limit noneconomic damages in a tort case, calls from your hometown will remind you that you were pledged to tort reform. Forty-six Senators and 196 House members have signed a "no tax increase" pledge for Americans for Tax Reform. Congressmen and Senators arrive in Washington committed on the budget, abortion, gun control, taxes, immigration, and the Iraq war. In short, Congress is so overorganized that the vote is fixed long before a bill is introduced, debated, and voted on. People wonder why there is no debate in Congress anymore. Congress is a fixed jury. As the media keeps the country overorganized, money controls the workings of Congress.

The live televising of Senate proceedings has guaranteed partisanship and confrontation. I'll never forget when television coverage commenced. It was at the time Sandra Day O'Connor was to be confirmed in the U.S. Senate. There was no opposition. The appointment had been reported unanimously from committee; the first woman to be appointed had been fully discussed. Ordinarily Supreme Court appointments without opposition would be confirmed in a couple of hours with the managers of the appointment and the Senators from the appointee's home state appearing on the floor. I was sitting in my office that Monday morning when the appointment was called for consideration on the floor of the Senate, and a staffer rushed in saying, "Strom just made a long talk about Sandra Day O'Connor and the value of women on the Court, and you'd better get down there and say something or they'll think you're against women." Of course I responded, going to the floor and talking, but the trouble is the rest of the Senate responded likewise. Instead of the two-hour confirmation, we didn't get Justice O'Connor confirmed until Thursday. Thereafter Newt Gingrich, in 1993 and 1994, addressed an empty chamber of the House every afternoon and evening, and it was covered live by C-SPAN. The loss of the House and the Senate by the Democrats in 1994 was attributed in large measure to Gingrich's unchallenged statements and appearances. From then on, we all learned the Gingrich lesson. With the twenty-four-hour news cycle, no Republican House member or Senator appears on the floor of the House or Senate without a challenging response by a Democrat and vice versa. TV requires us to be confrontational.

Today people have less trust in the President and Congress than ever. The biggest reason is the President and Congress constantly play games with the truth. The people know the truth:

1. Everyone knows there is no free lunch. The government in Washington must pay for the government it provides. Instead Washington runs government into the red by $500 billion a year for the past several years and tells the country deficits are being eliminated. The truth is that deficits are not being eliminated but only made to appear lower by applying the Social Security trust fund and other trust funds to the deficit. It's like paying off your MasterCard with your Visa card. The deficit is unchanged. Some years ago Denny McLain, the star pitcher for the Detroit Tigers, retired and headed a corporation. When the corporation got into financial difficulty, he used the company's pension fund to pay its debt. Of course this is a felony. McLain was charged, found guilty, served his time, and now, I understand, is doing well. I hate to draw attention to Denny, but I did so to make a point. At the time I mentioned this situation on the floor of the Senate: "If you pay off the company debt with the pension fund in the United States, you're guilty of a felony and will serve time. But if the Congress pays off the national debt with the Social Security Pension Fund, you get the Good Government Award." Then, as we borrow $2 billion a day from China and Japan to keep the government going, Washington tells us the economy is strong. Deficits may temporarily stimulate the economy, but they surely don't build a strong economy. Interest costs increase the national debt a billion dollars a day for nothing. President Ronald Reagan appointed the Grace Commission to look for waste in government. Now without looking we are increasing waste at the rate of $1 billion a day. It took the nation almost two hundred years of history, paying for all the wars from the Revolution to Vietnam, to reach a $1 trillion national debt under President Reagan in 1981. The national debt passed $9 trillion at the end of August 2007. Rather than eliminating the national debt by 2008 as Greenspan

had feared in 2001, in the seven years since 2001, the debt increased almost $3.5 trillion. Back in the 1970s, Senator Sam Ervin of North Carolina was trying to stimulate the economy by spending $5 billion for federal highways and bridges. He went into a labored analysis of the number of contractors involved with jobs created in the cement business, in the paving business, and how the economy would receive strong stimulation with $5 billion. We have been infusing the economy with $500 billion in hot checks each year for several years, and instead of growth we worry about a recession. As we keep the government on steroids, Vice President Cheney states, "Deficits don't matter." After the Vice President's statement, the Congressional Budget Office (CBO) reported in January 2005 that policy changes during Bush's first term had increased the incoming year's deficit by $539 billion. CBO attributed 37 percent of that amount to warfare and domestic security, 48 percent to tax cuts, and the rest to spending increases. People know that when you're operating in the red, tax cuts increase the deficit.

2. The charade of lowering the deficit with Social Security funds causes the false belief that "Social Security needs fixing." In 1983 the Greenspan Commission foresaw the retirement demand of "the baby boomers in the next generation" and recommended a high payroll tax. Revenues from this high tax have resulted in surpluses in the Social Security trust fund every year. Instead of recognizing these surpluses, politicians and journalists run aound saying, "Social Security doesn't have the money to take care of the baby boomers." On close examination one learns the truth. To look fiscally responsible, the government uses Social Security surpluses to report a smaller than actual deficit. The Social Security trust fund is invested by law in treasury bonds that earn interest. The government, in order to report a smaller deficit, acts as if these bonds are all indebtednesses of Social Security rather than of the government. But the bonds are the government's indebtednesses, not Social Security's. Social Security doesn't need fixing. The national debt needs fixing. The government needs fixing; that is, it must pay for the programs it provides. And, once and for all, we need for the President, the Congress, and the media to stop joining in this deception. I tried to stop it by recommending a VAT to pay down the debt. No support! The Social Security trust fund

remained off-budget until 1968, when Lyndon Johnson put Social Security on-budget. In 1983 Section 21 of the Greenspan Commission report on Social Security recommended that the Social Security trust fund again be removed from the unified budget. Pursuant to the Greenspan recommendations, I tried truth in budgeting by the enactment of Section 13-301 of the budget act, forbidding the President and Congress to report a deficit inclusive of Social Security trust funds. The President signed 13-301 into law. But each President and Congress violate this provision. The media joins in the violation by reporting a false deficit. No wonder a lack of trust.

3. Everyone knows that a nation engages in international trade to strengthen its production, its economy. Everyone knows that Corporate America's outsourcing has caused a loss of thousands of jobs in every state. As the nation loses production and jobs, the economy is weakened. Yet Washington insists on more free trade. The charade of "free trade" is the biggest reason for distrust in government. Americans, if nothing else, are a competitive people— "Yankee Traders." In 1945 the General Agreement on Tariffs and Trade for free trade promised an increase in manufacturing jobs. The Kennedy Round of 1962 promised an increase in jobs. The Tokyo Round in 1979 promised an increase in jobs. NAFTA in 1994 promised an increase in jobs. Permanent Normal Trade Relations with China promised an increase in jobs. Each time we've had a loss instead of an increase. In the last ten years, we have lost 3.5 million manufacturing jobs. But as jobs and production continue to be outsourced, Washington and Corporate America continue to tell us "free trade" increases jobs and production. No wonder there's a lack of trust.

We have been running a deficit in the balance of trade in excess of $700 billion for the past three years. Now we borrow so much from China and Japan to finance these deficits that they could control our trade policy. Japan's sell-off of our treasuries caused the stock market crash in 1987, according to incoming Secretary of Treasury Nick Brady.

For the United States, the trade war began on July 4, 1789, when the second act of Congress in its history was a tariff bill against England's protected manufacture. Protectionism no doubt began earlier, but—as it concerns the United States—it began in 1630 when the Mother Country required that all trade with the fledgling colonies be carried in British vessels. In 1769 the Townsend Act, exacting a tariff on tea and other articles, caused the famous Boston Tea Party. "Free-trade" Britain engaged in protectionism long before our freedom. Britain's protectionist trade policy with the colonies envisioned raw materials such as timber, rice, cotton, and indigo being imported from the colonies to England, where they would be used for manufactured goods exported back to the colonies. All kind of restrictions were put on the colonies prohibiting manufacture, even forbidding the printing of Bibles there. George Washington stated in his first message to Congress in 1789: "A free people should promote such manufactories, as tend to render them independent on others for essential, particularly military supplies." And Alexander Hamilton, responding to the Mother Country's policy of prohibiting manufacture in the colonies, wrote his famous *Report on Manufactures* (1790), setting a mercantilist or protectionist policy that built the United States into the industrial power of the world. Even John C. Calhoun championed a tariff act in 1816, stating in the House debate that "Liberty and the Union" of the United States depended upon the principle of protectionism. "Neither agriculture, manufacturers, nor commerce taken separately is the cause of wealth. . . . It flows from the three combined and cannot exist without each." Henry Clay, the subject of one of John Kennedy's "Profiles in Courage," stated on the floor of the Congress:

> Free Trade! Free Trade! The call for free trade, is as unavailing as the cry of a spoiled child, in its nurse's arms, for the moon or the stars that glitter in the firmament of heaven. It never existed; it never will exist. . . .
>
> Gentlemen deceive themselves. It is not free trade that they are recommending to our acceptance. It is, in effect, the British colonial system that we are invited to adopt.[1]

Abraham Lincoln, the Emancipator, was one of the biggest protectionists of all time. Protectionism was one of the issues that made Lincoln President. In 1862 he raised tariffs from 18 percent to 37 percent, and in 1864 he raised them again, to 47 percent—thus the debate on whether tariffs or slavery caused the Civil War. There is no question that the United States was built with tariffs, customs, and protection for the first hundred years. We didn't pass an income tax until 1913. The tariff-built industrial power of the United States at the beginning of the twentieth century is best described by Edmund Morris in *Theodore Rex,* his book on Teddy Roosevelt:

> This first year of the new century found her worth twenty-five billion dollars more than her nearest rival, Great Britain, with a gross national product more than twice that of Germany and Russia. The United States was already so rich in foods and services that she was more self sustaining than any industrial power in history.
>
> Indeed, it could consume only a fraction of what it produced. The rest went overseas at prices other exporters found hard to match. As Andrew Carnegie said, "The nation that makes the cheapest steel has other nations at its feet." More than half the world's cotton, corn, copper, and oil flowed from the American cornucopia, and at least one third of all steel, iron, silver, and gold.
>
> Even if the United States were not so blessed with raw materials, the excellence of her manufactured products guaranteed her dominance of world markets. Current advertisements in British magazines gave the impression that the typical Englishman woke to the ring of an Ingersoll alarm, shaved with a Gillette razor, combed his hair with Vaseline tonic, buttoned his Arrow shirt, hurried downstairs for Quaker Oats, California figs, and Maxwell House Coffee, commuted in a Westinghouse tram (body by Fisher), rose to his office in an Otis elevator, and worked all day with his Waterman pen under the efficient glare of Edison lightbulbs. "It only remains," one Fleet Street wag suggested, "for [us] to take American coal to Newcastle." Behind the joke lay real concern: The United States was already supplying beer to Germany, pottery to Bohemia, and oranges to Valencia.
>
> As a result of this billowing surge in productivity, Wall Street was awash with foreign capital. . . . Even the Bank of England had begun to borrow money on Wall Street. New York City seemed destined to replace London as the world's financial center.[2]

Protectionism built the United States into an industrial giant. The Smoot-Hawley tariff of 1930—blamed generally for the crash of the stock market and the Depression—was passed eight months after the crash of the stock market in October 1929. International trade at the time amounted to only 1.3 percent of the GDP as compared to 26 percent today. And Cordell Hull, who is credited with starting the "free trade" movement during the Woodrow Wilson administration, insisted that our trade policy be reciprocal. Reciprocity gave the nation a favorable balance of trade by 1933. President Franklin Roosevelt instituted protectionism for agriculture. President Eisenhower instituted protectionism for oil. President Kennedy instituted protectionism for textiles, and President Reagan instituted protectionism for steel, semiconductors, automobiles, machine tools, and motorcycles. Free trade as foreign aid took root with the Marshall Plan after World War II. When the Japanese attacked Pearl Harbor on December 7, 1941, Roosevelt, instead of suggesting that "we go shopping," put the country to work 24/7, including women. He rationed gas and foodstuffs, allocated materials for Ford to produce Sherman tanks and General Motors to produce B-24s, required curfews for conservation and safety, and increased taxes to pay for the war. "The Greatest Generation," including "Rosie the Riveter," won World War II. When the war ended, the United States possessed the only industrial production in the free world. Wisely we launched the Marshall Plan, sending our money, equipment, and expertise to rebuild Europe and the Pacific Rim. But in our zeal to conquer communism with capitalism in the Cold War, the government blended Marshall aid into trade policy, yielding to the protectionist policies of Japan and the recovering nations.

Foreign-policy experts from Woodrow Wilson on have insisted that free trade was the pathway to peace. The Council on Foreign Relations with the Trilateral Commission took over after World War II. On a trip to Japan in 1992, George H. W. Bush stated in his prepared remarks: "This century has taught us . . . that isolationism and protectionism lead to war and deprivation." On the contrary, when President Reagan put a 50 percent tariff on Japanese motorcycles, Harley-Davidson was saved. And when he threatened trade sanctions, he obtained voluntary-restraint agreements on steel, motor vehicles, computers, and machine tools; these agreements saved Intel, and we obtained Nucor Steel and a BMW plant in South Carolina. At the time Eastman Kodak brought a case against Fuji for dumping photographic paper in the United States—at 80 percent below cost. As a result we now have the multimillion-dollar Fuji production facility in Greenwood, South Carolina. Protection not only saves businesses, it creates new ones.

In 1969 I was making my second trip to Vietnam, and Mike Mansfield, the Senate Majority Leader, told me to call on Singapore's Prime

Minister Lee Kuan Yew, "the wise man of the East." Mansfield was a former professor of Latin American and Far Eastern history at the University of Montana. Lee and a couple of us Senators were discussing how the United States could not continue to bear the entire burden of defending the free world. Someone suggested that Japan pick up some of the cost, and I cautioned against Japan's developing an army or an air force. Then I suggested: "Let them have a navy and patrol the Pacific from the Philippines down to Australia, where there is no trouble. We can continue to patrol the Pacific from Japan, Korea, and up by Vladivostok." Lee immediately countered, "You wouldn't let them have nuclear?" I responded, "Of course not, I wasn't thinking of nuclear." Then I asked, "Would you trust the Germans with nuclear?" "Yes," said Lee. "They've learned their lesson; but not Japan. Japan teaches in its schools that the defeat in World War II was just a temporary setback. After the war Japan launched a policy of prevailing in the world economically." Five years ago Lee confirmed this warning when I called on him in Singapore with Senator Dick Shelby of Alabama. I wanted Shelby to hear it directly from former Prime Minister Lee. We talked to Lee for an hour in his apartment. Lee reiterated the fact that Japan was expanding its economic power and influence and then told of the unannounced visit of Hu Jintao, the incoming President of China. Hu had just visited Singapore, not called on Lee or any officials, and stayed with a friend, who took him around for a week. After Hu left, the friend told Lee that Hu wanted to see how Singapore, with a diverse population and no natural resources, managed to become a nation-state, strong economically. Then Lee added, "Now we'll have to watch China as it takes over the world economically." This is our challenge—not militarily but economically! Following the example of Japan, China has kept its markets closed except for products it doesn't produce. Even agriculturally it intends to predominate. As productive as we are agriculturally, there is no question three hundred million Chinese farmers can out-produce three million American farmers. Three years ago we had a deficit in the balance of trade with China in cotton. To keep the United States' favor, China exports its wheat to Korea so that it can import wheat from the United States. China, like Japan, has been anxious for U.S. technology. Lenovo of China has just bought IBM, "Big Blue," with all of its technology. Meanwhile the production and technology of the Boeing 777 is rapidly increasing in China. China started patenting its computer technology; we stopped it temporarily. Nevertheless with China's volume production, the Chinese article will become the product of trade. The majority of the key production of the Boeing 787, including the wings, is in Japan. Today the United States is a net importer of aircraft manufacture. China, Korea, and Japan keep their domestic markets closed and set competition for market share rather than profit in globalization. But America's transnationals continue to compete for profit, losing market share—even in our home market. Now we have a deficit in the balance of trade in advanced technology with China. More than half of the goods we consume in the United States have to be imported. What isn't outsourced is now being bought by Japan, China, and the Europeans with the cheap dollar. In the last ten years they have bought 8,600 U.S. companies at a cost of $1.3 trillion—many high techs such as Bell Labs to France and Westinghouse Nuclear to Japan, Votophone to Deutsche Telekom and Gateway to Taiwan. Finally the astronomical profits reaped from outsourcing are favored by our tax laws for reinvestment in China and India—not the United States.

The nation's security is in jeopardy. The security of the United States rests on a three-legged stool: one leg is the nation's values; the second is its defense; the third is its economy. The world has respected for years the sacrifices of the United States for individual rights, freedom, and democracy. But our preemptive invasion of Iraq has caused the world to question our values. Two million refugees have fled Iraq for Iran, Syria, Jordan, and Sweden. Another 2.3 million Iraqis have been displaced in-country. The Mideast thinks the United States is on a new crusade against the Muslim world. With Iraq we are creating rather than eliminating terrorism. The values leg is fractured.

The United States has always been respected as the world's superpower. Today the world knows the superpower will not use nuclear weapons to make war—only to defend itself. And the United States, cautious against casualties in Iraq, has caused the second leg, defense, to be challenged by guerrilla warfare. Outsourcing critical materials has put our defense supply chain in question. In 1991 the chairman of the Joint Chiefs of Staff, Admiral William Crowe Jr., said, "The U.S. defense industrial base is already in danger of becoming too dependent on foreign sources for strategic supplies." We had to await Japanese flat-panel displays to launch Desert Storm. We had to await Swiss crystals to invade Iraq. Recently China has come under suspicion of a cyber attack on the Pentagon. The company that provides the Pentagon with technology to prevent cyber attacks is 3COM. Responding to the charge, China attempts to buy into the company, so it can have access to the books, financial records, and company decisions. Ford is now buying parts in China. We don't have the manufacturing capacity to turn into war production, and we are losing more capacity every day.

As economic power gains control in world affairs, the economy leg is also fractured. Guerrilla war offset the superpower's Sixth Fleet and its nuclear bomb in Vietnam and is doing so again in Iraq. Today economic power is more controlling in foreign relations. In 1989 a subcommission of the Human Rights Commission passed a resolution to have the full commission examine China's human-rights violations in suppressing the student prodemocracy movement of Tiananmen Square. China, with its economic influence in the Pacific Rim and Africa, contacted its friends, and no hearing has been held. With globalization in today's world the superpower is not the military superpower but the economic superpower.

As a Senator and former Chairman of the Budget Committee, I have listened attentively for thirty-eight years to the economists— William McChesney Martin, Arthur Burns, Henry Kaufman, Paul Volcker, and Alan Greenspan. Now practically all the economists and President Bush say that the economy is fundamentally strong. Obviously I'm not an economist, but boosting the economy with $500 billion worth of hot checks each year for several years results in false growth and productivity. Normally the economy bounces back with real growth, but when stretched artificially year after year, the economy loses its elasticity and recedes into a recession. And the multiplying effect from people going back to work when the economy bounces back is lost when the work is outsourced.

I was taught that deficits disrupt the economy and cause waste. President Johnson left President Nixon with a budget surplus. But when we returned to deficit spending, we instituted the budget process, and we used to fuss at length over a deficit of $2 billion or $3 billion or more. Now we run $500 billion deficits and no one says anything. As Governor I struggled to create jobs. Now it has just been reported by the Bureau of Labor Statistics that we have lost 91,400 manufacturing jobs in South Carolina since President Bush took office—and 3.2 million manufacturing jobs nationwide. Today our country has fewer manufacturing jobs than in 1942. And the new jobs created—in health care, education, credit services, local government—provide fewer paid hours per week, pay lower wages, and offer fewer employer-provided benefits, such as health care and retirement savings. Of course, with the advances in technology and management, Americans now produce more than before. But the growth of production has not kept up with growth in the U.S. population and spending. Before 1983 U.S. manufacturers always produced more than the United States needed. But trade deficits in manufacturing in the past seven years total $3.1 trillion. And it is not just deficits in manufacturing. The United States is now a net importer of combined technology goods and intellectual property. That is, U.S. foreign earnings on intellectual property are not enough even to pay for imported technology goods much less for nontech goods such as oil and autos. This confirms my long-held belief that the once great industrial giant, the United States of America, is today not producing what she consumes. With a fiscal deficit of $3.4 trillion in the last seven years, debt-driven growth in the economy, soaring repayment obligations, and a falling dollar, how could anyone say that the United States is economically healthy? Martin Feldstein, chairman of the Council of Economic Advisers under Reagan, editorializes in the *Financial Times:* "A declining dollar helps growth and employment by raising exports and causing US consumers to buy domestic goods."[3] Has Feldstein been down on the docks and seen what we're exporting and what we're importing? Our exports are mostly goods such as foodstuffs, paper, and wood chips—no real manufacture. Has he been in a store? Only Chinese products. Economists are important to the economy. But when it comes to a recession, they look to see if there has been negative growth for the last two quarters. They look at the increase of productivity—but only of the remaining production, not the remains of the lost production from outsourcing. The nation is going out of business, and the economists are saying we're on the right track. As a government servant charged with developing a strong economy—with the United States having fewer than 14 million employed in manufacturing for the first time since June of 1950, having just lost 3.2 million manufacturing jobs in the last seven years, and with Ford and GM struggling and Toyota voted number one—don't tell me the U.S. economy is strong.

Instead of aggressively competing when the Cold War ended, we forfeited our economic might and failed to compete in the trade war of globalization. Today the presidential candidates talk of health care, energy, and infrastructure needs. But these domestic programs can't be paid for with an enfeebled economy. We must rebuild our industrial base and our economy. Hamilton wrote in his message to the House of Representatives in 1791 that "not only the wealth, but the independence and security of a Country, appear to be materially connected with the prosperity of manufacturers. Every nation . . . ought to endeavor to possess within itself all essential of national supply. These comprise the means of Subsistence, habitation, clothing and defense." Such strength internally has been overlooked in the rush to embrace "globalization," which has resulted in goods being produced cheaper offshore as our manufacturing base suffers, our workers are tossed overboard, and our economy languishes.

Corporate America has always led the way for the nation to have a strong economy. Henry Ford instituted a strong economy by doubling the minimum wage and providing health and retirement benefits for Ford workers. Our government followed that lead by enacting Social Security, Medicare, parental leave, plant-closing notice, and provisions for worker safety and the environment. After we enacted the Consumer Product Safety Commission, the officers of J. C. Penney Company met me on the fourteenth floor of their Lexington Avenue headquarters in New York and proudly showed me their test lab for monitoring the safety of their merchandise. I can still see that fish tank in the reception hall at Timken Roller Bearing in Gaffney, South Carolina. Timken didn't have just secondary treatment of washing the oil off the bearings; it had quadruple treatment, making the water clean enough for fish life as it poured into the fish tank. And Dupont was spending $2 billion to protect against acid rain.

Such initiatives show that industry in the United States took the lead to produce a high standard of living and community development. Corporate America, with the likes of the Ford Foundation, has supported local schools and colleges, cancer drives, charitable marathons, parks, and playgrounds. Responding to Corporate America's leadership on trade, the federal government went so far as to leave trade enforcement to industry. And industry kept Congress abreast of its needs to protect the nation's production. At the same time, the Federal Trade Commission kept watch to ensure our domestic market was open.

Beginning in the early 1990s, Corporate America's idol, Jack Welch, then CEO of General Electric, stated at an annual meeting that suppliers had to move the following year to Mexico or not be considered subcontractors for GE. "Squeeze the lemon" was his slogan in a policy to save labor costs. Emphasizing his loyalty to profits, rather than to his workers or to any country, he said that ideally Corporate America would have "every plant you own on a barge." Welch's words—coupled with the enactment of NAFTA in 1993—started the deluge of outsourcing.

Today Corporate America, instead of building in the United States, has gone to China and India. Unlike Henry Ford, who invested in U.S. workers, Corporate America slashes its workforce and cuts employees' health and pension benefits. General Motors establishes its Center for Advanced Science and Research not in Detroit, but in a $250 million corporate campus in Shanghai. U.S. firms abandon local communities. Intel, a leader in U.S. technology, outsources to China, and other companies follow suit. China is hustling industry and jobs as aggressively as southern Governors did back in the 1950s and 1960s.

Instead of enforcing our trade laws, Corporate America looks the other way. As American companies create jobs in China and India, they campaign for H-IB visas so cheap foreign engineers and technicians can enter the United States. By paving the way for educated foreign workers, our own companies have set the stage for qualified engineers and technicians in the United States to remain unemployed.

Worst of all Corporate America has turned into a "fifth column" in the trade war. It leads the fight against the Congress's attempts to regulate trade and provide protection for our production. Alan S. Blinder, a professor at Princeton and former Vice Chairman of the Federal Reserve Board, observed: "Economics is often a triumph of theory over fact." Warning that as many as forty million Americans could lose their jobs to lower-paid workers abroad in the next ten years, Blinder said: "What I have learned is anyone who says anything, even obliquely, that sounds hostile to free trade, is treated as an apostate."

Having led the charge for passage of five textile trade bills in the Senate, I know firsthand of what Blinder speaks. Each bill was killed by a President who lectured me on free trade. Today, if a Senator introduces a bill in Congress to enforce our trade laws or to protect our vital production, he or she will be pummeled by charges of "protectionism." Shouts of "free trade" will come from big banks (which make most of their profits outside the United States), the Council on Foreign Relations, the Trilateral Commission, the Conference Board, the Federal

Reserve, the transnationals with their corporate lawyers and lobbyists, the National Association of Manufacturers, the Business Roundtable, the Emergency Committee for American Trade, the National Foreign Trade Council, the American Farm Bureau, the United States Council for International Business, the National Retail Federation (with the retailers making a bigger profit on imported articles), the newspapers (who make a majority of their profits from retail advertising), and the United States Federation of Independent Business. Even the United States Chamber of Commerce joins in the chorus of "free trade" as it turns its favor from Main Street America to Main Street Shanghai. This is the crowd with campaign contributions. Members of the House and Senate need their contributions. You "don't bite the hand that feeds you." So Congressmen and Senators shout "free trade" too as they refuse to regulate trade—as they refuse to protect the economy. Outstanding Congressmen and Senators such as Marcy Kaptur of Ohio, Sander M. Levin of Michigan, Byron Dorgan of North Dakota, and Sherrod Brown of Ohio keep trying, but the opposition is formidable.

Candidates and Corporate America shy away from even raising the subject of trade in the presidential campaign. In 2007 I watched the early presidential debates to see if the nation's most important problems of jobs, outsourcing, and international trade would be discussed. I watched the first eight debates of the two parties. There was no mention of outsourcing jobs or international trade. Then in Iowa, where farmers have such a presence and are always looking to ship their products abroad, international trade was mentioned. Each candidate quickly affirmed that he or she wanted to protect agriculture but not start a trade war. They failed to acknowledge that we already are in a trade war—and not one question about outsourcing jobs. The outsourcing of automobile production caused Michigan to have and unemployment rate of 7.4 percent. In the debate held for just Republican candidates on January 10, 2008, there was bound to be a question on outsourcing. Never happened! Candidates were asked about the economy and each answered with a stimulus plan. John McCain stated that the lost automobile jobs would never come back, and Mitt Romney and Mike Huckabee said that they would bring the jobs back—but not how. A week later in South Carolina, where the textile industry has been outsourced, causing 6.6 percent unemployment, for two hours of questions on CNN's forum for Democratic candidates, there was no question about outsourcing jobs.

China will continue to have the advantage of a workforce with a lower standard of living than that in the United States. China is doing exactly what Japan has done in trade practice for fifty years. It is doing exactly what I would do if I were running China. It works. She is building her economy. Rather than raising a barrier to remove a barrier, rather than trading, the Congress and the candidates whine "free trade" and "be fair" while they avoid doing anything about our trade imbalance.

And the media is just as bad as the candidates. Where's the question: "Since we have been running deficits of $500 billion each and every year for the past five years, how do you intend to eliminate the $500 billion deficit? If your answer is 'cut spending,' detail the $500 billion in cuts." Where's the question: "How do you intend to stop the outsourcing of jobs and production?" Three days before the first presidential primary in Iowa, the *New York Times,* in a sum-up of the Republican and Democratic candidates' positions on the important issues of the campaign listed eight issues—not a one on outsourcing or trade. On the morning after President Bush delivered his State of the Union message, in *USA Today* under the headline "Reality Check: What Bush Said about Eight Big Issues," there was not one mention of outsourcing jobs on trade. Prior to Ohio and Texas in the presidential race, rather than mentioning the outsourcing of jobs and trading in globalization, it's been "The media doesn't ask, and the candidates don't tell."

As the economist John Kenneth Galbraith said, we have to "get the fraud out of free trade." We like to remember Patrick Henry's "give me liberty or give me death" and think that freedom was the cause of the American Revolution. But the trigger for the Revolution was trade, tariffs, the Boston Tea Party. That's why Article I, Section 8, of the U.S. Constitution delegates the regulation of foreign commerce to the Congress—not to the President.

Presidents today negotiate trade agreements, not to open markets but to protect Corporate America's foreign investment. The Ways and Means Committee in the House of Representatives and the Finance Committee in the Senate control trade regulations. These committees mostly comprise members protecting oil and farm interests. President Clinton and other Presidents win congressional approval for a trade deal by playing a round of golf with a committee member or by giving away a "pork" project in that member's district, and in return the trade agreement is reported from the Ways and Means or Finance Committee. Then under fast-track rules, both the House and Senate are required to vote up or down on the trade deals and are prohibited from offering amendments. This whole process means that trade is regulated by the President, not Congress. Lawmakers need to resume their responsibility for trade as set forth under the Constitution.

The fundamental role of government "to protect" is enunciated in the Constitution in the oath required of our President "to preserve, protect, and defend." Congress's foremost duty is to protect the people and the economy. But Congress is immunized from this duty by Corporate America's announcement that the world has entered into globalization. Tom Friedman, in his *The World Is Flat,* like the octopus escaping in a cloud of ink, escapes government in his cloud of ink. He describes in a most colorful fashion the breakthroughs in technology and advancements in communications and management techniques. Companies and countries produce their goods everywhere. Outsourcing is rampant. Every country is on its own. All a country can do to limit outsourcing, according to Friedman, is "educate," "educate." If he is talking higher education, we now have in the United States sixteen of the world's best research universities. If he is talking skills, I introduced a skills program in South Carolina almost fifty years ago that is producing a better quality BMW than Munich. Our problem is not a lack of educated people but a lack of jobs for educated people. Friedman never compares the cost of U.S. production to the cost of outsourced production—the cost of democratic-capitalist production to the cost of communist-controlled production. We have a capitalist regulatory government; China has a controlled government. The capitalist requires a minimum wage; the controlled, a maximum wage. The capitalist requires clean air; the controlled permits dirty air. The capitalist pays overtime; the controlled denies overtime pay. The capitalist requires safe machinery, a safe workplace; the controlled has unsafe machinery, an unsafe workplace. The capitalist prohibits child labor; the controlled allows child labor. The capitalist requires plant-closing notice and parental leave; the controlled prohibits both. The capitalist has a Federal Trade Commission to prevent price fixing; the controlled fixes a high price in the domestic market to induce saving and to accumulate a large profit, which the controlled government uses to subsidize manufacture. The capitalist has antitrust; the controlled is protrust. The capitalist has an open market; the controlled has a closed market.

The WTO permits the controlled government to rebate at export 17 percent of its production taxes; the WTO prohibits the capitalist government from rebating at export its production taxes, giving controlled production a 17 percent advantage. The controlled government subsidizes development of technology; the capitalist government has just repealed the Advanced Technology Program. The capitalist government refuses to protect its manufacture, trade, and economy; the controlled protects its manufacture, trade, and economy. China competes in trade; the United States refuses to trade. Where's the trade that's free?

Friedman concludes his treatise by saying, "The two greatest dangers we Americans face are an excess of protectionism . . . and excessive fear of competing in a world of 11/9 [the fall of the Berlin Wall] that prompts us to wall ourselves off in search of economic security." Today a country can't "wall" itself off because anything can be produced anywhere. With the satellite transferring finance and technology overnight, with Internet control of operation from any country, with air delivery of product in today's world, a trade wall, like the Great Wall of China, is obsolete. With the most open market in the world, America's worry is a lack of protection, not an excess of protection. And having the most productive workers, we don't have to fear competition in globalization. Our fear is that Washington government is not competing in international trade. Our fear is that Washington government is not protecting its manufacture and standard of living in globalization. In globalization David Ricardo's "comparative advantage" is no longer English woolens and Portuguese wine, but government. The world is still round. It is the United States government that is flat.

On taking office in 2001, instead of trading access to our vast market for access to China's market for U.S. exports, Bush went for voodoo-stimulating the market by cutting taxes or cutting revenue to raise revenue. Instead of paying for the wars in Iraq and Afghanistan, Bush and the Congress continued cutting taxes, causing deficits of $500 billion or more for several years. These trade and fiscal deficits forced us to borrow $2 billion a day, adding $3.5 trillion to the debt with interest costs of 5 percent, amounting to $200 billion. This forces us to waste $200 billion each and every year until the debt is paid. We are wasting the cost of Iraq and Afghanistan each year. This money could finance the nation's health care and infrastructure. After stimulating the economy with $3.5 trillion, we have ended up with a near-recession, causing the economists to suggest more stimulation.

Drunk on "deficit barley corn," the economists tell us to take another swig. Stimulating the economy is to give people money to spend for products, which increases jobs to produce products. Paul Craig Roberts, one of Ronald Reagan's economists, reports that 70 percent of products sold in Wal-Mart are produced in China. That means we will stimulate mostly China's economy. Alan Blinder, the Princeton economist, says that our principal export in the next ten years with free trade will be 30 million or 40 million jobs. So under President Bush and Tom Friedman's "Flat World, Free Trade," policy, we educate Americans for jobs going to China and borrow billions of dollars from China to stimulate the economy of China to create jobs in China. President Bush in the last seven years has stimulated the economy with tax cuts to create 5.6 million jobs at a cost of an increase of $3.5 million to the debt. That means we have to borrow $621,000 to create one job. No wonder everybody wants change.

Capitalism can be limited as in the United States with our controls for health, safety, wages, and antitrust; or it can be totally directed, subsidized, and protected as in Japan and Korea. The test is now on course to see whether totally controlled capitalism can work in Communist China. China's leaders are students. They have studied Japan, Korea, and Singapore and have determined to maintain an authoritarian control over their country's people and at the same time infuse China's economy with capitalism for the people's betterment and a strong economy. Of course, with 1.3 billion people, this is quite a task. The "have nots" become restless as they see the "haves" prosper. The task is to spread the betterment fast enough to withhold unrest, demonstrations, and revolt. To accomplish this, China needs a mammoth infusion of capital and technology. And guess what! Corporate America, with its outsourcing, is furnishing capital and technology as fast as it can. Worse—our government in Washington is helping as much as it can. Holding seminars in New York, the government tells American manufacturers to do as they are told by the Chinese government, and the Chinese government demands that Wal-Mart in China hire only Communists. Ironically, with a national mission to spread democracy, the United States is making Communism work. We need to sober up from our binge of "free trade" and domestic politics and take a break from our arrogance.

We are not in charge of the world. We think we are spreading democracy, but in fact we are creating and spreading terrorism with a preemptive war and the occupation of Iraq. We have made Israel less secure rather than more secure. At present we are not in charge of our own fate. Our infrastructure is crumbling; streets are littered with the homeless, many of whom are veterans; millions go hungry; and 47 million are without health care. We await foreign supplies to go to war, and we depend on China and Japan to finance our wars. We don't produce what we consume. Our principal manufactures, aircraft and automobiles, are mainly imported. What production remains from outsourcing is being bought up by foreign governments with the cheap dollar. We cut education, scientific and medical research. The only things on an increase are our national debt, oil prices, and prison population. As the strength of our democracy, middle America, disappears, the world's trust in America disappears.

For years Congress and Corporate America struggled to protect the nation's production and economy. Each time they were rebuffed by "free-trade Presidents" Johnson, Carter, Reagan, and George H. W. Bush. Then with President Clinton's NAFTA with Mexico, WTO with China, and PNTR with China, we've been hit with an economic Pearl Harbor in globalization. Like Roosevelt, we must build an economic superpower to become a military superpower. We've got to put America back to work. We must disenthrall ourselves from caterwauling about corporate greed. We drove Corporate America to outsource. Rather than whine "be fair," "be fair," "free trade," and cry about what China needs to do, we need to concentrate on what America needs to do.

We need to get to work on rebuilding the United States. We need to protect our high standard of living and make it profitable for Corporate America to invest and produce in the United States. Congress needs to

1. Organize the government to compete in globalization by merging the Department of Commerce, the Special Trade Representative, and the twenty-three entities now involved in trade policy into a new Department of Trade and Commerce. Trade treaties should open markets to our exports and protect America's vital production—not just protect Corporate America's foreign investment. The International Trade Commission should be abolished and its role absorbed by the International Trade Administration.

2. Reinvigorate the new Department of Trade and Commerce to apply the countervailing duty law.

3. Change tax laws that give incentives to invest abroad and adopt laws to give the incentive to invest in the United States.

4. Create the office of Assistant Attorney General for Trade in the Justice Department to enforce our trade laws.

5. Hire more customs agents. They are now overburdened with their responsibilities to deal with immigration, drugs, and homeland security. We need at least one thousand more customs agents to protect the transshipment and the safety of imported food, drugs, and textiles.

6. With the new office of Secretary of Trade and Commerce, require the Secretary to list those items vital to our national defense and set quotas or tariffs on critical materials to ensure their production in the United States.

7. Reinvigorate the office of the President of the United States to administer Section 1501 of PL 418, the 1988 Trade Act, which authorizes the President to set aside trade decisions in order to protect the nation's security.

8. Withdraw from the WTO as provided in the WTO charter. WTO is predominately an organization of poor developing countries to assist their development. China, which has the fourth largest economy, with a current account surplus between 12 percent and 13 percent of GDP and with a $1.5 trillion in foreign currency reserves, is treated as poor and developing. The United States is treated as rich and developed, and, with the U.S. having the same vote as Chad, there is no chance for a fair hearing. The WTO has already ruled that foreign tax provisions are not trade subsidies but that U.S. corporate tax provisions are subsidies. Moreover, Section 301 of the America Trade Act, which permits American firms to challenge nontariff barriers in foreign markets, is barred. We don't have time to become bogged down in endless appeals to the WTO.

9. Establish controls for sovereign wealth funds. We can't control our economy when foreign governments have an ownership stake in U.S. companies.

10. Replace the corporate income tax with corporate revenue tax. The change will correct the effects of "transfer pricing," a scheme by which foreign companies operating in the United States overcharge

their U.S. subsidiaries for parts, thus make no profit and pay no U.S. corporate tax.

11. Re-create the Office of Technology Assessment to advise Congress on new technology.

12. Repeal "fast track" consideration of trade legislation so that Congress can assume its constitutional role to regulate trade.

13. Enact a value added tax (VAT). We need the money. President Bush has just submitted his 2009 budget showing a projected deficit of $703 billion for this fiscal year, plus projecting a deficit of $759 billion for FY 2009 (see President's Budget: vol. 1, p. 166). That means that if we freeze spending or take this year's budget for next year, we would still have a deficit of $703 billion. We can cut some spending, but no one recommended $703 billion in spending cuts in my thirty-eight years as a Senator; and we've been playing games too long, acting as if new programs can be financed by just canceling Bush's tax cuts. Bush's $759 billion deficit for FY 2009 does not include war costs, and, of course, candidates for president are all promising health-care, infrastructure, research, and energy programs—a spending of billions. We need to move to pay-as-you-go government, paying down the debt rather than increasing it and wasting $1 billion a day in interest costs. Start with a 2 percent VAT so as not to shock the economy. It will have to be raised over time to remove the disparity in trade and eliminate the waste of a billion a day interest cost on the debt. It will take a year for the IRS to gear up for a VAT. Pending the equalization of the 17 percent disparity, enact a border equalization tax.

14. In the meantime, to slow the outsourcing, to begin trading, to create jobs enact an import equalization tax that equals the VAT plus the tariff charged by any trading partner.

Except for number 13, I have limited these recommendations to ones with strong bipartisan support so we can get something done.

Congress won't organize the government to compete and rebuild our economy until we first limit the money chase. Congress limited spending in campaigns and the money chase in a bipartisan vote in 1971 and again in 1974. Both times Republican President Richard Nixon signed into law limits on spending in campaigns. But the Supreme Court's convoluted decision in *Buckley v. Valeo* amended the First Amendment to the Constitution by equating free speech with money. I can tell you, as a Senator that voted both times for limiting spending in campaigns, the intent of Congress was to prohibit the buying of the office by either a candidate or a contributor. The principal intent of Congress was to prevent a rich young upstart from unseating an experienced senior Senator by buying the office. The Court agreed with Congress that a contributor couldn't buy the office. But it thwarted the principal intent of Congress by providing that a candidate could do just that.

For thirty years Congress, like a dog chasing its tail, has tried various ways to limit spending by both candidates and contributors—without success. Each attempt, like public financing, is rejected because, under *Buckley v. Valeo,* the rich can still buy the office. Or, required to match the spending of the rich candidate in public financing, Congress is reluctant to start an open-ended spending program for politics. More important, spending by 527 and other independent organizations will never be controlled until Congress is given the authority to control spending.

The Court has amended the First Amendment so that rich contributors' speech in campaigns is limited, but rich candidates have unlimited speech. For example Senator Arlen Specter of Pennsylvania, who is of limited means, couldn't match the spending of his opposition. He had an affluent brother, who was ready to contribute substantially to keep Arlen competitive in the race. Yet the Supreme Court said in *Buckley* that Arlen's brother's speech was barred, but that Arlen's opponent had all the speech he wanted. No leader in the Senate would call the Hollings-Specter Joint Resolution to limit campaign spending for consideration because members don't want to vote to restrict spending. Having an office in Washington is a tremendous advantage. Senator Specter and I laid in wait my last years in the Senate for the leadership to call any Joint Resolution for consideration so that we could call up our Joint Resolution as an amendment. But the leadership, realizing we would call our amendment, refused to call for consideration any Joint Resolution.

Each year the costs of campaigns go up and up. Ten years ago I had to raise $30,000 a week for six years to run my last campaign for the United States Senate. At the beginning of February this year, the leading presidental candidates of the two parties had already spent $100 million for the election in November. And one candidate had to put up $5 million of her own money to keep going. If you have to raise $100 million just to get halfway into a race for President of the United States, everyone must agree that the time and money required is ridiculous. Even worse, it is estimated that $3 billion will be spent on TV ads, as outside groups pour money into the presidential contest. The money and time required for political campaigns have become prohibitive.

In 2001 Michael Bloomberg spent $60 million of his own money to become Mayor of New York. Contemplating a run for the presidency, Bloomberg's political guru says, "If it happens, it's a $1 billion campaign."[4] Bloomberg is an outstanding public servant. But we can't always count on being lucky. Even outstanding public servants shouldn't be allowed to buy the office. Worthy candidates, knowing that public office can be bought, decline to run.

When I started in politics, all we had was free speech. Today TV commercials are the most expensive part of the campaign. Under *Buckley,* contributors are limited from paying the TV station for political commercials, but a candidate can buy all the TV time he wants. When he was drafting the First Amendment, James Madison never had in mind that free speech would be measured by money. The cost of campaigns has become so astronomical that it has almost vested the control of government in K Street's high-roller lobbyists.

It is sheer nonsense to say that a contributor does not influence the officeholder. I've tried for twenty years to control gratuitous violence on TV. Three times I've had such a measure reported out of the Commerce Committee by a vote of 20–1. But the Senators prevent their leaders from voting on such a measure on the Senate floor. I was once able to get my measure considered by the Senate as an amendment. It was shot down by the same Senators who had supported it in the committee. Fear of losing the contributions and support of Hollywood moguls kept the Senators from voting in favor of my measure.

I am the first to acknowledge that K Street lobbyists serve an important part of the political process. They are experts in particular disciplines and can help lawmakers understand often arcane proposals. But while lobbyists should have influence in the process, they must not control it. Lawmakers' constant quest for money in campaigns almost gives these hired guns control. These days the denizens of K Street— with their generous campaign contributions—can often be found drafting legislation and influencing when a vote is scheduled on it. They have too much influence.

Most contributors would be relieved by enactment of a constitutional amendment authorizing Congress to limit spending in elections. I know as a Senator that such a spending limit would be a relief. During my last few years in the Senate, I spent a third of my time raising money—and I wasn't even a candidate. As a former committee chairman, then ranking member, I was expected to raise $100,000 for the Democratic Senatorial Campaign Committee. I was expected to attend every Democratic Party fund-raiser. I was expected to attend every one of my committee members' fund-raisers. I had to give up policy committee lunches to go to my party's headquarters and spend two hours making calls to seek contributions. I had to attend breakfast fund-raisers and evening fund-raisers. I had to plan for and go to fund-raisers at the January break, at the February Washington-Lincoln Birthdays break, the March spring break, the Palm Sunday–Easter break in April, the Memorial Day break in May, the Fourth of July break, and on and on. Intermittently we would have fund-raisers and party retreats in Virginia, Maryland, Delaware, and Nantucket—as well as at the Super Bowls. Over on the House side I am told that chairmanships are no longer determined by seniority but by fund-raising abilities.

The Senate is known as the most deliberative body, but I had no time to deliberate and very little time to talk to other Senators and learn from their experiences. I had hardly any time to talk to the staff. The late Senator Richard Russell of Georgia said a Senator was given a six-year term—two years to be a statesman, two to be a politician, and two to be a demagogue. Now we take all six years to raise money. One's mind stays on the campaign for money. When it comes to the needs of the country, every Senator has been taught by his pollster: "Don't divide the voters; don't take a stand; don't say you're for or against." Whatever the question, whatever the issue, don't divide the voters. You can comment, but comment both ways, concluding "you're concerned," or "you're troubled." It's all hit-and-run politics. Hit on the issue and say you're "concerned." Don't lose the voter. Consequently we have one hundred Senators running around on the floor of the Senate "concerned" or "troubled." They are taught not to lead. And, with their minds mostly on money for their campaigns, nothing gets done.

I hadn't been in the Senate but for a few months when one morning, as I had just cast my vote, I got a tap on the shoulder. I looked up, and there was the most senior Republican Senator, John Cooper of Kentucky. Remember, I was seated in the next to the last seat for Democratic Senators in the corner of the Senate. In the middle of roll call, Senator Cooper had hastened all the way from the opposite side of the chamber to counsel: "Change that vote; change that vote." I did automatically. Senator Cooper explained that he was from horse country and knew the horsemen of South Carolina were for me—and I had just voted against their interests. He didn't want to see me lose their support. He knew I would have a hard time explaining a vote against them on an issue that was passing overwhelmingly. I thanked him profusely. That was when the Senate was a club. From then on, if it wasn't against South Carolina's interest, John Cooper of Kentucky had my vote. I became a fast friend of this All-American basketball player from Kentucky. His wife, Lorraine, and my Peatsy became close, and we socialized regularly on the weekends. This was typical. We used to have four or five Republican and four or five Democratic Senators rotate at one Senator's home each Wednesday night, taking potluck and having a wonderful time arguing about the happenings of the day. No more. In my last campaign, I'll never forget the fund-raiser against me in Washington. Every Republican Senator on my Commerce Committee, save Senator Ted Stevens of Alaska, attended. I had learned in the war that if you take care of your men, they'll take care of you. As Commerce Committee chairman for years, I took care of the Senators on my committee, be they Republican or Democrat. For example, one Republican colleague missed an important vote, causing his side to lose. I knew it was an innocent mistake, so I moved as a prevailing member to reconsider, let him vote, and my side lost. All the Senators understood. But if they've had a fund-raiser against you the night before, you don't feel like working with them on the floor of the Senate the next day.

Today in the Senate, there is total cleavage, almost confrontation. The Tuesday lunches for the political parties are to plot against each other. All for party control. No more Senate club. The Senate chamber is a boiler room for the campaigns. And the Democratic and Republican congressional campaign committees that pour in the campaign money congeal the confrontation.

The *Buckley v. Valeo* decision is similar to the *Plessy v. Ferguson* decision of 1896. In *Plessy* the Supreme Court found that "separate but equal" was equal. And for almost sixty years "separate but equal" was the law of the land. The Supreme Court finally sobered up in 1954 with *Brown v. Board of Education* and found that "separate but equal" was not equal and that segregation in public facilities was unconstitutional. In *Buckley v. Valeo* for the past thirty-five years candidate spending was free speech while contributor spending was not free speech. Now we must sober up and realize spending is not free—be it for a yard sign, a mailing, or a TV ad.

To repair the First Amendment from the damage caused by *Buckley v. Valeo,* we must enact an amendment to the Constitution to permit Congress to regulate or control spending in federal elections. I have tried for almost thirty years to win support for such an amendment. Time and again, we have been rebuffed by claims that such a change would infringe on the First Amendment. What we are doing is correcting an infringement on the First Amendment by the Supreme Court in *Buckley vs. Valeo.* And it is doable. Five of the last six amendments to the Constitution deal with elections, so our proposal is not a big stretch at all. The corruption of politics and government caused by *Buckley* must be corrected.

I hasten to emphasize that Senators and House members are not corrupt and are better at their jobs now than we were forty years ago. They are more informed and more conscientious. There are no drunks in Congress. Senators and Representatives are just caught up in a system corrupted by the Supreme Court. And we are suffering not because of a lack of leadership. Senator Harry Reid for the Majority and Senator Mitch McConnell for the Minority are excellent leaders. They are leading as their caucuses wish. The caucuses must wish that the cancer of money on the body politic be excised, or it won't happen.

My amendment doesn't mandate a particular solution. It just gives Congress the authority to limit spending any way it deems fit. If the future Congress reenacts what we enacted in an overwhelming bipartisan vote in 1971 and 1974, instead of being limited to $637,000 for a Senate race, I would be limited to $4 million for a statewide Senate race in South Carolina. While I could raise $4 million in South Carolina, I would have to fund-raise in Washington and travel across the country to fund-raisers for the $10 million that is required today. Contributions can come by mail or the internet. But the law ought to require that all fund-raising events must be instate. Senators and Congressmen are sent to Washington to legislate, not to fund-raise. With an amendment to the Constitution, spending by the parties and independent organizations could also be limited—as could, most of all, the time of campaigns.

Ideas, policies, programs all ought to predominate over money. But today there is no chance with the deluge of money in politics. The cumulative effect of special-interest money is prohibitive. Remove this effect by limiting campaign spending, and the money is still necessary but not controlling. The cumulative effect of Corporate America's conspiracy to outsource and forbid America's competing or trading in globalization is destroying our production and jobs. We suffer from Corporate America's abandonment of country to go anywhere for a profit. But their goal is profit, and they can't be faulted for seeking it. The President and the Congress are charged with building and maintaining a strong economy. So the government must make it profitable to invest and produce in the United States. To do this we must return to our founding principles. The Declaration of Independence set out our freedom from Great Britain and provided fo the rights of "the Free and Independent States." The "Free and Independent States" thereafter struggled for ten years to establish the federal government we have in Washington today. Our forefathers sought government, and we now have the government they sought. The country is in serious trouble, and we don't have the luxury of antigovernment politicking. It is our duty to make the government work. The very first bill passed by Congress created the seal of the United States. More important, the second bill was for a tax on trade or commerce. This protectionism didn't lead to war and deprivation (as free trade leaders have declared) but to economic growth and to the United States becoming the chief industrial power of the world. We need Alexander Hamilton, whose vision was not a nation of consumers but a nation of producers, of builders. We need to compete in globalization, to trade, and to rebuild America.

Once spending in campaigns is limited, the big boiler room of party politics in Washington will fade, and congressional politics addressing the country's needs will take over. With spending limits the government will be rescued from the grip of K Street. Senators and Congressmen will have time in Washington to do their work. They will have time to listen to constituents rather than contributors. They will be able to deliberate without the constant distraction of chasing money. Congressmen and Senators can go to work for the country rather than the campaign. Government will work again.

NOTES

Chapter 1. The Accidental Politician

1. Philip G. Grose, *South Carolina at the Brink: Robert McNair and the Politics of Civil Rights* (University of South Carolina Press, 2006), 47.

2. This description is drawn from the account in Nadine Cohodas, *Strom Thurmond and the Politics of Southern Change* (Mercer University Press, 1994), 231–32.

3. Grose, *South Carolina at the Brink,* 46.

4. The committee members in addition to me were Werber Bryan of Sumter, Walter Lake of Newberry, Joseph Mann of Greenville, H. Norwood Obear of Fairfield, and Joseph Spruill Jr. of Chesterfield.

5. "Person of the Year: Joseph F. Byrnes," *Time,* January 6, 1947.

6. Some of the educators who made the case for the sales tax were Guy Loggins of Richland County, Ryan Crowe of Sumter, and Ralph Durham of Colleton.

7. Among those who were instrumental in getting the measure passed was Ray Williams of Greenville, chairman of the conference, who was never slowed down by the fact that he was blind. He was lacking in sight but not in intellect as he had one of the sharpest minds. Senator T. B. Bryant of Orangeburg also was of particular help.

8. This account is drawn from Jack Bass and Marilyn W. Thompson, *Strom* (Public Affairs, 2005), 82–84.

9. Much of the description of the Summerton situation and the litigation is drawn from Glenn Cook, "First to Footnote," *American School Board Journal* 191 (April 2004); and from Darlene Clark Hine, "The *Briggs v. Elliott* Legacy: Black Culture, Consciousness, and Community Before Brown, 1930–1954," *University of Illinois Law Review* no. 2 (February 2005): 1059–72. The quotation from Judge Waring's decision comes from *Briggs v. Elliott,* 98 F. supp. 529, 547–48 (E.D.S.C. 1951).

10. Jim Newton, *Justice for All: Earl Warren and the Nation He Made* (Riverhead Books, 2006), 305.

11. Ibid., 304.

12. Ibid., 304–5.

13. Lewis P. Jones, *South Carolina: A Synoptic History for Laymen* (Sandlapper Publishing, 1971), 278.

14. James F. Byrnes, "The Supreme Court Must Be Curbed," *U.S. News & World Report* 40 (May 18, 1956).

Chapter 2. Taking Charge as Governor

1. Much of this account is drawn from my book *The Case Against Hunger* (Cowles, 1970), 20–21.

2. The description of my meeting with Bishop Hallinan and our efforts to catch the thugs is drawn from ibid.

3. Harold Evans, *The American Century* (Knopf, 1998), 435.

4. The group included Hampton G. Anderson of Anderson, Howard B. Carlisle Jr. of Spartanburg, Robert G. Clawson of Hartsville, R. M. Cooper of Wisacky, Robert B. Fickling of Blackville, Andrew D. Griffith of Orangeburg, J. C. Keys of Greenville, James B. Moore of Andrews, Connie R. Morton of Rock Hill, R. Roy Pearce of Columbia, Walter P. Rawl of Gilbert, Joseph P. Riley of Charleston, James C. Self of Greenwood, and Bernard Warshaw of Walterboro.

5. Walter W. Harper, interview by Herbert J. Hartsook, September 12, 1997, South Carolina Political Collections, University of South Carolina.

6. John West provided some of the details recounted here during an April 29, 2003, interview with Blease Graham of the John C. West Forum on Politics and Policy at the University of South Carolina.

7. The members of the Blue Ribbon Committee were Alvin F. Heinsohn of Charleston, J. Bonner Manly of Abbeville, Sapp Funderburk of Greenville, Clarence Rowland Sr. of Camden, J. Boone Aiken of Florence, and Chairman O. Stanley Smith Jr. of Columbia.

8. West provided details of the efforts to persuade Elgin to move to South Carolina in his 2003 interview with Graham.

9. Based on data on the Website of the South Carolina Department of Agriculture. http://www.scda.state.sc.us/virtualtour/broilers/broilers.htm (accessed December 12, 2007).

10. Council members included Harriet S. Mason, Thomas H. Pope, Huger Sinkler, Jennie C. (Mrs. J. A.) Henry, Brown Mahon, and Wiggins, chairman of the Atlantic Coast Line Railroad board.

11. The plants included four General Electric, four Westinghouse, three DuPont, two Owens Corning, and one each of Timken Roller Bearing, 3M, Lockheed, Michelin, Shakespeare, Elgin Watch, and Homelite, as well as the German steel plant at Georgetown.

12. Bass and Thompson, *Strom*, 126.

13. Charles H. Wickenberg Collection, South Carolina Political Collections, University of South Carolina.

14. This description is drawn from my book *The Case Against Hunger*, 25–26.

15. Ibid., 26.

16. Ibid., 25.

17. Rep. James Clyburn, interview by Kirk Victor, January 11, 2007.

18. Jack Bass and Walter De Vries, *The Transformation of Southern Politics: Social Change & Political Consequence Since 1945* (University of Georgia Press, 1995), 201.

19. For an excellent description of the integration of Clemson, see George McMillan, "Integration with Dignity," *Saturday Evening Post,* March 16, 1963.

20. Bass and Thompson, *Strom,* 177.

21. Ibid., 178.

22. "Cream Puff at Clemson," *Charleston News and Courier,* January 30, 1963, 6A.

Chapter 3. Getting to Know the Kennedys

1. See Arthur M. Schlesinger Jr., *Robert M. Kennedy and His Times* (Ballantine, 1978), 123. This comprehensive and excellent biography reports that "Kennedy grimly walked out." Similarly Evan Thomas, *Robert Kennedy: His Life* (Simon & Schuster, 1970), reports, "Grim-faced, young Kennedy walked out during the speech."

2. Thomas, *Robert Kennedy,* 73.

3. Ibid., 110.

4. Nick Bryant, *The Bystander: John F. Kennedy and the Struggle for Black Equality* (Basic Books, 2006), 116.

5. Ibid., 223.

6. This account is drawn in part from Coates Redmon, *Come as You Are* (Harcourt Brace Jovanovich, 1986), 14–16, which describes Gavin's speech and the ensuing call to Mike Feldman.

7. Ibid.

8. Ibid., 20.

9. This account of my interaction with Kennedy over his planned trip to South Carolina and my thoughts about the trip is drawn from *The Case Against Hunger,* 32–34.

10. Ibid. These quotations and the others from conversations with Senator Kennedy are from ibid., 33–34.

Chapter 4. Getting Started in the Senate

1. "Ex-Governor Feels 'Poor' in New Role as Attorney," *Charleston News and Courier,* January 18, 1963, 3C.

2. This analysis is among my papers at the South Carolina Political Collections, University of South Carolina. The papers do not identify the friend to whom I sent this analysis, and I can't recall who it was.

3. Much of this description of Lady Bird Johnson's tour comes from the excellent LBJ biography by Randall B. Woods, *LBJ: Architect of American Ambition* (Free Press, 2006), 542–44.

4. Nan Robertson, "First Lady Booed in South Carolina," *New York Times,* October 8, 1964, 32.

5. Woods, *LBJ*, 544.

6. Grose, *South Carolina at the Brink*, 8; "Russell Did Not Consult Sen. Johnston's Widow," *Charleston News and Courier*, April 23, 1965, 6D.

7. Bubba Meng, interview by Herbert Hartsook, January 21, 1992, South Carolina Political Collections, University of South Carolina. Meng was Senator Johnston's legislative assistant when he died and later became one of my long-serving staffers and friends.

8. Bass and Thompson, *Strom*, 196; Hugh E. Gibson, "Candidates and Offices to Be Plentiful in '66," *Charleston News and Courier*, April 23, 1965, 3A.

9. William E. Rone Jr., "Hollings Enters Race Attacking Russell," *State*, March 22, 1966, B1.

10. Ibid.

11. Jack Bass, "Strong Republican Bid Is Rejected by S.C. Voters," *State*, November 9, 1966, 1A.

12. Bass and Thompson, *Strom*, 194, 195. Fowler is quoted from an interview with Thompson, circa 1981.

13. Crawford Cook, interview by Herbert Hartsook, March 26, 1997, South Carolina Political Collections, University of South Carolina.

14. Much of this account of my dealings with Secretary Freeman on the tobacco issue is drawn from my account in *The Case Against Hunger*, 148–49.

15. Ibid., 149.

16. Ibid.

17. "We Lost Our Chance," *Ernest F. Hollings Reports to South Carolina*, October 1967.

18. Hollings, "Misled and Undermanned: The Truth on Iraq," *State*, November 9, 2003.

19. Hollings, *The Case Against Hunger*, 155. Much of my discussion of the power of the farm lobby is drawn from this book.

20. Ibid.

21. Ibid., 156.

22. Ibid.

23. Ibid.

24. Ibid.

25. Ibid., 20.

26. Ibid., 22.

27. Ibid., 147.

28. Ibid., 148. The description of this meeting with Shriver is drawn from my account in *The Case Against Hunger*.

29. Ibid.

30. Ibid.

31. Ibid., 150.

32. Ibid., 35.

33. Ibid., 36.

34. Ibid., 84.

35. Ibid., 42.

36. Ibid., 168.

37. Michael Barone and Grant Ujifusa, *The Almanac of American Politics 1982* (Gambit, 1982), 389; Robert Pear, "Proposed Food Stamp Cuts Are Assailed," *New York Times*, February 23, 1982.

38. Ibid.

39. Ibid.

40. This information is set out in "Hunger and Food Insecurity in the 50 States: 1998–2000," a report by the Food Security Institute, Ashley F. Sullivan, and Eunyoung Choi (Center on Hunger and Poverty, Brandeis University, 2002).

Chapter 5. Clement Haynsworth's Nomination to the Supreme Court

1. Cohodas, *Strom Thurmond*, 394.

2. Tom Wicker, *One of Us: Richard Nixon and The American Dream* (Random House, 1991), 496.

3. Letter to President Richard M. Nixon, May 28, 1969.

4. Ibid.

5. Speech, November 18, 1969.

6. John P. Frank's testimony is quoted in his *Clement Haynsworth, the Senate and the Supreme Court* (University Press of Virginia, 1991), 42.

7. Ibid., 41–42; see also 28 USC, section 455: "Any Justice or Judge of the United States shall disqualify himself in any case in which he has a substantial interest. . . ."

8. Frank, *Clement Haynsworth*, 52.

9. *Congressional Record*, October 7, 1969, S 28877.

10. Frank, *Clement Haynsworth*, 132.

11. Statement on Senate floor, October 8, 1987.

Chapter 6. The Early Fight to Protect the Environment

1. The Marine Resources and Engineering Development Act of 1966 was passed by both the House and Senate on June 2 (PL 89-454).

2. Edward Wenk Jr., "Creating the Stratton Commission—A Reprise," *Stratton Roundtable* (Marine Sciences Council), May 1, 1998, 17.

3. Ibid.

4. Wicker, *One of Us*, 510.

Chapter 7. The Supreme Court Corrupts Congress

1. My first wife, Pat, and I were divorced in 1970.

2. I spoke of our trip in comments on the Senate floor on September 14, 1971.

3. Richard Reeves, *President Nixon: Alone in the White House* (Simon & Schuster, 2001), 325.

4. Stephen E. Ambrose, *Nixon: The Triumph of a Politician 1962–1972* (Simon & Schuster, 1989), 615.

5. Ibid.

6. These figures come from Anthony Corrado, "Money and Politics: A History of Campaign Finance Law," in *Campaign Finance Reform: A Sourcebook,* ed. Corrado, abridged ed. (Brookings Institution, 1997).

Chapter 8. Imperial Nixon, Cautious Ford

1. Reeves, *President Nixon,* 566.

2. The discussion of Kennedy's efforts on this lawsuit is drawn from Adam Clymer, *Edward M. Kennedy: A Biography* (Morrow, 1999), 220.

3. *Congressional Quarterly Almanac* 29 (1973): 255.

4. The details of Muskie's move are laid out in an excellent account of developing the budget process: Joel Haveman, *Congress and the Budget* (Indiana University Press, 1978), 38–39.

5. Ibid.

6. Woods, *LBJ,* 228–29.

7. Details of the debate are drawn from *Congressional Quarterly Almanac* 30 (1974): 137.

8. Clymer, *Edward M. Kennedy,* 238.

9. Barone, Ujifusa, and Douglas Matthews, *The Almanac of American Politics 1976* (Gambit), 327.

10. Ibid., 771.

11. Much of the background of this legislative fight over fuel standards is drawn from *Congressional Quarterly Almanac* 31 (1975): 229–30.

12. Ibid.

13. Ibid., 230.

14. Ibid., 220.

Chapter 9. The Carter Years: A Time of Big Battles

1. Background on the debate over the Panama Canal Treaties is drawn from *Congressional Quarterly Almanac* 34 (1978): 379–97.

2. September 1979 newsletter to constituents.

3. See Robert G. Beckel, exit interview by David Alsobrook, December 3, 1980 (at the end of the Carter administration), President's Writer Staff.

4. Ibid.

5. The background data on votes is drawn from *Congressional Quarterly Almanac* 34 (1978): 379–97.

6. Associated Press, "Airline-Industry Deregulator Defends Outcome," *Chicago Tribune,* November 8, 1987, 13B.

7. The background of the debate is set out in *Congressional Quarterly Almanac* 34 (1978): 284–87.

8. Ibid., 287.

9. Background of the debate is drawn from ibid., 248–52.

10. Letter to Jimmy Carter, August 30, 1976.

11. The background of the Export-Import Bank legislation is set out in David M. Maxfield, "Congress Clears Extension of Export-Import Bank Life as Rider on

Banking Bill," *Congressional Quarterly Weekly Report* 36 (October 28, 1978): 3163; and Maxfield, "Ex-Im Bank Bill in Senate Becoming 'Christmas Tree,'" ibid. 36 (October 7, 1978): 2732. Senator Ribicoff's statement from the debate is in the *Congressional Record,* September 29, 1978, S 32584.

12. As reported in Pat Towell, "Carter Pressured to Speed Defense Spending Increase," *Congressional Quarterly Weekly Report* 37 (September 22, 1979): 2102.

Chapter 10. The Assault on Government

1. The background for this discussion of this budget process is in "$8.2 Billion Reconciliation Bill Cleared," *Congressional Quarterly Almanac* 36 (1980): 124–30.

2. For my description of this meeting with President-elect Reagan, see "A Funny Thing Happened on the Way to a New Beginning," undated document, Hollings Papers, South Carolina Political Collections, University of South Carolina. This document was a draft of my October 1981 newsletter to constituents.

3. *Congressional Quarterly Almanac* 36 (1980): 123.

4. The background of my offer to Domenici and his dealings with Reagan is set out in Hedrick Smith, *The Power Game: How Washington Works* (Random House, 1988), 357–58. See also David A. Stockman, *The Triumph of Politics* (Avon, 1986), 175–76.

5. Gail Gregg, "Reagan Plan Clears 1st Hurdle as Senate Budget Backs Cuts," *Congressional Quarterly Weekly Report* 39 (March 21, 1981): 499.

6. Ibid.

7. Laurence I. Barrett, *Gambling with History: Reagan in the White House* (Doubleday, 1983), 169–70.

8. Ibid., 170.

9. *Congressional Quarterly Almanac* 37 (1981): 252.

10. Ibid., 100.

11. William Greider, "The Education of David Stockman," *Atlantic Monthly,* 246 (December 1981): 46–47.

12. Barrett, *Gambling with History,* 171–72; Joseph White and Aaron Wildavsky, *The Deficit and the Public Interest* (University of California Press, 1989), 185.

13. White and Wildavsky, *The Deficit and the Public Interest,* 185.

14. Stockman, *The Triumph of Politics,* 199.

15. Barrett, *Gambling with History,* 156–158; Stockman, *The Triumph of Politics,* 207.

16. The background for this discussion of the passage of Social Security legislation is drawn from *Congressional Quarterly Almanac* 39 (1983): 219–26.

17. Peter McGrath with Eleanor Clift, Thomas M. DeFrank, Rich Thomas, Howard Fineman, Gloria Borger, and Christopher Ma, "The Deficit Rebellion," *Newsweek,* February 22, 1982, 22.

18. Ibid.

19. Ibid.

20. Cohodas, *Strom Thurmond*, 435.

21. *Congressional Record*, June 16, 1982, S 13796.

22. Ibid., S 13791.

23. Ibid., S 13794.

24. Ibid., S 13791.

25. Ibid., S 13796.

26. Ibid., June 17, 1982, S 14094.

27. Quotations from Chapman's ruling may be found in the *Congressional Record*, June 17, 1982, S 14124–25.

28. Ibid., S 14125.

29. Ibid., June 16, 1982, 13791.

30. Cohodas, *Strom Thurmond*, 479.

31. Peter W. Bernstein, "David Stockman: No More Budget Cuts," *Fortune*, February 6, 1984, 53.

Chapter 11. Attacking the Excesses of Reaganomics

1. Stockman, *The Triumph of Politics*, 8.

2. Ibid., 447.

3. Much of the background on this discussion of trade policy and politics is drawn from I. M. Destler, *American Trade Politics* (Institute for International Economics, 2005), 88–91.

4. *Congressional Quarterly Almanac* 41 (1985): 253.

5. Destler, *American Trade Politics*, 88.

6. This account of the background of the bill is drawn from *Congressional Quarterly Almanac* 41 (1985): 255–59.

7. Ibid., 258.

8. Destler, *American Trade Politics*, 89.

9. *Congressional Quarterly Almanac* 41 (1985): 259.

10. Mike Robinson, "Textile Forces, Jubilant at Senate Victory, Focus on Veto Threat," Associated Press, November 14, 1985.

11. Ibid.

12. Mark Hosenball, "Reagan Renews Import Vow," *Daily News Record*, September 22, 1983, 1.

13. Ibid.

14. Reagan's veto message is in *Congressional Quarterly Almanac* 41 (1985): 40D.

15. The background for this discussion is drawn from ibid., 459–68; and White and Wildavsky, *The Deficit and the Public Interest*, 429–67.

16. Smith, *The Power Game*, 662.

17. Warren B. Rudman, *Combat: Twelve Years in the U.S. Senate* (Random House, 1996), 68.

18. *Congressional Quarterly Almanac* 41 (1985): 467.

19. Smith, *The Power Game*, 664.

20. Newsletter to constituents, March 11, 1986.

21. Jonathan Fuerbringer, "Plan to Balance U.S. Budget by '91 Delayed in Senate," *New York Times*, October 5, 1985, 1.

22. Hollings, "Deficit Reduction: A Love Story; I Want a Divorce," *New York Times*, October 25, 1989.

23. *Congressional Quarterly Almanac* 42 (1986): 289.

24. The background for this discussion of the campaign finance battles in 1988 is drawn from *Congressional Quarterly Almanac* 44 (1988): 41–46.

25. *Congressional Record*, February 18, 1988, S 1724.

26. *Congressional Quarterly Almanac* 44 (1988): 46.

27. *Congressional Record*, February 18, 1988, S 1723.

28. The background for this discussion of the U.S.-Canada Free Trade Agreement is drawn from *Congressional Quarterly Almanac* 44 (1988): 222–28.

29. *Congressional Record*, September 19, 1988, S 24432.

Chapter 12. Missed Opportunities

1. Steve Gerstel, "Spending Freeze, New Tax Proposed," United Press International, January 26, 1989.

2. Ibid.

3. Ibid.

4. Lawrence J. Haas, "Bubbling VAT," *National Journal*, June 6, 1992, 1336–40.

5. Chris Delyani, States News Service, February 27, 1989; Hollings, "End the Budget Sham: Phony Figures and Wishful Thinking Won't Halt the Runaway Deficit," *St. Louis Post-Dispatch*, February 9, 1989, 3B.

6. *Congressional Quarterly Almanac* 45 (1989): 700.

7. Ibid.

8. John Markoff, "Pentagon's Technology Chief Is Out," *New York Times*, April 21, 1990.

9. This description of the background, the battle on Capitol Hill, and President Bush's veto is drawn from *Congressional Quarterly Almanac* 46 (1990): 219–22.

10. Ibid., 219.

11. Ibid., 220.

12. Ibid.

13. Ibid.

14. Allen William Smith, *The Looting of Social Security: How the Government Is Draining America's Retirement Account* (Carroll & Graf, 2004), 18–21, provides a good overview of my arguments in the Senate on Social Security.

15. Ibid., 21.

16. Ibid., 20.

17. "Confrontation in the Gulf: Excerpts from Iraqi Document on Meeting with U.S. Envoy," transcript of exchange between Ambassador Glaspie and Iraqi President Saddam Hussein, *New York Times*, September 23, 1990. The transcript was

provided by Iraqi government officials. A copy was provided to the *New York Times* by ABC News, which translated it from the Arabic. The State Department has declined to comment on its accuracy.

18. Jean Edward Smith, *George Bush's War* (Holt, 1992), 70, 68.

19. *Congressional Record,* January 3, 1991, S 11.

20. *Congressional Record,* January 4, 1991, S 314.

21. The four newly elected women Senators, all Democrats, were Barbara Boxer of California; Carol Moseley-Braun of Illinois, the first African American woman Senator; Dianne Feinstein of California; and Patty Murray of Washington. They joined Democrat Barbara Mikulski of Maryland and Republican Nancy Landon Kassebaum of Kansas. Democrat Ben Nighthorse Campbell of Colorado was the first Native American Senator in more than sixty years.

Chapter 13. The Early 1990s: From Budget Battles to Trade Wars

1. Bill Clinton, *My Life* (Knopf, 2004), 453.

2. Ibid., 460.

3. The background for Clinton's proposal is drawn from *Congressional Quarterly Almanac* 49 (1993): 85–89.

4. John M. Berry, "Greenspan Vows to Help Clinton; Fed Chairman Calls Deficit Reduction Proposals 'Positive Force,'" *Washington Post,* February 20, 1993, C1.

5. David Kaut, "Sparks Fly as Senate Budget Committee Takes Up Clinton Plan," States News Service, March 9, 1993.

6. Hollings, "Some Advice to the New Kid in Town: Just Remember that You're a 'New Democrat'; Democrats Have Long Been Smeared with the 'Tax-and-Spend' Label, but the 'New South' Governors Proved Their Fiscal Mettle," *Los Angeles Times,* June 27, 1993, M2.

7. *Congressional Record,* June 23, 1993, S 13796.

8. Ibid.

9. Bill Mintz, "Nip and Tuck: Senate OKs Deficit Plan," *Houston Chronicle,* August 7, 1993, 1.

10. John Kasich, "Reject This Tax-and-Spend," *USA Today,* August 4, 1993, 8A.

11. *Congressional Quarterly Almanac* 48 (1992): 154.

12. Gwen Ifill, "Clinton Uses Japan to Sell Mexico Pact," *New York Times,* October 21, 1993, 20.

13. *Congressional Record,* October 14, 1993, S 24704.

14. Background on the NAFTA debate and vote are drawn from *Congressional Quarterly Almanac* 49 (1993): 171–79.

15. David R. Sands, "Hollings, Clinton Vie as 'Good Friends,'" *Washington Times,* September 29, 1994, A11.

16. The witnesses included U.S. Trade Representative Michael "Mickey" Kantor; C. Fred Bergsten, director of the Peterson Institute for International Economics; Tom Donahue, secretary-treasurer of the AFL-CIO; Ambassador Abraham

Katz of the U.S. Council for International Business; Bruce Ackerman of Yale Law School; Laurence Tribe of Harvard Law School; Felix Rohatyn, an investment banker at Lazard Frères; consumer advocate Ralph Nader; Sir James Goldsmith, a member of the European Parliament; and Charles McMillion, president and chief economist of MBG Information Services, a business information, analysis, and forecasting firm.

17. *Congressional Record,* September 30, 1994, S 26969

18. Peter Behr, "World to Watch as Congress Votes on GATT; Proposed Trade Organization Opposed by Unusual Coalition," *Washington Post,* November 28, 1994, A1.

19. Destler, *American Trade Politics,* 228, 227; Alissa J. Rubin, "Dole, Clinton Compromise Greases Wheels for GATT," *Congressional Quarterly Weekly Report* 52 (November 26, 1994): 3405.

20. Destler, *American Trade Politics,* 228n63.

21. This description of the program is drawn from *Congressional Quarterly Almanac* 50 (1994): 221–23.

22. *Congressional Record,* March 7, 1994, S 3928.

23. Ibid.

24. Ibid., S 3929.

25. Ibid., May 27, 1993, S 11406.

Chapter 14. Protecting the Public Interest

1. *Congressional Quarterly Almanac* 50 (1994): 214.

2. George Hager, "Budget Battle Came Sooner than Either Side Expected," *Congressional Quarterly Weekly Report* 53 (November 18, 1995): 3503.

3. The background for our negotiations and the description of the legislation is drawn from *Congressional Quarterly Almanac* 51 (1995): 4-3–4-29.

4. Dan Carney, "Spate of Squabbles Leaves Bill's Fate Still Uncertain," *Congressional Quarterly Weekly Report* 53 (December 23, 1995): 3881.

5. *Congressional Quarterly Almanac* 51 (1995): 4-14, 4-17.

6. *Congressional Record,* February 12, 1999, S 1628.

7. James Shoch, *Trading Blows: Party Competition and U.S. Trade Policy in a Globalizing Era* (University of North Carolina Press, 2001), 235–36, 238.

8. Ibid., 234.

Chapter 15. The George W. Bush Years: Reckless Policies Divide the Country

1. William Neikirk, "Bush, Congress and Fed Aim to Thwart Recession," *Chicago Tribune,* January 16, 2001, 1.

2. Finlay Lewis, "Fed Chief's Testimony Stuns Democrats, Reshapes the Politics of Tax-Cut Debate," *San Diego Union-Tribune,* January 26, 2001, A1.

3. Hollings, "Reaganomics II: A Reckless Recipe for Fiscal Disaster," *Charleston Post and Courier,* March 5, 2001, 9.

4. *Congressional Quarterly Almanac* 58 (2002): 7-4.

5. *Congressional Quarterly Almanac* 60 (2004): 16-8.

6. The background for the discussion of Amtrak is in ibid., 16-7.

7. *Congressional Record,* November 19, 2002, S 11443.

8. This story was broken by Michael Isikoff and Daniel Klaidman, in "The Hijackers We Let Escape," *Newsweek,* June 10, 2002.

9. This background is drawn from *Congressional Quarterly Almanac* 58 (2002): 1-7–1-8.

10. Brent Scowcroft, "Don't Attack Saddam," *Wall Street Journal,* August 15, 2002.

11. Michael R. Gordon and Bernard E. Trainor, *Cobra II: The Inside Story of the Invasion and Occupation of Iraq* (Pantheon, 2006), 14.

12. Ron Suskind, *The Price of Loyalty* (Simon & Schuster, 2004), 72.

13. Gordon and Trainor, *Cobra II,* 16.

14. Richard A. Clarke, *Against All Enemies* (Free Press, 2004), 33, 31, 30–31.

15. Ibid., 18, 20.

16. Ibid.

Chapter 16. Making Government Work

1. Henry Clay, "In Defense of the American System, Against the British Colonial System," speech before the U.S. Senate, February 1832.

2. Edmond Morris, *Theodore Rex* (Random House, 2001), 20–21.

3. Martin Feldstein, editorial, *Financial Times,* October 15, 2007.

4. Jon Meacham, "The Revolutionary," *Newsweek,* November 12, 2007.

INDEX

Abdullah, King, 302
Abourezk, James, 187
Abramoff, Jack, 168
Abrams, Elliott, 293
Adams, John, 191
Advanced Technology Program (ATP), 235, 236, 322
Afghanistan: bin Laden's presence in, 292; Soviet invasion of, 198, 303; Taliban in, 302–3
AFL-CIO, 145
African Americans: and the Democratic Party, 100; educational opportunities for, 16–17, 23–25, 27–36; voting rights for, 11–13. See also *Briggs v. Elliott*; civil rights movement; racial tensions; voting rights
Agnew, Spiro, 136, 154, 174
agriculture. *See* farm lobby; tobacco farming
Agriculture, U.S. Department of, 132
airline deregulation, 187–88
airport security, 281–83
Albright, Jerry, 64
Allen, James, 161
Allott, Gordon, 164
al-Qaeda, 290, 294–95; in Iraq, 298
Americans for Tax Reform, 306
Amtrak, 286
anti-Catholicism: and John F. Kennedy, 87, 90–92, 95–96
antilynching law, 26, 42
Arab-Israeli War of 1973, 177
Arafat, Yasir, 292–93
Armstrong, William L., 241
Army Corps of Engineers, 153

Arn, Edward, 32
Arrants, J. Claytor, 36
Ash, Roy, 154
Ash Council, 154
AT&T, 266–67. *See also* telecommunications, legislation affecting
Ataturk, Kemal, 291
atomic bomb, 7
Attlee, Clement, 74
automakers lobby, 179
Aznar, José María, 295

Baird, Zoë, 248
Baker, Bobby, 94, 96, 124, 148
Baker, Howard, 185, 187, 203, 209
Baker, James, 219, 242
Balanced Budget Constitutional Amendment, 265
Bargmann, Betty, 44
Barnett, Ross, 3, 78–79
Barnwell Ring, 39
Barton, Thomas E., Jr., 55
BASF, 157
Bayh, Birch, 146, 147–48, 149, 200, 201
Beaufort-Jasper Comprehensive Health Center, 133
Beckel, Robert, 186, 187
Beckman, Dan, 78
Bell Atlantic, 270
Bellmon, Henry, 174
BellSouth, 270
Bentsen, Lloyd, 233, 246, 305
Bethea, A. W. "Red," 81–82
Biden, Joseph R., 164
Billings, Richard, 73
Bimson, Walter, 56–57

bin Laden, Osama, 283, 292, 296, 302–3
Blair, Frank, 77
Blair, James T., 93
Blair, Tony, 295
Blatt, Solomon, 39, 49
Bliley, Thomas J., 269, 270
Blinder, Alan S., 318, 323
Block, Herb, 148–49
Bloomberg, Michael, 328
Boggs, J. Caleb, 164
Boren, David, 150, 250
Bork, Robert, 150
Boston Tea Party, 310, 320
Boulware, Harold, 28
Brawley, Joseph W., 27, 28
Brennan, Terry, 86
Brennan, William, 128
Brewster, Danny, 126
Brezhnev, Leonid, 197
Briggs, Eliza, 29, 41
Briggs, Harry, 29, 41
Briggs v. Elliott, 2–3, 29–33, 41, 127
Brinkley, David, 240
Britt-Westbury case, 70
Brokaw, Tom, 271
Brown, Edgar, 37–38, 39, 49, 53–54, 81
Brown, Sherrod, 319
Brown, Walter, 53
Brown, Willie, 163
Brown v. Board of Education of Topeka, Kansas, 2–3, 32–33, 41, 331; impact of, 34–36; opposition to, 87–88, 97
Bruce, William R., 67
Bryan, Tom, 133
Buckley, James, 167
Buckley, William F., Jr., 51
Buckley v. Valeo, 5, 167–68, 227, 228, 264–65, 326–27, 328, 330–31
budgetary reform: under George H. W. Bush, 231–33; under Clinton, 246–51; under Nixon, 171–77; under Reagan, 201–9, 220–25, 231

Budget Enforcement Act of 1990, 241
Bullock, Bob, 277
Bumpers, Dale, 199
Burger, Warren, 142–43
Burke, Edmund, 186
Burns, Arthur, 315
Burns, Conrad, 282
Bush, Barbara, 239
Bush, George Herbert Walker, 5, 202–3, 230, 251, 312; Clinton's defeat of, 245; and economic issues, 238–39; and Operation Desert Storm, 242–44; as President, 231–45; and textile legislation, 237–38; warnings regarding Iraq, 298
Bush, George W., 125, 323, 326; and Iraq invasion, 289–302; as President, 276, 277–303; tax cuts sought by, 278–79, 322
Bush, Jeb, 293
Business Development Corporation, 57
Byrd, Robert, 189–91, 198, 222, 223, 227–28
Byrd, Willie, 23
Byrd-Boren bill, 227
Byrnes, James F., 3, 20–21, 27, 37, 39, 75, 116; and *Briggs v. Elliott,* 31; and *Brown v. Board of Education,* 34–35; and sales tax proposal, 23–25; as Secretary of State, 21–22
Byrnes, Maude Perkins Busch, 20, 22

Cable Act of 1992, 269
Calhoun, John C., 97, 310
Calio, Nicholas E., 281–82
Cambone, Steve, 293, 294
campaign finance legislation, 4–5, 165–69, 170, 227–28, 264–65, 326–32
Campbell, Leon, 55
Campbell's Soup Company, 66
Cannon, Howard, 187
capitalism, 6, 321–22, 323
Carnegie, Andrew, 311

Carolina Vend-A-Matic, 146

Carson City Silver Dollar bill, 196–97

Carter, Jimmy, 180, 238; and defense issues, 197–99; and the Panama Canal Treaties, 182–83, 186; as President, 181–200, 201, 216; Reagan's defeat of, 199–200; and SALT II agreement, 197–98; and tax credits for private education, 193; and trade policy, 194–95, 196–97

Carter, Rex, 46

Carter, Rosalynn, 181, 182

Case Against Hunger, The, 4, 131, 140

Catholicism. *See* anti-Catholicism

Cauthen, John K., 17, 48–49, 51, 52, 53, 81

Central Intelligence Agency (CIA), 287–88

Chafee, John H., 154, 233

Chalabi, Ahmed, 296–97

Chapman, Robert, 210–11

Charleston, S.C., 62–63

Charleston Harbor, 153

Cheney, Dick, 277, 293, 296, 308

Chiles, Lawton, 222, 223

China, 175; capitalism in, 323; economic growth in, 320, 325; human-rights violations in, 315; trade policies with, 275–76, 309, 313–14

Church, Frank, 200, 201

Churchill, Winston, 74

Civil Aeronautics Board (CAB), 187, 268

Civil Rights Act of 1957, 141

Civil Rights Act of 1964, 112, 113, 117

civil rights movement, 1–2, 11–12, 41, 75–79, 85. *See also* racial tensions

Clarendon County, S.C., 2–3

Clark, Mark W., 118, 287

Clark, Richard C. "Dick," 164

Clarke, Richard A., 294–95

Clay, Henry, 310

"Clean Break," 293–94

Clemson College (Clemson University), 66; integration of, 3–4, 36, 79–81, 83

Clendenin, John, 270

Clinton, Bill, 128, 245; and budgetary reform, 246–51; impeachment of, 273–74; as President, 246–65; and trade policy, 251–60, 275–76

Clinton, Hillary Rodham, 257, 273

Close, Bill, 195

Clyburn, Emily, 78

Clyburn, James E., 78

Cnossen, Sijbren, 233

Coastal Zone Management Act, 157

Cohen, William, 238, 294

Cohn, Roy, 86

Collins, Freddy, 190

Commerce, U.S. Department of, 324, 325

Congressional Budget and Impoundment Control Act of 1974, 173

Congressional Budget Office (CBO), 173, 308

Conklin, Otis, 115

Conlon, Charles, 19

Connor, Theophilus Eugene "Bull," 77

Consumer Products Safety Commission, 317

Contract with America, 266

Cook, Crawford, 118

Cooper, John, 330

Cooper, Lorraine, 330

Cooper, Robert M., 47, 57

Corporate Average Fuel Economy (CAFE) standards, 179

Cotton, Norris, 129

Cousteau, Jacques, 156

Cranston, Alan, 223

Cresap, McCormick and Padgett, 66, 67

Crisp, Lathan, 68–69

Croft, Croswell, 58

Crowe, William, Jr., 314

Culbertson, John Bolt, 130, 147

Cullen, Jim, 270

Culver, John, 187, 200, 201
customs agents, 325

Danforth, John, 226, 227, 236,
    262–63
Daniel, Charles E., 60, 98
Daniel International Construction
    Company, 60
Darman, Morton, 231
Darman, Richard G. "Dick," 231,
    232, 247
Daschel, Thomas A., 262
Davis, John W., 31, 33
Defense Advanced Research Projects
    Agency (DARPA), 235, 236
defense issues: under Carter, 197–99;
    and trade policy, 314–15. *See also*
    Gulf War (1991); Iraq
deficits. *See* budgetary reform;
    national debt; tax cuts
Deitzel, Paul, 56
DeLaine, Joseph A., 28–30, 41
DeLaine, Joseph A., Jr., 41
Democratic Party: changing nature of,
    74–75, 100, 128–129; and the
    1972 presidential campaign,
    162–65; in South Carolina,
    117–18
Democratic Senatorial Campaign
    Committee (DSCC), 162–65, 329
deregulation: of airline industry,
    187–88, 267; impact of, 234; of
    telecommunications industry,
    266–72
Detyens, Bill, 57
Dewey, John, 304
Dewey, Thomas E., 10, 98
Dillon, Douglas, 102
Dimery, Virgil, 132
Dingell, John, 269, 270
Dirksen, Everett, 145
DiSalle, Michael, 52
Dixiecrat Party, 13
Dobrynin, Anatoly, 160
Dodd, Chris, 223, 261–62
Dole, Robert, 146, 215, 218, 226,
    237 262; and food-stamp pro-
    grams, 139; as Majority Leader,

218, 226; and telecommunications
    legislation, 268, 269, 271; and
    trade policy, 257, 260, 261
Domenici, Pete, 197, 203, 207, 209,
    248
Donahue, Richard K. "Dick," Sr., 103
Donaldson, Sam, 240
Donaldson Air Force Base, 103
Donohue, Thomas, 275
Dorgan, Byron, 319
DuBridge, Lee A., 154
Duckworth, George, 274
Durkin, John, 176
Dusenbury, Julian, 18

Eagleton, Thomas, 149, 163
Earle, Willie, 26
economy: as aspect of national secu-
    rity, 315; Hollings's views on, 5,
    45–51, 309–26. *See also* trade
    policies
Edgefield County, S.C., 210–11
education: Hollings as advocate for,
    16–20, 23–27, 50–56, 67–68,
    191–93; for minorities, 16–17; rev-
    enue sharing for, 126; sales tax for,
    17–20, 23–27; and tax credits for
    private education, 191–93. See also
    *Briggs v. Elliott; Brown v. Board of
    Education of Topeka, Kansas;
    Plessy v. Ferguson*
Education, U.S. Department of, 193
Edwards, James, 176
Edwards, Robert C., 81
Edwards, Walter G. "Buck," 17, 57
Ehrlichman, John, 155
Eisenhower, Dwight D., 3, 33–34, 37,
    38, 88, 98, 144, 183, 312
El Al, 282
Elgin, S.C., 60–61
Elgin Watch Company, 60–61
Elliott, Roderick W., 29
Ellison, Blease, 26
Elmore v. Rice, 12
Energy, U.S. Department of, 177
energy issues, 177–80
environmental issues, 4, 152–58
Environmental Protection Agency, 157

Epps, Frank, 88
Epting, Heyward, 51–52
Ervin, Sam, 88, 172, 308
es' Stebbins, Jim, 62
Europe, trade policies of, 160, 229,
	258
Evans, Daniel, 218, 229
Exon, James, 225
Export-Import Bank Bill, 194, 196

Fall, Bernard, 106–7
farm lobby, 126–27
Faubus, Orval, 3
Federal Bureau of Investigation (FBI),
	288
Federal Communications Commission
	(FCC), 267, 268, 269
Federal Corrupt Practices Act of
	1925, 165
Federal Election Campaign Act of
	1971, 165–66
Federal Election Commission (FEC),
	167
Federal Emergency Management
	Agency (FEMA), 289
Federal Trade Commission (FTC), 317
Feith, Douglas, 293, 294, 295
Feldman, Myer "Mike," 98, 101, 102,
	103
Feldstein, Martin, 316
Felt, Harry, 123
Fields, Craig, 235, 236–37
Figg, Robert McCormick, 29, 31, 32,
	34, 128
Fonda, Avery, 54
Fonda, Henry, 33
Fong, Hiram, 145
Food for Peace, 4, 104
food-stamp program, 131–33, 138–39
Ford, Gerald, 183; Carter's defeat of,
	180; and energy policy, 179–80;
	Hollings's assessment of, 174,
	175–76; and inflation,
	174
Ford, Henry, 317
Fortas, Abe, 142, 144, 145, 146, 147,
	149
Fowler, Donald L., 118

Foxe, Fannie, 175
Frampton, Creighton, 15–16
Frank, John, 146
Frankfurter, Felix, 33
Freeman, Orville L., 102, 119–20
Freeman, Wayne, 81
Friedman, Thomas, 321, 322, 323
Frierson, Nelson, 8
Fulbright, J. William, 88
Funderburk, Sapp, 55
fund-raising, challenges of, 327–29,
	331, 332. *See also* campaign
	finance legislation
Furman, Alester, 143
Furness, Betty, 89

Galbraith, John Kenneth, 320
Gantt, Harvey, 3, 36, 79–83, 245
Garner, John Nance, 94
Gavin, James M., 100–101
General Accounting Office (GAO),
	224
General Agreement on Tariffs and
	Trade (GATT), 255–60, 309
Gerli, Paulino, 63
Gingrich, Newt, 266, 269–70, 271,
	274, 306–7
Glaspie, April, 242, 243
globalization, 313–26, 332. *See also*
	outsourcing; trade policies
Goldberg, David S. "Rocky," 9–10,
	15
Goldberg, William C., 45–46
Goldsmith, James, 258–60
Goldwater, Barry, 75, 112, 117, 141,
	176
Gordon, Michael R., 293
Gore, Albert, Jr., 250, 254–55,
	270–71
Gore, Albert, Sr., 87, 88
Gorton, Slade, 238
government: founding fathers' views
	on, 304–5, 310, 332; Hollings's
	recommendations for, 324–26;
	trust in, 307; waste in, 307
Grace, Peter, 58, 62, 212
Grace Commission, 212, 307
Graham, Bob, 283

Graham, Lindsey, 274, 299–300
Graham, Philip, 94
Gramm, Phil, 218, 221–22, 223, 229,
    239–40, 241, 244, 251
Gramm-Rudman-Hollings legislation,
    85, 176, 220–25, 240, 241
Gravel, Maurice R. "Mike," 163
Gray, Archie, 305
Greenspan, Alan, 201, 208, 247,
    278–79, 296, 315
Greenspan Commission, 208, 209,
    240, 309
Greenville Tech, 54–55
Greider, William, 206, 207
Gressette, L. Marion, 49
Griffin, Robert, 142, 146
Griffith, Andrew D., 56, 104
Grove, Andrew S., 55
Gulf War (1991), 243–44, 245
Gunn, David, 286

Hallinan, Paul, 44–45
Hamilton, Alexander, 310, 317,
    332
Harper, Walter, 47, 65
Harrelson, Roy, 63–64
Harris, Herky, 201
Harris, Hugh Pate, 118
Harris, Louis, 72, 98–99
Hart, Gary, 217, 222
Hart, Philip A., 173
Hartnett, Thomas F., 244
Haskell, Floyd, 164
Hastert, Dennis, 274
Hathaway, William, 164
Hawkins, Falcon, 111–12, 114
Haynsworth, Clement F., Jr., 141,
    143–50
Heilman, Bob, 17
Heinz, John, 238, 241
Helms, Jesse, 244, 293
Hemphill, Bob, 95
Henry, Patrick, 320
Herblock, 148–49
Heyerdahl, Thor, 156
Hickel, Walter, 155
Hinckley, John, Jr., 204
Hinton, James M., 28–29

Hipp, Francis M., 47, 48, 65
Ho Chi Minh, 123
Hodges, Kaneaster, Jr., 192, 193
Hodges, Luther, 47, 62, 64–65, 96
Holland, Kenneth L., 196
Hollings, A. G. "Bubba," 13–15
Hollings, Ernest F. "Fritz": as advo-
    cate for business development, 2,
    38, 40–41, 47–50, 55–67; as advo-
    cate for education, 16–20, 23–27,
    50–56, 67–68, 191–93; as advo-
    cate of sound fiscal policy, 48–50,
    171–77, 201–9, 213, 220–25,
    246–51, 278–79; as advocate of
    technical training, 52–56; as ad-
    vocate for technology, 234–36,
    262–64; as advocate for the textile
    industry, 194–96, 200, 218–20,
    229–30, 237–38; as advocate of
    Value Added Tax, 231–33, 308–9,
    326; on Afghanistan, 286, 289,
    295, 302–3, 326; and airline de-
    regulation, 187–88; and *Briggs v.
    Elliott*, 31–33, 35–36; and cam-
    paign finance reform, 5, 165–69,
    227–28, 264–65, 326–32; as can-
    didate for Governor, 39–40; as
    candidate for Lieutenant Governor,
    36–38; as candidate for President,
    212–13, 214–17; as candidate for
    S.C. House of Representatives,
    10–15; as candidate for U.S. Sen-
    ate, 72–75, 102–3, 115–18; as
    chairman of the DSCC, 162–65,
    329; defense as concern of,
    197–99, 244; and economic issues,
    5, 45–51, 309–26; and energy pol-
    icy, 177–80; and environmental
    issues, 4, 152–58; as Governor,
    35–36, 42–83; and Gramm-
    Rudman-Hollings, 220–25; and
    Haynsworth nomination, 141,
    144–45; hunger as concern of, 4,
    107–8, 109, 131–40; on Iraq, 6,
    125–26, 291–302, 314, 324, 326;
    and the Kennedy family, 72–73,
    84–110, 112, 117; and the Ku
    Klux Klan, 42–45; and labor-law

reform, 188–91; at law school,
8–9; military service of, 7, 74; and
Panama Canal Treaties, 4, 182–87;
and prison system, 68–71; and
product-liability legislation,
224–27; response of to racial tensions, 3–4, 11–13, 76–83; and
SALT agreements, 160–62,
197–98; and segregated schools,
35–36, 38–39; Senate committee
assignments of, 120; in the S. C.
House of Representatives, 15; and
telecommunications industry,
267–72; and trade policy, 217–20,
228–30, 251–61, 309–26; as trial
lawyer, 111–12; as U.S. Senator,
4–5, 106–9, 118–40; and the Vietnam War, 116–17, 118–19,
120–23, 124–25
Hollings, Rita Liddy "Peatsy," 159,
160, 182, 239, 281, 330
Holloway, James L., III, 184, 185,
186
Holtz, Lou, 56
homeland security, 280–86; role of
intelligence in, 286–89
Homeland Security, U.S. Department
of, 281, 287–88, 289
homosexuals, legislation affecting, 244
Hoover, Herbert, 101, 212, 287
Hoover, J. Edgar, 101
Hoover Commission, 212, 286–87
Howie, Thomas D., 256
Hu Jintao, 313
Huckabee, Mike, 319
Huddleston, Dee, 199
Hull, Cordell, 255, 312
Humphrey, Hubert, 84, 92, 98–99,
131, 139, 171
hunger: health problems associated
with, 135, 136–37; Hollings's con-
cern regarding, 4, 107–8, 109,
131–40
Hunter, Jim, 19
Hurricane Andrew, 289
Hurricane Katrina, 289
Hussein, Saddam, 242, 243, 291–92.
See also Gulf War (1991); Iraq

Inglis, Robert D., 272
Inouye, Daniel, 176, 199, 226
intelligence: and Iraq invasion,
289–92, 295–96; and national
security, 286–89
Interstate Commerce Commission,
268
Iran, U.S. hostages in (1979–80), 198,
199
Iran-Contra affair, 230
Iraq: authorization for invasion of,
289–90; Hollings's views on invasion of, 5–6, 125–26, 291–302,
314, 324; as perceived threat,
289–92. See also Gulf War (1991)
Israel: airline security in, 282; conflict
with Palestine, 292–93, 302; intelligence service of, 290, 291; security of, 299, 324

Jackson, Henry "Scoop," 161, 177,
197, 198
Japan, trade policies of, 217, 234,
258, 313, 314
Javits, Jacob, 145
Jefferies, Richard M., 51
Jefferies, Richard M., Jr., 51
Jefferson, Thomas, 304–5
Jeffords, Jim, 238, 279–80
Jenkins, Cambridge, 77–78
Johns, Jasper, 145
Johnson, Lady Bird, 94, 113–14
Johnson, Lyndon B., 87, 89, 105, 175,
238, 309; as President, 112, 116,
121, 315; presidential campaigns
of, 92–93, 112–14; Supreme Court
appointments of, 142; unpopular-
ity of, 118; as Vice President,
94–95, 96; and the Vietnam War,
123, 124
Johnston, J. Bennett, 222, 223, 250
Johnston, Olin D., 39, 72–74, 88, 91,
93, 95, 97, 102–3, 107, 114–15
Johnston, William, 39, 40, 73–74,
115, 116
Jolley, Robert A., Sr., 97
Jones, Phil, 135–36
Jordan, 243, 251, 302

Kahn, Alfred E., 187, 188
Kantor, Mickey, 261
Kaptur, Marcy, 319
Kasich, John, 251
Kaufman, Henry, 315
Keating, Kenneth, 106
Kefauver, Estes, 38, 87
Kemp, Jack, 215
Kemp-Roth proposal, 202, 206
Kennedy, Caroline, 110
Kennedy, Edward, 84, 85, 102, 172,
    178, 187, 198, 223; as candidate
    for President, 198–99
Kennedy, Ethel, 86–87, 95, 107, 110
Kennedy, John F., 65–66, 71–72, 130,
    237, 238, 310, 312; anti-Catholi-
    cism directed at, 87, 90–92,
    95–96; assassination of, 104–5,
    112; in debates with Nixon,
    96–97, 99; Hollings as supporter
    of, 87, 88, 90, 91–98, 103–4, 112,
    199; Hollings's friendship with,
    72–73, 84; presidential campaign
    of, 90–100; and racial tensions, 79
Kennedy, Robert F., 3, 82, 85, 90,
    125, 126; assassination of, 109–10,
    130; as candidate for U.S. Senate,
    106; Hollings's friendship with, 84,
    86–87, 95, 104, 107; after John F.
    Kennedy's assassination, 105; and
    Edward R. Murrow, 86
Kerrey, Bob, 250–51
Kerry, John, 223
King, Larry, 254
King, Martin Luther, Jr., 41, 77, 78,
    128; assassination of, 130
Kinports, Paul M., 27–28
Kissinger, Henry, 160, 161
Kreps, Muller, 49, 53
Kristol, William, 293
Kronsberg, Ed, 113
Ku Klux Klan, 3, 26, 42–45
Kuwait and Operation Desert Storm,
    242–44
kwashiorkor, 135

labor unions. See organized labor
Lane, Hugh C., 67

Lautenberg, Frank, 225, 282
Lee, Emma, 69
Lee, Robert E., 80
Lee Kuan Yew, 312–13
Legare, Allen, 12
Legge, Lionel K., 15
Leverette, Sarah, 8
Levin, Sander M., 319
Lewinsky, Monica, 272
Lewis, Gabriel, 186
Lewis, Woodrow, 9
Libby, Lewis "Scooter," 293, 294
Limehouse, John, 13–14
Lincoln, Abraham, 310
Lippmann, Walter, 304
Livingston, Otis, 19, 24
Livingston, Robert L., 274
lobbyists, 305, 328, 332. See also
    campaign finance legislation
Long, Russell, 166, 177–78, 193, 218
Lott, Trent, 293
Lowe, Charles Upton, 136, 137
Lucier, James, 142
Luke, David, 61
lynching, 26

Mabry, George L., Jr., 185
MacDougall, Ellis, 70
Macmillan, Paul, 28
Madison, James, 328
Magnuson, Warren, 152, 199, 201
Maliki, Nuri al-, 297, 298
Mann, James R., 97
Mansfield, Mike, 126, 149, 159, 160,
    171, 287, 299, 312–13
Manufacturing Extension Partnership
    Program, 235–36
marasmus, 135
Marchant, Pete, 54
Margolies-Mezvinsky, Marjorie, 250
Marine Mammal Protection Act, 158
Marshall, Thurgood, 3; as attorney
    arguing for voting rights, 11; and
    Briggs v. Elliott, 29, 30, 31–32, 33,
    127–28; Supreme Court nomina-
    tion of, 127–28
Marshall, Thurgood "Goody," Jr.,
    128

Marshall Plan, 312
Martin, Wade, 56, 65
Martin, William McChesney, 315
Mathias, Mac, 205
May, John Amasa, 25
Maybank, Burnet R., Jr., 75
Maybank, Burnet Rhett, 37
McAuliffe, Dennis P., 185
McCabe, Frank, 55–56
McCabe, Gordon, 115
McCain, Thomas C., 210, 211
McCain, John, 319
McCain-Feingold bill, 168, 265
McCarthy, Joseph R., 86, 286
McCaulay, Frank, 96
McConnell, Mitch, 228, 264–65,
    299, 331
McCormack, John, 88
McCullough, David, 183
McCutcheon, Hugh, 132
McDevitt, Sally Howie, 256
McGovern, George, 4, 104, 137,
    200, 201; and airline deregulation,
    187–88; as candidate for president,
    162–64
McIntyre, Jim, 201
McKissick, Ellison S. "Bubby," 195
McLain, Denny, 307
McNair, Robert E., 46, 52, 114–15
McNamara, Robert, 102
Meany, George, 145, 164–65
Meredith, James, 3, 78–79
Metzenbaum, Howard, 84
Mexico: democracy in, 303; working
    conditions in, 251–54
Meyer, Goldberg and Hollings, 9
Meyer, J. D. E. "Ernest," 8, 10
Michelin, 63
Miller, Jack, 164
Milliken, Roger, 195–97
Mills, Wilbur, 130, 174–75, 207
Mitchell, Andrea, 279
Mitchell, George, 237, 260, 261,
    268–69
Mitchell, John, 114, 143, 144, 148,
    152, 155
Monaghan, Sister Anthony, 44, 45,
    131, 133

Mondale, Joan, 182
Mondale, Walter, 216
Moore, Frank, 199
Moore, Joe, 123
Morocco, 159
Morris, Edmund, 311
Morse, Wayne, 126
Moss, Colie, 15
Mossad, 290
Moyers, Bill D., 123–24
Moynihan, Daniel Patrick, 191, 192,
    193
Mujahideen, 302–3
Mulroney, Brian, 228
Multilateral Trade Negotiations,
    194–95
Murphy, Beverly, 66
Murphy, Pat, 67
Murrin, Thomas J., 236
Murrow, Edward R., 86
Musharraf, Pervez, 302
Muskie, Edmund, 173–74, 197, 198,
    199
Myrtle Beach, S.C., 63–64
Myrtle Beach Sun, 63

National Association for the Advance-
    ment of Colored People (NAACP),
    12, 75, 76, 134
National Competitiveness Act, 262
National Council on Marine
    Resources and Engineering Devel-
    opment, 152
national debt, 5, 6, 307–8
National Environmental Policy Act,
    155–56
National Institute of Standards and
    Technology (NIST), 234–36, 262
National Oceanic and Atmospheric
    Administration (NOAA), 4,
    152–53, 154–55, 158
National Rifle Association, 165
national security, 314–15. See also
    homeland security
National Security Council (NSC), 286,
    287–88
Nelson, Gaylord, 200, 201
Netanyahu, Benjamin, 292–93, 299

Newbold, Greg, 295
Newman, I. DeQuincey, 76–77, 105, 134–35
news media, 304–5
Nickles, Donald L., 248
Nixon, Richard M., 4–5, 22, 38, 207, 315, 326; and budgetary reform, 171, 172; Congressional challenges to, 171–72; in debates with Kennedy, 96–97, 99; and environmental issues, 153–55; as President, 142–152, 159, 160; as presidential candidate against Humphrey, 141; as presidential candidate against Kennedy, 90, 95–97, 98; as presidential candidate against McGovern, 164; resignation of, 174; and SALT agreements, 160–62; Supreme Court nominations of, 142–44, 148; and Watergate scandal, 166, 171
North American Free Trade Agreement (NAFTA), 200, 251–55, 273, 309
Nunn, Sam, 198, 243, 250

Ocean Dumping Act, 157
O'Connor, Sandra Day, 306
O'Donnell, Kenneth, 92, 104
Office of Economic Opportunity (OEO), 132, 133
Office of Management and Budget (OMB), 138–39, 172, 173, 224
oil embargo, 177
oil lobby, 305
oil-depletion allowance, 178
Omnibus Budget Reconciliation Act of 1990, 241
O'Neill, Thomas P. "Tip," 163, 196–97, 208
OPEC (Organization of the Petroleum Exporting Countries), 177, 202
Operation Desert Storm, 242–44, 288–89, 291
organized labor: and Clinton, 252; and labor-law reform, 188–91; and Mexican workers, 253–54; as opponents of Haynsworth nomina-

tion, 145; as supporters of the Democratic Party, 164–65; and trade with China, 275
outsourcing, 5, 309, 314, 315–16, 318, 320, 321, 323. *See also* trade policies
Oxley, Michael, 271

Packwood, Robert, 191, 192, 193, 218, 229, 238, 251
Pakistan, 302
Palestine, 292–93, 302
Panama Canal Treaties, 4, 182–87; opposition to, 185–86
Panetta, Leon, 246, 258
Parker, John J., 145
Parker, Marshall, 45–46, 117, 130–31
Parks, Rosa, 41
Pate, W. W., 67
Patterson, John, 96
Peace Corps, 100–101
Pearl Harbor, attack on, 312
Pearson, Levi, 28, 41
Pepper, Claude, 203
Perle, Richard, 293–94, 295, 296
permanent normal trade relations (PNTR). *See* trade policies
Perot, Ross, 254–55
Perry, Matthew, 163
Petraeus, David, 296, 299–300
Plessy v. Ferguson, 16, 19, 30, 31, 33, 330
Plowden, Charlie, 37
polling, political, 72, 98–99
pollution. *See* environmental issues
Pope, Thomas H., 22, 95
port security, 283–85
Potter, E. C., 61
poultry industry, 66
Powell, Colin, 296, 302
Pressler, Larry, 269
prison system, 68–71
product-liability legislation, 224–27
Project for the New American Century, 293
protectionism. *See* trade policies
Prystowsky, Arnold, 15
Pyle National Company, 58

Qadir, Abdul, 301

racial tensions, 1–3; in South Caro-
    lina, 11–13, 26–36, 42–45, 75–83
rail security, 285–86
Ray, Harold, 70
Rayburn, Sam, 88, 94
Reagan, Ronald, 180, 183, 238, 307,
    312, 323; assassination attempt on,
    204–5; and budgetary reform,
    202–9; and cuts in government
    programs, 203, 211–12, 224; as
    President, 139, 150, 188, 199,
    201–13, 214–30; tax cuts advo-
    cated by, 202–3, 205–7
Reed, "Spider," 120–21, 123
Reid, Harry, 331
Regan, Donald, 209
Rehnquist, William H., 144, 148
Republican Party: S.C. Democrats
    switching to, 74–75, 117; victory
    of in 1994, 260–61
Reuss, Henry, 196
Reuther, Walter, 94
Ribicoff, Abraham, 94, 177, 195, 196
Ricardo, David, 322
Rice, Condoleezza, 294, 302
Richards, James Prioleau "Dick," 95
Richardson, Hamilton, 86
Ridge, Tom, 280
Riley, Joseph P., 64–65
Riley, Joseph P., Jr., 64
Riley, Richard W., 69
Riley, Ted, 95
Rivers, L. Mendel, 103, 136
Roberts, Dennis, 106
Roberts, Paul Craig, 323
Rockefeller, David, 194
Rockefeller, Jay, 282
Rockefeller, Nelson, 114
Rogers, Emory, 29
Rogers, William, 97, 160
Romney, George, 138
Romney, Mitt, 319
Roosevelt, Franklin D., 11, 20, 312
Roosevelt, Franklin D., Jr., 92
Roosevelt, Theodore, 311
Roth, William V., Jr., 197

Rudman, Warren, 221, 222, 223, 238
Rumsfeld, Donald, 290, 293, 294–95,
    296, 297
Rusk, Dean, 102
Russell, Donald, 39–40, 75, 79–80,
    111, 144; appointed U.S. Senator,
    114–15, 116
Russell, Richard Brevard "Dick," 88,
    120, 151, 171, 329

Sabah, Sheikh Jabir al-Ahmad al-, 302
sales tax for public education, 17–20,
    23–26
Salinger, Pierre, 163
Sanford, Terry, 87
Santayana, George, 291
Saudi Arabia, 242
savings-and-loan industry, 234
Schwartz, Victor E., 226–27
Schwarzkopf, Norman, 288–89
Scott, Hugh, 121, 145–46
Scowcroft, Brent, 290
Scrimshaw, Nevin, 136
seaports. See port security
Self, James C., 195
Senate, U.S.: and budgetary reform,
    171–77; camaraderie in, 170–71;
    and campaign finance reform,
    165–69; and energy policy,
    177–80; and environmental issues,
    152–58; and Haynsworth nomi-
    nation, 143–50; and labor-law
    reform, 188–91; and tax credits
    for private education, 191–93;
    televising of, 306–7
Senate Agriculture Committee,
    126–27, 139
Senate Appropriations Committee,
    173, 280, 302
Senate Armed Services Committee,
    120, 174, 198, 243, 288, 296,
    302
Senate Budget Committee, 201–2,
    205, 239–40, 241
Senate Commerce Aviation Subcom-
    mittee, 187
Senate Commerce Committee, 151,
    165, 178–79, 224, 226, 269, 330;

Senate Commerce Committee (*cont'd*) and homeland security, 284, 285, 286

Senate Defense Appropriations Subcommittee, 288, 290

Senate Finance Committee, 177–78, 256–58

Senate Finance Subcommittee on International Trade, 195

Senate Oceans and Atmosphere Subcommittee, 152, 153–58

Senate Permanent Subcommittee on Investigations, 86

Senate State, Justice, Commerce Subcommittee, 236, 280

Senate Subcommittee on Commerce Appropriations, 235

September 11, 2001, and homeland security policy, 280–86. *See also* bin Laden, Osama

Shaw, Eugene, 20

Shelby, Richard C. "Dick," 313

Shriver, Sargent, 101, 132, 133, 163

Simkins, Modjeska, 28–29

Singapore, 312–13

Sisters of Charity of Our Lady of Mercy, 44–45

Small, Robert, 115, 195

Smalls, Gene, 68–69

Smathers, George, 96

Smith, Gerard, 160

Smith, James, 54

Smith, Jean Kennedy, 56, 95

Smith, Margaret Chase, 164

Smith Corona, 58–60

Smith v. Allwright, 11–12

Smoot-Hawley Act, 255, 311

Social Security: funding for, 240–42, 308–9; and Gramm-Rudman-Hollings, 221; under Reagan, 203–4, 206, 207–8

South Carolina: business development in, 55–67; Democratic Party in, 117–18; economic growth in, 2, 46–48, 71–72; educational TV in, 51; and the global market, 2, 312; hunger in, 4, 107–8, 109, 131–40; insurance industry in, 67–68; integration in, 2–3; racial tensions in, 11–13, 42–45, 75–83; school segregation in, 27–30; tax increases in, 48–50; technical training programs in, 52–56; tourism in, 64

South Carolina Law Enforcement Division (SLED), 42, 79; integration of, 77–78

Southern Christian Leadership Conference (SCLC), 75

Southern Manifesto, 87–88

Southern Strategy, 22

Soviet Union, nuclear arms limitation agreements with, 159, 160–62, 197–98

Sparkman, John, 164

Specter, Arlen, 238, 327

Spence, Floyd, 46

Spong, William, 125, 164

Standard Oil Company, 58

Stans, Maurice, 155, 166

State Development Board (S.C.), 47, 65

Stennis, John, 88, 174, 198

Stevens, Ted, 282, 302, 330

Stevenson, Adlai, 32, 37, 38, 87, 88, 89

Stevenson, Adlai, III, 196

Stockman, David, 204, 206–7, 212, 215, 249

Stone, Eugene, 70

Strategic Arms Limitation Talks (SALT), 160–62, 197–98

Stratton, Julius A., 152, 153, 155

Stratton Commission, 152, 155

Strauss, Robert, 196

Strom, J. P. "Pete," 42–44, 45, 79, 81

Sullivan, Joseph P., 118

Summerton 60, 30, 41

supply-side economics, 203, 204, 206, 215, 249

Supreme Court, U.S.: and campaign finance legislation, 5, 167, 227, 264, 326, 327, 330–31; and school desegregation, 2–3, 16, 19, 24, 30–35, 41, 87–88, 192, 330–31; and tuition tax credits, 193; and voting rights, 11–12. *See also* Bork,

Robert; Burger, Warren; Fortas, Abe; Haynsworth, Clement, Jr.; Marshall, Thurgood; O'Connor, Sandra Day; Warren, Earl
Supreme Court decisions. See *Briggs v. Elliott; Brown v. Board of Education of Topeka, Kansas; Buckley v. Valeo; Plessy v. Ferguson; Smith v. Allwright*
Swearingen, John E., 58
Synar, Michael L., 224

Taft, Robert, 10, 11
Taliban, 302–3
Tanguy, Bob, 123, 183–84
tariffs. *See* trade policies
tax cuts: under George W. Bush, 278–79; under Reagan, 202–3, 205–7
Teapot Dome scandal, 165
technical training, 52–56
technology, emerging, 234–36, 262–64
telecommunications, legislation affecting, 266–72
textile industry, 52, 71, 101–2; legislation affecting, 129–30, 194–96, 200, 218–20, 229–30, 237–38
Thatcher, Margaret, 242–43
Thomas, Lowell, 21–22
Thompson, Bob, 273
Thurmond, Strom, 13, 22, 73, 75, 136, 185, 186, 306; as advocate of segregation, 82, 87; and Fortas nomination, 142; as Nixon supporter, 131, 141; switches to Republican Party, 112–13, 117–18; as U.S. Senator, 37, 82, 87, 95, 96, 116, 144, 164; and voting rights legislation, 209, 210, 211
Timmerman, George Bell, Jr., 38, 88, 89
tobacco farming, 119–20
Tocqueville, Alexis de, 304
Tolbert, Joseph W., 10–11
Torrijos Herrera, Omar, 182, 183
tort reform, 306

Townsend Act, 310
trade policies, 194–96, 200, 309–26; with China, 275–76, 313–14; under Clinton, 251–61, 275–76; defense as aspect of, 314–15; of Europe, 160, 229, 258; of Japan, 217. *See also* North American Free Trade Agreement; U.S.-Canada Free Trade Agreement
Trainor, Bernard E., 293
Trilateral Commission, 194, 312, 318
Trofimov, Yaroslav, 292
Troutman, Robert, 106
Truman, Harry S, 7, 13, 21–22, 51, 96, 175, 177, 287
Tsongas, Paul, 244
Tumbleston, Harold, 111
Turner, Nat, 17

Umstead, William B., 62
Underwood, Cecil, 96
United Auto Workers, 94
United Nations Security Council, 295
U.S.-Canada Free Trade Agreement, 228–29, 251
University of Mississippi, integration of, 78–79
University of South Carolina, School of International Business, 68

Valeo, Frank, 167
Value Added Tax (VAT), 231–33, 308–9, 326
Vance, Cyrus, 118–19, 197, 199
Vandiver, Ernest, 96
Veterans Bonus Bill, 18
Vietnam War: Hollings's views on, 4, 116–17, 118–19, 120–23, 124–25, 297; lessons from, 4, 125, 184, 298; Mansfield's views on, 299
Vinson, Fred, 31, 33
Volcker, Paul, 315
Volpe, John, 154
Voting Rights Act of 1965, 117, 209, 211
voting rights for African Americans, 11–13, 209–11

W. R. Grace & Company, 62, 212
Waddell, James M., 67
Wallace, George, 79, 81, 88–89
Wallace, O. T., 28
Wallop, Malcolm, 241
Waring, Elizabeth Hoffman, 30
Waring, J. Waties, 12, 13, 27, 30
Warner, John, 296, 302
Warren, Earl, 3, 33–34, 77, 142–43
Washington, George, 310
Washington, McKinley, 105–6
Washington-Williams, Essie Mae, 13
Watergate scandal, 166, 171
Watson, Marvin, 123
Weicker, Lowell, 58
Weinberger, Caspar, 222
Welch, Jack, 317–18
Wells, Isabelle, 54
Wellstone, Paul, 84
Wenk, Edward, 155
West, John, 45–46, 49, 52, 53, 60–61, 68
Westbury, Mrs., 70–71
Westmoreland, William C., 117, 119, 121–22, 123, 297
White, Theodore H., 92
Wickenberg, Charles, 73
Wiggins, Archibald L. M., 50–51, 67–68
Wilkins, Roy, 32, 34
Williams, Andy, 110

Williams, G. Mennen "Soapy," 94, 102, 104
Williams, Louie, 54
Willits, Oliver, 66
Willkie, Wendell, 11
Wilson, Charlie, 303
Wilson, Paul, 32–33
Wilson, Woodrow, 312
Winick, Myron, 136
Winthrop College, 17
Witt, James Lee, 289
Wolfe, Thomas, 112
Wolfowitz, Paul, 293, 294–95
Wolfson, Louis, 142
Women, Infants and Children (WIC) Program, 4, 109, 139–40
Wong, William, 77–78
Wood, J. Wilbert, 67
Wood, Kimba, 248
Workman, William D., 74, 117
World Trade Organization (WTO), 255, 257, 260, 261, 322, 325
World War II, 7
Wright, Charles Alan, 147
Wright, Ernie, 47, 58, 62, 65
Wurmser, David, 293, 294

Yarborough, Ralph, 305
Yeager, Chuck, 86

Zorinsky, Edward, 190

ABOUT THE AUTHOR

ERNEST F. "FRITZ" HOLLINGS has enjoyed a remarkable career in public service as a South Carolina legislator (1949–54), Lieutenant Governor (1955–59), Governor (1959–63), U.S. Senator (1966–2005), and U.S. presidential candidate (1983–84). A visionary workhorse, Hollings has focused throughout his career on putting government on a sound financial basis and promoting economic development to create opportunities. Recognized as a policy expert on the budget, telecommunications, the environment, defense, trade, and space, he is the author of the Coastal Zone Management Act (1972), the Ocean Dumping Act (1972), and the Automobile Fuel Economy Act (1975) and coauthor of the Gramm-Rudman-Hollings Deficit Reduction Act (1985). Hollings led in the creation of the Special Supplemental Nutrition Program for Women, Infants and Children in 1972 and passage of the Telecommunications Act of 1996.

Over the years, Hollings has been recognized with hundreds of awards received from a wide variety of organizations. Among these are Carolina Alumni Association's Distinguished Alumni (2007), Humanities Council^SC's Governor's Award (2007), S.C. Hall of Fame Inductee (2006), Columbia World Affairs Council's Global Vision Award (2004), United Black Fund of the Midlands' I. DeQuincey Newman Humanitarian Award (2002), National Association of Community Health Centers Service Award (six times), U.S. Business & Industrial Council's Defender of the National Interest (1997), S.C. Trial Lawyers' Association's Founders Award (1995), S.C. Jury Trial Foundation's Thomas Paine Award (1995) and Magna Carta Award (1992), Citizens Against Government Waste's Grace Caucus Award (1994), S.C. Chamber of Commerce's Sergeant William Jasper Freedom Award (1992), National Federation of Independent Businesses' Guardian of Small Business (seven times), Travel Industry Association of America's Tourism

Man of the Year (1990), NOAA's Appreciation Award (1989), Free
Congress Foundation's Sound Dollar Award (1988, 1989, and 1990),
Corporation for Public Broadcasting's Ralph Lowell Award (1988),
United Seamen Service's Admiral of the Sea (1988), Watchdogs of
the Treasury's Golden Bulldog Award (1988), Secondary and Post-
Secondary Education Association's Man of the Year Award (1987),
Martin Luther King Jr. Leadership Award (1986), S.C. Education
Association's Friend of Education (1974 and 1983), University of
South Carolina's Algernon Sydney Sullivan Outstanding Alumnus
(1982), American Association of Education and School Administra-
tors' "I Care" Award (1982), Association of the U.S. Army's James
Woodruff Award (1980), National PTA's President's Award for Distin-
guished Service (1979), New York Board of Trade's Textile Man of
the Year (1979), Northern Textile Association's Silver Medal (1979),
American Oceanic Organization's Neptune Award (1978), National
Wildlife Federation's Legislator of the Year (1975), S.C. Wildlife Federation's Conservationist of the Year (1974), National Oceanography
Association's Oceanography Man of the Year (1970), S.C. Commission
for Technical Education's Founder's Award (1963), U.S. Junior Chamber of Commerce's One of Ten Outstanding Young Men of the U.S.
(1954).